Leading-Edge Research in Public Sector Innovation

Leading-Edge Research in Public Sector Innovation

Structure, Dynamics, Values and Outcomes

Edited by
Eleanor D. Glor

PETER LANG

Oxford • Bern • Berlin • Bruxelles • Frankfurt am Main • New York • Wien

Bibliographic information published by Die Deutsche Nationalbibliothek.
Die Deutsche Nationalbibliothek lists this publication in the Deutsche
National-bibliografie; detailed bibliographic data is available on the Internet
at http://dnb.d-nb.de.

A catalogue record for this book is available from the British Library.

Library of Congress Control Number: 2017953987

Cover image: Pixabay.

Cover design: Peter Lang Ltd.

ISBN 978-1-78707-662-4 (print) • ISBN 978-1-78707-663-1 (ePDF)
ISBN 978-1-78707-664-8 (ePub) • ISBN 978-1-78707-665-5 (mobi)

© Peter Lang AG 2018

Published by Peter Lang Ltd, International Academic Publishers,
52 St Giles, Oxford, OX1 3LU, United Kingdom
oxford@peterlang.com, www.peterlang.com

This publication has been peer reviewed.

Printed in Germany

Thanks go to Dr Mario A. Rivera, Lead Editor of the Peter Lang Series Transamerican Studies: Social Justice, Identity and Public Policy, for his help in preparing the book proposal and its market research analysis.

Contents

Figures

Angelo Dossou-Yovo and Diane-Gabrielle Tremblay – Public Policy, Intermediaries, and Innovation System Performance: A Comparative Analysis of Québec and Ontario

Tables

Appendices

ELEANOR D. GLOR

1   Introduction: Creating a Contemporary Public Innovation Discipline

Government and nonprofit sector (public sector) innovation has been studied since the 1950s and has emerged into a strong cross-disciplinary research field, with its own schools of study. Innovation is studied in fields and organizations that are open to trying out new policies, programs or processes. During its publication since 1995, *The Innovation Journal: The Public Sector Innovation Journal* (TIJ), an electronic journal (<http://www.innovation.cc>), has published papers and books discussing theory, practice, public policy and administration, health, education, international/national/provincial/local governments and many other subjects. It has been in the forefront of studying new practices and approaches such as leadership, employee empowerment, policy informatics and collaboration. It is truly cross-disciplinary. This volume brings together sixteen essays originally published in TIJ.

TIJ has been a forum for discussion of theories, frameworks, and evaluations of public sector innovation; has demonstrated how interpretive, analytic, quantitative, and demographic methods can be applied to public sector innovation; and it has guided governments to more effective policies. TIJ has not adopted a field nor a school. Rather, it has published on a range of theories, subjects, and approaches. Nonetheless, it is now becoming clear that schools of study of public sector innovation are emerging. I am aware of several.

Early scholarly interest was in the *creation and early adoption* of innovations. This work began with study of the adoption of new ideas, practices, and technologies by American Midwestern farmers (e.g. Rogers, 1958). Innovators were considered the first few to adopt innovations in their systems (Rogers, 1995: 22). *The Innovation Journal* published two articles by Everett Rogers ("Complex Adaptive Systems and the Diffusion of Innovations" *and* "Evaluating Public Sector Innovation in Networks: Extending the Reach of the National Cancer Institute's Web-based Health Communication Intervention Research Initiative"). He was also a member of the Editorial Board of *The Innovation Journal* for several years. "Complex Adaptive Systems" is included in this volume.

Interest in the adoption of innovations led to studies of innovative state and provincial governments such as Minnesota, U.S.A (e.g. Poole, Van de Ven, Dooley and Holmes, 2000) and Saskatchewan, Canada (e.g. Glor, 1997, 2002). Interest in policy and program innovations was followed by interest in the innovation process and the observation of the S-curve of adoption (Rogers, 1995), published in the communications literature.

Interest in the adoption of innovation also developed into an interest in the dissemination or *diffusion* of policy innovations (Berry and Berry, 2013) and its communication (e.g. Rogers, 1995). Substantial quantitative research was conducted on the adoption of management innovations in local governments in the United Kingdom (Walker, 2006; Hartley, 2008) and the United States (e.g. Damanpour and Schneider, 2006; Walker, Damanpour, Devece, 2010). It used a different definition of innovation as an idea, practice or object that is perceived as new by an individual or other unit of adoption (Rogers, 1995, 11). Mark K. Warford, in Chapter 14 describes the history of the very early use of this definition and of the history of dissemination of innovation research.

Glor (2013), studying organizations implementing innovations, defined this approach to innovation as something new to the organization. As each policy, program or process that was new to the organization was adopted, it was considered an innovation. Other scholars also studied diffusion of policy innovations, especially among the American states (e.g. Walker, 1968; Gray, 1973; Berry and Berry, 1990; 1992; 2013), published primarily in political science journals. During the 1990s, the Ford Foundation funded innovation awards in five regions of the world (see more below). The Institute of Public Administration of Canada and the Commonwealth Association also introduced innovation awards. A number of scholars studied the results of awards in Canada (Glor, 1998; Bernier, 2014), the U.S.A (Borins, 1998), the United Kingdom (Hartley, 2008), and Brazil (Simtes and Goulart, 2006).

Most recently, interest in innovation has in some ways been replaced by interest in *resilience*. There are ways in which this is a more ideological approach. The City of Toronto, for example, under a right-wing mayor, implemented a resilience initiative as part of the 100 Resilient Cities pioneered by the Rockefeller Foundation. In an advertisement for a Chief Resilience Officer, it directed employees to support cutbacks and staff cuts, saying: "Lead the comprehensive assessment of current policy, planning and resilience activities, creating a compelling vision for Toronto's Resilience Strategy to drive engagement, understanding and commitment across all relevant community sectors" (advertisement circulated by the Institute of Public Administration of Canada, December 16, 2016). TIJ has published a number of articles on resilience, such as "Building Resilience in Public Organizations: The Role of Waste and Bricolage" by Steven Van de Walle (2014); "Innovation in the public sector: spare tyres and fourth plinths" by Wayne Parsons (2006); and "Protecting the Internet from Dictators: Technical and Policy Solutions to Ensure Online Freedoms" by Warigia Bowman and L. Jean Camp (2013).

These topics were paralleled by an interest in identifying the *effects of innovation*. Everett Rogers' two articles in TIJ were occupied with this. Eleanor D. Glor has laid out an agenda for research on the *fate of innovations and their organizations*. She has looked at them generally and when they change (summarized by Baum, 1996; Glor, 2013). This literature has been published primarily in the organizational studies journals. Scholars who studied organizational fate in government typically relied on government records, for example, United States Government Manual[1] and surveys of local governments in the United Kingdom (e.g. Walker, 2006; Hartley, 2008). Interest was also shown in the factors affecting those fates (summarized in Glor, 2013).

Throughout this scholarly history, there was an ongoing interest in *individual innovations and their adoption* (e.g. Simtes and Goulart, 2006; Ferreira, Farah and Spink, 2008 [Brazil]). A number of these authors came out of the Harvard School, which focuses on case studies, often using data

---

1   <http://www.usgovernmentmanual.gov/?AspxAutoDetectCookieSupport=1>

derived from public sector innovation awards. Many of these awards were funded by the Ford Foundation, which funded five innovation awards (e.g. Harvard, U.S.A Native Indian awards, Brazil, Philippines, South Africa). Sandford Borins, for example, studied groups of innovations, especially innovation award nominees, finalists, and winners (e.g. 1998, 2000). He argued that awards have identified enough innovations that the populations can be considered representative of public sector innovations generally (Borins, 2001). I disagree, and consider that innovation award finalists and winners may be an elite group of innovations and organizations which have more support from management and governments, more recognition, and may be more likely to survive longer than the average innovation. TIJ has published articles arguing that the demographics of adoption and effects of innovations on their target groups, organizations, communities, and populations need more study, especially effects on their populations (a population is, for example, all nonprofit day care centers in a region) (e.g. Glor, 2014; Glor and Rivera, 2015).

Eventually scholars grew interested in the impact of innovations. Mario Rivera, for many years the Senior Associate Editor of *The Innovation Journal*, was particularly interested in this topic, for example, in "Evaluating Public Sector Innovation in Networks: The National Cancer Institute's Web-Based Health Communication Intervention Research Initiative" (<http://www.innovation.cc/volumes-issues/vol9-iss3.html>).

No profile of public sector innovation research would be complete without a word about the iconoclasts. James Iain Gow (2014), in the Conclusion to this book, reviews and critiques a number of public sector innovation scholars. He sees Robert Behn as the main critic of public sector innovation, however. Behn's notions – managing by groping along and most of the knowledge needed to innovate being tacit – challenge the capacity for developing a field of innovation studies. (Gow, 2014: 6–7 (Chapter 17, this volume)). Howard A. Doughty too has been critical of innovation, especially its politics.

TIJ has published material from many of these schools. While the popularity of topics has in some cases come and gone, these topics remain of value in any attempt to understand public sector innovation. TIJ's contribution is important because it is the only journal publishing exclusively on public sector innovation, it publishes in both journal article and book form, it publishes in both English and French, and it provides a specific contribution because it focuses only on that subject.

The Innovation Journal: Publishing History

Up to volume 22, issue 1, 2017, publishing three times per year, and four in one year, in total TIJ has published (<http://www.innovation.cc/all-issues.htm>):

- 5 books
- 22 introductions
- 253 peer-reviewed (scholarly style) papers
- 149 discussion papers
- 66 case studies
- 22 review essays
- 195 book reviews

This is a total of 712 publications on public sector innovation in twenty-two years.

Comparison to Top-Ranking Public Administration Journals

Other journals also publish on public sector innovation. Scopus' *SCImago* uses the same method to identify citation of journals as Thompson-Reuters. As of the end of 2015 it identified the five electronic[2] journals

---

2   Pretty well all public administration journals now offer an electronic version.

in public administration receiving the most citations as *Administrative Science Quarterly*, *Journal of Public Administration Research and Theory*, *Educational Administration Research and Theory*, *Public Administration Review* and *Governance*, in that ranking.[3] Their articles on public sector innovation were reviewed as of fall 2016.

- *Administrative Science Quarterly* publishes on all sectors, not just the public sector. A review of its forty most recent articles on innovation revealed *none* on public sector innovation.
- *Journal of Public Administration Research and Theory* published a total of fifteen articles on innovation, eleven relevant to public sector innovation. TIJ published 465.
- *Educational Administration Quarterly* published no articles on public sector educational innovation. TIJ published two special issues on education, totalling sixteen articles.
- *Public Administration Review* published sixteen articles on public sector innovation from 1995 to 2015, the period parallel to the period when TIJ published (1995 to 2016).
- *Governance* published seven articles with "innovation" in their titles since it began publishing in 1998.

TIJ has published a total of 490 scholarly style papers, discussion papers, case studies, review essays, and five books. It has published many more articles on public sector innovation than the top ranking journals. TIJ has also, uniquely, published numerous articles on theory of public sector innovation, ethics of innovation, directions for research on innovation, and leading-edge topics such as innovation and complexity, policy informatics, development and the poor in developing countries, and employee, client, and citizen empowerment. These are topics the journals reviewed have not

---

3   These journals are followed, in citation rank, by *Journal of European Public Policy*, *Journal of Policy Analysis and Management*, *American Review of Public Administration*, *International Public Management Journal*, *Environment and Planning C: Government and Policy*, *Public Administration*, *Regulation and Governance*, *Review of Public Personnel Administration* and *Policy Studies Journal*.

addressed. Appendix 1.1 compares topics covered by the five comparison journals and TIJ. The comparison reveals that TIJ is the most important journal publishing on public sector innovation.

Over its twenty-two-year history, TIJ has explored many topics of interest to scholars, students, practitioners, and promoters of innovation. Appendix 1.1 compares the issues covered in major journals on the subject of innovation and whether they have been covered in TIJ. For PAR, which has covered public sector innovation the most, the year of coverage of public sector innovation is compared to when it was addressed in TIJ. TIJ has covered the same issues, and has usually covered them earlier. In addition, TIJ has addressed many more issues related to public sector innovation, such as innovation competences, designing innovation, innovation ethics, innovation and complexity, innovation in development, innovation antecedents, collaborative innovation, and innovation and organizational mortality. These are topics the top journals have not addressed in any quantitative or qualitative way that is close to TIJ's focus. Appendix 1.1 compares topics covered by the top five cited comparison journals and TIJ. TIJ is the most important journal publishing on public sector innovation.

Choosing Material for This Book

The wealth of material published by TIJ and the many topics covered presented a number of possible approaches to choosing chapters. Having considered several, papers were included with all of them in mind.

Publish material on popular or recent topics. Many topics addressed in TIJ are of ongoing interest in public administration and the field of study of innovation. A criterion was to make them even more available. These include topics such as conceptual frameworks (Chapter 3), innovation and ethics (Part II, Chapters 4, 5 and 6), leadership (Part III, Chapters 7 and 8), collaboration (Chapter 7; Part IV, Chapters 9, 10, 11), social issues (Part V, Chapter 12), policy issues (Chapter 15), and the performance of innovations (Chapter 16). These topics became the framework for the book.

Address gaps left by other journals. Because TIJ is devoted to public sector innovation, it has addressed issues not covered at all or not covered much elsewhere. Some of these topics were included, which had often been covered in special issues of TIJ, such as innovation theory, innovation research, designing innovation, innovation processes and tools, innovation ethics, use of informatics, innovations in governance, nonprofit governance models, innovation and the new public management, democracy and innovation, employee, citizen and client empowerment, educational and health innovations, innovations in leadership, and innovations in development. In this book, chapters are included on:

- innovation theory (Part I);
- innovation ethics (Chapters 4 and 5);
- innovations in leadership (Part III, Chapters 7 and 8).

Publish well-known and most-cited authors. Because these articles were expected to be of interest to readers, this criterion was followed by including the three most-cited papers. They are, in order of citations:

- Chapter 12: "Making a Difference: Strategies for Scaling Social Innovation for Greater Impact," by Frances Westley and Nino Antadze
- Chapter 13: "Complex Adaptive Systems and the Diffusion of Innovations," by Everett M. Rogers, Una E. Medina, Mario A. Rivera, and Cody J. Wiley
- Chapter 7: "Stewards, Mediators, and Catalysts: Toward a Model of Collaborative Leadership," by Chris Ansell and Alison Gash.

Address key issues in the study of public sector innovation. An attempt has been made to present a cross-section of the topics that represent an emerging field of study, such as theory (Part I, Chapters 2 and 3), innovative approaches (Part V, Chapter 12) and diffusion of innovations (Part VI, Chapters 13 and 14).

Represent regional and scholarly interests. A number of key scholars researching public sector innovation have created mini-schools studying key aspects of public sector innovation, in collaboration with their students and colleagues. They have been interested in such issues as collaboration (Eva Sorensen and Jacob Torfing, Denmark), use of information technology in the public sector and media (Ali Salman, Malaysia) and citizen empowerment (Cheryl Simrell King). More are outlined in Appendix 1.1. Collaboration is addressed substantially.

The book addresses these five themes. It has been grouped into eight topics: public sector innovation theory and frameworks, ethics of innovation, innovation leadership, complex networks, diffusion, social justice innovations, risk and performance, citizen participation, and public accountability.

What was not included. TIJ has published a good deal on the subject of organizational innovation, including the study and fate of public sector innovations and their organizations. The chapter chosen, "A Framework for Studying the Impact of Innovation," reflects this ongoing work program but a selection of these articles was impossible to achieve. There was also no attempt to reflect the learning from the books published by TIJ. The chapters included in this book are very close to the articles originally published in TIJ.

What is Included in This Volume

Part I addresses some of the components needed to create a theory of innovation. Chapter 2 considers key factors that might be influencing public sector innovation and presents a figure that outlines possible patterns that these factors might form. The patterns are explored further in Glor (2001, 2007). Chapter 3 identifies a framework for studying public sector innovation.[4]

---

4   Glor's additional work on theory of innovation is identified at <http://www.innovation.cc/editorial-board/glor.htm>.

Part II considers innovation and ethics, an important question for those doing new things. In Chapter 4 Jessica Word, Christopher Stream, and Kimberly Lukasiak discuss the dilemma faced by nonprofit organizations when required to spend resources on evaluation at the expense of programs. Their research employs the Right-versus-Right construct and examines the moral dilemma surrounding the mandates for performance evaluation and their impact on ethical decision-making. Mai Nguyen in Chapter 5 also discusses a dilemma inherent in accountability: the different understandings that governments and First Nations have of what is meant by accountability. While the Department of Indigenous and Northern Affairs Canada (INAC) understands accountability to be concerned with funding, First Nations believe accountability requires increasingly open and transparent dialogue between governments and affected communities, with a focus on accountability for performance. Mike Miles in Chapter 6 explores management values as a key element in change. A common dilemma in change programs focused on increasing employee participation is that managers have been trained that it is their role to make the decisions and solve the problems. Miles reports on a five-year change program carried out in the Department of Veterans Affairs Canada to shift the management culture in the direction of increased employee empowerment and participation and examines the critical role a four-day management values seminar played in convincing mangers that employees were interested in and capable of participation in work-related decision-making. This is particularly interesting because the Government of Canada is a labor union environment and has always actively protected its decision-making role.

Part III presents two other perspectives on leadership. Based on interviews with leaders in U.S. Workforce Investment Boards, in Chapter 7 Chris Ansell and Alison Gash identify three roles for leaders in collaborative engagement – stewards, mediators, and catalysts. Lilly Lemay in Chapter 8 also distinguishes different roles leaders play as they interact in complement at different levels of the organization. She proposes a conceptual model of the individual development of leadership in connection with the practice of collective and strategic leadership in the public sector, deriving, analyzing, and corroborating it with a case history of the career path and strategies of a senior public servant.

Part IV focuses on an innovation of keen interest – collaboration and networks. In Chapter 9, J. Travis Bland, Boris Bruk, Dongshin Kim, and Kimberly Taylor Lee develop a management perspective on the relationship between collaboration and innovation. Presenting an exploratory case study of the Texoma Regional Consortium, a regional partnership that brought together Texas and Oklahoma workforce development efforts, they suggest that the design, development, and institutionalization of specific mechanisms – integration, dialogue, and coordination –facilitate the use of the network form of governance for the specific purpose of public sector innovation. As communication technology becomes increasingly sophisticated and hierarchical, the complexity of public and private collective behavior increases and the information and communication needed to support healthy cities becomes more complex. Mary Ann Allison in Chapter 10 takes a complex adaptive systems perspective, itself an innovation, to set forth a framework for mediated urban nervous systems that facilitate shared understanding and collaboration at all system levels in urban areas. Chapter 11 is by Mie Plotnikof of Denmark, where there is a particular interest in collaboration and innovation. Plotnikof explores the collaboration process by examining design and implementation issues in collaborative governance, which involve stakeholders in problem solving and public innovation. She theorizes discursive aspects of such processes by conceptualizing and exploring the meaning negotiations through which collaborative governance designs emerge and change. The findings of a case study on local governments' efforts to innovate quality management in education through collaborative governance suggest that this form of governance is continually negotiated during both design and implementation phases. The chapter shows that a discursive approach offers concepts valuable for refining the understanding of the emergence of collaborative governance in practice.

Part V on innovative approaches is devoted to a discussion by Frances Westley, a well-known expert on social innovation, and Nino Antadze of scaling social innovation for greater impact. Their chapter explores the strategies and dynamics of scaling up social innovations, focusing on the challenge of scaling up social innovations in general and the dynamics of going to scale in particular.

Section VI takes two perspectives on diffusion of innovations. Chapter 13, whose authors include the dean of innovation, Everett Rogers, and the former Associate Editor-in-Chief of TIJ, Mario Rivera, alongside Una E. Medina and Cody J. Wiley, explores joint use of the diffusion of innovations model (DIM) and complex adaptive systems theory (CAS) to construct a hybrid model of induced change in population behavior. The chapter explores the actual and potential hybridization of these two systems theories, relying on illustrations from historical practical applications of DIM, particularly the STOP AIDS communication campaign in San Francisco, California. Rogers' diffusion of innovations model has become the standard, most widely used HIV/AIDS prevention education model in the world, based on his work in San Francisco. Mark K. Warford in Chapter 14 reports on a questionnaire study based on the Diffusion of Innovations in Education Model (DIEM), and synthesizes research on educational innovations. The study reported included foreign language teacher educators (N = 83) in eleven U.S.A south-eastern states. State mandates appeared to hinder rather than facilitate adoption; however, results supported the DIEM claim that innovation knowledge is associated with its adoption.

Part VII includes two chapters on innovation and performance, but should be read in conjunction with Part II. In Chapter 15, Angelo Dossou-Yovo and Diane-Gabrielle Tremblay focus on policy, intermediaries, and innovation system performance using two Canadian provinces, Québec and Ontario, as comparisons. Chapter 16 by Michael J. Dougherty, Pamela D. Gibson Goff, and Donald P. Lacy seeks ways to improve accountability and performance in local governments by successfully engaging the public. Their model learns from local examples in Virginia, Ohio and West Virginia to illustrate how this might be undertaken. Common factors include the need for flexibility, performance measures, renewal, monitoring, and review.

The Conclusion by James Iain Gow summarizes the current state of public sector innovation theory as expressed by Everett Rogers, Sandford Borins, Robert Behn, and Eleanor D. Glor. While Gow does not conclude that we yet have strong innovation theory, this book makes some contribution to its creation.

Bibliography

Baum, J. A. C. 1996. Organizational Ecology. Pp. 77–114 in Stewart R. Clegg, Cynthia Hardy & W. R. Nord, *Handbook of Organization Studies*. London, Thousand Oaks, CA, New Delhi: Sage Publications.

Bernier, L., T. Hafsi & C. Deschamps. 2014–2015. Environmental determinants of public sector innovation: a study of innovation awards in Canada. *Public Management Review*, 17(6): 834–856. http://dx.doi.org/10.1080/14719037.2013.867066

Berry, F. S., & W. D. Berry. 1990. State Lottery Adoptions as Policy Innovations: An Event History Analysis. *American Political Science Review*, 84(2): 395–415.

Berry, F. S., & W. D. Berry. 1992. Tax Innovation in the States: Capitalizing on Political Opportunity. *American Journal of Political Science*, 36(3): 715–742.

Berry, F. S., & W. D. Berry. 2013. Innovation and Diffusion Models in Policy Research. Chapter 9 in Paul Sabatier (ed.), *Theories of the Policy Process*. Boulder, CO: Westview.

Borins, S. 1998. *Innovating with Integrity: How local heroes are transforming American government*. Washington, DC: Georgetown University Press.

Borins, S. 2000. What Border? Public management innovation in the United States and Canada. *Journal of Policy Analysis and Management*, 19: 46–74.

Borins, S. 2001. Innovation, Success and Failure in Public Management Research. *Public Management Review*, 3(1): 3–17.

Bowman, W., & L. J. Camp. 2013. Protecting the Internet from Dictators: Technical and Policy Solutions to Ensure Online Freedoms. *The Innovation Journal: The Public Sector Innovation Journal*, 18(1), article 3 <https://www.innovation.cc/volumes-issues/vol18-no1.htm>.

Damanpour, F., & M. Schneider. 2006. Phases of the Adoption of Innovation in Organizations: Effects of Environment, Organization and Top Managers. *British Journal of Management*, 17: 215–236.

Farah, M., F. Santos & P. Spink. 2008. Subnational government innovation in a comparative perspective: Brazil. Pp. 71–92 in S. F. Borins (ed.), *Innovations in Government: research, recognition and replication*. Washington, DC: Brookings Institution Press.

Glor, E. D. 1997. *Policy Innovation in the Saskatchewan Public Sector, 1971–82*. Toronto, Canada: Captus Press.

Glor, E. D. 1998. Public Sector Innovation in Canada. Pp. 300–340 in R. Hoffman, D. Jurkowski, V. MacKinnon, J. Nicholson & J. Simeon, *Public Administration: Canadian Materials*, 3rd Edn. Toronto, Canada: Captus Press.

Glor, E. D. 2002. *Is Innovation a Question of Will or Circumstance? An Exploration of the Innovation Process through the Lens of the Blakeney Government in Saskatchewan.* Ottawa, Canada: The Innovation Journal: The Public Sector Innovation Journal <http://www.innovation.cc/books.htm>.

Glor, E. D. 2007. Assessing Organizational Capacity to Adapt. *Emergence: Complexity & Organization (E:CO)*, 9(3): 27–40.

Glor, E. D. 2013. Do Innovative Organizations Survive Longer than Non-innovative Organizations? Initial Evidence from an Empirical Study of Normal Organizations. *The Innovation Journal: The Public Sector Innovation Journal*, 18(3), article 1 <http://www.innovation.cc/volumes-issues/vol18-no3.htm>.

Glor, E. D. 2014. Studying the Impact of Innovation on Organizations, Organizational Populations and Organizational Communities: A Framework for Research. *The Innovation Journal: The Public Sector Innovation Journal*, 19(3), article 1 <http://www.innovation.cc/volumes-issues/vol19-no3.htm> (Chapter 3, this volume).

Glor, E. D., & M. Rivera. 2015. Proposal for Research on the Fate of Innovative Public Sector Organizations, Populations and Communities: A Research Synthesis and Prospectus, *The Innovation Journal: The Public Sector Innovation Journal*, 20(2), article 3 <http://www.innovation.cc/volumes-issues/vol20-no2.htm>.

Gow, J. I. 2014. Public Sector Innovation Theory Revisited. *The Innovation Journal: The Public Sector Innovation Journal*, 19(2), article 1 <https://www.innovation.cc/volumes-issues/vol19-no2.htm>.

Gray, V. 1973. Innovations in the States: A Diffusion Study. *American Political Science Review*, 67 (Dec.): 1174–1185.

Hartley, J. 2008. Does Innovation Lead to Improvement in Public Services: Lessons from the Beacon Scheme in the United Kingdom. Pp. 159–187, Chapter 9 in Sanford Borins (ed.), *Innovations in Government: Research, Recognition, and Replication.* Washington, DC: Ash Institute for Democratic Governance and Innovation, Harvard University and Brookings Institution.

Parsons, W. 2006. Innovation in the public sector: spare tyres and fourth plinths. *The Innovation Journal: The Public Sector Innovation Journal*, 11(2), article 1 <https://www.innovation.cc/volumes-issues/vol11-no2.htm>.

Poole, M. S., A. H. Van de Ven, K. Dooley & M. E. Holmes. 2000. *Organizational Change and Innovation Processes.* New York: Oxford University Press.

Rivera, M. A., & E. M. Rogers. 2004. Evaluating Public Sector Innovation in Networks: Extending the Reach of the National Cancer Institute's Web-based Health Communication Intervention Research Initiative. *The Innovation Journal: The Public Sector Innovation Journal*, 9(3), article 2 <https://www.innovation.cc/volumes-issues/vol9-iss3.htm>.

Rogers, E. M. 1958. Categorizing the Adopters of Agricultural Practices. *Rural Sociology*, 23(4): 345–354.

Rogers, E. M., Una E. Medina, Mario A. Rivera & Cody J. Wiley. 2005. Complex Adaptive Systems and the Diffusion of Innovations. *The Innovation Journal: The Public Sector Innovation Journal*, 10(3), article 1 <https://www.innovation.cc/volumes-issues/rogers-adaptivesystem7final.pdf> (Chapter 13, this volume).

Simtes, A. A., & O. M. T. Goulart. 2006. Brazil's National Award for Innovation in Education Management: An Incentive for Local Education Authorities to Improve Municipal Education Systems toward the Goals of the National Education Plan, *The Innovation Journal: The Public Sector Innovation Journal*, 11(3), article 6 <http://www.innovation.cc/scholarly-style/simoes6goular.pdf>.

Van de Walle, S. 2014. Building Resilience in Public Organizations: The Role of Waste and Bricolage, *The Innovation Journal: The Public Sector Innovation Journal*, 19(2), article 6 <http://www.innovation.cc/volumes-issues/vol19-no2.htm>.

Walker, J. L. 1969. The Diffusion of Innovations among the American States. *American Political Science Review*, 63(3): 880–899.

Walker, R. M. 2006. Innovation Type and Diffusion: An Empirical Analysis of Local Government. *Public Administration*, 84(2): 311–335.

Walker, R. M., F. Damanpour & C. A. Devece. 2010. Management Innovation and Organizational Performance: The Mediating Effect of Performance Management. *JPART*, 21: 367–386.

Appendix 1.1
Comparison of *The Innovation Journal** to Public Sector Innovation Coverage by the Five Most-Cited** Public Administration Journals

Rank and Journal	Innovation Topic Most Recent to Least Recent	Some Articles Covering the Same/Similar Topic in TIJ	List of TIJ Special Issues
1. *Administrative Science Quarterly* Total of forty articles	Most recent forty articles on innovation – none on public sector innovation		Innovation Research 15(3), 2010 Designing Innovation 8(1), 2003 Innovation Processes and Tools 8(4), 2003 Innovation Ethics 9(4), 2003
2. *Journal of Public Administration Research and Theory* Total of fourteen articles	Innovation types –framework 2008, 2009	2002 book 2015 book <http://www. innovation.cc/books. htm> 19(3), 2014, article 1 21(1), 2016, article 1	Policy Innovation – many articles Innovations in Governance 8(2), 2003 Nonprofit Governance Models 12(3), 2007, article 5
	Systems theory approach 2016	10(3), 2005, article 3 13(3), 2008, article 3. 13(3), 2008, article 9 18(3), 2013, article 3. 18(1), 2013, article 5 19(3), 2014, article 3	Complexity 13(3), 2008 Democracy 19(1), 2014 The Middle East 18(1), 2013 Quality Management 14(3), 2009
	Pro-business administrative reform 2009, 2016	4(3), 1999, article 1 12(3), 2007, article 7	Development and the Poor in Developing Countries 12(2), 2007 New Public Management 10(2), 2005

Rank and Journal	Innovation Topic Most Recent to Least Recent	Some Articles Covering the Same/Similar Topic in TIJ	List of TIJ Special Issues
	Public sector IT 2006, 2007, 2013	13(3), 2008, article 2 Implications for Malaysian Public Sector 16(3), 2011 20(1), 2015, article 3	Policy informatics 16(1), 2011 Challenges of Media and Communication 16(3), 2011
	Employee empowerment 2003, 2013	4(2), 1999, article 9	Employee Empowerment 9(1), 2004 Citizen Empowerment 10(1), 2005 Client Empowerment 13(1), 2008
	Role of managers 2009, 2011, 2016	9(2), 2004, article 10 9(2), 2004, article 4 6(2), 2001, article 4 9(1), 2004, article 3	Innovations in Leadership 7(3), 2002
	Collaboration 2003	11(3), 2006, article 2	Collaborative Innovation 17(1), 2012 Intersectoral Collaboration 18(2), 2013
3. *Educational Administration Quarterly* no articles	No articles on innovation	Innovation in Education Management Award, Brazil 11(3), article 6	Two special issues on educational innovation: 11(3), 2006 13(2), 2008
4. *Public Administration Review* sixteen articles 1995–2015 (twenty years)	Social media 2013	13(3), 2008, article 2 16(1), 2011, article 6 20(1), 2015, article 3	

Rank and Journal	Innovation Topic Most Recent to Least Recent	Some Articles Covering the Same/Similar Topic in TIJ	List of TIJ Special Issues
	New model for higher education 2013	5(3), 2010, article 5 16(3), 2011, article 9	Two special issues on educational innovation: 11(3), 2006 13(2), 2008
	Social innovation 2015	15(2), 2010, article 2	
	Nonprofits 2011	21(1), 2016, article 3	Efficient Management of Nonprofit Organizations 12(3), 2007
	State innovation USA 2007	Innovations in Education Management Award, Brazil 21(1), 2016, article 3.	
	IT 2011 Open innovation 2013	20(1), 2015, article 3	Special issue on Media and Communication, 16(3), 2011 Special Issue on Policy Informatics, 16(1), 2011
	Public entrepreneurship 2007	7(2), 2002, article 4 15(2), 2010, article 2 Social Entrepreneurship	
	Collaborative innovation 2013	11(3), 2006, article 2	Special issue on collaborative innovation 17(1), 2012
	Management innovation 2011	9(2), 2004, article 10 9(2), 2004, article 4 6(2), 2001, article 4 9(1), 2004, article 3	Leadership 7(3), 2002

Rank and Journal	Innovation Topic Most Recent to Least Recent	Some Articles Covering the Same/Similar Topic in TIJ	List of TIJ Special Issues
	Diffusion of innovation U.S.A cities 2004	11(3), 2006, article 6. Brazil.	
	Customer service and E-government 1996, 2004	3(3), 1998, Centrelink, Australia 16(1), 2011, article 4 16(3), 2011, article 9 21(2), 2016, article 4	OECD Health Care Reform 20(1), 2015
	Environmental management 1996	21(2), 2016, article 4 Chennai	
5. *Governance* 1998, year established, to 2015. seven articles (includes book reviews) with "innovation" in title	Networks 20(4), 2007	20(2), 2015, article 6 16(1), 2011, article 3 12(2), 2007, article 9 9(3), 2004, article 2 3(3), 1998, article 6 Book reviews: 17(1), 2012, article 10 14(2), article 6 10(3), 2005, article 3	
	France, Italy, Canada, Latin America, Australia (Centrelink), Israel–Taiwan–Ireland	Malaysia, Brazil, Germany, Canada, India, Australia (Centrelink), Israel	

Source: the author

* Index of The Innovation Journal issues at: <http://www.innovation.cc/all-issues.htm>

** Cited journals were identified from Scopus SCImago 2015, which uses the same measures as Thompson-Reuters

PART I

Innovation and Conceptual Frameworks

ELEANOR D. GLOR

2   Key Factors Influencing Innovation in Government[1]

ABSTRACT

This chapter represents the first step in an effort to answer three questions: If innovation occurred in patterns, (1) what would be the most important factors? (2) What would be the patterns (e.g. Glor, 2001a; 2014)? (3) What would be their implications (e.g. Glor, 2007; Glor, 2015a; 2015b) on fitness? Using a multi-disciplinary systems approach, the chapter integrates a number of relationships that affect innovation into three principal factors: the individual's motivation related to the innovation, the culture within the workplace as influenced by its exterior environment, and the challenge presented by an innovation. The chapter concludes by arguing that these three factors form patterns of behavior in government, thereby setting the stage for a subsequent paper that develops a typology for innovation and presents cases illustrating the typology. A hypothesis for further exploration is developed.

Introduction

How should innovation be conceptualized? This has been an important question for those who attempt to direct, to work within, and to understand organizations. While commonly recognizing that innovation is a mode of organizational change, and can be directed to some extent, philosophy, sociology, political science, social action theories and systems theory have each had their impact. Such concepts as contextualism, population ecology, organizational life cycles, power in organizations, political models of

---

1   *The Innovation Journal: The Public Sector Innovation Journal*, 6(2), 2001, article 1 <http://www.innovation.cc/volumes-issues/vol6-iss2.htm>.

change, social action theories, and the use of metaphor – for example, the organization as theater (Elkin, 1983; Wilson, 1992: 22) – have enriched descriptions of the process of change.

A number of these ideas, which are now being used to free up notions of innovation and change, are actually quite old. Heraclitis saw nature in constant change. The notion that individual perceptions have theoretical relevance goes back to George Herbert Mead. This concept was supported by Dilthey's concept of *verstehen*, and Weber's primary definition of sociology itself as a science aiming at *interpretative understanding* of social behavior with a view to creating explanation of its causes, its courses, and effects (Shils and Finch, 1949: 72). Likewise, such Weberian notions as empathy (*Einfuehlung*), experience (*Erleben*), and re-living (*Nacherleben*), the idea of *phenomenology* in the works of Husserl, and the whole tradition of German idealism from Kant onward, understood that sociology has many aspects, and that at least one of these carries the decidedly anti-positivistic theme of the humanistic disciplines (*Geisteswissenschaften*), namely that the natural sciences (*Naturwissenschaften*) and those approaches to social science that attempt to employ its methods are doomed to fail. In the humanistic-cum-idealistic tradition knowledge is internal, external, and people are intelligible despite their uniqueness and individuality (Coser, 1977: 244–247). Norbert Long's frequent metaphorical expression that administration is an *ecology of games* goes back more than fifty years (as Mandeville's analogy to bees goes back hundreds).

Still, by reintroducing these concepts, observers of innovation have been more able to see that organizations change all the time, to consider participants' subjective perception of organizational structures and situations, and to describe organizational functioning in terms of patterns rather than in terms only of static procedures, unambiguous products and pre-determined outcomes. Today an open systems approach is considered an appropriate framework for understanding the dynamics of innovation in organizations. Patterns reflect the relationships among people, structures, and ideas at work in an organization and integrate the effects of these major elements (Wilson, 1992). What is required now are steps toward an integrated theory to render these several concepts and diverse patterns comprehensible.

In 1990, Perry and Wise issued an explicit challenge to those who seek a new and more satisfying understanding of organizations: to develop a model that operationalizes linkages among individual values, task structure, organizational environment and outcome (Perry and Wise, 1990: 372). Everett Rogers (1995), the dean of innovation studies, had already attempted to identify the factors determining the rate of adoption of innovations. He focused on perceived attributes of innovations, type of innovation decision, communication channels, nature of the social system, and extent of change agents' promotion efforts. As well, Rogers and Eveland (1978) and Becker and Whisler (1967) identified the need for a theoretical framework that brought together external and internal factors, and structural and psychological factors.

This is the first of two chapters that are intended to respond preliminarily to these expressed theoretical needs by defining pivotal factors in innovation, distinguishing possible patterns in innovation, identifying examples of patterns, and exploring the nature of the problems, promises, and potential outcomes associated with the patterns. The current chapter is an inter-disciplinary look at adoption and implementation of innovation through the lens of three comprehensive factors that affect the innovation process: individual motivation, organizational culture and challenge of the innovation.

Individual Motivation to Innovate

It is not easy to choose one dynamic to represent the effect that the individual has in the organization. Some authors emphasize individual resistance to management initiatives, the effects of training and of individual empowerment. To set the stage for construction of a framework for innovation in organizations, this chapter uses the dynamic of motivation to represent the impact of the individual, in part because this concept addresses unconscious, conscious, and proactive relationships to innovation. Motivation is a concept frequently used to illuminate changes in behavior in the workplace.

Perry and Porter (1982) identified motivation as that which energizes, directs, and sustains behavior. They emphasized not only the amount of effort but also the direction and quality of the effort. The concepts of intrinsic and extrinsic motivation refine understanding of motivation (Dyer and Parker, 1975). Bandura (1986: 240–241) identified *intrinsic motivation* as comprising three types of relationship: one in which the consequences originate externally but are naturally related to the individual's behavior, a second in which behavior produces naturally occurring outcomes that are internal to the organism, and a third where a self-evaluative mechanism is at work. He suggested that pursuit of activities is lasting and least subject to situational inducements when the effects are either intrinsically related to the behavior or are self-provided. According to Thomas and Velthouse (1990), intrinsic task motivation is achieved in four ways: through meaning (value of work goal or purpose), competence (self-efficacy), self-determination (autonomy in initiation and continuation of work), and impact (influence on work outcomes). But motivation is also generated in a different way. *Extrinsic motivation* is motivation for behavior that is not representative of goals established by the individuals nor inherent in the behavior itself (Cofer, 1996). Extrinsic motivation is motivated by rewards and goals, and contrasts with the inherent reward of an act or self-determined goals characterizing intrinsic motivation (Cofer, 1996). The tools available to management such as giving direction and rewards would thus typically create extrinsic motivation. Perry and Porter defined the variables affecting (presumably mostly) extrinsic motivation as individual, job, work environment, and external environments, and identified four motivational techniques: monetary incentives, goal setting, job design (all extrinsic) and participation (which could be either intrinsic or extrinsic).

Much of the motivational literature has concentrated on employees within business and industrial organizations. Based on a study of the differences in rankings for eight reward categories among a sample of 210 employees of public, private, and hybrid organizations, Wittmer (1991) found significant differences among public and private employees with regard to preferences for higher pay, status, and helping others. Perry and Wise also studied the motivation of public servants. They explored the possibility that there is a unique public service motivation, defined as "an individual's predisposition to respond to motives grounded primarily or uniquely in public institutions and organizations" (Perry and Wise, 1990:

368–369). This led them to identify three analytically distinct types of public service motivation. *Rational motivation* is grounded in individual utility maximization; it includes such motivations as the desire to participate in the formulation of good public policy, commitment to a program because of personal identification with it, and conscious or unconscious advocacy for a special interest. Norm-based motivation is based on idealism, and includes such motivations as the desire to serve the public interest, patriotism, a sense of duty to the government as a whole, and a commitment to social equity, defined as enhancing the well-being of minorities. *Affective motivation* is commitment based on personal identification with a program that develops out of such factors as conviction about its social importance, service to society, and Frederickson and Hart's (1985) patriotism of benevolence, a combination of caring about the government's values and caring about others. In a subsequent study, Perry (1996, 1997) identified four constituent dimensions of public service motivation: attraction to public policy making, commitment to the public interest and civic duty, compassion, and self-sacrifice, although he found little difference between a four-dimension model and a three-dimension model that did not include self-sacrifice. Personally, I find Perry and Wise's formulation comprehensive and more descriptive of public servants as I know them.

In an empirical study of the motivation of 421 managers to adopt information technology innovations in forty-seven municipalities, Perry et al. (1993) found that three categories of managers – top managers, other department and division heads, and information system managers –shared two major motivations, the desire to *improve productivity* and *enhance service*. They did not find professionalism or innovation to be important motivators, nor that managerial motivation was determined purely or even primarily by environmental factors. Altruism was more important than self-interest as a motivation (Mansbridge, 1990); control was not more important than production efficiency (Hannaway, 1987). Likewise prestige and professional status were not more important than service and efficiency.

This research suggests that these public servants are motivated by both intrinsic and extrinsic motivation. The types of motivation fall into two basic categories: some – such as Perry et al.'s (1993) norm-based, affective, rational, commitment to the public interest, civic duty, compassion, self-sacrifice, altruism, self-interest, and control – derive from the personal belief or need systems of the public servants involved, and according to Thomas and Velthouse's definition (1990) could be considered to be intrinsically motivated. Others – such as productivity, service, and arbitrary rewards and goals – relate to the external world and could be considered to be extrinsically motivated. The authors suggest that a complex interaction of experience, personality, and environment determine motivation.

The concepts of intrinsic and extrinsic motivation have a passive flavor about them. People have somehow become like that: how, why, and how the condition is maintained are not illuminated. Even Bandura's self-efficacy is a condition. Amitai Etzioni postulated a more active approach, which can be seen to be linked to the German tradition of searching for subjective meanings that impel action (Coser, 1977: 247). According to Etzioni, *individual consciousness* allows the individual to be aware and pay attention. This is a relationship, since awareness is always of something. *Societal consciousness* creates a generalized capacity to be aware on the part of societal actors, in part through an aggregation of individual members' consciousness, but also through institutionalization of awareness on the collective level, for example, through the creation of sub-units charged with *paying attention* (Etzioni, 1971: 224–225).

Organizational Culture and Innovation

Etzioni recognized the importance of both individual and collective consciousness in producing autonomy and innovative behavior. He identified three types of consciousness that contributed to action: consciousness of the environment, the acting self, and controlling overlayers. He pointed to the *normative–cognitive pattern* that provides an evaluative structure for action. The capacity to innovate is related to the capacity for autonomous direction and action, growing out of individual self-consciousness, self-identity, values, commitment, knowledge, and power. Self-conscious actors can also be expected to be less well integrated into their societal systems, communities (and presumably, organizations), to be more instrumental and manipulative than others and to have slower reactions. They can also be expected to be more creative, to engage in less trial-and-error behavior when confronted with a new problem, to design solutions, to be more transformable and more utopian (Etzioni, 1971: 225–229).

> Making a societal unit more conscious of its societal environment, its structure, its identity, and its dynamics is part of the process of transforming a passive unit into an active one. Consciousness is an essential prerequisite for the active orientation: Although actors can act with limited or even no consciousness, we expect in this case that they will tend to realize fewer of their goals. On the other hand, an increase in consciousness *alone* implies mainly an increase in symbolic activity, and hence, if other elements such as commitment and power are lacking, the societal unit may not be more active. (Etzioni, 1971: 229)

The social environment in an organization is sometimes referred to as its organizational or corporate culture. Like the concept of motivation, the concept of organizational culture is commonly used to describe the social environment in a workplace. Corporate culture, according to Cummings and Huse, is "the pattern of basic assumptions, values, norms and artifacts shared by organization members." These cultural elements are "generally taken for granted and serve to guide members' perceptions, thoughts and actions" (Cummings and Huse, 1989: 421, 71). Artifacts are visible manifestations of the other levels of cultural elements and include observable behaviors of members, structures, systems, procedures, rules, and physical aspects (Cummings and Huse, 1989: 421). Similarly, Schein defined organizational culture as "a pattern of basic assumptions – invented, discovered, or developed by a given group as it learns to cope with its problems of external adaptation and internal integration – that has worked well enough to be considered valid and, therefore, to be taught to new members as the correct way to perceive, think, and feel in relation to those problems" (Schein, 1985: 9). Culture should be understood at three levels, according to Schein: Artifacts (the visible level-constructed physical and social environment), values, and basic underlying assumptions. Assumptions are likely to be taken for granted, and are less conscious than observed behavioral regularities, norms, dominant values, organizational philosophy, rules of the game or feelings and climates. Schein sees *organizations or groups* as "open systems in constant interaction with their many environments," consisting of "many subgroups, occupational units, hierarchical layers and geographically dispersed segments" (Schein, 1985: 7). While the management literature has tended to treat organizational culture as a malleable instrument for improving performance (Peters and Waterman, 1982; Deal and Kennedy, 1982), organizational development studies usually consider culture a network of shared meanings (Turner, 1971; Smirchich, 1983) or a structure of symbols that is quite constant (Silverman and Jones, 1976; Burawoy, 1979).

From both Etzioni's sociological perspective and the organizational development perspective, an important aspect of organizational culture is thus its understanding of power within the organization. Filby and Willmott (1988) perceived work culture as a medium and an outcome of the reproduction of a structure of power relations. With a critical, emancipatory intent, Burrell and Morgan (1979) saw *cultural myth* as a tool used to reflect and reproduce, in codified forms, relations of domination. Some innovation research has emphasized the role of structure and process as reflections of power and authority in organizational cultures. Rogers and Eveland (1978: 191–192) suggested components of structure were control or authority structure, centralization or decentralization, complexity (represented by level of knowledge, expertise, and professionalism), formalization (represented by codification of jobs), communication integration (identified by the degree to which the members of a system are interconnected by interpersonal communication patterns), organizational slack, and organizational efficacy. Individuals who provide an organization with openness are called cosmopolites – usually these were regarded as managers, but working level staff were also found to have networks exterior to the organization. Both internal and external structure were seen as important.

If an innovation creates a reaction in individuals, affects motivation and creates change in organizational culture through its modifications of structure, process, and power, it also creates a direct challenge to members of the organization. An innovation presents itself to staff as a challenge and/or an opportunity. Although the challenge presented by an innovation could be defined as risk, the management literature tends to treat *risk* as challenges to management, without much reference to working level staff. In the interests of comprehensiveness, this chapter introduces the concept of challenge instead, in order to address the phenomenon faced by both – working level staff and management. This approach allows more issues to be addressed.

Magnitude of Challenge

Challenges and opportunities come in many forms. At the personal level they are found in the amount of money, time, work, and psychic energy that would be given or received to implement the innovation. Losses or gains might be implied. Losses and gains can be personal, involving loss of power, money, status, and respect, or they can be public, involving failure, career consequences, public scrutiny and/or negative media attention. The magnitude of change involved in the innovation also presents a challenge to employees. Change, especially change that affects an employee personally, is often disruptive.

The characteristics of innovations that affect the rate of adoption as identified by Rogers and Eveland (1978) can be considered challenges. They include the relative advantage of the innovation compared to what it is superseding, the compatibility with existing values and past experience of the implementers, the complexity both in terms of understanding and use, their testability, and the observability of the results. Rogers and Eveland identified advantage and compatibility dimensions, and found they contained both a potential perceived implication of commitment to further change and a threat of change. They acknowledged that each individual in the organization could have a different perception about the challenge or opportunity. Consider, for example, the reallocation of power. For some more power is welcome, for others it is not. For some loss of power is a large challenge, for others it is a relief. It was because of recognition of challenge that communication was seen as a vital component of dissemination.

Nadler and Tushman (1986) reflected the challenge in innovation when they offered their distinction between two types of change. They differentiated between incremental and strategic change, defining incremental change as changing pieces or components of the organization and strategic change as involving most of the organization's parts and features.

Strategic change is more challenging to the people affected and the organization than incremental change. Hickson et al. (1986) developed a system of classification for magnitude of change that is applicable to the perception of staff. They described four degrees of change: status quo, expanded reproduction, evolutionary transition and revolutionary transformation. Table 2.1 outlines their framework for understanding degrees of change. While status quo and expanded reproduction are usually concerned with operational decisions and produce incremental change, evolutionary transition and revolutionary transformation primarily involve strategic and policy decisions and require a shift in the current ways of operating or thinking about the organization's functions. Although status quo does not have much potential to describe innovation, some innovations affect the status quo very little while other innovations change it a good deal. Hickson et al.'s classification provides a framework that can be used for thinking about change as predicted and perceived by the members of the organization.

Table 2.1: Degrees of Organizational Change

Degree of Change	Operational/ Strategic Level	Characteristics
Status quo	Can be both operational and strategic	No change in current practice
Expanded Reproduction	Mainly operational	Change involves producing more of the same
Evolutionary transition	Mainly strategic	Change occurs within existing parameters of the organization (e.g. change, but retain existing structure, technology, etc.)
Revolutionary change	Predominantly strategic	Change involves shifting/redefining existing parameters. Structure and technology likely to change, for example.

Based on: D. J. Hickson, R. J. Butler, D. Cray, G. Mallory and D. C. Wilson. 1986. *Top Decisions: Strategic Decision Making in Organizations*. Oxford: Blackwell; San Francisco: Jossey-Bass, as summarized in David C. Wilson. 1992. *A Strategy of Change: Concepts and Controversies in the Management of Change*. London and New York: Routledge, p. 20.

Embedded in the challenges identified by Rogers and Eveland (1978), Nadler and Tushman (1986) and Hickson et al. (1986) is the question of whether power can be expected to change for those affected by the change. If power will change, especially if it will change considerably, the challenge is heightened. Power is a complex concept that is treated by psychologists as a motivating factor or expectancy belief state internal to the individual. It fulfills the need for self-determination and a sense of personal efficacy (Bandura, 1977a). In the psychological conceptualization, power has its base within motivational disposition, is closely related to the concept of personal empowerment, and could be considered an element of intrinsic motivation.

While psychologists focus on personal empowerment, sociologists and political scientists see power as influence and control over sanctions. Most analysts start with Max Weber's (1968) definition of power: The probability that a person can carry out his or her own will despite resistance. Bierstedt (1974) saw power as force or the ability to apply sanctions. It included the potential, not just the actual use of force, that is, the application of sanctions, and was distinguished from influence. Power was inherently coercive and implied involuntary submission, whereas influence was persuasive and implied voluntary submission. Dahl's (1963) work was also based on Weber's definition: power was exercised whenever one party affected the behavior of another, thus fusing the force and influence dimensions. An unused potential was not power, because power implied successful use of the potential. Wrong (1968) was also grounded in Weber: he held that the behavior of others could be altered either by potential power or by use of power (actual power). Compliance is often based on the target's subjective expectation that the potential can and will be used when necessary. Groups and individuals may control resources that can be developed into a base for power or the base can be left dormant and undeveloped: Attention should be paid to the subjective nature of power and the processes of power acquisition. Bacharach and Lawler (1980: 13–26) regarded power as a sensitizing device.

Challenges are factors that create resistance to adoption of an innovation. Albert Bandura (1977b) identified challenges such as perceived risks, negative self-evaluation, various social barriers and economic constraints.

He suggested that challenge is counterbalanced by influences encouraging adoption, such as stimulus inducements, anticipated satisfactions, positive self-evaluation, observed benefits, and experienced functional value, which can be revealed through pilot and demonstration projects. If the positive benefits are perceived as dominant, the net magnitude of challenge will be low, if negative perceptions predominate, innovation will be seen as a major challenge.

Discussion

Motivation and Innovation

Motivation to innovate is treated in this chapter as the reason people become willing to adopt the sense of the need to change in the workplace. Whether and how individuals become motivated to innovate is important for the fate of innovations. As discussed above, innovation motivated by the requests, demands, and direction of superiors will likely create extrinsic motivation and innovation motivated by meaning, competence, self-determination and impact (Thomas and Velthouse, 1990) will likely produce intrinsic motivation. For the purposes of creating a framework for innovation, action, change, and innovation can thus be thought of as being motivated one of two ways: *intrinsically*, growing out of individual drive and commitment, and *extrinsically*, due to direction, pressure or encouragement.

Like the Perry et al. (1993) research, most study of innovation in organizations has focused on the role of managers in deciding to adopt an innovation. The current study seeks to include the role of all staff, because in some organizational cultures front-line staff play a major role in identifying and choosing innovations, and also because they are usually the ones responsible for implementing innovations. Many innovations falter at the implementation stage, making the essential role of implementers apparent. Like the motivation to adopt, the motivation to implement innovation has not, unfortunately, been studied much (Rogers and Eveland, 1978).

The phenomenon at work seems clear, however – intrinsically motivated staff are empowered. While empowerment has been defined a number of ways, the most empowering strategies seem to be personal enablement and participation, generating self-efficacy, power, and intrinsic motivation, while the least empowering strategies are delegation by third parties of powers and responsibilities to middle managers and front line staff (Glor, 2001b), generating extrinsic motivation. Since motivation affects the objectives served, as described by Perry et al. (1993) and Perry and Wise (1990), it also has an impact on the effort expended and the quality of work. People are more likely to persevere in tasks, work harder, and do higher quality work if they are intrinsically motivated (Lepper and Greene, 1975; Deci and Ryan, 1985; Harackiewicz and Elliot, 1993). External rewards can have the opposite effect desired, by causing intrinsic motivation to decline (Lepper and Greene, 1975; Eisenberger et al., 1999; McGraw, 1978). The motivation created has implications, as well, for the level of creativity of the ideas produced. Theresa Amabile has identified the factors that promote problem solving or personal creativity. Although group factors were not shown to do so, with one exception – qualities of the group assisted creativity – personal characteristics did relate to creativity: specific personality traits, self-motivation, special cognitive abilities, a risk orientation, diverse experience, expertise in the area, social skill, brilliance, and naiveté. The qualities of problem solvers that inhibited creativity, on the other hand, were lack of motivation, lack of skill, inflexibility, external motivation, and lack of social skills. Individual creativity was enhanced, in other words, by domain-relevant skills, creativity-relevant skills and *intrinsic task motivation*. The intrinsically motivated person was more creative than someone who was extrinsically motivated (Amabile, 1988: 142–143).

While intrinsically motivated people are committed to different objectives, work harder, produce better quality work, and are more creative, they may also be more willing to change. For an individual who is intrinsically motivated, individual needs and wants are met, and s/he is engaged. Some people are frequently intrinsically motivated, are more often self-actualized (Maslow in Lowry, 1973), and actively position themselves where they can work on their personal interests. Other people can become intrinsically motivated, given a suitable, supportive environment within which to work.

Given that people are differently motivated in relation to innovation and that these differences should have implications for innovation, is there any indication of how people are typically motivated when innovating? In his survey of 217 Ford Foundation–Harvard University American Innovation Award finalists, Sandford Borins found that 48 per cent of the innovations were initiated by frontline workers and middle managers (Borins, 1998). On the other hand, from the perspective of the other half of the applicants studied, the innovations were initiated by agency heads, politicians, interest groups, nonprofit groups, and individual citizens, people outside the immediate work unit. In his survey of the members of the Institute of Public Administration of Canada, J. Iain Gow found most members of IPAC – Canadian academics and employees of Canadian federal, provincial, municipal, and territorial governments – looked to senior staff to develop innovative ideas (Gow, 1991). In the Gow study, more than half of the innovations were initiated organizationally from above those who would implement them, while among Borins' finalists it was 41 per cent. Initiation and/or direction to innovate from senior staff or politicians enhance extrinsic motivation for working level staff and do not fully engage intrinsic motivation, individual effort, creativity, and commitment.

At the same time, in a hierarchical organization like government, central agency and senior management support is crucial to secure the approval necessary to implement an innovation. Central decision-takers are most likely to approve an innovation if they themselves are intrinsically motivated by it. If motivation, creativity, and acceptance are to be maximized, the creation of intrinsic motivation and control at both the frontline and at the center becomes a core problem for innovation in organizations generally and in government in particular.

Intrinsic and extrinsic motivation thus have important implications for innovation. Innovation is probably affected by the types of objectives sought by the individual and the motivation created in the individual, both in terms of how creative the options identified are and how interested the person is in the innovation. But innovation is not solely affected by what happens internal to the individual. It is also affected by the social environment – the collective attributes of the work environment or organizational culture and how it manages itself. While individual motivation and organizational culture can be seen as being interdependent (Bandura, 1977b: 206), it is also useful to consider the ways in which they are independent.

Organizational Culture

Many change models are built from the perspective of management. Some explore how leaders can overcome individual and collective resistance to change (e.g. Maurer, 1996; Strebel, 1996; Collins, 1999). These are defined here as *top-down* approaches. Other models of change take *bottom-up* approaches. Many quality models, for example, emphasize the role of staff in identifying quality problems and solutions; satisfying customers, suppliers, and investors (in the private sector); and controlling resources. Quality models also focus on culture change but emphasize frontline staff and leaders working together cooperatively. Participative models, too, suggest non-managerial staff have a cardinal role to play in change (Cotton, 1993).

Top-down change models are the most common. Schein (1985) saw organizational cultures as being created by leaders, asserting:

> Organizational cultures are created by leaders, and one of the most decisive functions of leadership may well be the creation, the management, and – if and when that may become necessary – the destruction of culture ... there is a possibility ... that the only thing of real importance that leaders do is to create and manage culture. (Schein, 1985: 2)

The function of culture is to solve the group's problems of survival and adaptation to an external environment, and integration of internal processes to ensure capacity to continue to survive and adapt (Schein, 1985: 50). Schein perceived organizations as going through three developmental phases, during which the function of culture and the change mechanisms vary. During birth and early growth, culture is the glue that holds the organization together and socialization is a sign of commitment. Change occurs through natural evolution and managed revolution by outsiders. During organizational midlife, new subcultures are spawned, key goals and values are lost, and an opportunity to manage the direction of change is presented. Change mechanisms include planning change and organization development, technical seduction, scandal and explosion of myths, and incrementalism. During organizational maturity, markets mature or decline, the organization is internally stable or even stagnates, and there is a lack of motivation to change. The culture becomes a constraint on innovation, preserving the glories of the past as a source of self-esteem and defense. Change occurs through transformation, where some key aspects of the culture change, or through destruction. The change mechanisms are coercive persuasion, turnaround, reorganization, destruction, and rebirth (Schein, 1985: 271–272).

Lewin's top-down change model used *forces at work*. He identified driving forces for change as new personnel, changing markets, changing attitudes, internationalization, social transformations and new technology. Restraining forces included fear of failure, loss of status, inertia/habit, strength of culture, rigidity of structure, lack of resources, contractual agreements and strongly held beliefs and recipes for evaluating activities (Lewin, 1951). According to Lewin, most of the driving forces come from outside the organization, while most of the restraining forces, many of which – such as strongly held beliefs – are cultural, come from within. Since he recognized very few internal driving forces for change, he can be recognized as seeing the need for top-down change. The concepts of *change management and the manager as a change leader* are two other top-down models of change. While putting management of individuals at center-stage in change might lead to the conclusion that individuals have an important role to play in bringing innovation about, such models usually involve implementing preconceived models of change and achieving a particular set of expected, predetermined, and desired outcomes. The approach of empowering managers to plan for change tends to ignore wider forces and implications of actions, including the implications for staff.

Peters and Waterman's (1982) excellence model is a structural approach and also top-down. Although critical of bureaucratic structure, the excellence model suggests that structure is important for performance and recommends a decentralized, project-based organizational design. In a causal, unidirectional, *one best way* approach to organization – a concept first developed by Frederick Taylor and used for design of assembly lines – change, organizational structure, and culture are linked, and culture is manipulated through its structure. For Peters and Waterman the organization is decentralized to achieve change. Project-based organizations that place individuals at the center of organizational attention are seen as those that succeed. While people are emphasized, the culture requires almost fanatical devotion from employees. Individual choice is limited and the culture is not recognized as having a contextual role for change. Despite its decentralization, the excellence approach remains top-down (Wilson, 1992: 75). According to top-down approaches, a combination of culture change, human resource management and total quality management are said to be key to organizational performance and produce employees who share values and give of their best at work.

While top-down cultural approaches became a central theme in management and organization literature during the 1980s, some authors were critical of this approach. In their skeptical article about culture, Alvesson and Willmott (1996) referred to the potential for the prescriptions of corporate culture to have subjugating and even totalitarian implications, and pointed to the benefits of and the need to work for autonomy, self-conscious formulation of values, and democratic practices. The need for critical thinking to set the stage for encouraging emancipation in the workplace are highlighted. They advocated a bottom-up culture.

Compared to a structural approach, an interpretive view of culture uses the perspective of the individual to define the situation and is bottom-up. The important factors are the interpretive and cognitive processes by which individuals support change, facilitate it, or attempt to disrupt it. While symbols, language, and interpretation are essential to both the structural and interpretive approaches, through the interpretive approach corporate culture is personalized. The change process is seen as fueled by a variety of interpretations, each of which contributes to or detracts from spurring action, creating vision and sustaining energy in those participating. An interpretive view recognizes more permanency in culture and is bottom-up. Change can be seen internally to the organization in several other, bottom-up ways – occurring, for example in an open system, a population ecology or organizational life cycles (Wilson, 1992: 41–49). The structural and interpretive approaches are not mutually exclusive, however – both structure and interpretation are at work in an organization – neither the organization nor the individual is the sole element considered in organizational culture. As well, broader societal and institutional values affect change in organizations. They bring to bear such issues as the sense of individualism or community, the power distance that is acceptable, and the degree to which uncertainty is or is not tolerated.

Handy (1986) recognized both top-down and bottom-up cultures: Of his four types of organizational culture, based on the division of labor, power and role cultures can be seen as top-down while task and people cultures can be seen as bottom-up. A power culture is centrally controlled by a single individual or group that determines the culture, and favors and nurtures strong individuals. In role cultures processes are subject to rule, precedent, and regulation, and people are organized in a pyramid, with large power distance and reduced ambiguity. The culture of the task or business project is often found in decentralized, consensual organizations that favor group over individual work in matrix structures. A culture of people or professionalism favors individualism, avoids bureaucratization and large power distances, and often lacks structure.

The culture-based change models described above have been grouped into top-down and bottom-up cultures. A culture that supports staff, pays attention to their ideas, creates strategies for and implements those ideas is a bottom-up culture. One that provides direction to innovate from above – for example, from leaders, managers or cabinet ministers – is top-down. These are fundamentally different approaches that could be expected to affect the outcomes of innovation. But staff's responses to an innovation are not just a function of their internal states and their organization's culture. They are also affected by their relationship to the innovation itself.

Challenge

The challenge of an innovation rests both in the power that must be exercised to bring it about and in the changes in the granting, transfer or sharing of power that are implied by its implementation. It is possible to draw a distinction between minor and major challenges. *Minor challenges* are expected by the participants to involve low personal threat, incremental change, status quo or expanded reproduction, and no or minor changes in power. *Major challenges* are expected by the participants to involve high personal threat, strategic change, evolutionary transition or revolutionary transformation, and changes in power relationships within the government or vis-a-vis groups outside the government. Part of the role of a leader in introducing innovation is to find strategies for reducing the magnitude of the challenges presented by innovation.

Values influence decisions about magnitude of challenge. What happens in government is affected by the values of public servants and also by political and ideological input to decisions. Those involved in decisions bring their own values to play in the decisions, although the values are often not made explicit, especially in the public service context, where employees (at least under some governments) are expected to be politically neutral. Instead, values and political beliefs remain part of the tacit information that employees bring to discussions. An innovation that moves in a direction not valued by the participant is more of a challenge than a change in a valued direction. A right-winger, for example, would find pro-business innovations less of a challenge than expansions of the social safety net; a left-winger would have the opposite response.

Are These the Right Factors?

Acknowledging that it is not really possible to reflect reality fully in three dimensions, there are at least three good reasons for representing it this way. First, many students of organizations (Bandura, Schein) have identified these factors as fundamental to change in organizations. Students of innovation such as Perry and Wise (1990) have seen innovation through similar lenses. Second, Everett Rogers' five factors (Table 2.2) can be dovetailed into two of these three. The nature of the social system and type of innovation decision can be seen as represented in organizational culture, while the perceived attributes of innovation, communication channels and extent of change agents' promotion efforts can be seen as part of the challenge and efforts to diminish the challenge. Rogers does not emphasize the role of the individual, as this author does. Lastly, by combining

Table 2.2:   Rogers' Variables Determining the Rate of Adoption of Innovations

Variables Determining Rate of Adoption	Dependent Variable Explained
I. Perceived Attributes of Innovations 1. Relative advantage 2. Compatibility 3. Complexity 4. Trialability 5. Observability	Rate of Adoption of Innovations
II. Type of Innovation-Decision 1. Optional 2. Collective 3. Authority	Rate of Adoption of Innovations
III. Communication Channels (e.g. mass media or interpersonal)	Rate of Adoption of Innovations
IV. Nature of Social Systems (e.g. its norms, degree of network interconnectedness, etc.)	Rate of Adoption of Innovations
V. Extent of Change Agents Promotion Effects	Rate of Adoption of Innovations

Based on: Everett M. Rogers. 1995. *Diffusion of Innovations. Fourth Edition*. New York and Toronto: The Free Press, pp. 206–208 and Figure 6–1.

the dynamics into and limiting the analysis to three factors, it is much easier to use and to see the effect of these factors in creating patterns of innovation. These patterns are discussed in a subsequent paper (see Glor, 2001a). Still, it is appropriate to ask: Are motivation, culture, and challenge independent of each other?

Relationships among the Factors

Some observers treat motivation as a part of or even a by-product of the environment, culture or management style of the organization. These same observers typically emphasize the role of the manager or leader in generating culture and employee motivation and de-emphasize the beliefs, commitments, and actions that employees bring to the workplace. Culture and management can influence motivation, as recognized by the concept of extrinsic motivation. Schein (1985), on the other hand, would say that culture helps define management and vice versa, so management and culture cannot be separated. Likewise, Bandura in his concept of self-efficacy (Bandura, 1977a; 1997) and Czikszentmihalyi in his concept of flow and the concept of intrinsic motivation all belie the idea that motivation is entirely determined by context. These authors suggest that motivation is an individual characteristic and, at least sometimes, an internally generated phenomenon. Perry and Wise (1990: 368–369) confirmed the independence of motivation with their three sources of motivation – rationality, norms, and feeling – all three of which, this author has suggested, could induce intrinsic motivation.

To be able to perceive the possibility of intrinsic and extrinsic motivation, the individual and the community/culture must be conceived as having, at least to some extent, an independent existence. New public management critics of public servants serving personal interests on the job also recognize that employees can be internally motivated, albeit that the critics prefer to diminish and control such independence. Bandura described the social learning perspective, in which psychological functioning is a reciprocal interaction among personal, behavioral, and environmental determinants. He concluded that it has not been especially informative to try to gauge the relative importance of these factors (Bandura, 1977b: 194). While the precise influence of personal motivation and organizational culture is unclear, both affect innovation.

The same argument can be made for the relationship between challenge and the other factors. The challenge faced by an individual is a function not only of the dynamics identified earlier, but also of motivation and culture. For someone who is extrinsically motivated and works in a top-down culture, innovation may seem more of a challenge than for someone who is intrinsically motivated and works in a bottom-up culture. While at one level these factors are independent, they also influence each other.

These types of interrelationships are recognized by systems analysis that identifies patterns, not causal relationships. The three factors – individual, culture, and challenge – can be understood as interacting in patterns. Each interaction is unique, yet the interactions tend to form into patterns, perhaps in a manner conceptually similar to those produced by chaos theory. The enormously complex behavior represented by the individual, culture, and challenge may thereby be seen as assuming recognizable shapes. The three factors of motivation, culture, and challenge are interrelated to form patterns in Figure 2.1, and the patterns are named. These patterns are examined and some evidence is offered that the patterns exist in Glor (2001a).[2]

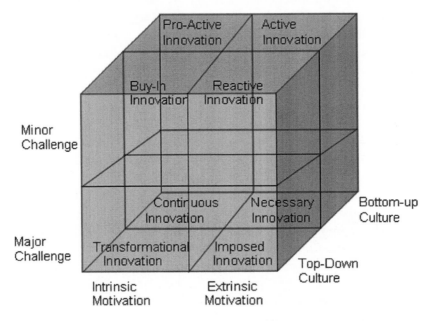

Figure 2.1: Innovation patterns, based on source of motivation, organizational culture, and magnitude of challenge. Courtesy of: *The Innovation Journal: The Public Sector Innovation Journal.* Used with permission.

The Relationship between Organizational and Societal Culture

So far this discussion of organizational innovation has looked only within the organization. But organizations cannot be separated completely from society. Robert Putnam, for example, has argued that societies have

2   These patterns have been expanded upon in Glor (2001a, 2007, 2015a, b).

long-established ways of functioning – hierarchical or democratic ways in the Italian context (Putnam, 1993). It is possible that organizations have long-established ways of functioning, as well, that are extremely difficult to change.

Putnam's work on civic culture and its relationship to good government and innovation raised the issue of whether or not organizational culture and societal culture are related. Do hierarchical and elitist societies tend to have hierarchical and elitist organizations? Similarly, do participative and democratic civic societies also tend to have participative and democratic organizations? Although this chapter cannot articulate a position on this question, the source of the culture of governmental and private organizations is an important one for future consideration. If it were true that organizations tend to replicate society's patterns of authority, and that methods of interacting within organizations mirror methods of communicating in societies, organizations could be expected to create vicious and virtuous circles internally. This would help to explain the innovation adoption patterns of organizations.

Etzioni suggested there are two essential links between the level of societal consciousness and societal capacity for innovation and transformation: "One concerns the building of new structures and systems; the other involves the 'unlocking' of old ones" (Etzioni, 1971: 240). The capacity to build new structures and systems grows out of a capacity to transcend the self, to design new patterns, and to direct efforts toward their realization. The most significant factor that interferes with this process is subscription to views that conceal options, often associated with conservative ideology. Etzioni acknowledges that transformation almost always involves a power struggle. He expects increased consciousness of *existing societal morphology* to be associated with more effective unlocking and easier transformation because increased societal consciousness is associated with increased personal willingness to change, elites more conscious of societal patterns are more able to innovate and design alternate ones, and societal patterns are at least partly symbolic, and so can be changed somewhat through increased consciousness. Moreover, the conditions under which the capacity for transformation is high are determined in part by the extent to which the environment is changing (Etzioni, 1971: 238–243).

Conclusion

Because staff often are not intrinsically motivated by innovation (either because their intrinsic motivation is not induced by the government's action or because of an organization's management style), a stream of management theory, research, and practice has been occupied with the question of how to encourage or persuade staff to become more creative and innovative (Amabile, 1988; Basadur et al., 1982). Private sector companies, moreover, are actively using creativity enhancement techniques to accomplish this goal. One journalist reported that half of the firms in the U.S.A. had used such techniques in 1997 (Johnson, 1998). Creativity techniques attempt to draw on tacit knowledge and encourage staff to realize connections with their intrinsic motivators. Unlike private industry, governments are not using creativity enhancement techniques much. While public servants often feel committed to their work, this is primarily self-generated through intrinsic motivation because governments as organizations do not often seek to encourage creativity nor induce intrinsic motivation very much.

Motivation speaks to inputs, culture addresses the environment, while the magnitude of challenge addresses risk for the people in an organization and the difficulties realizing an innovation. The advantage of a model that integrates motivation, environment, and risk is that it allows the linkages among the three factors to be made more apparent. The purpose of this exercise is to help generate discussion and theory building about the major factors at work in innovation. An hypothesis is suggested:

> How people are motivated, the culture of an organization and the magnitude of challenge are primary relationships in determining patterns of innovation.

The factors suggested – motivation, culture, and magnitude of challenge – interact in an organization. The next step is to examine the nature of the patterns they form.

Further research must address additional issues. First, it must deal with the likelihood that these factors are not really bifurcated, and so should be considered to be along a continuum. If the factors are arranged on a continuum, the patterns would lean toward categories rather than fitting solidly within them. Some implications are discussed in Glor (2001b, 2007, 2015a, b). Second, are some factors more important than others? Bandura has suggested, for example, that the inclination to adopt innovations is best considered "in terms of controlling conditions rather than in terms of types of people" (Bandura, 1977b: 54). The implication might be that organizational culture is more important than motivation or challenge in determining adoptive behavior. Third, each of the categories requires further exploration. Is the individual role in innovation best expressed in terms of motivation or, for example, should it be considered in terms of roles played in relation to innovation? Or, perhaps certain players are important at specific points: champions, leaders, and implementers play different roles in innovation – perhaps the former is most important at the acquisition stage, while the latter is at the implementation stage. Fourth, what other factors are important in the successful adoption and implementation of innovations? Bandura (1977b: 50–51), for example, has identified modeling as the medium by which most people are influenced both to acquire and to adopt innovation. Is the role model therefore crucial? Fifth, is the collective way of doing things best expressed as a culture? Lastly, the concepts of top-down and bottom-up cultures also need to be explored further. They seem to parallel Putnam's high and low civic capital concepts: Is there such a thing as social capital in an organization? Consideration needs to be given to these alternate concepts and approaches.

Bibliography

Alvesson, M., & H. Willmott. 1996. *Making Sense of Management: A Critical Introduction*. London: Sage Publications.

Amabile, T. M. 1983. *The Social Psychology of Creativity*. New York: Springer-Verlag.

Amabile, T. M. 1988. A Model of Creativity and Innovation in Organizations. *Research in Organizational Behavior*, 10: 123–167.

Bacharach, S. B., & E. J. Lawler. 1980. *Power and Politics in Organizations*. San Francisco, CA: Jossey-Bass Publishers.

Bandura, A. 1977a. Self-efficacy: Toward a unifying theory of behavioural change. *Psychological Review*, 84: 191–215.

Bandura, A. 1977b. *Social Learning Theory.* Englewood Cliffs, NJ: Prentice-Hall.

Bandura, A. 1986. *Social Foundations of Thought and Action: A Social Cognitive Theory.* Englewood Cliffs, NJ: Prentice-Hall.

Bandura, A. 1997. *Self-efficacy:the exercise of control.* New York: W. H. Freeman.

Basadur, M., G. B. Graen, & S. G. Green. 1982. Training in Creative Problem-Solving: Effects on ideation and problem-solving in an industrial research organization. *Organizational Behavior and Human Performance,* 30: 41–47.

Becker, S. W., & T. L. Whisler. 1967. The innovative organization: A selective view of current theory and research. *Journal of Business,* 40: 462–469.

Bierstedt, R. 1974. *The social order.* 4th Edn. New York: McGraw-Hill.

Borins, S. 1998. *Innovating With Integrity: How Local Heroes Are Transforming American Government.* Washington, DC: Georgetown University Press.

Brewer, G. A., S. C. Selden & R. L. Facer II. 2000. Individual Conceptions of Public Service Motivation. *Public Administration Review* 60(3) (May/June): 254–264.

Burawoy, M. 1979. *Manufacturing consent.* Berkeley: University of California Press.

Burrell, G., & G. Morgan. 1979. *Sociological paradigms and organisational analysis.* London: Heinemann.

Capra, F. 1996. *The Web of Life. A New Scientific Understanding of Living Systems.* Toronto, New York, London: Anchor Books, Doubleday.

Cofer, C. N. 1996. Extrinsic Motivation. In Benjamin B. Wolman (ed. in chief), *The Encyclopedia of Psychiatry, Psychology, and Psychoanalysis.* New York: Henry Holt and Company.

Collins, J. 1999. Turning Goals into Results: The Power of Catalytic Mechanisms. *Harvard Business Review,* July–August: 70–82.

Coser, L. A. 1977. *Masters of Sociological Thought.* 2nd Edn. New York: Harcourt Brace Jovanovich.

Cotton, J. L. 1993. *Employee Involvement: Methods for Improving Performance and Work Attitudes.* Newbury Park, London: Sage Publications.

Cummings, T. G., & E. F. Huse. 1989. *Organization development and change.* 4th Edn. New York: West Publishing.

Czikszentmihalyi, M. 1990. *Flow: The Psychology of Optimal Experience.* New York: Harper & Row.

Dahl, R. A. 1963. *Modern Political Analysis.* Englewood Cliffs, NJ: Prentice-Hall.

Deal, T., & A. Kennedy. 1982. *Corporate culture: the rites and rituals of corporate life.* Reading, MA: Addison-Wesley.

Deci, E., & R. M. Ryan. 1985. *Intrinsic motivation and self-determination in human behavior.* New York: Plenum Press.

Dyer, L., & D. F. Parker. 1975. Classifying outcomes in work motivation research: An examination of the intrinsic–extrinsic dichotomy. *Journal of Applied Psychology,* 60: 455–458.

Eisenberger, R., L. Rhoades & J. Cameron. 1999. Does Pay for Performance Increase or Decrease Perceived Self-Determination and Intrinsic Motivation? *Journal of Personality and Social Psychology*, 77(5): 1026–1040.

Elkin, S. L. 1983. Towards a Contextual Theory of Innovation, *Policy Sciences*, 15(4) (August): 367–384.

Etzioni, A. 1971. *The Active Society: A Theory of Societal and Political Processes*. New York: The Free Press.

Filby, I., & H. Willmott. 1988. Ideologies and Contradictions in a Public Relations Department: The Seduction and Impotence of Living Myth. *Organization Studies*, 9(3): 336.

Frederickson, H. G., & D. K. Hart. 1985. The Public Service and the Patriotism of Benevolence. *Public Administration Review*, 45 (Sept/Oct): 547–553.

Glor, E. D. 1998. What Do We Know About Enhancing Creativity and Innovation? A Review of Literature. *The Innovation Journal: The Public Sector Innovation Journal*, Collected June 1, 2017 at: <http://www.innovation.cc/all-issues.htm>.

Glor, E. D. 2001a. Innovation Patterns. *The Innovation Journal: The Public Sector Innovation Journal*, 6(3) (July), article 2 <http://www.innovation.cc/volumes-issues/vol6-iss3.htm>.

Glor, E. D. 2001b. Ideas for enhancing employee empowerment in the government of Canada. *Optimum: The Journal of Public Sector Management*, 30(3–4): 14–26.

Glor, E. D. 2007. Assessing Organizational Capacity to Adapt. 2007a. *Emergence: Complexity & Organization (E:CO)*, 9(3): 27–40.

Glor, E. D. 2015a. Building Theory about Evolution of Organizational Change Patterns. 2015. *Emergence: Complexity & Organization (E:CO)*, 16(4).

Glor, E. D. 2015b. *Building Theory of Organizational Innovation, Change*, Fitness and Survival. Ottawa, Canada: The Innovation Journal: The Public Sector Innovation Journal <http://www.innovation.cc/books/20_2_1a_glor_fit_organizations.pdf>.

Gow, J. I. 1991. *Learning from Others: Administrative Innovations among Canadian Governments*. Toronto and Ottawa: The Institute of Public Administration of Canada and the Canadian Centre for Management Development, Government of Canada.

Handy, C. B. 1986. *Understanding Organizations*. Harmondsworth, UK: Penguin.

Hannaway, J. 1987. Supply Creates Demand: An Organizational Process View of Administrative Expansion. *Journal of Policy Analysis and Management*, 7(1): 118–134.

Harackiewicz, J. M., & E. J. Andrew. 1993. Achievement of goals and intrinsic motivation. *Journal of Personality and Social Psychology*, 65(5): 904–915.

Hickson, D. J., R. J. Butler, D. Cray, G. Mallory, & D. C. Wilson. 1986. *Top Decisions: Strategic Decision Making in Organizations*. Oxford: Blackwell; San Francisco, CA: Jossey-Bass.

Johnson, T. 1998. Inventive Purveyors of Unorthodox Methods for Brain Teaser: Fostering corporate creativity have got a few organizations thinking. *The Globe and Mail Report on Business Magazine* (December): 76–84.

Kaplan, H. I., & B. J. Sadock. 1991. *Synopsis of Psychiatry. Sixth Edition*. Baltimore, MA: Williams and Wilkins.

Lepper, M. R., & D. Greene. 1975. Turning play into work: Effects of adult surveillance and extrinsic rewards on children's intrinsic motivation. *Journal of Personality and Social Psychology*, 31(3): 479–486.

Lewin, K. 1951. *Field Theory in Social Science*. New York: Harper and Row.

Lowry, R. J. (ed.). 1973. *Dominance, Self-Esteem, Self-Actualization: Germinal Papers of A. H. Maslow*. Monterey, CA: Brooks/Cole Publishing Company.

McGraw, K. O. 1978. The detrimental effects of reward on performance: A literature review and a prediction model. Pp. 33–60 in M. R. Lepper and D. Greene (eds), *The hidden costs of reward*. Hillsdale, NJ: Erlbaum.

Mansbridge, J. J. (ed.). 1990. *Beyond Self-Interest*. Chicago, IL: University of Chicago Press.

Maurer, R. 1996. *Beyond the Wall of Resistance: Unconventional Strategies that Build Support for Change*. Austin, TX: Bard Books.

Nadler, D. A., & M. L. Tushman. 1986. *Managing Strategic Organizational Change: Frame Bending and Frame Breaking*. New York: Delta Consulting Group.

Perry, J. L. 1996. Measuring Public Service Motivation: An Assessment of Construct Reliability and Validity. *Journal of Public Administration Research and Theory*, 6(1): 5–22.

Perry, J. L. 1997. Antecedents of Public Service Motivation, *Journal of Public Administration Research and Theory*, 7(2): 181–197.

Perry, J. L., K. L. Kraemer, D. E. Dunkle & J. L. King. 1993. Motivations to Innovate in Public Organizations. Pp. 294–306 in B. Bozeman (ed.), *Public Management: The State of the Art*. San Francisco, CA: Jossey-Bass Publishers.

Perry, J. L., & L. R. Wise. 1990. The Motivational Bases of Public Service. *Public Administration Review* (May/June): 367–373.

Perry, J. L., & L. W. Porter. 1982. Factors Affecting the Context for Motivation in Public Organizations. *Academy of Management* Review, 7(1): 89–98.

Peters, T. J., & R. H. Waterman. 1982. *In Search of Excellence*. New York: Warner Books.

Putnam, R. D., with R. Leonardi & R. Y. Nanetti. 1993. *Making democracy work: civic traditions in modern Italy*. Princeton, NJ: Princeton University Press.

Rogers, E., with J. D. Eveland. 1978. Diffusion of innovations perspectives on national R&D assessment: communication and innovation in organizations. Pp. 275–297 in P. Kelly and M. I. Kranzberg (eds), *Technological Innovation: A Critical Review of Current Knowledge*. San Francisco, CA: San Francisco Press.

Schein, E. H. 1985. *Organizational Culture and Leadership*. San Francisco, CA: Jossey-Bass.

Shils, E., & H. Finch (eds). 1949. *Max Weber on the Methodology of the Social Sciences*. New York: Free Press.

Silverman, D., & J. Jones. 1976. *Organisational work; the language of grading and the grading of language*. London: Collier/Macmillan.

Smirchich, L. 1983. Concepts of culture and organizational analysis. *Administrative Science Quarterly*, 28(3): 339–358.

Strebel, P. 1996. Why Do Employees Resist Change? *Harvard Business Review* (May–June): 86–92.

Thomas, K. W., & B. A. Velthouse. 1990. Cognitive elements of empowerment: An "interpretive" model of intrinsic task motivation. *Academy of Management Review*, 15(4): 666–681.

Treasury Board Secretariat. 1996. *Managers' Guide for Implementing Quality Services*. Ottawa, Canada: Government of Canada.

Turner, B. 1971. *Exploring the industrial subculture*. London: Macmillan.

Weber, M. 1968. *Economy and Society: An Outline of Interpretive Sociology* (3 vols), ed. Guenther Roth and Claus Wittich. New York: Bedminster Press.

Wilson, D. C. 1992. *A Strategy of Change: Concepts and Controversies in the Management of Change*. New York and London: Routledge.

Wittmer, D. 1991. Serving the People or Serving for Pay: Reward Preference among Government, Hybrid Sector, and Business Managers. *Public Productivity and Management Review*, 14(4) (summer): 369–383.

Wrong, D. H. 1968. Some Problems in Defining Social Power. *American Journal of Sociology*, 73(6): 673–681.

ELEANOR D. GLOR

3 A Framework for Studying the Impact of Innovation on Organizations, Organizational Populations, and Organizational Communities[1]

ABSTRACT

This chapter develops a framework for studying the impact of innovation on organizations, arguing there are four main aspects to this impact that require four different approaches: (1) successful and unsuccessful cases of implementation of individual innovations that achieve/do not achieve their chosen objectives; the effects of innovations on (2) employees, (3) organizational functioning, and (4) organizational structures. Accordingly, it frames the research within four possible research approaches (case studies, people, functions, structures). The approaches focus on the impact (1) of individual innovations on individual issues and organizations, organizational populations, and organizational communities; (2) on people; (3) of inputs and organizational adaptation; and (4) impacts on structures and survival of organizations, populations, and communities. The framework identifies definitions suitable for each approach, what each approach is most suited to studying, their levels of analysis, suitable methodologies and measures, and the types of impacts each is capable of revealing.

Introduction

While private sector, nonprofit sector and public sector innovation has been vigorously promoted for two generations, the impacts of innovation have not been determined. When the impacts of innovation have been addressed, the focus has tended to be the effect on economic performance at

1 *The Innovation Journal: The Public Sector Innovation Journal*, Volume 19(3), 2014, article 1 <http://www.innovation.cc/volumes-issues/vol19-no3.htm>.

the firm (Evangelista and Vezzani, 2010) and country levels (Sapprasert and
Clausen, 2012). During this period, the primary focus of public sector innovation has been strategies and methods to reduce use of public resources,
create agencies and privatize government functions (the New Public
Management, NPM), not the impact of the innovations. Several authors
have noted the lack of attention to the impacts of the set of innovations
known as NPM (Christensen and Laegreid, 2006: 2; Pollitt, 2001: 480).
Damanpour (1991: 584), who mostly studies the private sector, recommended expanding the scope of innovation studies to include evaluation
of the consequences of innovation.

The innovation literature has tended to focus on the successful implementation of innovations and making appropriate tactical choices about
when to innovate and when to delay/selectively adopt innovations (de
Lancer Julnes and Holzer, 2001). There is much to be learned from innovations that fail but they are difficult to research (e.g. Glor, 1997). In
determining the effect on organizational survival, a clear distinction must
be made between innovations that are not fully implemented or that fail
and ones that are fully implemented and accomplish their objectives. As
well, organizations have many other objectives, for example, supporting
employees, achieving organizational objectives, assuring organizational
survival. This chapter's objectives are to identify ways to determine the
impact of innovations on their organizations and to develop a research
framework for doing so. The term *impact* is defined to include *both* the
results of the innovation's intervention (outcomes) and the broader effects
of the innovation. The chapter builds a framework for research on the
impact of innovation on organizations addressing both the impact of
individual innovations and innovations' impacts on organizational people,
functioning, and structures. Each approach is seated within a different
conceptual paradigm. The paradigms are described, then the chapter
develops an approach and explores innovation within each paradigm, by
discussing the different definitions of innovation used by each approach,
what each is most suited to studying and the issues that can best be studied within it, levels of analysis implied, methodologies and measures
that could be used, and the impacts that can best be studied within each
approach.

Organizational Concepts

The framework is loosely based on Burrell and Morgan's (1979) four organizational paradigms: interpretive, radical humanist, functionalist, and radical structuralist. The interpretive paradigm describes, explains, diagnoses, and understands. The radical humanist paradigm describes, critiques, and seeks to change – critical analysis grew out of it. The functionalist paradigm searches for regularities, tests in order to predict, and controls and maintains the status quo. Theoretical interests are relationships, causation, and generalization. Theory-building occurs through causal analysis. The radical structuralist paradigm identifies sources of domination and persuades in order to guide revolutionary practices. It focuses on domination, alienation, macro forces and emancipation. While the objectives of innovation are not typically radical, Burrell and Morgan's paradigms help to create a conceptual framework for determining the impact of innovation on its people, organizations, innovative populations and communities.

The approaches used in this chapter study case studies, people, organizational functioning and structure. *Case studies* examine the ethnography of the innovation and its organization by studying individual examples of innovations and develop hypotheses based on their findings. The focus is individual innovations and innovating organizations. *People-focused* (humanist) research considers the effects of innovation on the people developing and implementing innovations (personnel, elected officials, managers), the people in the organization (how they do their work, loss or creation of jobs, effects on careers, how it affects their lives, impact on families, their empowerment to innovate, rewards and punishments for innovation, impact on people outside the organization – clients and geographic, ethnic, and other communities in which the innovation occurs). It also examines the effects on clients and the public. *Functionalist* research scrutinizes organizational functions and the determinants of organizational mortality but assumes minimal change. Innovation could be a function of selection factors such as resources, politics, location, organizational age and size, and environmental and ecological processes that correlate with organizational mortality (Baum, 1996; Singh, House and Tucker, 1986a; Singh,

Tucker and House, 1986; Camison-Zornoza et al., 2004). Structuralist research (which will be called *structural* in this chapter) analyzes innovations' organizations, structural components, institutions, populations, communities, and innovation as a tool for adaptation that affects organizational survival and mortality rates (March, 1991; Nohria and Gulati, 1996; Damanpour and Gopalakrishnan, 1999). These four approaches and the issues they most effectively address are discussed in the sections that follow. The framework is outlined in Appendix 3.1.

Case Study Approach

The case study approach investigates individual innovations, innovating organizations, innovative populations and innovation communities. *Individual innovation* case studies increase their value by being matched with others in the same innovation categories (e.g. income security innovations, informatics innovations) and/or with normal[2] organizations. This approach is most suited to studying the innovation process in detail and from this information, developing hypotheses. It can be used for both short- and long-term studies. Typically it has described unique high-profile innovations, but this is not a necessary use. Case studies can identify the innovation adoption process, organizational and authority structures, policies, resources, environments, types (functions) of innovations adopted, impacts of specific innovations, and organizational survival or mortality. *Innovative organizational populations* are studied through the types and numbers of innovations created/implemented, types of jobs created/lost, niches (types of populations adopting types of innovations), and their demographics. The *organizational communities* supporting innovations

---

2   In defining normal organizations, Glor excluded outliers, organizations known to
      have extreme levels of factors being studied. Normal organizations introduce some
      innovations but not many innovations.

(Astley, 1985; Astley and Fombrun, 1987; Hunt and Aldrich, 1998) are important to the successful approval, implementation, and maintenance of innovations. They, the role they play and their fate should be described.

Employing common definitions of innovation, researchers should identify *innovation(s)*, preferably all of the innovations of an organization, department (ministry) or population/government, whether or not fully implemented; internal impacts, including whether they attracted public, political, and client group praise/criticism; effect on the target issue; whether and how the innovation(s) was of sufficient impact to affect the organization (e.g. consumption of resources, access to and allocation of personnel, independence, organizational level, change in power balance); impact on the role, status, independence, and prestige of the organization within the population/government, and the organization's survival or mortality, at its own level and the levels above it (see next paragraph). Mortality should be measured by whether the organization remained or disappeared from a full record (Glor, 2011). Researchers should record the size of the innovation because the size at which an innovation begins to affect the fate of an organization is not known. If the innovation was part of a group of related innovations, they should also be examined (e.g. Government of Saskatchewan's Native initiatives [Glor, 1997, 2000]).

Researchers need to describe the *organization, subunit, organizational pattern, population, and community* that implemented the innovation, the organization and level affected, and how, and, if the innovation was at the program level, report what happened to the program, its organization, and the organizations one level below and two levels above it. The structural possibilities for innovation implementation range from an existing unit asked to implement a small innovation to a new organizational unit/division/directorate/department/agency created to implement a large innovation. An innovation will presumably affect most the organization implementing it, but there are exceptions. If there is a one-to-one ratio between an innovation and a structure, the innovation will be easier to track.

Research on the implications of being innovative organizations should describe the impact of the innovation(s) on the issue the innovation was introduced to address and on the fate of individual innovations, innovators, and organizations. It should consider whether there was an impact on the population and the geographic and organizational communities. Research should seek out innovation case studies where there is a plausible link between an organization being innovative and surviving/disappearing. These should be matched with case studies of normal organizations. Organizations should thus be studied in sets of four cases – innovations whose organizations survived/disappeared and normal organizations which survived/disappeared. There is much information and many dynamics to understand in such case studies such as tombstone data (description of the innovation, number of innovations, niche, etc.), ratio of innovations to normal activities (budget, number of employees), founding and mortality dates, current status, size, population density, why the organization/ population innovated/did not innovate, time in each stage and what occurred (introduction of innovation, full implementation, impacts), membership of the community. The link between innovation and its impacts and orga-nizational/population/community survival/mortality should be explored in detail and other factors that influenced impacts and survival/mortality should be identified as well. Cases need to be paired and compared for key issues such as age, size, budget, number of employees, function(s), period addressed, and dominant political and management ideologies. The fate of employees should be identified and compared to that in normal organizations.

Innovation case studies should be used to develop hypotheses about innovations and about the impacts of innovation on organizations. Glor (2008a) developed some concepts, their properties and theories of public sector organization innovation. Strauss and Corbin (1998) are experts on how to do this. Others have also developed theories, such as Damanpour and Schneider (2006, 2009). Innovation case studies should also be used to classify innovations if possible.

In terms of measurements, Glor (2001a, b; 2007a, b; 2008a, b; 2015) developed measures for organizational patterns that could be used and *The Innovation Journal* suggests what issues should be covered by case studies. Authority structure can be identified from the organizational chart. Influence may be measureable through environments. Because it is very difficult to secure case study-type information for large numbers of innovations, it is important that case studies record data such as funds and number of staff allocated to the innovation and what proportion they represented of their organizations' resources.

While case studies will not provide representative information for all types of possibilities, numerous case studies will allow researchers to determine the range of possible results. If very few were found, for example, where innovation was a factor in the survival/mortality of the population or community, this would suggest innovation is not a factor.

Effects on People Approach

What are the kinds of effects innovations could have on people within the organization and how can they be measured? While a considerable amount of attention is given to impacts of innovation on organization functioning (considered in the next section), the focus is rarely shone on the impacts of innovation on people. Kiefer, Hartley, Conway and Briner (2015), studying employees' experience of innovation-related organizational changes, compared to their experience of cut-backs, found the experience was more positive.

People are the most important factor. Innovations and organizations are the creation of the people who work there, who pay for it, and who receive its benefits. Innovation effects on employees can be studied through numbers of employees, personnel budgets, personnel policies, work technologies, empowerment strategies, employee testing and surveys, career paths, interviews, cultural assessments, and equivalent information for the innovation, organization population, geographic and organizational community. Innovation effects on people outside case studies can be explored through budget and personnel reallocation, service statistics, and measures of organizational impact on its objectives. The innovations studied need not only be limited to individual innovations but could be major initiatives as well. Work-related legislation and enforcement must also be understood. If it is true as suggested for the private sector, that 75 to 80 per cent of innovations fail, this also has a major effect on people.

Innovations have an effect on clients and organizational communities helping to achieve the innovation and its goals, and on the geographic in which the innovation occurs. Staff perspectives can be measured through organizational reports, employee and management interviews and surveys. Interviews with people who are both happy and unhappy with the innovation should be conducted. Both management and working level personnel and current and recently retired employees could be interviewed. Numbers and types of personnel, their perspectives on the innovativeness of their organization and the organizational pattern, and the steps required to create an innovation should be recorded at the time the innovation exists or shortly thereafter. Internal documents and surveys should be employed to determine staff perspectives. Data indicating impacts should be collected.

A focus on people should reveal people's perspectives on innovation, their motivation toward it, how it affects their careers and those of others, the effect of innovators on others in the organization, and on their clients and organizational communities. It should also outline the profile of employees, the employment situation in the environment, the working conditions and dynamics within the workplace and with clients, and employees', clients', organizational and geographic community's quality of life.

Functional Approach

Antecedents of innovation and the impact of innovation on organizational functions have been studied the most extensively, through correlates of innovation with environmental and organizational characteristics and functioning. These can be and sometimes have been treated as selection factors for survival (Baum, 1996). Organizational evolutionists (e.g. McKelvey and Aldrich, 1983; McKelvey, 1994) consider factors such as resources, environments, and niches that select for survival. For example, Boin, Kuipers and Steenbergen (2010) examined the role of institutional design in the survival of American New Deal public organizations, finding that design's role was sometimes positive and sometimes not, as the design changed over time.

Damanpour and Wischnevsky suggested "innovation adoption contributes to organizational success but is not necessarily the primary success factor" (2006: 275). An innovative outcome *is* the primary success factor for innovation-generating organizations (Damanpour and Wischnevsky, 2006: 275, Table 2; Tornatzky and Klein, 1982). Where innovation is not the primary success factor for organizations, innovation would be one of several factors contributing to organizational survival: they would all need to be studied to determine the relative importance of innovation. Researchers need to determine whether the innovation was necessary to survival of functions and what the linkages were between organizations that adopt more innovations and organizational survival. A functional perspective therefore fits better with a focus on organizational management than a focus on people or organizational survival.

Organizational evolutionists such as Hannan, Freeman, Carroll, Baum, Oliver, Singh, Boin and others take a different view, seeing innovation and change as the manner in which organizations evolve. They have found selection factors that correlate with increased/decreased organizational mortality (e.g. organizational age, size, resources, embeddedness, competition, location in capital city or close to the executive, politics, niche width, population density, change) (e.g. Freeman and Hannan, 1983). In a very few studies, survival analysis (time series, survivor function, hazard rate) was used to identify differences in the fate of organizations that changed compared to organizations that did not change within study populations and across populations (e.g. Singh, House and Tucker, 1986; Hannan and Carroll, 1992; Peters and Hogwood, 1988). In most studies, organizations that changed had higher mortality rates in the short and adolescent term, but settled into similar rates to older organizations as the survival period got longer (Amburgey, Kelly and Barnett, 1993; Baum, 1996; Damanpour, 1991; Singh, House and Tucker, 1986; Singh, Tucker and House, 1986).

Quantitative measures of determinants assessed by correlation have identified factors associated with adoption of innovation and many determinants of innovation have been established.[3] The fate of innovating organizations and organizational communities has rarely been considered.

Structural Approach

The structural approach to studying impacts of innovation focuses on organizational, organizational population and community structures, and their demographics. The study of organizations within populations is demographic. Carroll and Hannan (2000) identified the conceptual organizing principles of demography as:

---

3   Damanpour (1991) analyzed twenty-three mostly private sector quantitative studies of
     determinants and moderators related to organizational innovation and recommended
     studying type of innovation and stage of adoption, but as secondary contingencies
     (intermediate variables) between primary contingencies and organizational char-
     acteristics. Damanpour and Wischnevsky recommended comparing "the units that
     succeed in *generating* innovations with those that do not, and the units that succeed
     in *adopting* innovations with those that do not" (2006: 286). Type of organization
     and scope of innovation were important determinants of innovation. Positive and
     negative statistically significant associations at the 0.05 level were found between the
     mean correlations of the three-paired types for specialization, functional differentia-
     tion, professionalism, managerial attitude toward change, and technical knowledge.
     Camison-Zornoza et al. (2004: 350) found types of organization and organizational
     size correlated significantly with innovation. The associations between organizational
     variables and innovativeness were not distinguished significantly among the private,
     nonprofit and public sectors, but were by the type of organization (manufacturing,
     service, nonprofit sector) and the scope of innovation (low, high).[3] Damanpour
     (1991: 583) suggested it was no longer necessary to replicate the results for variables
     with strong significant results, such as specialization, functional differentiation and
     external communication in a unidimensional study of innovation. To develop theories,
     Damanpour recommended studying type of organization (industry, sector, structure,
     strategy), variance in environmental threats and opportunities for different types of
     organizations, and multidimensional innovation studies to better understand the
     combined effects of different factors (contingencies) on organizational innovative-
     ness (Damanpour, 1991: 582–583).

(1) a population perspective; (2) focused on the vital events of birth and death; (3) concentrated on the flows of events in time and the implications of events for population structure – age is the master clock ... beginning with calculation of age-specific hazards (or rates), followed by comparisons of the rates across time and among various groups; (4) individuals are related back to the population through counting of events and distributional measures of the population such as the mean and variance in age; and (5) models of demographic systems possess a coherent and consistent internal logic that permits demographers to move freely among the parts and levels of the system ... vital rates and population characteristics are used ... to derive implications for population change and stability. (Glor, 2013: 4–5; summary of Carroll and Hannan, 2000: 25–26)

Besides permitting exploration of the link between innovation and survival, tracking demographic data for innovative organizations and organizational populations would allow comparison with normal/static organizations and their populations.

Organizations are like the net that holds meat together, providing a context within which activities occur, and a structure within which planning can be done, funds allocated, people hired, products made and programs and services delivered. They are essential to the implementation of innovations and their having an impact. Both a functional and a structural perspective treat innovations as a source of adaptation – most organizations must adapt to survive and if organizations do not adapt, they may not survive. Considered this way, change and innovation are essential to organizational survival. The key survival factor is not likely to be whether the organization invented the innovation (unless in the business of inventing innovations), but rather whether an organization fully implemented the innovation(s) and achieved the results intended. Securing approval and implementation are probably more difficult for innovators and early adopters than for later adopters of innovations but full implementation and achieving results can most plausibly link the innovation's and the organization's structural survival in the short term. Being in the business of inventing innovations is probably more common in the private sector than the nonprofit and public sectors except in government research councils and innovative governments. An innovative government requires an innovation development function.[4]

4 The innovative Saskatchewan government, for example, planned innovations in its Executive Council, departmental research and planning groups, and programs. In

Innovation and organizational *mortality* is usually defined as disappearance from the record (demonstrated by Glor, 2013). Innovation may lead to the appearance or disappearance of organizations: for example, Glor and Ewart (2016) traced the fate of five innovations and their organizations. Disappearance should be treated as organizational mortality, because organizations that disappear are usually undergoing a major change in mandate – changed mandates, more/less responsibility, elimination of mandate – and structure, personnel, conditions of employment and accountabilities. Structural changes can often be traced, even after the fact, but internal changes can rarely be tracked after the fact (as demonstrated by Glor and Ewart, 2016). Internal changes that are not reflected in official documents have the disadvantage of only being traceable by word of mouth and early tracking but many researchers are suspicious of first-hand accounts. Because organizational survival is a long-term issue, researchers typically have variable, limited, and inconsistent access to information about internal changes. Internal changes are unlikely to be documented publicly. A demographic approach, on the other hand, can explore the consequences of innovation for all types of organizations, thus contributing to comparability.

Demography is the study of populations and is measured by founding and mortality rates. According to Glor, normal populations are "ones that include a full population (preferably) or close to it or are representative of a full population and are therefore suitable for establishing a standard. Ideally, a normal mortality rate is determined by calculating the mean mortality rate of the population over its full lifespan" (Glor, 2013: 5). Glor (2013) identified the demography of normal organizational populations by sector and found organizations generally have low mortality rates and sectors (private, nonprofit, public) have fairly similar mortality rates, with the public sector having the highest (Glor, 2013). It is not known, however, how long organizational populations, especially innovative ones, tend to exist nor whether they exist for similar or different periods of time in different historical eras. We do not know whether organizations survive shorter periods now than in the past, whether organizations exist longer

---

Saskatchewan Health, employees were asked for written proposals for innovations. In the public health area, five were approved but two were not successfully implemented.

in some countries than others, nor whether organizations that innovate thereby decrease or increase their mortality rates.

Glor's (2013) review of the organizational demography literature for normal organizations and summary of the results by sector offers a comparable measure of performance (also Walker, 2004) for innovative organizations and populations in the three sectors, especially the public sector. The demographics of innovative organizations, populations, and communities have not been studied much. An exception is a small pilot of five innovations and their organizations from the Government of Saskatchewan conducted by Glor and Ewart (2016). Measures of organizational innovativeness could include number of innovations and the adoption ranking of the innovations by the organizations, populations, and communities. The number of inventions generated, what they were, and their details should also be recorded. All should be made available in databases (see Conclusion).

Organizational communities also need study. An organizational community is the community (network, collaboration) of individuals and organizations supporting implementation and legitimacy of an innovation or a package of innovations (Astley, 1985; Drazin and Schoonhoven, 1996). Without one, the innovation may not be approved, be implemented, or survive. Such communities include for example, those lobbying for the innovations, governments (departments) with similar interests, and businesses/nonprofits providing supplies and credibility to the innovation. They may have previously implemented the innovation(s) or may support future implementation and expansion (e.g. implementation of NPM was supported by the Organization for Economic Cooperation and Development, International Monetary Fund and World Bank).

Research Approaches

The framework used (Appendix 3.1) for researching the impact of innovation addresses each of the four approaches and the nature of an appropriate definition of innovation, its focus, what each is most suited to studying, suitable level(s) of analysis, appropriate methodologies and measures, what is likely to be affected, and what can be studied. Gioia and Pitre (1990) recommended doing multi-paradigm theory-building: this framework suggests a way to do so. Choice of organizational paradigms and approaches is largely determined by what researchers are interested in studying but eventually all of these issues should be covered.

Table 3.1 outlines some thoughts on what each of the levels of research might reveal. Data are typically collected at the level of, one level below and one above the level of the structure being studied, for example, if the

Table 3.1: Research Approaches

Research Methodology	What Each Could Reveal
1. Matched case studies of innovations or innovations and non-innovations	– What the issues are in specific organizations – What innovation looks like in organizations, to verify definitions – Effects of innovation on its organizations – The answer to "Is it possible to measure …?" (e.g. organizational innovativeness in the way defined) – Possible theories of innovation – How normal and innovative organizations differ/are similar
2. a. Studies of people	– Employees' opinions and perspectives – Statistics collected by the organization + magnitudes and trends – In-depth understanding of issues, factors, history, etc. – Numbers of employees engaged/laid off due to the innovation and their fate
b. Matched case studies of innovative and normal organizations and populations	– What normal and innovative populations look like, to verify definitions – Determine how normal/static and innovative populations differ and are similar – What the issues are in specific populations – Effects of innovation on some organizations, organizational populations and communities
3. Correlations	– Innovation, organizational and environmental characteristics and other factors that correlate with organizational innovativeness
4. Demography of innovative organizations	– Demographic profile of innovative organizations, organizational populations, communities – Compared to normal organizational populations (public sector, other sectors)

object of study is an organization, data are collected about innovations, sub-organizations, the organization to which the innovation reports, and the level above that. Research would ideally be conducted sequentially, but it is also valuable to do some of each type, which is what has been done to date.

Discussion

A number of the debates in innovation studies could be informed by these approaches. For example, Downs and Mohr (1976) suggested that the determinants found have been unstable across studies. Damanpour, on the other hand, concluded that "the effects of determinants on organizational innovation are not necessarily unstable across different studies" and that Downs and Mohr's (1976) prescriptions "are better suited to studies in which the focus is on the innovation rather than the organization" (Damanpour, 1991: 582). Damanpour nonetheless emphasized the need for studies of single innovations and their adoption process, which "are essential to understanding the generation, development, and implementation of innovations in organizations. Multiple-innovation studies are also needed" (Damanpour, 1991: 582). This framework should help researchers clarify when each focus is needed.

This approach would help identify organizational characteristics and factors that facilitate innovation adoption and thus build theory. "Theory accumulation and theory building in the field of organizational innovation is possible ... more elaborate research toward developing reliable theories should be conducted" (Damanpour, 1991: 582). Damanpour (1991: 583–584) recommended (1) using his innovation results to guide selection of independent variables in research, to consider more than one dimension and to include variables from several categories (e.g. individual, organizational, environmental); (2) a comprehensive list of innovations related to all parts of an organization should be studied;[5] (3) a change of focus from a few

5   Glor (1997, 2002) and colleagues did this for the Government of Saskatchewan, a population.

unrelated innovations (e.g. awards) or sets of innovations of the same type (e.g. surveys) to groups of related innovations (e.g. Glor and Ewart, 2016); this would draw a link between innovativeness and organizational effectiveness. Such studies need to be longitudinal and multidimensional and would require both substantial resources and collaborative efforts.

Conclusion

This chapter identified a conceptual structure for researching and some of the factors important to determining the impact of innovations. It suggested that four kinds of research are needed – case studies, studies of impacts on people, quantitative studies of relationships between innovations, antecedents, and organizational factors, and demographic studies of organizational, organizational population and community fate. Impacts cannot, however, be determined through one research program in one country – they need to be assessed in numerous organizations and populations, as was done with normal organizations, before conclusions can be drawn. The research framework would be useful for conducting comparable research and for assuring research is cumulative and would make possible comparisons of innovations to each other, innovations to normal activities, innovative organizations to normal or static ones, innovative organizational populations to normal ones,[6] and innovation communities to normal organizational communities. To assure comparability, researchers should coordinate their efforts and adopt common definitions, concepts, theories, methodologies, and measures. Researchers need to be conscious of the definitions

---

6   While it would be easier to find results comparing innovative and static populations, comparison to normal populations is recommended because it will be easier to find information on a normal population than a static one, if there is such a thing. Identifying and isolating static populations would be even more difficult than identifying and isolating innovative populations. Normal populations will presumably be introducing some but not many innovations.

used by others and explicit about their own. By standardizing definitions, research could be clearer, and relationships and theories could be tested more effectively. Comparison of organizations, populations, communities, and countries would be possible if common definitions and research protocols were used. Some research programs are already in place, for example international LIPSE[7] and research on smart and liveable cities programs. There is no program on the effect of public sector innovation on its organizations, organizational populations and/or organizational communities. There is no equivalent in the public sector to the private sector European longitudinal Community Innovation Survey (CIS),[8] but there should be.

To explore the effect of innovations on their organizations, populations, and communities, researchers require: (1) an ability to identify innovations and distinguish innovative organizations from laggards (terms developed by Rogers, 1995); (2) an understanding of the factors involved in organizational survival (requiring in-depth case study, people, and correlation research); (3) accessible databases of information about innovative organizations, organizational populations and organizational communities, including dates of founding and disappearance from the record. Researchers also need to collect the information needed to determine whether (1) an innovation had an impact on an organization's survival, and (2) organizational and population fate was related to its innovativeness in whole or in part, rather than to other factors such as leadership or political selection.

The most valuable research for achieving an understanding of the impacts of innovation (some of which has already been done) would be systematic (1) numerous comparisons of matched case studies of innovative and normal organizations, using clear, measureable definitions; (2) numerous studies of the effect of innovation on people; (3) studies of the antecedents correlating with organizational survival and mortality and determining whether innovation is adaptive for survival; and (4) studies of the impacts of innovation on organizational structures and innovation's effect on demographics, by examining the fate of innovations, innovative

7   Learning from Innovation in Public Sector Environments (<http://www.lipse.org>)
8   For example, Evangelista and Vezzani, 2010 (Italy); Sapprasert and Clausen, 2012 (Norway).

organizations, their populations and their innovation communities. Since there is already a substantial literature on the fate of normal organizations and populations, once the fate of enough innovative organizational populations are determined, it should be possible to compare the demographics of normal and innovative organizational populations.

Demographic analyses require large databases of innovations, organizations, innovative organizational populations and innovation communities. There is information in government budget estimates and sometimes in other documents but there are no inclusive databases for innovations and their organizations. A few surveys of dissemination of innovations can be accessed, for example, the biannual survey conducted by the ICMA of top management, querying adoption of specific innovations. Since this information is not now systematically collected, researchers in cooperation with interested organizations such as government central agencies, professional associations or international agencies should develop accessible databases of the development, approval, implementation, effects, feedback, and survival of innovative organizations for entire organizational populations and communities that would allow consideration of the demographics of innovative organizations and whether innovation has been adaptive for organizations, populations, communities. Similar normal populations should be identified and compared to the innovative populations and communities.

Bibliography

Amburgey, T. L., D. Kelly & W. P. Barnett. 1993. Resetting the Clock: The Dynamics of Organizational Change and Failure. *Administrative Science Quarterly*, 38(1): 51–73.

Astley, W. G. 1985. The two ecologies: Population and community perspectives on organizational evolution. *Administrative Science Quarterly*, 30: 224–241.

Astley, W. G., & C. J. Fombrun. 1987. Organizational Communities: An ecological perspective. *Research in the Sociology of Organizations*, 5: 163–185.

Baum, J. A. C. 1996. Chapter 1.3: Organizational Ecology. Pp. 77–114 in S. R. Clegg, C. Hardy & W. R. Nord (eds), *Handbook of Organization Studies*. Thousand Oaks, CA: Sage Publications.

Baum, J. A. C., H. J. Korn & S. Kotha. 1995. Dominant Designs and Population Dynamics in Telecommunications Services: Founding and Failure of Facsimile Transmission Service Organizations, 1965–1992. *Social Science Research*, 24: 97–135.

Boin, A., S. Kuipers & M. Steenbergen. 2010. The life and death of public organizations: A question of institutional design? *Governance: An International Journal of Policy, Administration and Institutions*, 23(3): 385–410.

Brook, A. No Date. The Structure of Ethical Positions on the Environment. Conference remarks. Accessed June 22, 2017 at: <http://http-server.carleton.ca/~abrook/ENVRNETH.htm>.

Burrell, G., & G. Morgan. 1979. *Sociological paradigms and organizational analysis*. London: Heinemann.

Camison-Zornoza, D., R. Lapiendra-Alcami, M. Segarra-Cipres & M. Boronat-Navarro. 2004. A Meta-Analysis of Innovation and Organizational Size. *Organization Studies*, 25: 331–361.

Carroll, G. R., & M. T. Hannan. 2000. *The Demography of Corporations and Industries*. Princeton, NJ: Princeton University Press.

Christensen, T., & P. Laegreid (eds). 2006. *Autonomy and Regulation: Coping with Agencies in the Modern State*. Cheltenham, UK: Edward Edgar.

Damanpour, F. 1991. Organizational Innovation: A meta-analysis of effects of determinants and moderators. *Academy of Management Journal*, 34(3): 555–590.

Damanpour, F., & J. D. Wischnevsky. 2006. Research on innovation in organizations: Distinguishing innovation-generating from innovation-adopting organizations. *JET-M*, 23: 269–291.

Damanpour, F., & M. Schneider. 2006. Phases of the Adoption of Innovation in Organizations: Effects of Environment, Organization and Top Managers. *British Journal of Management*, 17: 215–236.

Damanpour, F., & M. Schneider. 2009. Characteristics of Innovation and Innovation Adoption in Public Organizations: Assessing the Role of Managers. *JPART*, 19(3) (July): 495–522.

Damanpour, F., R. M. Walker & C. N. Avellaneda. 2009. Combinative Effects of Innovation Types and Organizational Performance: A Longitudinal Study of Service Organizations. *Journal of Management Studies*, 46(4) (June): 650–675.

Damanpour, F., & S. Gopalakrishnan. 1999. Organizational Adaptation and Innovation: The Dynamics of Adopting Innovation Types. Pp. 57–80 in K. Brockhoff, A. Chakrabarti & J. Hauschildt (eds), *The Dynamics of Innovation: Strategic and Managerial Implications*. New York: Springer-Verlag.

Downs, G. W., & L. B. Mohr. 1976. Conceptual Issues in the Study of Innovation. *Administrative Science Quarterly*, 21: 700–714.

Drazin, R., & C. B. Schoonhoven. 1996. Community, Population and Organization Effects on Innovation: A Multilevel Perspective. *Academy of Management Journal*, 39(5): 1065–1083.

Evangelista, R., & A. Vezzani. 2010. The economic impact of technological and organizational innovations: A firm-level analysis. *Research Policy*, 39 (1): 1253–1263.

Freeman, J., & M. T. Hannan. 1983. Niche Width and the Dynamics of Organizational Populations. *American Journal of Sociology*, 88(6): 1116–1145.

Gioia, D. A., & E. Pitre. 1990. Multiparadigm Perspectives on Theory Building. *Academy of Management Review*, 15(4): 584–602.

Glaser, B. G., & A. Strauss. 1967. *The Discovery of Grounded Theory: Strategies for Qualitative Research*. Chicago: Aldine Publishing Company.

Glor, E. D. 1998. Public Sector Innovation in Canada. Pp. 300–340 in R. Hoffman, D. Jurkowski, V. MacKinnon, J. Nicholson & J. Simeon (eds), *Public Administration: Canadian Materials*, 3rd Edn. Toronto, Canada: Captus Press.

Glor, E. D. 2000. *Is Innovation a Question of Will or Circumstance? An Exploration of the Innovation Process through the Lens of the Blakeney Government in Saskatchewan*. Ottawa, Canada: The Innovation Journal: The Public Sector Innovation Journal. Accessed June 22, 2017 at: <http://www.innovation.cc/books.htm>.

Glor, E. D. 2001a. Key Factors Influencing Innovation in Government. *The Innovation Journal: The Public Sector Innovation Journal*, 6(2) (March), article 1. Accessed June 22, 2017 at: <http://www.innovation.cc/volumes-issues/vol6-iss2.htm>.

Glor, E. D. 2001b. Innovation Patterns. *The Innovation Journal: The Public Sector Innovation Journal*, 6(3) (July–November), article 2. Accessed June 22, 2017 at: <http://www.innovation.cc/volumes-issues/vol6-iss3.htm>.

Glor, E. D. 2002. Is Innovation a Question of Will or Opportunity? The Case of Three Governments. *International Public Management Journal*, 5: 53–74.

Glor, E. D. 2007a. Assessing Organizational Capacity to Adapt. *Emergence: Complexity & Organization (E:CO)*, 9(3): 27–40.

Glor, E. D. 2007b. Identifying Organizations Fit for Change. *The Innovation Journal: The Public Sector Innovation Journal*, 12(1), article number 6. Accessed June 22, 2017 at: <http://www.innovation.cc/volumes-issues/vol12-no1.htm>.

Glor, E. D. 2008a. Toward Development of a Substantive Theory of Public Sector Organizational Innovation. *The Innovation Journal: The Public Sector Innovation Journal*, 13(3), article 6. Accessed June 22, 2017 at: <http://www.innovation.cc/volumes-issues/vol13-no3.htm>.

Glor, E. D. 2008b. Identifying Organizational Patterns: Normative and Empirical Criteria for Organizational Redesign. *Journal of Public Affairs Education (JPAE)*, 14(3): 311–333.

Glor, E. D. 2011. Patterns of Canadian Departmental Survival. *Canadian Public Administration*, 54(4) (December): 551–566.

Glor, E. D. 2013. Do innovative organizations survive longer than non-innovative organizations? Initial evidence from an empirical study of normal organizations. *The Innovation Journal: The Public Sector Innovation Journal*, 18(3), article 1. Accessed June 22, 2017 at: <http://www.innovation.cc/volumes-issues/vol18-no3.htm>.

Glor, E. D. 2014. Building Theory about Evolution of Organizational Change Patterns. *Emergence: Complexity & Organization (E:CO)*, 16(4): not paginated <https://journal.emergentpublications.com/>.

Glor, E. D. (ed.). 1997. *Policy Innovation in the Saskatchewan Public Sector, 1971–82.* Toronto, Canada: Captus Press.

Glor, E. D., and G. Ewart. 2016. What Happens to Innovations and Their Organizations? *The Innovation Journal: The Public Sector Innovation Journal*, 21(3), article 1. Accessed June 22, 2017 at: <http://www.innovation.cc/volumes-issues/vol21-no3.htm>.

Gopalakrishnan, S., & F. Damanpour. 1994. Patterns of generation and adoption of innovation in organizations: Contingency models of innovation attributes. *Journal of Engineering and Technology Management (JET-M)*, 11: 95–116.

Gopalakrishnan, S., & F. Damanpour. 1997. A Review of Innovation Research in Economics, Sociology and Technology Management. *Omega, International Journal of Management Science*, 25(1): 15–28.

Gow, J. I. 1994. *Learning from Others, Administrative Innovations among Canadian Governments.* Toronto, Canada: The Institute of Public Administration of Canada and Ottawa, Canada: Canadian Centre for Management Development.

Hannan, M. T., & G. R. Carroll. 1992. *Dynamics of Organizational Populations: density, legitimation, and competition.* Oxford: Oxford University Press.

Hannan, M. T., & J. Freeman. 1977. The Population Ecology of Organizations. *The American Journal of Sociology*, 82(5) (March): 929–964.

Hannan, M. T., & J. Freeman. 1984. Structural inertia and organizational change. *American Sociological Review*, 49: 149–164.

Hawley, A. 1968. Human Ecology. Pp. 328–337 in D. L. Sills (ed.), *International Encyclopaedia of the Social Sciences.* New York: Macmillan.

Hunt, C. S., & H. E. Aldrich. 1998. The Second Ecology: Creation and Evolution of Organizational Communities. *Research in Organizational Behaviour*, 20: 267–301.

Jick, T. 1993. *Managing Change: Cases and Concepts.* Homewood, IL: Irwin.

Kiefer, T., J. Hartley, N. Conway & R. B. Briner. 2015. Feeling the Squeeze: Public Employees' Experiences of Cutback- and Innovation-Related Organizational Changes Following a National Announcement of Budget Reductions. *Journal of Public Administration Research and Theory*, 25(4) (October): 1279–1305.

Kuipers, B. S., M. Higgs, W. Kickert, L. Tummers, J. Grandia & J. Van der Voet. 2014. The Management of Change in Public Organizations: A Literature Review. *Public Administration*, 92(1): 1–20.

Lancer Julnes, P. de, & M. Holzer. 2001. Promoting the utilization of performance measures in public organizations: An empirical study of factors affecting adoption and implementation. *Public Administration Review* 61(6): 693–708.

McKelvey, B. 1994. Commentary: Evolution and Organizational Science. Pp. 314–326 in J. A. C. Baum & J. V. Singh (eds), *Evolutionary Dynamics of Organizations*. New York, Toronto, et al.: Oxford University Press.

McKelvey, B., & H. Aldrich. 1983. Populations, Natural Selection, and Applied Organizational Science. *Administrative Science Quarterly*, 28(1) (March): 101–128.

March, J. G. 1991. Exploration and exploitation in organizational learning. *Organization Science*, 2: 71–87.

Nohria, N., & R. Gulati. 1996. Is Slack Good or Bad for Innovation? *Academy of Management Journal*, 39(5): 1245–1264.

OECD. 2010. *Measuring Innovation: A New Perspective.* Paris: Organization for Economic Cooperation and Development. ISBN 978-92-64-05946-7 (print), ISBN 978-92-64-05947-4 (PDF).

Olsen, J., & G. Peters (eds). 1996. *Lessons from Experience: Experiential Learning in Administrative Reform in Eight Democracies.* Oslo: Scandinavian University Press.

Osborne, D., & T. Gaebler. 1992. *Reinventing Government: How the Entrepreneurial Spirit is Transforming the Public Sector.* Reading, MA: Addison Wesley.

Peters, G. B., & B. W. Hogwood. 1988. The Death of Immortality: Births, Deaths and Metamorphoses in the U.S. Federal Bureaucracy 1933–1982. *The American Review of Public Administration*, 18(2) (June): 119–133.

Poel, D. H. 1976. The Diffusion of Legislation among the Canadian Provinces: A Statistical Analysis. *Canadian Journal of Political Science*, 9(4) (December): 605–626.

Pollitt, C. 2001. Clarifying Convergence. *Public Management Review*, 4(1): 471–492. ISSN 1471–9037.

Pollitt, C., & G. Bouckaert. 2000. *Public Management Reform: A Comparative Analysis.* Oxford: Oxford University Press.

Pollitt, C., G. Bouckaert & E. Löffler. 2006. *Making Quality Sustainable: Codesign, Codecide, Coproduce, Coevaluate.* Report of the Scientific Rapporteurs, 4QC Conference, Tampere, Finland, 27–29 September. Retrieved March 5, 2010 from: <http://www.4qconference.org/en/4qc_evaluation_index.php> (no longer accessible).

Rogers, E. M. 2005. *Diffusion of Innovations, Fourth Edition.* New York: The Free Press.

Roness, P. G. 2007. Types of State Organizations: Arguments, Doctrines and Changes beyond New Public Management. Pp. 65–88 in T. Christensen & P. Lægreid (eds), *Transcending New Public Management. The Transformation of Public Sector Reform.* Aldershot, UK: Ashgate.

Rousseau, D. M. 1985. Issues of Level in Organizational Research: Multi-level and Cross-level Perspectives. *Research in Organizational Behavior*, 7: 1–37.

Sapprasert, K., & T. H. Clausen. 2012. Organizational innovation and its effects. *Industrial and Corporate Change*, 21(5): 1283–1305. doi:10.1093/icc/dts023

Singh, J., R. House & D. Tucker. 1986. Organizational Change and Organizational Mortality. *Administrative Science Quarterly*, 31(4) (December): 587–611.

Singh, J., R. House & D. Tucker. 1986. Organizational Legitimacy and the Liability of Newness. *Administrative Science Quarterly*, 31(2): 171–193.

Sorensen, E., & J. Torfing. 2012. Introduction: Collaborative Innovation in the Public Sector. *The Innovation Journal: The Public Sector Innovation Journal*, 17(1), article 1. Collected June 22, 2017 at: <http://www.innovation.cc/volumes-issues/vol17-no1.htm>.

Strauss, A., & J. Corbin. 1998. *Basics of Qualitative Research: Techniques and Procedures for Developing Grounded Theory*. Thousand Oaks, CA: Sage.

Tornatzky, L. G., & K. J. Klein. 1982. Innovation characteristics and innovation adoption-implementation: A meta-analysis of findings. *IEEE Transactions on Engineering Management*, 29(1): 28–45.

Walker, R. M. 2004. *Innovation and Organizational Performance: Evidence and a Research Agenda*. Advanced Institute for Management Research Working Paper Number 2. London: AIM Research. Accessed January 16, 2014 at: <http://www.aimresearch.org> (no longer accessible).

Walker, R. M. 2013. Internal and External Antecedents of Process Innovation: A review and extension. *Public Management Review*, 1–25. DOI:10.1080/147190 37.2013.771698. Retrieved July 25, 2017 from: <http://dx.doi.org/10.1080/147 19037.2013.771698>.

Wettenhall, R. 2003. Exploring Types of Public Sector Organizations: Past Exercises and Current Issues. *Public Organization Review*, 3: 219–245.

Wischnevsky, D. J., & F. Damanpour. 2008. Radical strategic and structural change: occurrence, antecedents and consequences. *International Journal of Technology Management*, 44(1/2): 53–80.

Appendix 3.1: Research Framework for Studying Impacts of Innovation on Organizations, Populations and Communities

Organial Approach	Case Studies	People	Functional	Structural
Definitions of innovation and Innovative organization	– Unique to each organization that does it (OECD, 2010) – Innovative organizations are ones that introduce popular innovations (see awards programs) – An innovative organization introduces many innovations (Glor)	– Unique to employees, management, geographic community, people being served, organizational population, country – Contributes to an important national effort (e.g. war effort) – An innovative organization introduces innovations beneficial to employees and others	– Something new to an organization – An innovative organization achieves the same objectives in new ways	– Something new to the population (government) and/ or organizational community – An organization that achieves new objectives in new ways – An innovative population/ community introduces many innovations
Focus of study	– Identifying, understanding, classifying and developing hypotheses about innovations, innovative organizations, populations, communities	Employees, employees' families, clients, geographic communities	– Innovations that enhance management control – Incremental innovations – Occasional radical innovations	– Innovative organizations, organizational populations, organizational communities – Innovative organization achieves new objectives in new ways

Organi'al Approach	Case Studies	People	Functional	Structural
Approach most suited to	– Understanding in detail individual innovations, processes, stakeholder motivations, organizational patterns – Building hypotheses – Short- and long-term – Unique, high-profile innovations[9]	Understanding innovation's impact on people – Innovations affecting employees – Short- and medium-term	– Understanding the adaptation process in relation to management's objectives – Understanding and maintaining the status quo, esp. at the level of mgmt and objectives – Short- and medium-term (Damanpour, Walker and Avellaneda, 2009)	– Understanding innovations' impact on: organizational structure, demographics – Comparing across systems – governments, countries, organizational communities (Rousseau, 1985) – Longitudinal studies
Levels of analysis	One organizational level in one to four organizations at a time	– Organizational culture – Employee and mgmt motivation – Personnel of organization – Work technologies – Work-related legislation, regulations, enforcement	– Vertical and horizontal organizations within the population – What the organization does/produces – Organizational and management needs, products, organizational environments – Same innovations across organizations (i.e. dissemination of innovations)	Organization, organizational population and community – Organizational and population environment

9   Thus answering the question "why this innovation?."

Organizal Approach	Case Studies	People	Functional	Structural
Methodology: Study...	– Ethnography of individual innovations and their organizations – Qualitative, develop grounded and substantive theory (Glaser and Strauss, 1967; Strauss and Corbin, 1998) – Comparable if match-ed pairs of similar innovations or organizations	– Surveys – Testing – Personnel systems – Supports to employees (e.g. paternity leave; employee counselling; unemployment insurance, health, disability, sickness and accident insurance)	– Normal organizations doing a few innovations – Population ecology: selection mechanisms (Hannan and Freeman, 1977) – Correlation of selection factors with organizational and population survival, impacts on structures	– Changes in organizational structure – Changes in organizational populations, communities – Comparison with normal populations
Types of data	Award winners Individual case studies	– Employee surveys – Employee testing – Geographic community statistics – Interviews	Management surveys	– Organizational history – Organizational demographic data
Measures	– Descriptions of dynamics, processes, issues in innovations, people's roles, context, results, organizations, geographic communities – Code analysis	– Variety among personnel's backgrounds, gender – Number of employees of each type – Geographic community employment and unemployment	– Resources (number of personnel, expenditures and revenues), internal and external environment – Survival analysis	– Organizational founding, changes, length of survival, mortality – Hazard rates and ratios – Mortality rates – Individual innovation adoption rankings

Organizal Approach	Case Studies	People	Functional	Structural
	– Comparison with other innovation's/organizations' results	– Working conditions and dynamics		– Population and community innovation adoption rankings – Organizational population and commun- ity mortality rates
Impacts of Innovation on …	– Innovation process – Characteristics of innovations and innovators (e.g. ideological, saved $) Impact on: – Objective – Organizational structure, population, community – Fate of individual innovators, organiza- tions, populations, communities	Quality of life of employees, geographic community, country – Impact on fate of innovators – Impact of innovators on other staff	Organization's ability to function and adapt – Capacity to control – Survival/mortality of organizations not a focus – Innovation as contributing to a function – Population dynamics (e.g. Baum, Korn and Kotha)	Survival/mortality of organizations and organizational populations and communities

Organ'al Approach	Case Studies	People	Functional	Structural
Issues which could be studied ...	– Innovation, organization, how it functions – Organization culture – How innovation challenges affected the organization – Was the innovation fully implemented? – Did it accomplish its objectives? – Did and how did it affect its organization?	– Empowerment – Participatory management – Organizational networks, collaborations (Sorensen and Torfing, 2012) – Motivations – Effects of innovation on careers	– Innovations' and orgs' functions, resources, etc. necessary to develop and implement innovations – Implementation challenges – Stages of innovation implementation – Innovative organizations	– Innovations' effects on their and other organizations – Innovative organizations – Innovation's/community's effects on their populations – Fate of organizations sponsoring innovations – Fate of innovations, organizations

PART II

Innovation and Ethics

JESSICA WORD, CHRISTOPHER STREAM,
AND KIMBERLY LUKASIAK

4   What Cannot Be Counted: Ethics, Innovation, and Evaluation in the Delivery of Public Services[1]

ABSTRACT

Outcome evaluation has been a significant innovation in the delivery of public services and the management of nonprofit organizations. Evaluation is meant to provide an engine to innovate programs by providing actionable information. Most existing research has focused on compliance with mandated performance evaluations with little consideration of the implications of these mandates.

In the nonprofit setting, administrators often must choose between spending on mission achievement and contracting out to acquire necessary expertise to measure performance. The irony is accountability requirements affect the organization's ability to achieve its mission and can hinder a nonprofit's capacity to provide services to clients. This generates an ethical dilemma for individuals within organizations – they are *forced* to choose between client needs and organizational performance.

This inherent dilemma is analyzed in this chapter. The research employs the Right-versus-Right construct (Kidder, 2005) and examines the moral dilemma surrounding the mandates for performance evaluation and their impact on ethical decision-making. These theoretical constructs aid in the identification of ethical and management dilemmas that relate to performance evaluation and impact an organization's mission. This assessment is timely given pressures to do more with less.

1   *The Innovation Journal: The Public Sector Innovation Journal*, Volume 16(2), 2011, article 2 <https://www.innovation.cc/volumes-issues/vol16-no2.htm>.

Introduction

Outcome evaluation has been one of the most significant innovations in the management of organizations in the last twenty years. This major innovation has shaped the delivery of public services through the use of performance measurement and program evaluation. Certainly, government has always been accountable to their constituents for what they do and how they use resources. However, with the recent economic turmoil there has been a resurgence of the *right to know* attitude among citizens over the past decade. Many different methods are employed in an attempt to demonstrate quality and performance in the administration of public and nonprofit organizations. Most recently, the idea of program evaluation and the reporting of the performance measures to external users has been the favored method for creating public accountability. Program evaluation is now occurring nationwide. It is conducted at the top levels of the federal government down to the smallest local governments and has been instituted in the nonprofit sector as well.

The recent focus on accountability in part stems from the reinventing government and the new public management movements (Behrens and Kelly, 2008). These reforms have led to significant changes in the methods for public service delivery. The reforms included the considerable use of contracting out of public services to be delivered by the nonprofit sector.

Government contracts often required nonprofit organizations to comply with extensive accountability and performance measurement reporting. Previous research has primarily been directed at compliance with mandated program performance evaluations and consequently little consideration has been given to the implications of these mandates. Mandated performance evaluations often create multiple and competing systems of accountability that make both management and ethical decision-making difficult. It is especially true of organizations that have varied programs, funding sources, and stakeholders, all of whom hold the organization accountable.

In terms of public perception, innovation should be a core activity of the public sector. The goal is to help public services improve performance and increase public value; respond to the expectations of citizens and adapt to the needs of users; increase service efficiency and minimize costs. The public sector *has* been successful at innovation in the past (Hamson, 2004). How to seek out and foster innovation in all public programs is crucial to continual development and improvement: only half of all innovations are initiated at the top of organizations. Maintaining diversity of staff, paying attention to the needs and expectations of users and frontline staff, and promoting formal creativity techniques are all valuable tools to ensure innovation is sought. Our research seeks to understand the link between three issues facing the implementation of programs through nonprofit organizations, innovation, and ethics.

Often in the nonprofit setting, managers are forced to choose between spending money on achieving the mission or contracting to acquire the expertise necessary to adequately measure performance toward achieving the mission. The tangle of accountability requirements can affect the organization's ability to achieve its mission because it can hinder a nonprofit employees' capacity to provide services to clients. This generates a secondary ethical dilemma for individuals within these agencies when they are forced to choose between a client's needs and organizational performance demands (Connor- Snibbe, 2006; Minkoff and Powell, 2006). Current literature aimed at examining evaluation from the perspective of funders and nonprofit organizations largely ignores the ethical implications of performance evaluations and assumes an evaluation is always appropriate (Ebrahim, 2009). The prevailing perspectives lack critical consideration of the ethical issues and tradeoffs that are inherent in the practice and implementation of evaluations.

The lack of concern regarding ethical issues related to evaluations seems to stem from the underlying belief that information always leads to better decision-making. However, research has also shown that organizations tend to gather more information than they can consume (Feldman and March, 1981) and often the data collected is not employed to make more informed decisions (Behrens and Kelly, 2008). This chapter analyzes the inherent dilemmas that stem from accountability systems implemented by service providing nonprofits. This chapter uses the Right-versus-Right construct developed by Rushworth Kidder (2005) and examines the moral dilemma surrounding the mandates of performance evaluation and the impact on ethical decision-making and management. These theoretical constructs will aid in the identification of ethical and management dilemmas as they relate to performance evaluation and the impact on an organization's mission, management, and values. This examination is especially timely given the recent economic crisis, which has created an increased demand for services with fewer resources to meet additional demands.

The growing conflict between an organization's ability to serve its clients; while being held accountable via evaluative measures raises interesting ethical questions: Is the growing emphasis on measuring performance detracting from the ability of nonprofit organizations to effectively serve their clients and mission? Do administrators have the necessary skills to navigate these ethical dilemmas? What ways might the evaluation process help or hinder the process of innovation in public sector service delivery? These questions are explored in this chapter through the use of heuristic decision models. Specifically, Kidde's (2005) Right-versus-Right model and decision-making rules are employed as a tool to examine ethical dilemmas and suggest some possible means to analyze these dilemmas in practice.

Accountability in Nonprofit Organizations

Accountability comes in many forms but for the purpose of our discussion we will define accountability as "the process of holding actors responsible for actions" (Fox and Brown, 1998: 12). The current practice of accountability in nonprofit organizations has undergone significant change as the nonprofit sector itself has grown and become more involved in the delivery of services for the public sector. First, we will examine the evolution of accountability in the nonprofit sector. Second, we will discuss different methods and types of accountability. Finally, we will discuss some of the tensions that emerge from current accountability practices, which are both mandated and voluntary in the nonprofit sector and some of the implications of these tensions using the Right-versus-Right framework.

Evolution of Nonprofit Accountability

The recent emphasis on performance evaluation in nonprofit organizations largely began in the 1990s as a response to changes in practice by governments and other funding organizations (Behrens and Kelly, 2008). The change in government standards was largely driven by the reinventing government movement as embodied by the Government Performance and Results Act in 1993. The change in evaluation practice in nonprofit organizations was largely led by the United Way in 1996. The primary critique of these efforts has focused on the low quality of the evaluations preformed and the lack of useful data collected by nonprofits and funders (W. K. Kellogg, 1998; Connor- Snibbe, 2006; Behrens and Kelly, 2008).

Prior to the current emphasis on accountability, nonprofit organizations were largely held accountable through their own boards of directors and legal mandates defined in the tax code or service delivery contracts. The shift toward a greater emphasis on performance evaluation is, in part, due to elevated mistrust of nonprofit organizations by the public and government officials, which stem from nonprofit scandals involving the United Way's misuse of funds and the Red Cross's handling of September 11, 2001 donations (Glaser, 1993; Conner-Snibbe, 2006). Additionally, corporate scandals surrounding organizations like Enron and WorldCom further shook public trust in organizations and led to public pleas for increased fiscal and operational transparency through the passage of the Sarbanes-Oxley Act (2002), which applies in limited ways to nonprofit operations.

Additionally, policy changes stemming from the reinventing government movement and the Government Performance and Results Act (1993) introduced management techniques to government and nonprofits that emphasized accountability in the administration of grants, contracts, financial records, and operations. This approach to funding oversight emphasizes greater transparency in terms of organizational outcomes (Menzel, 2005) as well as accountability for financial management. Increased emphasis on outcomes has been transferred to nonprofit organizations through contract and funding requirements and has resulted in a cultural shift in the management of nonprofit organizations (Frumkin, 2002). As nonprofits mature and begin to transition from volunteer-based to more professionalized, cultural shifts occur and conflicts can become more apparent and difficult to manage.

A local organization, which engages in an afterschool youth sports programs for at risk children, has been affected by these emerging trends to increase program transparency and accountability. This particular non-profit has been providing services for over twenty years. Their mission is to provide a safe after school environment for local children by offering a sanctuary to a population within the community that is at high risk to join gangs, participate in violence, and/or use drugs. The nonprofit created a program that encourages fitness and self-actualization, with an intended outcome of keeping the kids out of gangs by encouraging and inspiring them to graduate from high school. During this nonprofit's history, both societal and economic changes have transpired, causing the organization to falter in its ability to provide services. Additionally, they have suffered relational impacts on their ability in obtaining funding to sustain the organization. For example, over the years the nonprofit had been provided free space to conduct its fitness classes for youth – generally having few issues of gaining support or funding to obtain space. However, due to changing requirements, the founders had to mortgage their personal home to pay for a permanent location to ensure they were able to continue conducting classes for the youth. This shift largely occurred because the inability of the nonprofit to keep up with changing demands of donors and funders for increased formalization and professionalism, which caused the organization to lag behind other larger organizations in their capacity to report on outcomes of the services provided.

Accountability requirements of funders often involve complex data collection and analysis. As the complexity of nonprofit organizations increased, so did the need for additional professionalism, training, and specialized education to support these activities. Increased professionalism in general has led to better management of programs and organizations, but has also been a source of concern (Hwang and Powell, 2009). The increase in professionalization creates a large contrast in management capacity between small informal nonprofit organizations and larger formalized nonprofits. The larger more professionalized and formalized organizations tend also to be more open to external pressures that divert time and resources away from core missions and change the culture of organizations.

The cultural change, in part, comes with an increased focus on quantitative measurement of program accomplishments. The focus on measurement can be helpful in allowing organizations to improve programs, policies, and outcomes. But, the intensive focus on measurement may also change the nature of who chooses to work for these organizations and lead to the replacement of passionate amateurs with those more able to deal with the technical demands of quantifying and measuring results and outcomes (Hwang and Powell, 2009). Often these professionals have managerial and business rather than substantive backgrounds that are more connected to service delivery. This can create a tension between administrators and those that work directly in the service delivery arena. A manager of a local nonprofit which runs group homes for children explained that often those individuals that work directly with the children resist taking time away from their substantive duties to "fill out paperwork." The agency has also struggled with making the measurement a meaningful management tool since so much of what is done with these children is hard to quantify and often it is hard to isolate what makes a difference in terms of outcomes.

The focus on rational and managerial techniques such as evaluation also results in diversion of resources from direct service delivery to activities that are being added in order to capture and analyze data instead of undertakings that directly deliver public services. The diversion of resources may further frustrate direct service employees who see the direct impact of decreased resources on the lives of individuals served by the organization. The diversion of resources may also be less visible and take the form of less time for employees to interact with clients because of the need to "fill out paperwork" to assure data is collected, in order to measure program attributes. These data collection efforts may be especially difficult for organizations to justify to front-line employees if the data collected is externally mandated and not used to improve organizational practices or outcomes.

Another unintended consequence of evaluation is that mandated performance evaluations of individual programs with multiple funding sources often focus on programs rather than whole organizations or systems. The focus on programs for budgeting and funding reasons forces the compartmentalization of information and the optimization of programs, not organizations. This is further complicated by the way in which most nonprofit organizations are funded, with grants or donations specifically focused on particular programs or populations, which may allow some programs to thrive while others with less stable funding sources struggle to continue within the same organization.

Types of Accountability

Accountability can and often does come in different forms and holds different meanings. Ebrahim (2003) points out accountability can be both an internal and external phenomenon. Internal accountability and external accountability often create tensions for managers struggling between loyalty to their internal stakeholders and responsibilities to external stakeholders. External accountability is usually defined by individuals that are not directly involved in the delivery of programs or services and is usually the result of funding or licensure requirements. In contrast, internal accountability is led by those directly involved with the organization and can, at times be too narrowly concerned with organizational issues.

External accountability also can be further divided into two distinct types of accountability, identified as legal and moral accountability. The first, legal, or compliance-based accountability ensures that rules are followed and punishes those that fail to adhere to preset standards or procedures (Jos and Thompkins, 2004). Compliance-based evaluation is mainly focused on ensuring that the process and procedures set forth in the grant or contract are carried out. This often involves formal reporting or site visits from grantors. Often compliance-based accountability, such as the publication of nonprofit informational returns with the IRS, rely on transparency to ensure ethical behavior (Adams, Balfour and Reed, 2006). The emphasis on transparency often results in critiques of nonprofit executive salaries in local newspapers to alert the public in hope that either the board will be shamed into acting or the public will take their donations elsewhere. However, these types of critiques are often overlooked by the public and fail to take into account if leadership is a key factor in the performance of that organization. Often, the critique of executive pay in nonprofits is somewhat myopic and fails to understand the size and complexity of the job of nonprofit managers or the comparability of nonprofit salaries with salaries for similar jobs in the public and private sectors.

In contrast, the second type, moral or ethical accountability requires broader responsibility to not only comply with mandates, but also requires concern for the "general welfare" (Dwivedi and Jabbra, 1988). Adhering to moral accountability standards means individuals and organizations behave within their conscience and care not only for the end results, but also the means chosen to reach goals (Dicke and Ott, 1999). Under this model, the end results are important, but equally important is how performance is achieved. Organizations with a social justice mission must serve that mission in a broader way, including promoting social justice for their own employees through providing adequate living wages and healthcare benefits. A social justice organization that is ethically accountable must not only serve its clients in a way consistent with its mission, but also be an example in the way it conducts operations and treats staff.

The difference between legal and moral accountability in terms of outcomes for individuals and communities can be significant. One striking example of these differences is found in explorations of moral inversion. The concept of moral inversion refers to situations in which "something evil has been redefined convincingly as good" (Adams and Balfour, 2004: 4). Often moral inversions are masked through technical rationality, which elevates the rational mindset over all other forms of reason. Technical rationality in part increases the risk of moral inversion simply because of the specialization of knowledge which resulted from increased professionalism. In order for individuals and organizations to appear professional and rational they must comply with standards and adopt techniques that are scientific and rational. The desire to comply with professional and rational standards in turn creates a greater threat of moral inversion. The end of professionalism becomes a good in and of itself. We as professionals often fail to question rational practices and assume that instrumental practices are neutral and legitimate (Dillard and Ruchala, 2005). The elevation of rationality in the nonprofit sector increases the danger that managers will lose sight of the care-based thinking expressed in missions and fail to value those things which cannot be measured (Hwang and Powell, 2009). A common example of moral inversion in the nonprofit sector deals with issues of employee's misuse of funds or fraudulent diversion of resources (Greenlee, Fisher, Gordon and Keating, 2007).

Often organizations cover up these incidents to protect the organization's image in an effort to keep donors or funders from losing faith in the organization's ability to manage resources. Similar trade-offs are possible in evaluation, where the good of the organization is put above the good of the mission or the good of those being served.

Ethical Issues of Accountability

There are many ethical dilemmas inherent in performance evaluation, which can impede management capability to make choices outside of data gathered. The first can arise from the organization implementing the evaluation itself, which draws resources away from serving the mission. The second involves difficulties in determining what should be evaluated and the method(s) of identifying and documenting the expected/anticipated outcomes. The uncertainty many nonprofit managers face, in terms of outcome complexity and determining what to evaluate, may pressure managers to cherry pick only those goals which are achievable or easily measured.

The third is the issue created by the evaluator who may not have the necessary skills to properly perform the evaluation. Poorly implemented evaluations may result in decisions that unfairly reward or punish organizations and the individuals that they serve based upon biased or incomplete data. Ethical dilemmas are also inherent within the context of economic and political environments, in which nonprofit managers may feel pressure to embellish results or withhold bad news. There are many reasons why outcomes may be altered, for self-interest in an effort to protect careers, or to protect the organization. Most likely it is to protect the livelihoods of employees and the programs that managers feel are important to the community and the populations they serve.

In addition to the ethical dilemmas, the cost of carrying out an evaluation is expensive in terms of time and resources consumed, which means shifting already stretched resources away from services and the organiza-tion's mission. Mandates to evaluate are almost always the result of funders who often do not understand the potential costs of their demands. Most donors are unaware of the layers of accountability faced by organizations, this causes a tangle of demands, on organizations, created through multiple funding streams (Connor-Snibbe, 2006; Martin and Ketner, 1997). Most funding sources demand reports and data collection often requiring the use of different information, forms, and file structures. Even when nonprofits perform the necessary evaluations, the funders are often only interested in how their money was spent and the performance of a particular program or agency, which seems to have little bearing on future funding decisions (Conner-Snibbe, 2006). The information created through the evalua-tion process seems to add little value to the decision-making processes of funders or managers of nonprofit organizations. Nonprofits fearing the loss of funding cannot complain or change these mandates because they fear losing vital support.

Evaluations are often unfunded and mandated with little understand-ing of what is entailed in the evaluation process (Conner-Snibbe, 2006; Ebrahim, 2009). While an ideal evaluation often involves the tracking of outcomes for programs, this is often difficult and costly since "the only surefire way to show that a program is helping people more than they could have helped themselves is to conduct expensive and lengthy studies involving control groups" (Connor-Snibbe, 2006). While true experimental designs are likely the best choice for demonstrating causality of programs to outcomes, most evaluations fall short of this ideal due to expense, legal issues, and ethical concerns. Instead, large volumes of data are collected. Since there is little understanding of the difficulty and cost associated with measuring a program's impact, the resulting data can be both useless and misleading (Conner-Snibbe, 2006). The resulting system leads to no significant change in helping the social sector improve its programs or the outcomes for its clients or for services offered. Another unintended con-sequence is that the overhead costs for the organization often increase as a result of the expertise required, further impacting missions. Evaluation takes greatly needed resources, specifically money and staff, away from the programs designed to meet mission mandates.

Additionally, the high costs necessary to carryout quality evaluations can also make nonprofit organizations less competitive than other organizations that are either less concerned about quality or have larger operations. Evaluation costs, since they are not part of direct program delivery, raise overhead expenses especially for small to medium nonprofit organizations. The imposition of program evaluations therefore can have an overall impact of decreasing the competitiveness of individual nonprofits because many donors and funders use overhead costs as an indicator of organizational efficiency. The downward pressure on overhead costs is likely limiting the capacity and quality of many nonprofit organizations in various areas (Urban Institute, 2004). In the context of attempting to keep costs low, it is unlikely that most organizations can afford to implement and analyze performance data adequately or to make costly adjustments suggested by evaluations, which might be necessary in the light of performance data.

Other ethical dilemmas become apparent through the reporting of evaluation findings. Evaluation findings often exaggerate program successes while downplaying negative findings or outcomes. The tendency of evaluations to exaggerate program success stems, in part, from the difficulty in measuring outcomes in many areas of the nonprofit world. The difficulty in measuring outcomes also results from the fact that often the social problems nonprofit organizations attempt to address are messy, complex, and handled across organizational boundaries and addressed through multiple programs. Issues faced by individuals that are receiving assistance from nonprofit organizations often are multi-faceted and require a range of services and expertise. For example, domestic violence victims often need medical and counseling care in addition to legal, housing, and employment assistance. It is unlikely that any one agency has the ability to address every aspect required to create a successful outcome and the range of services administered makes it very difficult to determine the direct impact of any individual agency, program, or service. In the face of uncertainty about causality of outcomes, many funding organizations defer to the expertise of individual nonprofits in defining and measuring outcomes. This may tempt some agencies to pick measures, which inflate their performance. Additionally, this system allows bad news to be diffused or go unreported, since it can often be explained by the performance of a group of organizations or a system rather than a single program or agency.

Right-versus-Right Dilemmas

The Right-versus-Right dilemma is one of the most common ethical dilemmas faced by individuals seeking to make tough decisions in which there is no clear right answer. These dilemmas are often the result of two intersecting values or issues that meet in such a way that policies or regulations provide little to no guidance. Right-versus-Right dilemmas are very different from Right-versus-Wrong choices because of the lack of clarity about the appropriate ethical path in these situations. In the case of a Right versus Wrong, there is almost always some clear guidance from laws, regulations, and policies that can be helpful in making decisions. In Right-versus-Right dilemmas, individuals have to choose between ideals such as Truth versus Loyalty, Individual versus Community, Short-Term versus Long-Term and Justice versus Mercy (Kidder, 2005). Below the discussion examines how each of these common Right-versus-Right dilemmas are encountered by nonprofit managers in the course of evaluation.

Truth versus Loyalty

Truth-versus-Loyalty dilemmas are those situations in which individuals are asked to choose between honesty and loyalty to some group, individual, or ideal. These situations occur when individuals are asked to decide how much information to divulge or what information should be included in reports and documentation. This comes into play in the area of accountability when a nonprofit manager must decide between divulging potentially damaging information about an agency to remain truthful with funders or protecting the organization by exposing internal concerns or operational short-comings that are beyond the agency's control. Often the temptation is to simply report the information that will present the organization in the best light and to strategically avoid discussion of real problems or "near misses" that reveal the weaknesses of the organization. Telling the truth is the most ethically defensible position, however it might be damaging to the agency's reputation, especially if other agencies the organization competes against choose to do otherwise. In this case, telling the truth may undermine the ability of an organization to compete with others that are gaming the system or falsifying information to gain the advantage in competition for resources.

Individual versus Community

The Individual-versus-Community dilemmas are situations when an organization is asked to choose between the well-being of a single individual over the well-being of the community, as a whole. This dilemma can be reframed in terms of a single organization versus the well-being of the entire community. Often nonprofit managers are pushed to put the well-being of an entire community over the well-being of their organization. An example of this can be seen in a local nonprofit organization which was ordered by a particular funding source to make organizational changes or forfeit funding. The funder wanted the organization to join a larger network of youth service organizations to increase community capacity. In this case, the nonprofit said "No." This situation provokes the following questions: (1) What level of authority should a funder have over an organization? (2) Is it acceptable for a funder to mandate specific changes within an organization or threaten withdrawing funds? It has made other funders more leery of donating to this organization. Is it right that nonprofits should have to choose between the interests of the community and the interests of their organization?

The push to put organizational interests behind those of the community often come through appeals to collaborate with other organizations or to merge nonprofit organizations to avoid duplication of services. The push to intertwine organizational interests often comes through funder and government appeals to collaborate and/or merge with other nonprofit organizations in an attempt to avoid duplication of services.

While the idea to put the health of the community before the health of the organization is appealing to many funders, it is often somewhat short-sighted in terms of considering the long-term health of communities. Often, the argument to outsource services previously provided by government to nonprofits is predicated on the idea that nonprofit organizations operate in a competitive marketplace and this creates more efficient and effective services through competition. The push to collaborate and merge non-profit organizations to reduce duplication of services may lead to reduced competition and innovation in terms of service delivery.

Short-term versus Long-term

The need to balance short-term outcomes versus the long-term outcomes is one that is often encountered in the public policy arena and delivery of public goods and services. In order to help public officials maximize their re-election chances, often nonprofit organizations providing services, on behalf of government, are pressured to produce short-term results on programs that may in fact only payoff many years down the road. An example of this is shown in the Las Vegas communities' public-run hospital, the University Medical Center (UMC). The hospital has faced budget short falls for years, coupled with an increasing indigent population; this has created numerous issues for the organization. The board of County Commissioners overseeing the hospital's operations conducted a review of converting the current hospital from a not-for-profit to a non-profit, teaching or for-profit hospital. Each option provided a different set of challenges. Ultimately, consensus among the Commissioners was that it would become a teaching hospital, though the outcome was never implemented. This was the easiest of the options to implement, causing the least amount of political conflict. However, it was not necessarily the best option for the Las Vegas community; the best option would have taken a significant amount of time and effort. In the end, the community would have realized the most benefits selecting one of the other options. In some extreme cases, the push for short-term outcomes can actually handicap the ability of organizations to produce long-term results for the individual-client and the communities that they serve because of the relative costs of creating these short-term outcomes. Many accountability standards push nonprofit organizations to maximize the short-term outcomes of clients and others over the long-term health of the community and individual clients.

An example of the inherent trade-offs between short-term and long-term results can be seen in many of the measurement decisions being made around nonprofit evaluation. Often governments and elected officials want to see the short-term results of a program to ensure that their investment in the nonprofit agency is in fact paying off. However, many social service and educational programs require a longer time horizon than the typical contract period between governments and contractors (Bozeman, 2002; Letts, Ryan and Grossman, 1997). In many instances, such as early childhood education, the resulting progress by a particular client group may not be apparent until long after the work of an agency is completed. The longer time horizon also increases staff time, costs, and difficulties in measuring outcomes. The need to produce measurable results may force many nonprofits to only provide services that have demonstrable short-term outcomes and ignore more difficult to measure service areas, in favor of those that show expedited measurable results. This forces a choice between the long-term results that might be achievable but not measurable and the short-term results, which are easily measurable but are less impactful on clients and communities.

Justice versus Mercy

Justice versus Mercy is the ethical dilemma which arises when organizations are asked to choose between attempting to evenly apply rules and make exceptions in cases that involve extraordinary circumstances, which would make application of the rule seem cruel or unfair to an individual. A prime example of the difficulty in applying rules consistently or with mercy often comes in examining some of the difficult situations that arise when income cutoff points are set for social or healthcare services for the poor. Often individuals miss the cut-off point by earning only a few dollars more than allowed and are denied access to vital services such as food stamps or healthcare. From a justice perspective, the only fair way to administer the program is to apply rules consistently across all cases. A mercy perspective would compel managers to resist disqualifying an individual from needed services or medical care based on the difference of a few dollars, which does not increase their ability to pay for services independently.

Justice-versus-Mercy dilemmas are often the most problematic for nonprofit organizations that are the implementing arms of governmental policies and programs. Legal accountability requires that organizations implement programs and policies as defined by government. These legal requirements and the qualifications of clients often make merciful actions difficult to justify. But ignoring mercy often goes against the very mission that the nonprofit organization was set up to serve. In order to serve both ends, formal programming that is funded by government is often administered from a justice perspective while informal norms or wrap around programs that are funded through donations and other fundraising efforts are administered to serve more merciful ends.

Resolving Two Rights

The most difficult decisions faced by both organizations and individuals occur when they are faced with decisions in which they are forced to choose between two competing principles or rights. These ethical dilemmas are not easily resolved and create difficult trade-offs. Often, the answers to these questions create high levels of uncertainty that are not easily governed by a normal or single set of ethical guidelines or principles. For this reason, Kidder (2005) argues that these types of dilemmas are best resolved by applying three different perspectives from moral philosophy.

Kidder (2005) states the three principles outlined below are drawn from the traditions of moral philosophy. The three decision rules listed are particularly useful in analyzing Right-versus-Right issues. Each gives us a way to test the twin rights of a dilemma. Kidder called these decision rules: ends-based, rule-based, and care-based. The three decision rules are outlined below.

(1) *Ends-based thinking.* Ends-based thinking, concerned with the results of a decision, is a utilitarian approach commonly described by the phrase, "the greatest good for the greatest number" (Brousseau, 1998). The

utilitarian weighs decisions based on the consequences. In other words, if things turnout well, you made the right decision. Kidder (2005) states that it demands a human/social/societal cost-benefit analysis, determining who will be hurt and who is helped and measuring the intensity of that help. It is a staple of public policy debates; most policies are crafted with utilitarian tests in mind (Kidder, 2005). However, ends-based thinking has been highly criticized, since no one can really be certain about the future outcomes that today's decisions will create and often times unforeseen or unintended consequences can carry heavy costs.

(2) *Rule-based thinking.* Rule-based thinking, by contrast, seeks to identify and apply the rule that if obeyed, would make the world the kind of place we all want to live in (Brousseau 1998). It differs from ends-based thinking by denying the possibility that the result or consequence of any decision can in fact be known – or evenly properly estimated. What is right for the rule-based thinker can universally be applied everywhere, across the board. How the situation turns out is of little interest: What matters is the fundamental precept that underlies the decision (Kidder, 2005). Kant explains: "Act only on that maxim through which you can at the same time will that it should become a universal law." Simply put, follow the principle you want others to follow. Ask yourself, "If everyone in the world followed the rule of action I am following, would that create the greatest good or, in Kant's words, the greatest worth of character" (Kidder, 2005)?

(3) *Care-based thinking.* Care-based thinking derives from the concept of the Golden Rule: *Do unto others as you would have them do unto you* (Brousseau 1998). By putting yourself in the other person's position, you are encouraged to take their perspective into account. It is a principle of reciprocity, best seen by imagining a reversal of roles with others around you. It partakes of a feature known to philosophers as reversibility: In other words, it asks you to test your actions by putting yourself in another's shoes and imagining how it would feel if you were the recipient, rather than the perpetrator of your actions (Kidder, 2005).

Care-based thinking is often associated with the Judeo–Christian Tradition. The Bible (Matthew 7:12) states that "all things whatsoever ye would that men should do to you, do ye even so to them." This idea appears at the center of all the world's religious teachings. While some philosophers, including Kant, have disputed its standing as a practical principle, it is for many people the only rule of ethics they know, deserving consideration for the moral glue it has provided over the centuries (Kidder, 2005).

The goal of this research is to demonstrate how focus on different stake-holders in the nonprofit setting (the client, the community, and organization) may inherently create challenges for managers in the area of creating ethical evaluation practices when using the heuristics above. Each of these decisions rules can be applied to allow managers to identify possible solutions to management and ethical dilemmas as they relate to performance evaluation and the impact on organizational mission, management, and individual morale.

There are dangers if you only use one approach and complete ethical consideration calls for an exploration of all three heuristics before a final decision is reached. This, however, can also raise a dilemma for individuals making the decision. The decision may not be as easy as having two out of three heuristics substantiate a decision. Ultimately, these heuristics are only guides and ultimately the decision made will depend upon the experience and ethical values of individuals, since different individuals applying these rules can reach very different conclusions and use different weighting scales and factors.

Conclusion

Nonprofit administrators are faced with balancing the demands of funders with those of serving their clients. This often leads to a conflict that can be examined more clearly by using the decision-making model outlined in this chapter. By better balancing the ethical dilemmas faced by nonprofit administrators, better public services and understanding of the needs of communities and nonprofit organizations are possible along with a higher level of trust of services by funders and clients. Our analysis makes several key points. First, nonprofit organizations must work hard to find the balance between need for services and need for knowledge (or data). What is best for the clients and what is best for an evaluation often conflict in practice. Therefore, nonprofit administrators will have to determine an appropriate and acceptable balance in today's environment.

Second, nonprofit organizations should advocate for greater consistency and resources for accountability. When it comes to accountability, it is important for nonprofit organizations to have the resources available to carry out an evaluation plan. At times, this may mean they have to demand from funders the resources necessary to comply with accountability requests. Additionally, the mandated evaluations take up slack resources that are necessary to make the very adjustments and innovations that can become apparent during the evaluation process.

Third, and connected to the previous point, is the importance of educating funding organizations of tradeoffs inherent in accountability. Many nonprofit organizations do not have the capacity to meet funder and organization mission demands. Funding entities need to be educated regarding the varying nonprofit capacities. The most successful relationships between funders and nonprofit organizations are when both entities understand that evaluation is not a "gotcha" system, but a learning system that can help the organization identify what works and what does not, so as to continue with and improve on what is working and repair or replace what is not working. In rare cases, evaluations can provided a nonprofit organization the ability to make a strong case for change, but that is only when the evaluations really take into account the real outcomes of the agency and demonstrate needed changes in a way that does not create a loss of faith with funding organizations.

Fourth, the current system restricts honesty of organizations about failures and inhibits real growth in terms of management, due to worry of funders who do not want to be associated with failure. Within most organizations, failure to meet performance goals results in a comprehensive review of problems and solutions. Ideally, it is important for an organization to establish a culture that is based on understanding the reality of human error and striving to innovate. But this is easier said than done, especially in today's fiscal environment. For many nonprofit organizations, barely able to fund current service delivery levels, the fear of admitting mistakes or shortcomings in operations is frightening. Many believe that evaluation is simply about proving the success or failure of a program. This conventional wisdom assumes that success is implementing the perfect program and never having to hear from stakeholders again – the program will now run itself perfectly. This does not happen in real life. From our experiences and analysis, success is remaining open to continuous feedback and adjusting the program accordingly. Evaluation gives continuous feedback and funders must be open to this iterative process in order to create real solutions to social issues faced by communities.

Finally, a focus on evaluation, without the resources or expertise needed, often leads to collection of data that is easy to collect but does not offer meaningful information about program outcomes. In today's era of information overload, it is possible to collect too much data.

Advanced technology facilitates this tendency. If nonprofit organizations do not have the capacity to carry out evaluation plans, then it is tempting to take advantage of the myriad data resources available via the internet or to simply produce information that is already collected by the organization, but is not connected to outcomes. Certainly, many nonprofit organizations can offer access to and collection of data, but many often struggle with sufficient analytical capacity, which prevents them from ensuring that their results are meaningful and are taken seriously.

In our work with nonprofits organizations, many have cautioned against repeating their initial mistake: collecting data simply because the data were available to be collected, or because having large amounts of data looked good. Instead, organizations need the capacity to choose data and performance measures that can help describe organizational performance, direction, and accomplishments; and then use these to improve services for clients and stakeholders. Collecting the wrong data limits our ability to make good decisions and change programs in ways that will be effective.

The current system of accountability aimed at programs rather than at the nonprofit sector as a whole possibly has the overall impact of worsening several weaknesses inherent within the nonprofit sector. Kramer (1981, 265) identified four characteristic vulnerabilities: formalization or institutionalization, goal deflection, minority rule, and ineffectuality. Over time, formalization takes away the flexibility that made nonprofit organizations attractive alternatives to government's service delivery. Evaluation procedures and the level of professionalization required to carry out accountability processes have an overall impact on the level of flexibility. Nonprofits weighted down by accountability requirements may have difficulty innovating or adapting to emerging social conditions (Ebrahim, 2005). Even the best of standards tend to create some rigidity in systems that had previously been dominated by care-based ethics.

The emphasis on evaluation may also create a process which enhances the dangers of goal deflection. Goal deflection refers to the slow process of an organization being distracted from its mission by means such as fundraising or grant attainment. The process of collecting the data and competing for the next grant becomes more important than the services delivered or the lives of clients that are changed. The final and probably most troubling is that all this concern over performance may actually result in a less innovative and effective nonprofit sector. The focus on short-term outcomes and increased rigidity may actually limit the ability of nonprofit organizations to effectively navigate increasingly complex and sticky social problems.

Our analysis suggests that legal accountability often interferes with the ability of organizations to provide services at the same quality and level demanded by moral accountability. This suggests that policy makers and managers need to carefully examine the impact of evaluations and accountability imposed on organizations in terms of the considering the potential negative impacts that evaluation mandates can have upon service to the mission.

Bibliography

Adams, G. B., & D. L. Balfour. 1998. *Unmasking administrative evil.* Thousand Oaks, CA: Sage, Inc.

Adams, G. B., D. L. Balfour & G. E. Reed. 2006. Abu Ghraib, Administrative Evil, and Moral Inversion: The Value of "Putting cruelty First." *Public Administration Review*, 66(5): 680–693.

Behrens, T. R., & T. Kelley. 2008. Paying the piper: Foundation evaluation capacity calls the tune. *Nonprofits and evaluation: New Directions for Evaluation*, 119: 37–50.

Bozeman, B. 2002. Public-Value Failure: When Efficient Markets May Not Do. *Public Administration Review*, 62(2): 145–161.

Brousseau, P. L. 1998. *Ethical Dilemmas: Right vs. Right. The Ethics Edge*. Washington, DC: International City/County Management Association.

Conner-Snibbe, A. 2006. Drowning in Data. *Stanford Social Innovation Review* (Fall): 39–45.

Dicke, L. A., & J. S. Ott. 1999. Public agency accountability in human service contracting. *Public Productivity and Management Review*, 22(4): 502–516.

Dillard, J. F., & L. Ruchala. 2005. The rules are no game: From instrumental rationality to administrative evil. *Accounting, Auditing and Accountability Journal*, 18(5): 608–630.

Dwivedi, O. P., & J. G. Jabbra. 1988. Public service accountability. *Public Service Accountability*. West Hartford, CT: Kumarian Press, Inc.

Ebrahim. A. 2003. Making sense of accountability: Conceptual perspectives for northern and southern nonprofits. *Nonprofit Management and Leadership*, 14(2): 191–212.

Ebrahim, A. 2005. Accountability myopia: Losing sight of organizational learning. *Nonprofit and Voluntary Sector Quarterly*, 34(1): 56–87.

Ebrahim, A. 2009. Placing the normative logics of accountability in "thick" perspective. *American Behavioral Scientist*, 52(6): 885–904.

Feldman, M. S., & J. G. March. 1981. Information as Signal and Symbol. *Administrative Science Quarterly*, 26(2): 171–186.

Fox, J. A., & L. D. Brown. 1998. *The struggle for accountability: The World Bank, NGOs, and grassroots movements*. Cambridge, MA: MIT Press, Inc.

Frumkin, P. 2002. *On Being Nonprofit: A Conceptual Policy Primer*. Cambridge, MA: University of Chicago Press.

Glaser, J. 1993. *The United Way Scandal: An Insider's Account of What Went Wrong and Why*. New York: John Wiley and Sons Inc.

Greenlee, J., M. Fischer, T. Gordon & E. Keating. 2007. An investigation of fraud in nonprofit organizations: Occurrences and deterrents. *Nonprofit and Voluntary Sector Quarterly*, 36(4): 676–694.

Hamson, N. 2004. Why Innovation Doesn't Work: And what to do about it. *The Innovation Journal: The Public Sector Innovation Journal*, 9(1), article 8. Accessed June 21, 2017 at: <http://www.innovation.cc/volumes-issues/vol9issue1emp-emp.htm>.

Hwang, H., & W. W. Powell. 2009. The rationalization of charity: The influence of professionalization in the nonprofit sector. *Administrative Science Quarterly*, 54(2): 268–298.

Jos, P. H., & M. E. Tompkins. 2004. The accountability paradox in an age of reinvention: The perennial problem of preserving character and judgment. *Administration and Society*, 36(3): 255–281.

Kearns, K. P. 1996. *Managing for Accountability: Preserving the Public Trust in Public and Nonprofit Organizations*. San Francisco, CA: Jossey-Bass.

Kem, J. D. 2006. The use of the "Ethical Triangle" in Military Ethical Decision Making. *Public Administration and Management*, 11(1): 22–43.

Kidder, R. M. 2005. *Moral Courage*. New York: Harper Collins Publishers.

Kim, S. E. 2005. Three Management Challenges in Performance Improvement in Human Services Agencies: A Case Study. *International Review of Public Administration*, 10(1): 83–93.

Kramer, R. M. 1994. Voluntary agencies and the contract culture: Dream or nightmare? *Social Service Review*, 68(1): 33–60.

Letts, C. W., W. Ryan & A. Grossman. 1997. Virtuous capital: What foundations can learn from venture capitalists. *Harvard Business Review* (March–April): 36–44.

Light, P. C. 2000. *Tides of Nonprofit Reform: A Report on the Nonprofit Public Service*. Washington, DC: Brookings Institute Press.

Martin, L. L., & P. M. Ketner. 1997. Performance measurement: The new accountability. *Administration in Social Work*, 21(1): 17–29.

Menzel, D. C. 2005. Research on ethics and integrity in governance: A review and assessment. *Public Integrity*, 7(2): 147–168.

Minkoff, D. C., & W. W. Powell. 2006. Nonprofit mission: Constancy responsiveness or deflection. Pp. 591–611 in W. W. Powell and R. Steinberg, *The Nonprofit Sector: A Research Handbook*. New Haven, CT: Yale University Press.

Nicholson-Crotty, S., N. A. Theobald & J. Nicholson-Crotty. 2006. Disparate measures: Public managers and performance-measurement strategies. *Public Administration Review*, 66(1): 101–113.

Pesch, U. 2008. Administrators and accountability: The plurality of value systems in the public domain. *Public Integrity*, 10(4): 335–344.

Urban Institute. 2004. Getting What We Pay For: Low Overhead Limits Nonprofit Effectiveness. *Nonprofit Overhead Cost Project Brief No. 3* (August). Available at: <http: http://www.urban.org/uploadedpdf/311044_nocp_3.pdf>.

W. K. Kellogg Foundation. 1998. *The W. K. Kellogg Evaluation Handbook*. Battle Creek, MI: W. K. Kellogg Foundation.

MAI NGUYEN

5 Consulting No One: Is Democratic Administration the Answer for First Nations?[1]

ABSTRACT

Governments and First Nations have different understandings of what is meant by accountability. While the Department of Indigenous and Northern Affairs Canada (INAC) understands accountability to be concerned with funding, First Nations believe accountability requires increasingly open and transparent dialogue between governments and affected communities; that is, accountability for performance. However, accountability for performance did not occur in the 1980s with the implementation of the New Public Management (NPM) model, which focused on treating citizens like consumers. Through the use of Canadian court cases, this chapter argues that the lack of accountability for performance has created serious political, economic, and social implications that have denied First Nations communities rights and control over their destinies (Shoucri, 2007: 103). As such, accountability for performance can be achieved through greater consultation between First Nations and governments at the initial stages of policy-making, as advanced in the democratic administration framework.

Introduction

In 1996, the Office of the Auditor General (OAG) of Canada reported in the *Study of Accountability Practices from the Perspective of First Nations* that governments and First Nations have different understandings of what is meant by accountability. While the Department of Indigenous and Northern Affairs Canada (INAC) – formerly known as Indian and Northern Affairs Canada (INAC) – understood the department's mechanism of accountability to remain in the form of accountability for funding provided by the

---

1   *The Innovation Journal: The Public Sector Innovation* Journal, 19(1), 2014, article 7 <https://www.innovation.cc/volumes-issues/vol19-no1.htm>.

federal government, First Nations believed accountability required increasingly open and transparent dialogue between the department and the people it affects. That is, accountability for performance means that government action must achieve high results in terms of citizens' expectations (Behn, 2001: 10). Specifically, First Nations expect to know how funds are being allocated and implemented, be part of the initial stages of policy-making and, more importantly, that program results meet First Nations' expectation. With this in mind, this chapter has two focuses. First, this chapter argues that accountability for performance can be achieved through greater consultation at the initial stages of policy-making (a-priori policy). This type of engagement is advanced in the democratic administration model which ultimately stipulates that greater participation by citizens in government affairs will led to greater citizen-centered policy outcomes.

Second, this chapter argues that the focus on accountability for funding rather than the focus on accountability for performance has created serious political, economic, and social implications that have denied First Nations communities rights and control over their communities (Shoucri, 2007: 103) (summarized in Figure 5.1). Given that the rights of First Nations communities derive from the *Indian Act, 1876* and Section 35 of the *Canadian Constitution Act, 1982*, and because the Canadian system entrusts the judiciary to be the guardians of the Constitution and mediator between state and society (Shoucri, 2007: 100), recent Canadian Court cases (*Mikisew Cree v. Canada*, 2005; *Ermineskin v. Canada*, 2009; and *Pikangikum v. Canada*, 2002) are the instrument of analysis.

It is important to know that First Nations communities are culturally unlike other Canadian citizens and because of this the programs the communities depend on require greater culturally specific attention. This attention is best provided by First Nations communities and not white-Canadian bureaucrats – a problem that is recognized by INAC (Turcotte and Zhao, 2004: 11). However, First Nations continue to be excluded from the decision-making process. It is on this point that this chapter theorizes that the model of democratic administration, with an emphasis on greater participation by First Nations communities, will allow for greater accountability for performance. But what is democratic administration? And why has the lack of implementation been detrimental to First Nations? This chapter attempts to answer these questions.

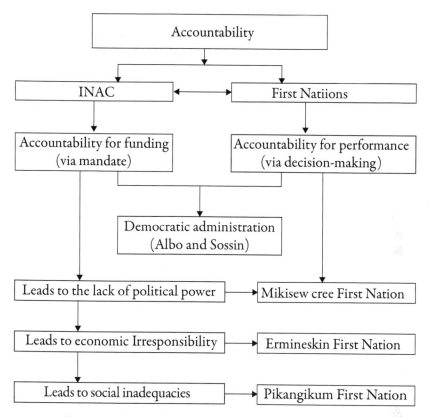

Figure 5.1: Accountability within the democratic administration framework. Source: the author.

Accountability within the Democratic Administration Framework: Review of the Literature

Public sector reform can often be situated along the political spectrum. The New Right and the New Left advocate greater public involvement in the policy-making process but differ on how and why the public is involved. What has materialized is a differing view on what governments should be doing for citizen. While the New Right, often associated with New

Public Management (NPM), focuses on making governments effective and responsive to citizen demands, the New Left, often associated with democratic administration theory, focuses on curving out a new space for citizens in the policy-making process. What has been the driving force behind these two ideologies?

Beginning with the former, since the 1970s, NPM has been the management model of choice for bureaucratic reform in advanced industrial countries (Britain, United States, Canada, Australia, etc.). The shift from the bureaucratic organization to the post-bureaucratic organization of NPM stipulates that governments should operate more like a business by adopting private-sector characteristics. This has been in line with both the theories of "managerialism" and the public choice model deriving from the field of economics (Atreya and Armstrong, 2002). Some of these characteristics include a transition from: organization-centered to citizen-centered; rule-centered to people-centered; independent action to collective action; status-quo-oriented to change-oriented; process-oriented to results-oriented; centralized to decentralized; budget-driven to revenue-driven; and monopolistic to competitive (Kernaghan et al., 2000: 3). The list is extensive, and numerous external factors (globalization, technological revolution, etc.) as well as internal factors (debt reduction, changing political culture, etc.) drive public sector reform. Within this framework, the call for greater public participation (often described as participatory democracy) has led to the demand for greater accountability between governments and citizens (Kernaghan et al., 2000: 180).

However, proponents of democratic administration (Ostrom, 1974; Albo, 1993) argue that public sector reform towards the New Public Management model has not fulfilled its mandate to be more effective and accountable (Albo, 1993). Since the ascendance of neo-liberalism, Canadian governments have taken up the New Right approach to public sector reform, which has restructured the bureaucracy to emphasize more choice for citizens/consumers in purchasing public goods and services, an increasingly decentralized bureaucracy, and a bureaucracy immune to the needs of the market (Sossin, 2002: 87). Lorne Sossin (2002: 86) notes that the restructuring of bureaucracy has returned public administration, especially in the fields of social welfare, to communities (via the downloading of responsibilities). However, Sossin (2002: 86) is ultimately critical of this approach for which he states, "It may tend to improve the quality and lower the price of goods and services in question (at least at first), but it does not lead to substantive citizen influence over the decision-making process."

In other words, within the New Right accountability is embodied in the ability to give citizens "choice" rather than "voice." Many argue (King et al., 1998; Turnball and Aucoin, 2006; Catt and Murphy, 2003) this approach is problematic because citizen input is sought only after important policy decisions have already been made and therefore, disguised by a veneer of legitimacy. Eric Otenyo (2006: 12) correctly states that "NPM and its derivative policy outcomes, especially the shrinking state has not in any meaningful way translated into democratic enlargement." The New Left attempts to rectify this problem by focusing on mechanisms of accountability that are embedded in the ability to make the bureaucracy more open and democratic by allowing citizens a voice during the initial stages of policy-making. This will allow for greater democratic governance and ultimately better policy outcomes.

According to Greg Albo (1993), the true essence of accountability to the public cannot be fully realized without the participation of citizens. He argues (1993: 28) that accountability should operate horizontally and believes that the operations of the public sector should ultimately be held accountable to the people, the true users of public services. Unlike the NPM theory, this approach views the people as a collectivity rather than a collection of individual "consumers." Furthermore, understanding the people as a collectivity is the true premise of democratic citizenship. Though he does not explicitly label it so, it is embodied in what can be called the "control from below" model. This model suggests a shifting of power at the center to bring all public servants in line with the reform agendas, and a level playing field for all participants, which allows everyone from frontline workers, to ministers, to interest groups, to be involved in the formation and implementation of policies (Albo, 1993: 28). More importantly, the "control from below" model requires a working relationship and continuous dialogue (often in the form of consultation) between the producers and the users of government services.

Along similar lines, Sossin (2002: 91) states that the premise is "simply that every bureaucratic setting can and should be evaluated according to how fully the goals of participation and accountability have been achieved." This is unlike NPM in which the bureaucratic settings are evaluated based on service delivery and cost-cutting mechanisms. Within the democratic administration model, Sossin advocates for accountability that sees citizens as having increased participation in the development of public policy (2002: 87). This means that the public sector is accountable to ensure the inclusion of citizens in the initial stages of policy formation and implementation. As Sossin (2002: 88) states, "the goal is to transform administrative action into a shared enterprise between citizens and officials, in which each have a stake in the fairness and justness of bureaucratic decision-making, and each accountable to the other, and to the public, for holding up their end." Sossin's understanding of accountability is that which hopes to be realized by First Nations and their dealings with the state.

According to First Nations communities, accountability should be based on the ability of INAC to provide greater mechanisms of accountability for performance to First Nations communities. This can be achieved in several ways, such as self-government arrangements, co-management boards, and creation of lands and reserves. More importantly, this can be achieved through the implementation of the democratic administration model, specifically through the implementation of stronger methods of consultation a-priori policy-making. The rationale for this is historically justified since the state has imposed itself on Aboriginal affairs. This imposition has generally occurred without the input or participation of Aboriginal groups during the policy-making process and has adversely affected First Nations communities both historically and to date. More than ever, First Nations communities, dissatisfied with the workings of representative democracy, are actively staking their right to be consulted on matters that directly affect them. As a result, First Nations communities are initiating a new political relationship with the Canadian state.

This changing relationship dates back to the drafting of the Trudeau *White Paper, 1969*, which was the beginning of Aboriginal mobilization, and continued with the affirmation of Aboriginal and Treaty rights in Section 35 of *The Constitution Act, 1982*, resulting in the "duty to consult" stemming from legal cases such as *Haida Nation v. British Columbia* (Minister of Forests – 2004 SCC 73) and *Mikisew Cree First Nation v. Canada* (Minister of Canadian Heritage – 2005 SCC 69). Accountability for performance is important for First Nations because they endeavor to remove the reigns of colonialism and work towards political inclusion for self-determination. As Helen Catt states:

> Democratic decision making as a means of obtaining self-governance to fulfill the ideal that no person should be deciding for another is an important strand of argument in justification for democracy ... The other strand to the argument of self-government is that all decisions should be made only after each person has had an opportunity to express their view. Only if the decision is made by all is it legitimate. (Catt, 1999: 8)

To this end, decision-making power through the consultation process is a step towards political inclusion and thus, self-determination for First Nations communities. As the Public Service 2000 Report (1990) states, "Effective consultation is about partnership. It implies a shared responsibility and ownership of the process and the outcome." Without a sharing of the enterprise, governments will continue to impose their agenda on participants through a veneer of legitimacy, or what they call consultation. Therefore, First Nations communities have staked their right to be consulted on matters that directly affect them.

First Nations communities recognize the lack of state consultation and are taking their right to participation in policy-making to the Supreme Court of Canada (SCC), whom over time has ruled in favor of First Nations communities. To date the SCC has clearly stated that the Crown must engage in a "distinct consultation process" (*Mikisew Cree First Nation v. Canada*, supra notes 2 and 4) with First Nations. That is, First Nations cannot be treated as mere stakeholders; rather, their concerns must be addressed in a distinct consultation process. Dwight Newman states that legally acceptable and good consultation:

> ... must be initiated at an appropriate stage, such that there is meaningful discussion about a particular strategy or plan. There must be an identification of the Aboriginal communities potentially affected and an identification of contact people in those communities. There must be appropriate forms of notice given and further information made available where necessary for meaningful consultation. (Newman, 2009: 63)

However, it is this accountability which has been seriously lacking since INAC's inception and has created serious political, economic, and social implications for First Nations communities.

Inferences from Data: The Political, Economic and Social Consequences

INAC (2008) is responsible for two mandates, *Indian and Inuit Affairs* and *Northern Development*. Combined, both mandates support Canada's Aboriginal and northern peoples in the pursuit of healthy and sustainable communities and broader economic and social development through the provision of financial funds (accountability for funding) (INAC, 2008). According to the *Indian and Inuit Affairs* mandate, INAC is empowered to, negotiate comprehensive and specific land claims and self-government agreements on behalf of the Government of Canada; oversee implementation of claim settlements; deliver provincial-type services such as education, housing, community infrastructure and social support to Status Indians on reserve; manage land; and execute other regulatory duties under the *Indian Act* (INAC, 2008). The *Northern Development* mandate stems from statutes including the *Department of Indigenous Affairs and Northern Development Act*, modern treaties north of 60 degrees, and from statutes dealing with environmental or resource management (INAC, 2008).

In this section of the chapter three historical legal cases (*Mikisew Cree v. Canada*, 2005; *Ermineskin v. Canada*, 2009; and *Pikangikum v. Canada*, 2002) are examined to highlight the lack of accountability for performance and its consequences on specific First Nations communities. Court cases are the instrument of analysis because courts are mediator between state and society. As Liora Salter (1993: 89) argues, those seeking democratic administration and accountability are facing a losing battle and, "greater reliance should be placed upon the courts to handle some of the responsibilities that regulators now assume in order to promote accountability." First Nations recognize the importance of the Canadian legal system and have taken their battles straight to the courts. The following section examines the political, economic, and social implications that have arisen because of a lack of consultation a-priori policy-making.

The Political Failures of Consultation

Albo (1993: 31) states that political power is, "the ability to control and shape one's life and community." However, increased political power has been slow to bear fruit for First Nations communities. Recognizing this, the 2002 *Report of the Auditor General of Canada* criticized INAC for lack of consultation with First Nations communities and advocated for greater consultation which will lead to better programming and effective outcomes based on the concerns of First Nations. As the Report (OAG, 2002: 23) states,

> Reporting, both financial and non-financial, is an essential element of the account-ability relationship between the federal government and First Nations. The federal government needs to attest to effective spending of funds ... This work will also support First Nations in community planning, program evaluation and assist program service delivery.

Unfortunately, since this report not much has changed. More disconcerting is that the lack of consultation by Canadian governments breaches the Crown's legal duty to consult with First Nations pursuant under section 35(1) of the *Canadian Constitutional Act of 1982*. This is illustrated through the *Mikisew Cree First Nation v. Canada* (2005) Supreme Court of Canada (SCC) case in which the group was not properly included in the policy-making process on an issue which directly affected them. More importantly, this case was instrumental in setting the precedent for the legal "duty to consult."

The Mikisew Cree First Nation case against the Minister of Canadian Heritage stemmed from a breach of the Treaty 8 agreement between the group and the Crown (*Mikisew Cree First Nation v. Canada*, 2005: 3). In 2000, the federal government approved a winter road which ran through the group's reserve. After protest from the Mikisew Cree the road was modified, without consultation, to be built around the reserve's outer boundary (*Mikisew Cree First Nation v. Canada*, 2005: 4). The Mikisew Cree held that the building of such a road would interfere with their rights to hunt, trap, and fish which is protected under Treaty 8 (*Mikisew Cree First Nation v. Canada*, 2005: 3) and that this road would affect their traditional lifestyle because it crossed a number of trap lines and hunting grounds (Newman, 2009: 13). More importantly, the unilateral decision to build the road breached the Crown's duty to consult and accommodate Aboriginal peoples (*Mikisew Cree First Nation v. Canada*, 2005: 3). As the SCC judges state:

> The Crown did not discharge its obligations when it unilaterally declared the road realignment would be shift from the reserve itself to a track along its boundary. It failed to demonstrate an intention of substantially addressing aboriginal concerns through a meaningful process of consultation. (Mikisew Cree First Nation v. Canada, 2005: 6)

In other words, what occurred was a lack of consultation resulting in the group's diminished capacity to affect policy in two ways. First, the group was not consulted at the initial stages of the policy-making process. As the trial judge stated, "Parks Canada did not consult directly with the First Nation about the road, or about means of mitigating impacts of the road on treaty rights, *until after important routing decisions had been made*" (emphasis added, Lawson Lundell Aboriginal Law Group, 2005). Second, consultation after the fact was not sufficient to affect the policy outcome. As the trial judge stated:

> The realignment ... was not developed in consultation with Mikisew. The evidence of Chief George Poitras highlighted an air of secrecy surrounding the realignment. Parks Canada admitted it did not consult with Mikisew about the route for the realignment, nor did it consider the impacts of the realignment on Mikisew trappers' rights. (Mikisew Cree First Nation v. Canada, 2005: 16)

On this point, the building of a winter road, according to Mikisew, would have had adverse effects on the group which were not known to Parks Canada due to a lack of consultation.

In light of this SCC decision, in February 2008 INAC created an *Action Plan on Consultation and Accommodation*. This action plan (INAC, 2007) is expected to achieve some of the following results:

Federal officials are equipped with the tools needed to discharge the legal duty to consult; Creation of a federal policy on consultation that addresses policy and legal challenges and that reflects the participation of First Nations, Metis and Inuit groups in its development; and Better coordination of Canada's consultation approaches (INAC, 2007).

Though this appears to be a step forward, it is not clear at what stage of the decision-making process would First Nations communities be consulted. Consultation after the important decisions have been made would not result in greater accountability or political power because First Nations would not be given a voice a-priori policy design. Therefore, public consultations occur after the fact would only be used to justify policy choices which have already been made (Sossin, 2002: 93).

The Economic Failures of Consultation

This section will examine the *Ermineskin Indian Band and Nation v. Canada* (1998) case in which monies were mismanaged by the Government of Canada. A lack of consultation between INAC and the Ermineskin Indian Band resulted in the mismanagement of funds derived from the Band's revenues. Though the Band did not win this case, this case does illustrate that the lack of consultation between INAC and the Ermineskin Band resulted in the loss of significant monetary interest which would have been gained through better investment of the Band's revenues.

The *Indian Act* of 1876 made First Nations communities ward of the state by empowering the Crown with a fiduciary obligation towards the communities. In the *Ermineskin Indian Band and Nation v. Canada* case, the band, governed by Treaty 6, alleged the Crown failed to fulfill this duty when it failed to diversify, through investment, the band's oil and gas royalties and when it calculated and paid interest on such royalties (*Ermineskin Indian Band and Nation v. Canada*, 1998: 4). The SCC (*Ermineskin Indian Band and Nation v. Canada*, 1998: 5) stated that, "Samson and Ermineskin filed statements of claim ... alleging that the Crown's fiduciary obligations required it to invest oil and gas royalties received on behalf of the bands as a prudent investor would, that is, to invest the royalties in a diversified portfolio."

Unfortunately, in this case the SCC held that the Crown did not have the obligation or authority to invest the bands' royalties pertaining to the Crown's fiduciary duty, as well as under section 35(1) of the *Constitution Act*, 1982, because there is no treaty right to investment by the Crown (*Ermineskin Indian Band and Nation v. Canada*, 1998: 4). This SCC decision ruled in favour of the Crown and the band did not receive any additional money. However, the point of contention according to the SCC is that:

> In 1969, the Crown decided to tie the rate of interest to the market yield of government bonds having terms to maturity of ten years or over. Discussions took place ... between the Crown and leaders of various bands and a new Order in Council was enacted in 1981. (*Ermineskin Indian Band and Nation v. Canada*, 1998: 4)

Here, the Crown already made the most important decision which was to tie the rate of interest to the market yield of government bonds without consulting with the group. In addition, there was no further consultation with the band in regards to how the money would be managed post-1970s. In this case, the band was not given the ability to make important economic decisions a-priori factual through consultation. The Assembly of First Nations' (AFN) Regional Chief Littlechild (2009) responded to the SCC decision stating, "We are obviously very disappointed in today's decision. It may point to the need for a mechanism through which First Nations that want control over their trust monies are able to take that control."

In other words, it is evident that there exists a tension between what the Crown believed its fiduciary duty to be and what the band expected of the Crown in regards to investment. This difference has meant that First Nations, specifically the Ermineskin Indian Band, has had little control over their finances which has resulted in a significant loss of funds.

The Social Failures of Consultation

INAC is responsible for providing social programs and services to First Nations communities in the areas of health, education, housing, community infrastructure and other poverty measurements. On this front First Nations have not made significant strides. The 2009 Assembly of First Nations' (AFN) report, *Federal Government Funding to First Nations: The Facts, the Myths and the Way Forward*, states that First Nations rights are accessed through federal funding and are categorized into three areas: comparable services; lawful obligations; and self-government (AFN, 2009). Comparable services consist of services of at least equal quality to those provided to other Canadians by federal, provincial, and municipal governments (AFN, 2009). However, AFN (2009) states that, "living conditions on many First Nations reserves are notoriously inadequate. In order to arrive at some equality of outcomes with the rest of Canada, existing policy must change." This problem can be attributed to the actions of the federal government in its attempts to download programs and responsibilities to First Nations communities. However, many First Nations communities lack the capacity to implement specific programs in their communities and this has led to social inadequacies as was demonstrated in the *Pikangikum First Nation vs. Canada* (2002) Federal Court case.

In 2000, the Pikangikum First Nation entered into a Comprehensive Funding Agreement (CFA) with INAC, which was in effect from April 2000 to March 2001 (*Pikangikum First Nation vs. Canada*, 2002: 05). According to INAC (2007), "CFA is a program-budgeted funding arrangement INAC enters into with Recipients for a one year duration and which contains programs funded by means of Contribution – reimbursement of actual expenditures; Flexible Transfer Payment – formula funded and surpluses may be retained provided terms and conditions have been fulfilled; and/or Grants." CFAs allow First Nations to deliver social and economic programming directly, and in the case of the Pikangikum First Nation, without external interference to support First Nation groups in achieving self-government, economic educational, cultural, social needs and aspirations (*Pikangikum First Nation vs. Canada*, 2002: 3).

However, during the 2000–2001 fiscal year INAC became concerned about Pikangikum's ability to properly administer projects and programs because the community continued to experience problems relating to infrastructure (*Pikangikum First Nation vs. Canada*, 2002: 4). For example, in late 2000 there was a significant flood at the water treatment plant due to older equipment that was never properly managed (*Pikangikum First Nation vs. Canada*, 2002: 4). Additionally, the Pikangikum School was closed for almost a year as a result of a fuel spill when the shut-off valve of the fuel tank was not turned off (*Pikangikum First Nation vs. Canada*, 2002: 4). Due to apparent mismanagement, on November 17, 2000, INAC notified the Pikangikum First Nation that the department intended to appoint a third-party manager to oversee the terms of the CFA and if the band did not cooperate funding would cease to commence (*Pikangikum First Nation vs. Canada*, 2002: 05). Upon notice, INAC went ahead with its decision and transferred the delivery of services and programs to A. D. Morrison and Associates Ltd. This decision was taken to trial for judicial review.

The Pikangikum First Nation submitted that INAC unilaterally breached the terms of the CFA without adequately specifying what conditions led the department to be concerned (*Pikangikum First Nation vs. Canada*, 2002: 7). In addition, the band (*Pikangikum First Nation vs. Canada*, 2002: 7) argued that INAC knew the water treatment plant was never completed, was vulnerable to accidental flooding, many of the infrastructural deficiencies preceded the band's control over the services, and actually were a direct result of previous planning by INAC. More importantly, the lack of consultation between INAC and the band led to: "The program and service infrastructure at Pikangikum First Nation [was] not operating normally; The First Nation has been removed from any input into the development of its major capital infrastructure; The First Nation does not have the funds to deliver department services ..." (*Pikangikum First Nation vs. Canada*, 2002: 8). With this evidence presented to the court, the Federal Court ruled in favor of the band noting that Indian Affairs Minister Robert Nault breached the duty of procedural fairness. However, for the purposes of this chapter the ruling is less important than the circumstances under which the ruling took place.

In this case, INAC mistakenly allowed market empowerment to be equated with political empowerment without providing mechanisms of accountability for performance. Essentially, accountability for performance would have required INAC to ensure that services and programs were comparable to those services of other Canadian residents (*Pikangikum*

First Nation vs. Canada, 2002: 02). However, the Pikangikum First Nation was not equipped with the necessary tools and capacity to fulfill the terms of the CFA. In addition, when INAC became concerned with the band's performance the department reneged on its commitment and unilaterally imposed external control over the band's affairs. The lack of consultation resulting in the department's unilateral decision created serious social service problems for the band as mentioned above. Though INAC was essentially following its mandate, the department did so without providing the band the capacity necessary to succeed in implementing the CFA.

Conclusion

Over the past several decades INAC has provided First Nations communities with substantial financial funding which has not been largely contested. However, this form of accountability has not translated into accountability for performance. The lack of accountability for performance has created political, economic, and social implications that have prevented First Nations from gaining control over their communities, and consequently, their destinies. Ultimately, this has inhibited democratization and First Nations' self-determination. Therefore, the next logical step for First Nations communities is to demand greater participation in consultation during the initial stages of policy-formation. Involvement a-priori policy-formation will lead to greater First Nations specific and appropriate programs. The clear lack of consultation between INAC and First Nations communities has created tensions between the two players resulting in a relationship based on a lack of trust. This lack of trust has not led to effective policies and/or meaningful compromises. Therefore, a renewed relationship must be based on an equal partnership between the two which can be achieved through the New Left perspective of democratic administration. That is, INAC is accountable to First Nations for results and First Nations are responsible to INAC for participating in consultation and ultimately, responsible to its members for results. Newman is optimistic that:

Consultation embodies the possibility of genuinely hearing one another and seeking reconciliations that work in the shorter-term while opening the door for negotiations of longer-term solutions to unsolved legal problems. Those potentially engaged with consultations, whether governments, Aboriginal communities, or corporate stakeholders, ought to bear in mind not only their doctrinal legal position but the longer-term prospects for trust and reconciliation that will enable all to live together in the years ahead. (Newman, 2009: 64)

Some headway has been made on this front. On November 2008, INAC stated that it will implement a plan to improve the way Aboriginal individuals and communities are supported and will enhance program effectiveness and accountability by focusing on areas such as:

Education and housing; development of legislative frameworks that will empower Aboriginal Canadians and Northerners to make their own decisions ... and support their community's development; and special attention to those who are most vulnerable ... by establishing family violence shelters and ... protect the property rights of First Nations women in cases where relationships fail. (INAC, 2008)

In addition, INAC (2008) stated it would focus on creating effective partnerships between governments, First Nations, and other third parties. However, a framework for empowering First Nations with the ability to be effective partners has yet to be established. Therefore, until First Nations communities are provided with the tools necessary to control and manage their communities, either through greater consultations, increased funding, better self-government arrangements, etc., many of the action plans put forth by governments pay little more than lip-service to the issue of accountability for performance.

Bibliography

Albo, Greg. 1993. Democratic citizenship and the future of public management. Pp. 17–33 in G. Albo, D. Langille & L. Panitch (eds), *A Different Kind of State? Popular Power and Democratic Administration*. Toronto, Canada: University of Toronto Press.

Assembly of First Nations. 2009. *Federal Government Funding to First Nations: The Facts, the Myths and the Way Forward.* Accessed April 1, 2014 at: <http://64.26.129.156/cmslib/general/Federal-Government-Funding-to-First-Nations.pdf> (no longer available).

Atreya, B., & A. Armstrong. 2002. A review of the criticisms and the future of new public management. *Working Paper Series.* Melbourne, Australia: Victoria University. Accessed July 15, 2017 at: <http://vuir.vu.edu.au/169/1/wp7_2002_atreya_armstrong.pdf>.

Behn, R. 2001. *Rethinking Democratic Accountability.* Washington, MD: Brookings Institution Press.

Catt, H. 1999. *Democracy in Practice.* New York: Routledge.

Catt, H., & M. Murphy. 2003. What voice for the people? Categorising methods of public consultation. *Australian Journal of Political Science*, 38(3): 407–421.

Congress of Aboriginal Peoples Report. 2006. *Where does the money go? Proactive disclosure of grants and contributions for Aboriginal Peoples.* Ottawa, Canada: Congress of Aboriginal Peoples. Accessed April 1, 2014 at: <http://www.abo-peoples.org/wp-content/uploads/2013/01/where_moneygo.pdf> (no longer available).

Diebel, L. 2009. *Bureaucrats indifferent to Indian Affairs fiasco. Toronto Star*, March 17.

Ermineskin Indian Band and Nation *v.* Canada, [2009] 1 S.C.R. 222, 2009 SCC 9.

Federal Court of Canada. 2002. *Pikangikum First Nation vs. Canada (Minister of Indian and Northern Affairs).* Manitoba, Canada: Federal Court of Canada – Trial Division.

Accessed August, 11 2017 at: <http://www.constitutional-law.net/index.php?option=com_mtree&task=viewlink&link_id=224&Itemid=9>.

Haida Nation v. British Columbia (Minister of Forests), [2004] 3 S.C.R. 511, 2004 SCC 73.

INAC (Indian and Northern Affairs Canada). 2007. Backgrounder – Action plan on consultation and accommodation. Accessed August 3, 2017 at: <http://www.aadnc-aandc.gc.ca/DAM/DAM-INTER-HQ/STAGING/texte-text/intgui_1100100014665_eng.pdf>.

INAC. November 30, 2007. Comprehensive funding arrangement national model for use with First Nations and Tribal Councils for 2008–2009. Last modified September 15, 2010. Accessed August 3, 2017 at: <http://www.aadnc-aandc.gc.ca/eng/1100100010085/1100100010087>.

INAC. 2008. *Aboriginal consultation and accommodation: Interim guidelines for federal officials to fulfill the legal duty to consult.* February. Ottawa, Canada: INAC. Accessed April 1, 2014 at: <http://www.aadnc-aandc.gc.ca/eng/1100100014664/1100100014675> (no longer available).

INAC. 2008. Mandate, roles, and responsibilities. Ottawa, Canada: INAC. Accessed August 3, 2017 at: <https://www.tbs-sct.gc.ca/rpp/2008-2009/inst/ian/ian01-eng.asp>.

Kernaghan, K., B. Marson & S. Borins. 2000. *The New Public Organization*. Toronto, Canada: The Institute of Public Administration of Canada.

King, C., K. Feltey & B. O'Neill Susel. 1998. The question of participation: Toward authentic public participation in public administration. *Public Administration Review*, 58(4): 271–291.

Littlechild, W. 2009. Assembly of First Nations "very disappointed": by Supreme Court of Canada decision in Samson and Ermineskin. CNW. February 13. Accessed July 15, 2017 at: <http://www.newswire.ca/en/story/528313/assembly-of-first-nations-very-disappointed-by-supreme-court-of-canada-decision-in-samson-and-ermineskin>.

Mikisew Cree First Nation v. Canada (Minister of Canadian Heritage), [2005] 3 S.C.R. 388, 2005 SCC 69.

Newman, D. 2009. *The duty to consult – New relationships with aboriginal peoples*. Saskatoon, Canada: Purich Publishing Ltd.

Office of the Auditor General of Canada (OAG). 1996. Chapter 13: Study of accountability practices from the perspective of First Nations, in *September 1996 Report of the Auditor General of Canada*. Ottawa, Canada: OAG. Accessed April 1, 2014 at: <http://publications.gc.ca/collections/collection_2015/bvg-oag/FA1-1-1997-eng.pdf> (no longer available).

Office of the Auditor General of Canada. 2002. Chapter 1: Streamlining First Nations reporting to federal organization, in *December 2002 Report of the Auditor General of Canada*. Ottawa, Canada: OAG. Accessed July 15, 2017 at: <http://www.oag-bvg.gc.ca/internet/English/parl_oag_200212_01_e_12395.html>.

Office of the Auditor General of Canada. 2009. Chapter 4: First Nations Child and Family Services Program – Indian and Northern Affairs Canada, in *May 2008 Report of the Auditor General of Canada*. March. Ottawa, Canada: OAG. Accessed July 15, 2017 at: <http://www.fncaringsociety.com/sites/default/files/docs/402_PACP_Rpt07-e.pdf>.

Ostrom, V. 1974. *The Intellectual Crisis in American Public Administration*.

Otenyo, E. 2006. Vincent Ostrom's Democratic Administration and New Public Management in East Africa. Paper presented at the Indiana University's Workshop in Political Theory and Policy Analysis Conference: "Vincent Ostrom: The Quest to Understand Human Affairs" (in honor of Vincent Ostrom's work and life), May 31 – June 6, 2006. Indiana University, Bloomington, Indiana.

Panitch, L. 1993. Different kind of state? Pp. 2–16 in Greg Albo, D. Langille & Leo Panitch (eds), *A Different Kind of State? Popular Power and Democratic Administration*. Toronto, Canada: University of Toronto Press.

Salter, L. 1993. Capture or co-management: Democracy and accountability in regulatory agencies. Pp. 87–100 in Greg Albo, D. Langille & Leo Panitch (eds), *A Different Kind of State? Popular Power and Democratic Administration.* Toronto, Canada: University of Toronto Press.

Shields, J., & B. Evans. 1998. *Shrinking the state: Globalization and public administration reform.* Halifax, Canada: Fernwood Publishing.

Shoucri, R. 2007. Weaving a third strand into the braid of aboriginal–crown relations: Legal obligations to finance aboriginal governments negotiated in Canada. *Indigenous Law Journal* (at the University of Toronto), 6(2): 95–123. Accessed August 3, 2017 at: <http://ilj.law.utoronto.ca/sites/ilj.law.utoronto.ca/files/media/ilj-6.2-shoucri.pdf>.

Sossin, L. 2002. Democratic administration. *Handbook of public administration in Canada.* Toronto, Canada: Oxford University Press.

Turcotte, M., & J. Zhao. 2004. A portrait of aboriginal children living in non-reserve areas: Results from the 2001 Aboriginal Peoples Survey, catalogue no. 89-597-XIE. Ottawa, Canada: Statistics Canada Housing, Family and Social Statistics Division. Accessed July 15, 2017 at: <http://www.statcan.gc.ca/pub/89-597-x/2001001/index-eng.htm> (website indicated available on request).

Turnball, L., & P. Aucoin. 2006. *Fostering Canadians' role in public policy: A strategy for institutionalizing public involvement in policy.* Ottawa, Canada: Canadian Policy Research Networks. Accessed August, 3 at: <http://rcrpp.org/documents/42670_fr.pdf>.

Tuscaloosa, AL: The University of Alabama Press.

United Nations Development Programme (UNDP). 2001. *UNDP and indigenous peoples: A policy of engagement.* Accessed July 15, 2017 at: <http://www.undp.org/content/undp/en/home/librarypage/environment-energy/local_development/undp-and-indigenous-peoples-a-policy-of-engagement.html>.

MICHAEL MILES

6 The Process of Engagement: Examination of Management Values as a Change Strategy in Veterans Affairs Canada[1]

ABSTRACT

One of the most difficult issues of change programs is how to get started. Motivating initial steps related to the change involves convincing those affected by the change that they should become actively involved in achieving the change goals. A frequent dilemma of change programs focused on increasing employee participation is that managers have been trained that it is their role to make the decisions and solve the problems. Employees, they believe, are not capable and, in many cases, not interested in participating in managerial tasks.

This research study examines a five-year change program carried out in the Department of Veterans Affairs Canada to shift the management culture in the direction of increased employee empowerment and participation. It examines the critical role that a four-day management values seminar played in convincing mangers that employees were interested and capable of participation in work-related decision-making. The study concludes that the structured examination of managers' personal beliefs and values related to employees, employee involvement, and change management processes was a critical element in motivating managers to implement change initiatives in support of the project goals.

Introduction

> "If only it weren't for the people, the God-damn people," said Finnerty, "always getting tangled up in the machinery. If it weren't for them, earth would be an engineer's paradise."
>
> — VONNEGUT (1952: 59)

1   *The Innovation Journal: The Public Sector Innovation Journal*, 9(1), 2004, article 2 <http://www.innovation.cc/volumes-issues/vol9issue1emp-emp.htm>.

Issues related to "the people" tend, for the most part, to absorb the highest percentage of management time and energy in the overall scheme of organization life. This is true mostly because, unlike dollars or other physical assets, people are not mere quantitative entities to be manipulated at will. They think, feel, judge, and act based on things they value – ideals, goals, outcomes, and processes – all of which are complex entities for the individual manager to track and take into consideration as he or she leads the organization. The conundrum remains, however, that it is through the successful management of people that managers succeed or fail in the achievement of organization goals. Shingen Takeda, a feudal lord and administrator from the province of Kai in Japan, felt so strongly about this that he maintained, when questioned about his lack of progress in building fortifications, that "the people are the moat, the people are the stonewalls, the people are the castle" (Imai, 1975: 63). With this conviction in mind, he never built a castle of his own, but instead focused on the involvement of his people and responsiveness to their needs as a strategy to administrative success.

In modern organizations fortress building does not represent current official strategy, though some would say that informally it represents one of the prime goals of less-effective managers. Even outside of the context of building castles, however, Takeda's principle still appears to apply. Regardless of the elegance of the organization design or the brilliance of the strategy, it is still the people (in this case the employees and managers considered together) who must accept and implement it for success to evolve. Thus it is largely a factor of how effectively managers harness and engage the human component of the organization that determines how successful the organization becomes.

Literature on organization productivity points strongly to a positive correlation between employee involvement and empowerment and increases in multiple measures of organization effectiveness (Applebaum et al., 2000; Belanger, 2000; Drucker, 1999; Pil and MacDuffie, 1996). Research undertaken by Peters and Waterman (1982) stressed that managerial efforts to influence the motivation, morale, and productivity of employees by listening to what they think or value and involving them directly in corporate decision-making represent one of the key differentiating factors between excellent and mediocre companies. The literature suggests that this very process itself – the involvement of the employees in organizational decision-making – represents a critical practice differentiating merely effective and superbly productive organizations (Collins, 2001).

The difficulty with empowerment from the perspective of organizational power is at least two-fold. In a world framed by the assumption of limited power, empowerment of one party implies the disempowerment of another. The typical loser in the empowerment scenario is the first line and middle level management group, both of whom generally are divested of decision-making authority in favor of increased rank and file decision-making in typical empowerment initiatives. For supervisors who have worked many years to reach the point of being able to make operational decisions see their hard-won authority – and associated status – eroded by the empowerment movement. Supervisory resistance to employee empowerment is understandably high. Given the supervisor's access to managerial decision-makers in the planning and early implementation stages or empowerment efforts, this resistance can quickly evolve into rear-guard actions designed to block or frustrate the success of empowerment initiatives.

A second dilemma flows from the managerial culture associated with the basic assumptions underlying the concept of a managerial hierarchy. Most supervisors have only experienced an organizational system in which decisions were deferred to superiors at a higher level in the managerial hierarchy. Their deeper level assumptions hold that hierarchy of decision authority is a natural and necessary condition for organizational effectiveness. Even when faced with valid and convincing research data supporting the position that decisions can be delegated effectively to lower levels of the organization with resulting increases in productivity, managers and supervisors who have not personally experienced the effectiveness of such a system fail to embrace empowerment.

The Change Agent's Question

Through what processes do men and women alter, replace, or transcend patterns of thinking, valuation, volition, and overt behavior by which they have managed and justified their lives into patterns of thinking, valuation, volition, and behavior which are better oriented to the realities and actualities of contemporary existence, personal and social, and which are at once more personally fulfilling and socially appropriate?

—KURT LEWIN (1998)

Their personal experience does not support the data and traditional managerial wisdom contradicts it.

Allied with the managerial bias is the overwhelming experience base of employees whose typical day-to-day experience of work reinforce both Fayol and Taylor's fundamental managerial principle of the distinct division of responsibilities between management (including supervisors) and employee. Traditional employee experience – and accumulated expectation – is that managers will plan, organize, direct, and control while employees implement. While the experience of more leading-edge, high-performance organizations contradicts the necessity of this particular differentiated arrangement of work roles, the personal experience of employees reinforces both the "natural" nature of the division as well as the potential advantages to the employee of a relatively passive role in the job. Limited decision-making responsibilities easily equates to limited accountability for results determined by those same decisions.

Research carried by Auclaire and Archambault (1980) and reinforced by the literature of organizational effectiveness (Hackman and Oldham, 1980; Collins, 2001) supports the conclusion that employees in general value the opportunity to use their cognitive abilities in the workplace – to actively participate in the analysis, planning, and decision-making processes associated with their specific jobs. The Auclair and Archambault research further suggests that, to the extent that both managers and employees have opportunities to use these valued skills within the context of their work responsibilities – labeled "judgment at work" – organization performance will be above par and morale will be high.

The operating dilemma represented by the finding in the literature is one of implementation: how can an organization successfully engage supervisors in a shift from a more traditional hierarchical management approach to a more full involvement of all levels in the management of the enterprise? Literature on organizational change suggests a variety of meta-strategies useful in approaching this end (Benne and Chin, 1985; Miles et. al., 2002). Best practice analysis points in the direction of a combination of the use of information, power, and some form of personal experience that challenges the current values and beliefs of those involved in the change as the optimal strategy (Rokeach, 1970; Benne and Chin, 1985; Miles, 2002).

The research documented in this chapter examines the impact of a five-year effort by the Canadian Federal Government Department of Veterans Affairs (DVA) to broaden the participation of employees in decision-making and problem-solving on the job. The declared goal of the initiative was to shift the overall management culture of the organization in the direction of increased joint participation of managers and employees in the daily management of work-related activities. The change process utilized a four-day Management Values Seminar (MVS) that confronted managers and supervisors with their own biases against this end. The content of the seminar itself challenged participants to reconsider empowerment-related alternatives. This chapter outlines the thinking behind the design of the seminar, summarizes the impact of attendance based on post-implementation evaluation, and suggests additional research considerations in relation to approaches to organizational change efforts focused on increasing employee involvement through empowerment in the workplace.

Method

In keeping with the overall strategy of the Department to bring about a shift in the management culture of the organization, the Management Values Seminar was envisioned as a first step in the movement of the Department of Veterans Affairs toward implementation of a philosophy of management consistent with maximum involvement of employees in the decision-making elements of their jobs. The overall Departmental change strategy outlined in Table 6.1 highlights a number of desired outcomes related to the seminar and follow-up activities in terms of immediate, intermediate, and long-term time frames.

The research approach adopted by this study was designed to measure the extent to which attendance by managers at the Management Values

Table 6.1: Veterans Affairs Organization Renewal Strategy

Input	• Management Values Seminars (MVS) • Consultant follow-up and support
Intended Immediate Impacts	• Improved knowledge/skills of managers • Managerial values challenged (cognitive dissonance) • Managers motivated to attempt change initiatives within work groups
Intended Intermediate Impacts	• Projects undertaken to improve work environment and job design • Increased employee participation in decision-making
Intended Long-Term Impacts	• Improved work group effectiveness and productivity • Increased individual productivity and satisfaction • Departmental philosophy of management as a prevailing condition in DVA

Seminar (MVS) had been instrumental in bringing about the two desired intermediate level impacts:

(1) managerial initiative to undertake projects to improve work environment and job design in individual work units; and
(2) increased employee participation in decision-making related to their individual jobs.

The study design was developed to enable inference to be made about the causal link between participation in the seminar and increased activity of departmental managers in relation to the above two outcome areas.

A variety of choices and dilemmas are encountered when planning any form of assessment program related to organization change. For this particular research study, the fact that DVA is a functioning organization responding in real-time to both internal political realities and external environmental pressures strongly influenced the final choice of both the research design and questionnaire instrument used. It also resulted in a number of limitations to the final design itself, factors impacting to some extent on the level of internal validity of the study and the ability to generalize results to other organizations. Key to these was the internal political processes related to implementation of the change across five regions of the country and under the direction of five strong and independent managers. Their personal styles and decisions related to the speed and breadth of participation in the MVS, and proved to be a critical factor in the penetration of the change within their individual geographic areas of responsibility. This in turn resulted in some regions being more represented in final questionnaire completion.

Design of Questionnaire Instruments

Measurement of the impact of the seminar was carried out through administration of two structured questionnaires, one designed for distribution to the management group members who had participated in (or were eligible for participation in) the seminars, and the other to a sample group of employees. Sample size of the management category was 408 respondents while that of the employee group was 300. This represented a 100 per cent sample of manager participants of the values seminar and a 10 per cent sample of employees selected from work unit groups spread throughout the Department. Sampling procedures for the employee group were designed so that work units and individual respondents were selected randomly within categories to ensure that all major constituent groups (geographical, language, gender, and organizational) would be represented. All members of the employee group of respondents worked for managers who were eligible for participation in the MVS. As such, the total sample of employee respondents was in a position to give direct feedback concerning changes introduced by their superiors subsequent to seminar attendance.

In their overview of instruments and procedures for measurement of organizational change initiatives, Lawler, Nadler and Mirvis (1983) indicate that there are eleven distinguishable types of instruments or procedures for the collection of information. Based on the goals of the current research as outlined above, the study carried out in relation to the MVS used a modified version of the "Change-Implementation and Goal-Attainment

Questionnaire" approach outlined in the Lawler, Nadler, and Mirvis' typology. It is described as "a questionnaire employed to obtain employee views about the implementation of changes [in the workplace]. Questions are developed to determine the extent to which employees perceive improvements or other changes in their jobs." The particular form of questionnaire is focused on initiatives carried out in situations where multiple factors could be perceived to influence outcome objectives. The intent of its design is to focus respondent attention on the potential for linkage between one or a subset of factors and a particular change initiative.

The final design resulted in manager and employee questionnaires highlighting content areas covered by the seminar itself. Respondents were requested to indicate, through the process of checking off listed categories of interventions, the variety of types of changes introduced or being implemented in their work areas (structured checklist approach). The questionnaire also allowed participants to specify an open number of additional change initiatives not specifically highlighted in the MVS itself but which modeled the spirit of the intended results in the direction of increased participation and empowerment of employees. Nominated choices were directly related to elements of job enrichment and work-group communication improvement strategies, on-the-job decision-making, and intrinsic motivation techniques. All of these strategies had been mentioned in the seminar as core mechanisms to increase employee involvement and as mechanisms which competent managers frequently employed to achieve high levels of employee performance and satisfaction.

In addition, managers were asked to indicate the extent to which the Management Values Seminar was influential in their decision to implement change initiatives and to pinpoint other factors which were significant in helping or hindering the introduction of new ideas in their work groups. Employees were asked to indicate changes introduced by their managers by checking off a list of possible initiatives similar to that provided to managers and to confirm whether changes had been introduced before or after their managers had participated in the MVS. The research intent was to establish a temporal connection between the seminar and introduction of change activities. Statements by the managers concerning the impact of the study were matched with those of the employees concerning changes implemented. An assumption of the study, based on the Lawler, Nadler and Mirvis typology, was that if initiation occurred subsequent to the seminar and managers indicated positive impact of the seminar, attendance had been instrumental in motivating the new activity or behavior.

Results

Analysis of New Initiatives Implemented Subsequent to Attendance at the MVS

The first segment of the survey instrument focused on immediate follow-up discussions and agreements for activity between participants and their direct supervisors. Questionnaire responses indicated that of the 412 respondents, 247 had attended the seminar while 165 had not yet had an opportunity to do so. These figures confirm that, with the exception of a few newly promoted or transferred managers, all management staff down to the supervisory level in the Department had attended the seminar over the previous three-year period. The remaining supervisors were scheduled to attend the seminar in the upcoming year.

Of the sample of 247 managers who attended the seminar, 128 (52 per cent) indicated that they had taken the initial step of discussing the seminar with their immediate supervisors while the remaining 118 (approximately 48 per cent) indicated that they had not undertaken this recommended initiative as of the date of the survey (see Table 6.2).

Given the existing hierarchical culture of DVA, the change initiative planning team recommended that most important initial action that participants could take would be to discuss their reactions and ideas concerning the MVS with their immediate supervisors. Responses to the questionnaire instrument indicated that approximately 50 per cent of seminar participants undertook this initial follow-up activity. Results of these discussions generated a variety of potential options for action in keeping with the intent to increase employee participation. These are summarized in

Table 6.2. Although a number of these initial ideas pointed in the direction of gathering more information and increasing supervisor and employee understanding of the significance of employee involvement, over 25 per cent of follow-up activities identified focused on immediate implementation of work-group planning and work redesign initiatives directly. The topics discussed clearly reflect the content covered by the seminar (as outlined by both the pre-prepared survey checklist and the unstructured "other" comments).

Table 6.2: MVS Seminar Attendance and Initial Management Follow-Up

	Actual/Potential
Number of Managers Attending Seminar	247/412 = 60%
Attendees Holding Follow-up Discussion with Immediate Supervisor as suggested in MVS Seminar	128/247 = 52%
Follow-up Activities Discussed:	Frequency:
• Have additional staff attend seminar • Meet as management team to determine follow-up strategy • Undertake individual work-group planning sessions • Undertake work redesign activities • Gather data (using mini-surveys) on current issues related to employee involvement • No decision reached as a result of meeting • Other	104 80 55 57 26 25 17

Although immediate follow-up to the seminar through discussion with peers and supervisors was important, the goal of the seminar was to motivate actual ongoing change activity at the working level, initiated as a result of the participants' seminar experience. Data generated by the management participants in the MVS indicated that 197 participants (80 per cent) initiated some form of

I feel that I can't say enough positive things about the MVS. For me it opened many doors and gave me a new perspective on *me* and others. I have discussed the seminar with my staff. Trust and open feedback are more visible and continuing to develop. It is not all sunshine and roses. But at least I understand more easily now why my great ideas bombed out. Sometimes I have even caught myself being unfair and biased – OUCH.

— SEMINAR PARTICIPANT

change initiative subsequent to attendance at the seminar. Descriptions of the types of change introduced are summarized in Table 6.3. Analysis indicates that the activities initiated focus directly on broadening employee input to decision-making through changes in the structure of planning and decision-making meetings, new division of work responsibilities/job redesign, creation of local "change committees" to capture employee ideas, restructuring of meeting agendas to facilitate idea discussion, development of change proposals for consideration by senior management, and a variety of additional initiatives generally designed to build employee involvement.

Among the miscellaneous items added in the "other" category were the following: having more study days with employees, leaving decisions that the manager does not have to make up to the discretion of the employees, including staff to a greater degree in goal-setting and work-planning, and altering the format of staff meetings from information-dissemination sessions to team participation sessions.

As part of the research strategy, a parallel questionnaire was distributed to a sample of 300 employees in units whose managers had attended the seminar. Analysis of much of the data generated by this instrument resulted in conclusions of limited utility for a number of reasons. For example, in the question asking whether the immediate supervisor of the respondent had attended the MVS, 45 per cent indicated that they did not know. Another questionnaire item asked respondents to indicate whether change activities had been initiated in their work units. Although 50 per cent of the respondents indicated that activities had occurred, approximately 55 per cent of this number failed to indicate whether such initiatives had begun before or after attendance at the seminar. As a result, the intent of the study to use employee data to confirm management responses was limited to some extent. Nevertheless, some of the descriptive data generated through the use of this instrument does prove useful in confirming patterns established through the management survey results. This data is summarized in Table 6.3 along with the management statements of changes initiated. Review of the table confirms that employee experience of changes being introduced into their work group closely parallel the claims of management related to the types change initiatives implemented.

Table 6.3: Change Initiatives Undertaken Subsequent to MVS

Participants Initiating Change Initiative Subsequent to Attendance at MVS	197 (80%)	
Follow-up Activities Discussed	Frequency	
	Noted by: Managers	Noted by: Employees
• introduction of more frequent idea-generation and decision-making staff meetings	157	97
• new division of work responsibilities/ job redesign	128	111
• creation of local "change committees"	38	40
• restructuring of meeting agendas to include employee idea discussions	46	35
• preparation of change recommendations for transmission to senior management	39	17
• other	24	14
Sample size	247	217

The sheer number of follow-up activities occurring subsequent to the MVS suggests a level of impact from attendance at the seminar. The MVS itself stressed the theme of opening up opportunities for employee use of judgment in either decision-making or problem-solving roles. Table 6.4 summarizes content areas addressed in the seminar and the perceived usefulness of each as judged by the participants.

Many of the follow-up activities attempted mirror the seminar content areas directly, especially the attempts to increase the frequency with which staff meetings became opportunities for employees to generate ideas and participate in decisions related to their jobs. Under the category of "other," respondents highlighted several additional content areas of particular usefulness. These included extending decision-making power to individuals in relation to their own jobs, understanding the impact of personal values on how individuals approach people and work situations, and the importance of being able to make mistakes without fear of disproportionate punishment.

Table 6.4: Perceived Usefulness of Topics Covered in the MVS

Topic	# of Participants Indicating Topic was Useful Total sample N = 247
• Extending "judgment" down the hierarchy	174 (71%)
• Involving work groups in generating ideas about better ways to do jobs	176 (71%)
• Sharing planning, organizing, and controlling aspects of jobs with employees	149 (60%)
• Respecting individual positions in the reporting structure	109 (44%)
• Developing "internal commitment" of employees to job	105 (43%)
• Creating jobs to allow "whole tasks"	80 (32%)
• Beginning change efforts with small issues and moving up to larger ones	62 (25%)
• Other	16 (7%)

Responses of participants in the seminar indicate that the vast majority (219 of the total sample of 247 participants) found the ideas and approaches covered in the seminar to be useful in a practical sense in their work environment. By far the most useful was the cluster of content areas dealing with the dynamics and mechanisms of participative management, with special focus on the seminar theme of extending the use of judgment to employees in their jobs. When questioned about the specific actions that participants took in the general areas outlined in Table 6.3, the most frequently cited new practices undertaken included the training of employees in new skill areas to accept broader responsibility, redesigning jobs to allow for individual responsibility for whole tasks, staff rotation across responsibility areas, and the creation of small teams of employees with responsibility for whole tasks. A large number of respondents (51 per cent) attempted general change activities in broad areas of job and work design. Specific initiatives undertaken are outlined in Table 6.5.

Table 6.5: New Practices Reflecting MVS Content Introduced into the Workplace

New Practice	Frequency (Total sample N = 247)
• Training of staff in new skill areas for broader responsibility	125 (51%)
• Staff rotation across responsibility areas	101 (41%)
• Work teams given overall responsibility for whole tasks	48 (19%)
• Redesigned individual jobs as whole tasks	83 (34%)
• Regular information gathering from staff about current issues	120 (49%)
• More frequent total staff meetings	113 (46%)
• Regular supervisor-employee meetings	62 (25%)
• Spending time with work groups to reinforce current effective practices	115 (47%)
• No new changes introduced	20 (8%)

Analysis of the Relationship between Attendance at the Seminar and Participant Willingness to Initiate Change Activity

Research data analyzed to this point has focused on the details of individual follow-up activities and new practices introduced subsequent to the seminar. A simple overview of activities, however compelling, is not sufficient evidence to lead to the conclusion that there is a causative relationship between attendance at the seminar and subsequent initiation of change activities. With this in mind, questionnaire respondents were asked to indicate directly by means of a seven-point scale the extent to which their participation in the MVS had been a motivating factor – in their individual decisions to introduce work group improvement activities. Results of the response to this question are outlined in Table 6.6.

Statistical analyses of the responses received to this question indicate that the mean response to this item was 4.82 on the seven-point scale, with a standard deviation of 1.62. Given that the question was phrased such that any response above the base of 1.00 indicated some degree of connection between attendance at the seminar and motivation to introduce work group change activities related to the VS, the pattern of response indicated above suggests a strong relationship between the two variables. Analysis of

Table 6.6: Participant Perception of Motivational Impact of MVS on Introduction of Change Initiatives

| | *Not at all a Related Factor* | | | | | *The Key Related Factor* | |
	I	*2*	*3*	*4*	*5*	*6*	*7*
Responses (raw #'s)	9	13	29	22	65	60	27
Per Cent of Total	4.0	5.8	12.9	9.8	28.9	26.7	12.0

Note: Total sample size N = 247 (nil responses N = 22)

cross-tabulation between participants' self-report on motivational impact of seminar and self-report on whether they did or did not attempt follow-up activities (Table 6.7) strongly supports this conclusion.

Analysis of Table 6.7 indicates that as the degree of self-reported motivational impact of the MVS rises, so does the absolute number of managers who choose to implement follow-up activities. The comparison between the ratio of numbers of participants who indicated they did and did not undertake follow-up activity when viewed as a factor of their position on the seven-point scale is even more compelling in its suggestion of relationship between attendance at the seminar and the decision to implement change. For those who indicated that their attendance at the seminar was not at all related to their decision regarding implementation of work-improvement activities, the number of managers who did initiate activities trailed those who did not (four respondents undertook activities compared to five who did not, representing a ratio of 1:1.25 for responses at this point on the seven-point scale). From this point on, however, as the self-reporting of managers indicates that the seminar influenced their decision to change, the ratio of managers implementing activities compared to those who did not increase at all points on the scale except one. This is consistent with the degree to which participants indicate that the seminar represented a motivating force in their decision to proceed with follow-up. As indicated in Table 6.7, the probability of such a relationship being due to chance is 0.011. The described level of relationship between these two factors thus appears fairly strong.

Table 6.7: Cross-Tabulation of Participant Self-Reports of Implementation of Change
Initiative and Motivational Impact of Seminar

Participant Self-Reported Impact of Seminar as Motivating Willingness to Attempt Change Initiatives ⬇	Participant Attempted Change Initiative		
	Yes	No	Ratio Yes/No
Not at All Related (1)	4 (1.8%)	5 (2.3%)	1:1.25
(2)	9 (4.1%)	3 (1.4%)	3:1
(3)	23 (10.5%)	6 (2.7%)	3.75:1
(4)	16 (7.3%)	6 (2.7%)	2.66:1
(5)	56 (25.5%)	8 (3.6%)	6.25:1
(6)	54 (24.5%)	5 (2.3%)	10.8:1
The Key Factor (7)	23 (10.4%)	2 (0.9%)	11.5:1

Valid Cases N = 220   185   35   5.29:1
Probability due to Chance = 0.011

A number of respondents added supplementary comments related
to the issue of the relationship between their implementation of change
initiatives and participation in the seminar. Several indicated that they
were already practicing the principles outlined in the MVS. For some such
individuals, as noted in Table 6.7, there was little connection between the
seminar and ongoing positive management practice at the work group
level. More representative of this group, however, were comments similar
to that which noted: "The seminar has reinforced a basic management style
and has rounded off a few corners." In keeping with the positive overall

reaction to the seminar, therefore, it appears that participation both moti-vated participants to introduce practices which were new to their work area and served to reinforce and further encourage the efforts of a number of participants who were already implementing management practices in keeping with the approach outlined by the seminar itself.

Discussion

Change interventions such as the MVS represent real-life experiments in approaches to management of employees. Such programs impact partici-pants in a variety of ways, depending on their background, values base, experience, and working situation. Given the complexity of the multiple factors involved in change, the dilemma for the change manager is to moti-vate people – managers and employees alike – to change. The MVS was designed based on the assumption underlying much of the traditional and current literature of change (Benne and Chin, 1985; Lewin and Gold, 1998; Argyris, 1970; Kanter, 1983; Beckhard and Harris, 1980) that change is generally motivated by a need to resolve some experienced uncertainty or dissonance around current beliefs, concepts, expectations, or accepted behavior patterns. Lewin referred to this process as "unfreezing," Beckhard developed a formula in which he termed the initial change motivator "dis-satisfaction," and Argyris referred to the disconfirming process as the "gen-eration of valid data."

Underlying the three models of change noted above is an operat-ing principle which maintains that change will not occur unless there is motivation to change. The MVS was the primary mechanism used in the Department's strategy to motivate the required shift in thinking among participants. The seminar focused on encouraging participants to openly and in depth consider their values, biases, preconceptions, and fears related to employee empowerment and participation. The process of this examina-tion confronted participants with credible sets of information contradict-ing their own beliefs, experiences, and expectations. The seminar process was designed to raise questions in their minds concerning the accuracy or validity of their preconceptions related to employee empowerment. The intent was to raise a level of uncertainty – the suspicion that their current beliefs and associated managerial behavior – may have been inadequate. Once raised, this sense of "self-doubt" opens the door for the introduction of alternative frameworks of understanding and guiding participant experience through the process of resolution of the resultant cognitive dissonance (Zimbardo and Ebbesen, 1970; Beckhard, 1997).

Theory associated with the concept of cognitive dissonance (Festinger, 1957; Harmon-Jones and Mills, 1999) supports the prediction that the magnitude of tension generated by the combination of credible data associated with managerial best practices supporting employee empowerment and the data, also presented in the seminar, that employees are highly interested in participation, would be sufficiently high to produce initial motivation to explore alternative managerial behavior options. Motivation for the initial steps in the change process would have been achieved, to be built upon by subsequent steps of the change program, including introduction of change initiatives in the work units.

Based on the research data, it would appear that participation in the MVS was indeed a significant factor in motivating change in the behavior of seminar participants concerning the involvement of employees in work group planning and decision-making activities. Data drawn from the study questionnaire clearly confirms, in general, the significance of the seminar in relation to manager motivation to undertake change activities focusing on increased employee involvement. Responses of seminar participants to a direct question in relation to this issue confirm that respondents overwhelmingly felt that the seminar was a least minimally influential in stimulating changes in their approaches to involving staff. As indicated in the results section of this chapter, the mean response on the seven-point scoring scale related to the question on the motivational impact of the MVS was 4.84. On the basis of such a clear statement drawn from the total seminar participant group, the impact of the seminar in relation to motivation of follow-up change activities must be acknowledged. This conclusion is further reinforced by the sheer number of follow-up activities undertaken by respondents subsequent to their participation in the seminar itself. In addition, a very large number of questionnaire respondents (74 per cent) indicated that their participation in the MVS was one of the key factors motivating and guiding the introduction of new ideas in their work area.

The vast majority of managers indicated that they were clearly influenced by the MVS to undertake change activities. In the sense that the intent of the seminar design was to motivate a rethinking of beliefs about employee empowerment and participation, the seminar succeeded – at least at the level of behavior – in achieving its intended goal. Although the same certainty of impact is not confirmed by data gathered from the non-management segment of the questionnaire sample, there is at least some recognition by this group that shifts in the direction of the changes proposed by the seminar did occur subsequent to their managers' attendance at the MVS. Management respondents confirmed this data, indicating that they had acted on the new information to which they were exposed in the seminar by attempting a variety of change initiatives related to seminar content upon return to their home work units.

Conclusion

The reality of change processes carried out within functioning organizations is such that many factors are usually significant in the successful implementation of a change program. Organizations exist as systems, resulting in the fact that changes in any one element of the system must be reflected in resultant changes in or support from other significant parts of the system. Data generated by the follow-up survey instrument completed by participants in the MVS highlighted a number of factors which respondents clearly felt were significant to the successful implementation of the DVA management change program. Although these do not detract from the results outlined above concerning the significance of the MVS in motivating change efforts, they broaden the scope of understanding concerning implications for future change programs or research efforts.

Most impassioned among the comments offered by respondents in addition to those directly related to the MVS itself were those concerning senior management's involvement in the development of the seminar process and overall change program. Although large numbers of seminar participants indicated an increased interest subsequent to attending the MVS in undertaking initiatives highlighted by the seminar content, feedback received through the research study questionnaire consistently stressed the importance of higher level management's support for such activities as a prerequisite for follow-up initiation. Fully 95 per cent of DVA managers (both those who had attended the seminar and those who had not) indicated that this was a key factor in facilitating the introduction of new ideas at the working level.

Indications of the significance of this factor represent an important planning element in change programs of the large- scale nature represented by the DVA values seminar project. Respondents' indication that higher level management's support of the change effort is a significant factor is important in an additional sense as well. Peters and Austin (1985: 333) observed that higher managements' priorities – including what they will or will not support – are transparent regardless of what they say. The questionnaire follow-up of the MVS clearly demonstrates that this reality was alive and active in DVA. The public actions of more senior managers in relation to daily management activities became, for many seminar participants, influential in their decision as to whether they should attempt seminar follow-up activities.

Implications of the above data suggest the need for additional research into the role of senior management leadership of change initiatives. In particular, the impact of leader example as a critical factor in subordinate commitment to change represents potential fertile ground for further research activity. Additionally, the impact and significance of public involvement of senior leadership in the design and delivery of elements of the change process also represents an important area for future examination. DVA seminar participants commented specifically on the positive impact of the presence of top management at seminar sessions and noted this level of participation as a sign that "they were serious this time." Studies of the impact and strategy of senior level participation in elements of the change initiative could well result in some formative guiding principles related to this element of change leadership theory.

The change program reviewed in this study, especially the MVS element, assumed that managers resisted adoption of participative management not exclusively because they did not understand it at a rational level, but more significantly because they did not feel any personally relevant pressures to make the effort. The MVS provided an experience for participants which caused them to question their personal and professional beliefs concerning employee participation. In addition, the model which formed the base of the seminar reinforced that the most competent managers tended to operate on the basis of principles generally defined as "participative management." In a sense, the seminar operated on the assumption that the decision to become more participative as a manager is a decision of the heart, not of the head, although both components are involved. Results of the study tend to indicate that this assumption has some validity. It would appear that once managers are engaged at the level of values and convinced of the validity of an approach based on dialogue which either confirms or questions aspects of their personal values, their level of energy and creativity for implementing change activities rises dramatically, within the limitations of support from their organizational environment. The conclusion is that values and beliefs are at the heart of the decision to empower. As such, focused exploration of these human elements may be an underutilized strategy in the move toward increased employee involvement.

Bibliography

Applebaum, E., T. Bailey, P. Berg & A. Kalleberg. 2000. *Manufacturing Advantage: Why High Performance Work Systems Pay Off.* Ithaca, NY: ILR Press.

Argyris, C. 1970. *Intervention Theory and Methods: a Behavioral Science View.* Reading, MA: Addison-Wesley.

Auclair, J., & G. Archambault, 1980. Unpublished data genetrated by the Bilingualism and Biculturalism Commision in 1965 and gathered longitudinally between 1965–1980. Personal conversations.

Beckhard, R. 1997. *Agent of Change*. San Francisco, CA: Jossey-Bass.

Beckhard, R., & R. Harris. 1980. *Organizational Transitions*. Reading, MA: Addison-Wesley.

Belanger, J. 2000. *The Influence of Employee Involvement on Productivity: a Review of Research*. Ottawa, Canada: Applied Research Branch, Human Resources Development Canada (HRDC).

Benne, K. 1976. The process of re-education: an assessment of Kurt Lewin's views. Pp. 315–331 in W. Bennis, K. Benne & R. Chin, *The Planning of Change*, 3rd Edn. New York: International Thompson Publishing.

Benne, K., & R. Chin. 1976. Strategies of Change. Pp. 7–32 in W. Bennis, K. Benne & R. Chin, *The Planning of Change*, 3rd Edn. New York: International Thompson Publishing.

Collins, J. 2001. *Good to Great: Why some companies make the leap … and others don't*. New York: Harper Business.

Drucker, P. 1999. Knowledge Worker Productivity: The Biggest Challenge. *California Management Review*, 41(2): 79–94.

Hackman, J., & G. Oldham. 1980. *Work Redesign*. New York: Pearson Education POD.

Harmon-Jones, E., & J. Mills (eds). 1999. *Cognitive Dissonance: Progress on a Pivotal Theory in Social Psychology*. Washington, DC: American Psychological Association (APA).

Herzberg, F. 1966. *Work and the Nature of Man*. Cleveland, OH: World Publishing Company.

Imai, M. 1975. *Never take Yes for an Answer*. Tokyo, Japan: Sirnul (Simul) Press.

Kanter, R. 1982. Dilemmas of Managing Participation. *Organizational Dynamics*, 52(3): 5–16.

Kanter, R. 1983. *The Change Masters*. New York: Simon & Schuster.

Lawler III, E. E., D. A. Nadler & P. H. Mirvis. 1980. Organizational Change and the Conduct of Assessment Research. Stanley E. Seashore (ed.), *Assessing Organizational Change*. New York: Wiley.

Lewin, K., & M. Gold (eds). 1998. *The Complete Social Scientist: a Kurt Lewin Reader*. Washington, DC: American Psychological Association (APA) Press.

Lovell, R. (ed.) 1994. *Managing Change in the New Public Sector*. Harlow, Essex, UK: Longman Information and Reference.

Michael, S. R., F. Luthans, G. Odiorne, W. Burke & S. Hayden. 1981. *Techniques of Organization Change*. New York: McGraw Hill.

Miles, Michael, A. Thangaraj, D. Wang & H. Ma. 2002. Classic Theories – Contemporary Applications: A comparative study of the implementation of innovation in Canadian and Chinese Public Sector environments. *The Innovation Journal: The Public Sector Innovation Journal*, 7(3), article 2. Accessed August 3, 2017 at: <http://www.innovation.cc/volumes-issues/vol7-iss3_leadership.htm>.

Peters, T., & N. Austin. 1985. *A Passion for Excellence*. London: William Collins & Sons Ltd.

Peters, T., & R. Waterman. 1982. *In Search of Excellence*. New York: Free Press.

Pil, F., & J. MacDuffie. 1996. The adoption of high involvement work practices. *Industrial Relations*, 35(3): 423–455.

Rokeach, M. 1973. *The Nature of Human Values*. New York: Free Press.

Vonnegut, K., Jr. 1952. *Player Piano*. New York: Delacorte Press.

Zimbardo, P., & E. Ebbesen. 1970. *Influencing Attitudes and Changing Behavior*. Reading, MA: Addison-Wesley.

PART III

Leadership and Innovation

CHRIS ANSELL AND ALISON GASH

7 Stewards, Mediators, and Catalysts: Toward a Model of Collaborative Leadership[1]

ABSTRACT

Leadership is an important ingredient in successful collaboration. Collaborative leaders typically play multiple facilitative roles to encourage and enable stakeholders to work together effectively. Building on the existing literature on collaborative governance and interviews with leaders of U.S. Workforce Investment Boards, we identify three facilitative roles for collaborative leaders. *Stewards* facilitate collaboration by helping to convene collaboration and maintain its integrity. *Mediators* facilitate collaboration by managing conflict and arbitrating exchange between stakeholders. *Catalysts* facilitate collaboration by helping to identify and realize value-creating opportunities. The salience of these roles may vary with the circumstances and goals of collaboration. In situations of high conflict and low trust, for example, collaborative leaders may emphasize steward and mediator roles. In situations that require creative problem-solving, the catalyst role may become much more central. Distinguishing these three collaborative leadership roles is critical and an important step to building a contingency model of collaborative leadership.

Introduction

In 1998, President Bill Clinton signed into law the Workforce Investment Act (WIA). Much like the welfare reform enacted only two years earlier, WIA promised to revolutionize the *work* of workforce development.

---

1   We thank Eva Sørensen, Jacob Torfing, Tamara Metze, an anonymous reviewer, and participants in an American Society for Public Administration (APSA) panel on collaborative innovation for their feedback on earlier versions of this paper.

Although the federal government had long been a supplier of workforce training programs under programs enacted through the Job Training Partnership Act (JTPA) or the Comprehensive Employment and Training Act (CETA), these programs offered a patchwork approach to job training. According to former Labor Secretary Alexis Herman, these programs were "never fully brought into alignment with other components of the 'system.'" Consequently, federally funded job training programs were largely scattered – offering clients limited access to services, career advice, quality job information data, and skills training. It was hoped that through coordination and co-location at the service-delivery level (e.g. one-stop shops), consumers would have easier access to every element of the workforce development system, from simple job searches to receiving advice on career planning, to enrolling in basic more advanced skills training. However, coordination of service delivery was only one of the problems plaguing an increasingly dysfunctional workforce system, so policymakers also mandated a more comprehensive strategy of collaboration. The WIA placed control of each local workforce area (established by governors) in Workforce Investment Boards (WIBs), which would be jointly governed by labor unions, community colleges, training providers, locally elected officials, industry leaders, and social service providers. These stakeholders were to develop collaborative strategies to create a more effective workforce system.

Despite this mandated collaborative framework, large variations developed in the degree, scope, type, and breadth of collaboration among workforce development areas. Some workforce development areas practiced *pro forma* collaborative governance – presenting only enough of a veneer of collaboration to please local and federal officials. Others surpassed this by implementing micro-collaboratives – supplementing the WIB's governance with smaller project-based forms of collaborative governance. A small but growing number of WIBs engaged in more extensive collaborative governance. In each of these cases, leaders played a critical role in shaping the depth and extent of WIB collaboration. Leaders of the most collaborative WIBs, for example, have begun to reassess what one referred to as the "little fiefdoms" established by governors under WIA – workforce areas established along political rather than economic lines. These leaders are looking at the potential for true regionalism to address the impending shortfall of WIA funds and are establishing longer-term collaboratives with other workforce boards.

This chapter builds on our earlier work (Ansell and Gash, 2008) that found that leadership is an important variable in explaining the success or failure of collaborative governance. Based on a meta-analysis of the collaborative governance literature, we found that many case studies and a number of important theoretical studies pointed to the importance of leadership. In this chapter, we "drill down" into this leadership variable to develop a more fine-grained view of the role of leadership. In doing this, our goal is to expand upon a "contingency approach" to collaborative governance. A contingency approach assumes that there is no single "best way" to exercise collaborative leadership, but that different tasks, goals, and contexts will place distinctive kinds of demands on leaders. In some collaborations, for example, the primary challenge facing leaders may be to cultivate sufficient trust among stakeholders to allow them to engage in fruitful deliberation; in others, the primary challenge may be to help an already functioning community of stakeholders engage in more innovative and creative problem-solving. Different kinds of leadership skills or types of leaders may be called upon to meet these challenges. Although we do not focus explicitly on innovation, we believe our contingency approach is a useful first step in understanding the aspects of leadership that are critical in promoting collaborative innovation.

To develop this analysis of collaborative leadership, we supplement an extensive review of recent scholarship with interviews with ten workforce development leaders conducted in August 2011. We identified these workforce leaders, who represent program managers, board directors, and partners from geographically diverse workforce development regions, through conversations with consultants to and participants in a recent Department of Labor-funded project exploring various aspects of workforce leadership (see <http://www.enhancingworkforceleadership.org>) Workforce development provides an ideal policy backdrop to explore collaborative leadership. First, both the nature of workforce development – its inherent reliance on the combined efforts of educators, employers, social service providers, and economic developers – and its current statutory framework essentially require that workforce development leaders operate collaboratively. As one leader offered:

> There is no way to get anything done without collaboration. It is central to anything in workforce development. And it was designed to be collaborative ... [Collaboration] is second nature.

Second, in many ways, workforce development provides a textbook example of the contingent nature of collaborative governance. In our earlier work (Ansell and Gash, 2008), we argued that antecedent and exogenous conditions can affect collaborative success. The workforce leaders we interviewed reinforced this claim, pointing out that the success of collaboration depends on a number of often exogenous factors. "We should be okay when collaboration isn't working," said one leader. "Don't do it. It's okay – collaboration isn't always good." In their descriptions of their own personal and programmatic successes, interviewees pointed to four conditions that influenced the efficacy of their leadership: access to resources; the strength of relationships with current and potential partners; regional, state, and local governance and service delivery infrastructures; and historical perceptions of workforce development shared by industry and economic development stakeholders.

Third, at its best, workforce development can be a locus of innovation. Legislative calls for local autonomy coupled with opportunities and incentives for economic competitiveness make workforce development an ideal policy arena to examine the degree to which collaborative leaders operate as innovators or change agents and the conditions that facilitate or impede this process. Many of the leaders we consulted, for instance, referenced collaboration as the key to remaining competitive in a future marked by shrinking budgets and slow job growth. As one workforce leader observed:

> Increasingly it is about competitive resources and being prepared as a region to be competitive and we are more competitive regionally together and we have demonstrated that through millions in grants. We are feeling like when we do work together it makes us more competitive and enhances our capacity to sustain after grants are done.

To successfully lead such efforts, leaders must often have particular attributes and skills and they must often develop specific strategies. In the remainder of the chapter, we try to specify these attributes, skills, and strategies, drawing on both the collaborative governance literature and our interviews with workforce leaders.

The Importance of Leadership for Collaborative Governance

Our original paper suggested that the key adjective that can be used to describe collaborative leadership is "facilitative." Although collaboration may be mandated, collaboration is typically voluntary. In addition, as Crosby and Bryson (2005) have emphasized, collaboration operates in a "shared power" world in which different stakeholders control distinct resources and have their own distinct bases of power and authority. In this voluntary, shared power world, it is clear that leaders do not "command" in the same way that they might in a hierarchical organization. Leaders may bear responsibility for *steering* collaboratives toward efficient service delivery, consensus, or creative problem-solving, but they must work within the constraints imposed by voluntary action and shared power. Typically, then, their role is to facilitate rather than to direct. In this sense, collaborative leadership is similar to what the network literature calls "metagovernance" (Sørensen and Torfing, 2009). In exploring the details of collaborative leadership, our goal is to identify and analyze different aspects of this facilitative role.

The tricky part of analyzing leadership is that it tends to be a "residual" category. Leadership is typically involved in all aspects of collaborative governance, from inception through completion. Leadership is often the most visible aspect of group action and leaders assume responsibility for collaborative outcomes, both good and bad.

Leaders are often the "proximate cause" of success and failure of collaboration, but their ability to work effectively often depends on other less proximate factors. For all these reasons, there can be a tendency to "load" too much of the explanatory weight on a leadership variable (as suggested by classic criticisms of the "great man" view of history), while outcomes may in fact be due to less visible and less proximate factors. One of the implications is that it is difficult to separate leadership influences from the whole fabric of collaboration. Emerson, Nabatchi and Balogh (2011) argue that leadership, as an essential driver of the collaborative governance process, should be kept conceptually distinct from "system context" in which collaborative governance unfolds. We entirely agree with this point. However, it is important to recognize that leaders act *in* and *through* the system context – or as Huxham and Vangen (2000) put it, in and through the "leadership media" of structures, processes, and participants. For example, should we attribute successful trust-building to effective leadership or to the trust-building process? It is often difficult to assign ultimate responsibility.

Another challenge in leadership research is how widely to conceive of leadership. Much of the contemporary leadership literature has clearly moved away from a "command-oriented" view of the leadership role and has embraced a more "distributed" view of leadership. This is especially appropriate in the "shared power" context of collaborative governance (Huxham and Vangen, 2000; Morse, 2008; Ospina and Foldy, 2010; Crosby and Bryson, 2010). However, as the view of what counts as leadership expands, the role of "leaders" can become blurred, adding to the tendency to load explanatory weight on the leadership variable. We acknowledge that leadership can be exercised by many stakeholders at many different levels of action. But we focus our analysis of leadership on the role of "key leaders" who initiate, guide, or steer the collaborative process. Crosby and Bryson (2005) argue that two distinct kinds of leaders are necessary for successful collaborative governance: champions and sponsors. The champion provides the direct day-by-day leadership to move a collaborative process forward, while a sponsor stands behind the scenes, but deploys authority and resources to support the collaboration. Our own analysis of facilitative leadership focuses largely on champions – those key leaders who play a day-to-day role in initiating, guiding, and steering collaborative governance.

In our earlier work, we identified two different *styles* of leadership in collaborative governance. One style of leadership stresses the neutrality and professionalism of collaborative leaders. Such leaders are often trained facilitators and their leadership typically stresses their function as neutral mediators in the collaborative process. Typically, these trained facilitators come from outside the community of stakeholders, which guarantees their neutrality and independence from any stakeholder. The neutral facilitator has no particular vested interest in the outcome of negotiations, but serves a professional role to facilitate improved collaboration. The second style of leadership we dubbed "organic," to stress that these leaders come from within the community of stakeholders. Organic leaders often straddle different stakeholder groups and are often intimately familiar with and connected to stakeholders in the community. What they lack in professional facilitator training, they often make up for in subject matter expertise or local knowledge. They may not be neutral with respect to collaborative outcomes, but generally have an overriding interest in promoting collaboration. Both the professional facilitator and the organic leader can serve as "honest brokers," but they have different strengths and weaknesses as leaders.[2] Professional facilitators have advanced skills in mediation and a legitimacy that arises from their neutrality and independence. But they often lack social capital or authority within the stakeholder community. Organic leaders have the opposite set of strengths and weaknesses. Their strength arises from their local knowledge and relationships, but they may have a harder time convincing stakeholders of their neutrality and may lack the skills to facilitate complex negotiations. In this chapter, we further elaborate on the character of collaborative leadership by distinguishing three different roles for facilitative leadership: steward, mediator, and catalyst.

Leadership Roles for the Collaborative Leader

Huxham and Vangen (2000: 1161) define collaborative leadership as "making things happen." Facilitative leadership might be described as helping others to make things happen. In keeping with our contingency

---

2   In contrast with our earlier work, we have slightly changed the language used here to describe these two leadership styles in order to clarify that both types of leaders may be "honest brokers."

perspective, we suggest that there are a number of different ways to help people to make things happen and they can be broadly captured by the terms "steward," "mediator," and "catalyst." Simply put, a steward is someone who facilitates the collaborative process by establishing and protecting the integrity of the collaborative process itself; a mediator is a leader who facilitates by helping to arbitrate and nurture relationships between stakeholders; and a catalyst is someone who helps stakeholders to identify and realize value-creating opportunities. Building on the existing literature on collaborative leadership and incorporating our findings from interviews with workforce leaders, Table 7.1 summarizes our central findings about each of these leadership roles. In the remainder of the chapter, we discuss each role in detail in terms of how they relate to antecedent conditions, systems context, and the goals of collaboration.

Steward

In our previous work, we found that leaders play a critical stewardship role in the collaborative process and are important for establishing and maintaining the integrity of that process (Ansell and Gash, 2008; see also Chrislip and Larson, 1994). Although stakeholders are encouraged to "take ownership" of the collaborative process, this often takes considerable work and time. At early stages of the collaborative process, in particular, leaders "represent" the collaborative process as a whole and they exercise authority in the name of the collaboration – something that no single stakeholder can unilaterally do. Scott's recent study of collaborative health reform in Georgia describes the key leader as follows:

> He was a highly respected lawyer and elected official in the community; his stature
> brought credibility to the process and signified its importance to Georgians; and he
> also ensured that the process was bipartisan by inviting other members of the House of
> Representatives from different political parties to join the working group as their time
> permitted and kept them fully informed as the process unfolded. (Scott, 2011: 446)

In this example, we see that this organic leader played an iconic role in establishing the collaborative process. He lent his considerable legitimacy

Table 7.1: Collaborative Leadership Roles

Collaborative Leadership Roles	General Definition	Skills and Strategies	Distinctive Role of Neutral Facilitator	Distinctive Role of Organic Leader
Steward	Establishes and protects integrity of the coll. process	– Lends reputation and social capital to convene process – Establishes inclusiveness, transparency, neutrality, and civic character of process – Manages image and identity of collaborative	Professional facilitator may be more important in establishing ground rules than in initially convening the process	Organic leader may be critical in convening a collaborative process, because organic leader has reputation and social capital to invest
Mediator	Arbitrates and nurtures relationships between stakeholders	– Serves as "honest broker" in mediating disputes – Facilitates construction of shared meaning – Restores process to positive interaction – Builds trust among stakeholders (specific strategies depend on goals and baseline trust)	Professional facilitator role may have an easier time establishing credentials as "honest broker"; professionals often have sophisticated communication and negotiation skills	Organic leaders may be more effective in intervening to move difficult processes forward; may have context-specific knowledge valuable for adjudication
Catalyst	Identifies value-creating opportunities and mobilizes stakeholders to pursue them	– Engages in 'systems thinking' – Frames or reframes problems – Creates mutually reinforcing link between collaboration and innovation	Professional facilitators are probably less likely to engage in catalytic leadership	Organic leaders are likely to draw on contextual knowledge and unique relationships to act catalytically

in the community to the collaborative and he symbolized the possibilities for collaboration. Note, however, that this leader was also a Republican representative in the Georgia House of Representatives and hence his bipartisan "honest broker" role depended on the perception that he was not simply structuring collaboration to advance his partisan interests. At the same time, we note that it probably would have been more difficult for a neutral professional facilitator to establish the initial legitimacy of collaborative healthcare reform, because he or she would have no social capital to "lend" to the establishment of the process.

Page (2010) identifies "convening stakeholders" as one of three distinct leadership tactics, along with framing the agenda and structuring deliberation. The role of stewardship is to help establish the "integrity" of the collaborative process. We can return to our Georgia healthcare example to provide an illustration of how leadership can work to establish this integrity. Scott (2011) refers to the key leader as a "convenor" who sought to develop an inclusive process with wide representation of stakeholders. This leader also convened the process in a "neutral" setting, remained neutral with respect to the outcome of the collaboration, and "provided a broad framing of the working group's goal – transparency, inclusiveness, and outcome effectiveness" (Scott, 2011: 446). He also "kept the process moving and on track through all its phases" (Ibid.). By attending meetings and being actively involved, he "visibly demonstrated his ongoing and consistent commitment to the collaborative process" (Ibid.). In all of these roles, this leader was acting as a steward of the collaborative process by helping to establish and maintain the integrity of the process itself.

What is interesting about the Georgia case is that this organic leader shared the leadership process with leaders who came closer to the professional facilitator model.[3] The "convenor" drew on the neutral facilitation skills of the faculty of the Georgia State University College of Law. These faculty leaders saw themselves as providing a public service as neutral facilitators as well as legal expertise on the issues related to the healthcare issues

---

3   Following Crosby and Bryson (2010), it is tempting to distinguish these roles as "sponsor" versus "champion," yet because of the convenor's active engagement, the boundary between these roles is not clear cut.

at stake (suggesting a kind of hybrid between the neutrality of a professional facilitator and the expertise of an organic leader). As Scott notes, the law faculty were not trained as facilitators and this might have been a liability. But they made up for this lack of training by hard work and good will. Scott (2011: 448) notes that they successfully nurtured a "constructive climate for collaboration." As the process became more conflictual, they also sought to ensure the representation of different perspectives and voices and took steps to maintain the transparency of the process by circulating information to all stakeholders. They also sought to ensure that all stakeholders had an opportunity to exercise their voice during the deliberations. As Scott (2011: 450) writes:

> By being so transparent about what was going on at every step in the process through giving everyone the same information and opportunity to comment and participate actively in the revisions, they established an atmosphere of fair play and confidence that there were no "back-room deals" being cut between meetings. Their transparency and consistently respectful attitude to divergent voices allowed for trust to develop among the participants.

The role of these more neutral facilitators was also to some extent iconic for the collaborative process. Scott notes that by being consistently prepared, they served as role models for the participants.

Workforce development leaders take on a similarly iconic role while also attempting to positively position the collaborative in the minds of the public. This involves both maintaining, as the public face of the collaborative, a strong personal reputation with stakeholders and in the community, as well as marketing the products and outcomes of the collaborative. To maintain a strong personal image as stewards of the collaborative, workforce leaders constantly worry about the degree to which their identity as a stakeholder in the workforce community conflicts with or impedes that of the collaborative. In so doing they also attempt to model the ideal of power-sharing for their stakeholders. Credit-sharing served as the main vehicle for this goal. Each of the leaders we interviewed strived to reject the impulse to credit-claim for themselves or their individual organizations and instead to elevate the status of their partners and stakeholders:

> You have to have a level of humility and not always be out front. [...] It takes a very particular kind of leader – a leader has to be confident that the

work that they do is valuable without public recognition ... a leader has to be one who likes to plant seeds and see it grow and to see the benefits of your contribution germinate in a way that makes the system better – that has to be enough of a reward ... a leader has to have a personality and value system that is aligned with that frame of mind.

During interviews, leaders repeatedly stressed that collaboration fundamentally requires that partners not only compromise on program and policy preferences, but also on accomplishments. "In this environment," explained one leader, "identity becomes really important. Identity and collaboration can be really challenging. While everyone knows that it is a good way to get things done you don't get the same level of credit."

Leaders need to model for their stakeholders both the process and the promise of credit-sharing. "Partners," explained one leader, "know what they want to accomplish, but they aren't aware of what they are willing to give up in return." A strong leader will practice this in both small and significant ways. For some, this entails deliberately altering a status quo that consistently privileges larger, politically powerful workforce areas to benefit smaller, isolated workforce regions. As one urban leader described:

> Some challenges for us happen at the regional level – [our county] and the four counties had formed years ago a regional WIB collaborative. There was an agreement that we would not compete against each other for grants, that we would collaborate whenever possible, and that we would meet monthly. The challenge is the footprint of [our county] relative to the other counties. If [our county] is involved we always get the lion's share of resources so we have intentionally in different instances taken a step back and allowed our other counterparts to serve as the lead organization. There are a number of statewide projects that are regional and we have decided "okay" the administrator of the funds is going to be another county, not us. We want them to be seen as a leader.

Some leaders have even opted to reduce their share of funding to better the collaborative and the community. One leader, for instance, elected to share a grant opportunity with his regional partners rather than applying for it on his own – despite the fact that his organization was all but assured by the funder that they would receive a sizable grant as a single applicant. "We will have less money coming to our board area," he explained "but we are willing to do that for the sake of the regional collaborative." Over time, explained the workforce leaders we interviewed, this focus on credit- and resource-sharing will earn leaders (and their organizations) the respect of partners. This, in turn, has the potential to expand opportunities for the collaborative.

The need for self-awareness extends to all areas where the collaborative operates, be it a board meeting, a social event, or a private meeting between parties not associated with the collaborative, recalls one leader of a state level meeting unrelated to workforce development:

> At the meeting I was conscious about not doing most of the talking and deferring to my colleagues. Even if I had an idea I would pause to make sure that other people had a chance to speak. This is something that I have learned over time, having made mistakes – going to a meeting and talking more than I should have.

Collaborative leaders often present themselves as humble, observant, and thoughtful. In their role as stewards, workforce leaders also devote significant resources to managing the image of the collaborative. As public relations specialists, workforce leaders must look for ways to sell the collaborative to potential stakeholders or to the public. Sometimes this can be as simple as building or maintaining a positive reputation, but often it requires more deliberate strategies. One leader explained that the success of their collaborative centered, to a large degree, on keeping "our name in the public through events that will help keep the public educated as to how we can help them."

To maintain a positive image and keep the focus on the needs and accomplishments of the collaborative rather than any single organization, workforce leaders stressed the importance of issue or needs-focused rhetoric. A strong leader will help the collaborative develop a "common understanding of ... the issue" and will remind participants that they are "negotiating for everyone's happiness." Some rely on this strategy to help attract previously disinterested – but nevertheless critical – partners. As one leader noted, a new issue might be introduced "in terms of the advantage it could have for individuals and the positioning of the city and region by having a stronger skilled workforce who could fill jobs in the local and regional area."

In conclusion, collaborative leaders facilitate collaboration by serving as stewards of the collaborative process itself and often of the community they represent. By developing and promoting the legitimacy of collaboration and by ensuring that the process is indeed collaborative, leaders establish the basic framework in which collaboration unfolds. This stewardship role shades into the role of leaders as mediators.

Mediator

A second role for collaborative leaders is to serve as a mediator or broker between different stakeholders. This mediation role grows out of the basic structure of collaborative governance, with its context of voluntary participation and shared power. Since stakeholders hold diverse perspectives and interests, they often do not see eye-to-eye. Much of the impetus for collaborative governance, in fact, grows out of the movement for alternative dispute resolution and conflict management. Therefore, leaders are called upon to facilitate positive exchanges between different stakeholders through adjudication of conflict, to arbitrate between different positions, to stabilize the conditions for positive exchange, and to promote trust-building. In bemoaning current trends to privilege efficiency over process, one workforce leader argued that "it takes relationship building and trust and you can't short-circuit those items because it is a human endeavor." This remains true even when a collaborative has the advantage of strong pre-existing relationships among its leaders and participants. Communicating and maintaining good will among stakeholders is still a priority – despite its often time consuming and challenging nature. One leader (a self-described "business and process guy") noted:

> We tried to put together this shared framework to parse out the flow of industry engagement. Something that emerged in this conversation is that there is angst in one county about losing their identity to [our workforce area.] There has been a couple of days of back and forth meetings – we are trying to clear the air to get to a place where we can move on ... you have to constantly work at it even though we are all very good friends ... But overall we will get to a place where we have a defined way of figuring out how, why and if we work together.

This quote demonstrates the important role collaborative leaders have in mitigating and managing conflict (Crosby and Bryson, 2010).

Collaborative efforts often fail because leaders are unable to manage bitter conflict between stakeholders. Matthews and Missingham (2009: 1054) describe the failure of collaborative governance in the Wombat Forest in Australia in these terms:

> Interviewees reported that meetings often included screaming matches, people breaking down into tears, and disrespect for participants. Two Working Group representatives stated that much of the infighting was among men "puffing their chests." When meetings digressed to verbal conflict, neither the chairperson nor the [Department of Sustainability and Environment] [DSE] made significant attempts to intervene or protect the volunteers. The DSE's ability to manage the group may have been compromised by the atmosphere of conflict between the DSE and certain community members that had been initiated before the [Community Forest Management] process began.

This quote also suggests, however, that the failure to manage high levels of conflict cannot simply be "loaded" on the variable of leadership. A range of factors and antecedent conditions stack the deck against effective conflict mediation. Even the most skillful mediators may have had difficulty overcoming the conflict in this situation. This case also suggests how the steward and mediator roles may interact. The inability to mediate, in this case, was linked to an erosion of the integrity of the collaborative process itself.

Institutional or infrastructural features may work against the effectiveness of mediation. Often the success of workforce leaders as mediators is contingent upon the position of their organization within the larger workforce system and the infrastructure of the state workforce system – factors that are largely beyond a leader's control. Despite what one leader described as the "natural" requirement for collaboration in workforce development, quite a few leaders feel that the system is designed to thwart all but the most superficial forms of collaboration. One leader attributed his struggles with promoting regional collaboration to the state infrastructure mandated by WIA:

> There are incentives by WIA against collaboration – within a workforce region there are incentives to collaborate, but across boards there aren't. There is a fractured system. It doesn't encourage regional collaboration and economies are not the same as political boundaries of the workforce system. So automatically you set up these disconnects.

While institutional fragmentation creates the need for mediation, it can also make it exceedingly difficult to achieve in practice.

Effective conflict mediation is sensitive to stakeholder perceptions that collaborative leaders are acting as "honest brokers." As a result, we find a tension between the neutral professional facilitator and the organic leader roles. Conflict tends to breed distrust and leaders can easily become a target of this distrust, undermining their ability to mediate conflict. In the Wombat Forest case, the selection of an organic leader interacted with the distrust associated with spiraling conflict to undermine the legitimacy of leadership:

> In the Wombat initiative there was a government-appointed [Community Development; CD] officer and a committee appointed chairperson. The CD officer was the former president of the Wombat Forest Society and had for years been conducting campaigns for sustainable logging in the Wombat. From the government's perspective, appointing the former WFS president as the CD officer was a natural choice, due to his support for continued sustainable logging, his long history in the forest, and his existing networks. The CD officer had also lobbied the government to implement the CFM model, because he saw it as an opportunity to bring everyone to the table and resolve the community conflict over the logging issue. Although the CD officer appeared to be a good choice for the government, he was not well received by all stakeholders. The CD officer's history on the contentious issue of logging in the Wombat meant that he brought a particular commitment to the process. Due to this commitment, some participants in the process were ideologically opposed to him from the beginning. (Matthews and Missingham, 2009: 1059–1060)

In this case, the collaborative leader's commitment to collaboration, substantive knowledge, and community social capital did not overcome stakeholder distrust of his bias for certain positions.

While it is difficult to draw a strong conclusion from a single case, a neutral professional facilitator might have made more progress in overcoming the distrust in the Wombat case. But there may simply be a dilemma here; facilitative leadership typically must become more interventionist as stakeholders become less able to work together or to make progress in consensus building (Ansell and Gash, 2008). In general, we suspect that organic leaders are in a better position to take this interventionist role, because of their knowledge of local conditions, substantive expertise, and community social capital. One workforce leader, for example, recalled the value of recruiting the collaborative's first president from within the community: "Because of [the new president's] social capital, we were able to move projects more effectively and we had that level of trust that wouldn't have been there had we hired someone from another community." Yet, as the Wombat forest case demonstrates, an organic leader may also find it difficult to establish legitimacy as an honest broker.

A second aspect of the mediating role is what we refer to as "arbitrage." Given the different perspectives and interests that stakeholders have, collaborative leaders must facilitate the communication and translation of perspectives. Even if conflict is not high, stakeholders may still have considerable trouble in understanding each other and in aligning their perspectives. As Crosby and Bryson (2010) observe, collaborative leaders must often play the role of facilitating the construction of shared meaning between stakeholders. For instance:

> [I]n a workforce collaborative, one of the key techniques or qualities for a leader is to adjust all the information that is coming in and condense it to the common denominators. Take away Dave or Sally's specific set of issues and have a set of data that represents the group not the individuals. It takes particular skills to do that and keep the group cohesive and not alienate folks at the table.

Professional facilitators are often trained to facilitate the process of communication. However, organic leaders may sometimes have the specific legitimacy and knowledge that enable them to most effectively serve this role. Here is an example from Crosby and Bryson (2010: 21):

> Randall Johnson had been a local planner and critic of MC projections, so he could speak the language of local planners and be seen as a legitimate champion of better regional solutions that addressed local needs and concerns. In short, he could work well with policy makers, planners, and technical personnel.

Johnson was effective at arbitrage because he "could speak the language of local planners." However, leaders may also benefit from a certain professional distance from local affairs. As one workforce leader pointed out: "[Collaborative leaders] have to sort of separate themselves from whatever their current programs or resources are and listen."

A third mediating role collaborative leaders are called upon to play is what we will call a "stabilizer" role. Collaborative governance is a dynamic process and is prone to "deviation amplification" or "negative feedback" (as in "vicious cycles"). Thus, a key leadership role is to intervene to prevent these negative dynamics or to restore more positive interactions. Workforce development leaders call the stabilizer a "connector." Connectors must be able to assert themselves into the conversation to point out flaws or problems concerning partners.[4]

In describing the need for "iterative adjustment" of leadership tactics, Page (2010: 261) offers a hypothesis, grounded in his case study evidence, which also comes close to describing the "stabilizer" role:

> When collaborative processes become difficult or trying, stakeholders draw negative interpretations about one another's intentions or abilities and about the legitimacy, distributional equity, or integrative potential of the initiative. In turn, understandings of public problems and collaborative opportunities diverge. Changes in leadership tactics that respond to these negative interpretations by improving convening and deliberation processes may reshape the stakeholders' understandings and perceptions of the legitimacy and distributional equity of collaboration.

When collaboration engenders negative dynamics, the mediator must act as a stabilizer, who dampens down the negative consequences of interaction and helps to restore collaboration to more positive interactions.

A final mediating role that facilitators play is trust-building, which might be seen as a particularly important case of an intervention to restore collaboration to a positive feedback cycle. Trust-building is also one critical way to intervene to manage conflict, since destructive conflict like that seen in the Wombat Forest is likely to be ameliorated by greater trust. The importance of collaborative leaders in engaging in trust-building is widely recognized (Crosby and Bryson, 2010; Vangen and Huxham, 2003).When

---

4   As one leader suggested, this can be a real struggle with stakeholders who are essentially peers, colleagues, or even friends rather than contractors or employees: "A lot of triangulation happens. A lot of 'this partner isn't doing what we need to do so how do we make it work' instead of just talking. Workforce leaders are good at running organizations but not always good at being up front at the table. These are people that we care about – they aren't vendors or providers – and it makes the communication really difficult."

stakeholders lack relationships with each other, a positive relationship with the collaborative leader can fast-track trust-building with other members of the collaborative.

Vangen and Huxham (2003) suggest that the precise tactics for managing trust in collaboratives will depend on how ambitious collaborative goals are and on the prior level of trust. Where goals are modest and baseline trust is weak, they suggest a "small wins" approach that helps stakeholders identify measurable gains that can build trust. Often this may require leaders to develop specific activities or events designed to showcase the promise of the collaborative – even if those activities are unnecessary to the overall substantive goals of the collaborative. For instance, one workforce leader described his efforts to maintain participation in a collaborative comprised of rural community residents and leaders. Representatives from smaller communities were beginning to lose faith in the collaborative as the benefits were perceived as accruing primarily to stakeholders in larger towns. In order to sustain committed participation from these smaller communities – which was vital to the goals of the collaborative – he had to take time to develop activities that advantaged smaller towns, even when these activities did not align with the specific tasks of the collaborative. "It is important to create local activities," he stated "where [these communities] benefit from the boost rather than something we do just to make the town or county more successful. That isn't just words – it is activities."

Where goals are modest and more baseline trust is present, collaborative leaders should attend closely to factors that could derail this trust, such as power imbalances and stakeholder instability. Where goals are more ambitious and where baseline trust is weak, collaborative leaders should engage in exploration of where and with whom trust might be built. Finally, where goals are ambitious and baseline trust is present, collaborative leaders should provide for transparent communications, promote shared ownership of the process, and other strategies that nurture trust. In some respects, this last category describes features that we have attributed to the stewardship role. In other respects, this category builds on features of the mediator role we have already described.

Catalyst

The third role for collaborative leaders is to serve as a catalyst for effective and productive collaboration. The importance of leadership for catalyzing collective action and collaboration is also well represented in the literature (Luke, 1997; Mandell and Keast, 2009; Morse, 2010). This catalytic role is sometimes captured by describing this leadership role as "entrepreneurial" (Weber, 2009; Morse, 2010). The catalytic role goes beyond a mediating role in the sense that it must often engage with the substantive content of negotiations with the aim of identifying and exploiting opportunities for producing value. Morse (2010: 243) sums up the catalytic role of leaders of several successful collaborative projects in North Carolina:

> Opportunity is the key variable in all three of the cases. Leaders such as Gibson saw in the set of conditions in front of them an opportunity to do something different. They saw opportunity for integration. This perhaps lies at the core of what it means to be a catalyst. In order for integration ... to even be possible, someone has to imagine the process of coming together to create something new. Thus, the vision of public value is often dependent on these individual leaders, the entrepreneurial boundary spanners, unsatisfied with the status quo and willing to take risks to realize something better.

To recognize these opportunities, Crosby and Bryson (2010) argue that collaborative leaders must engage in "systems" thinking, surveying the existing and emerging constraints and opportunities.

Collaborative leaders have limited capacity to act unilaterally. Therefore, their catalytic interventions must work through the actions of stakeholders. One instrument at their disposal is problem framing or definition. Leaders cannot dictate problem definition, but they can help stakeholders identify and invent productive framings. One way they can do this is by helping stakeholders "surface" underlying assumptions and beliefs and to identify alternative framings (Feyerherm, 1994). Assisting with the reframing of problems that lead to stalemate and intractable conflict is one important role for collaborative leaders (Crosby and Bryson, 2010). Ospina and Foldy (2010) identify five leadership practices important for the "bridging" work inherent in collaborative governance: Prompting cognitive shifts (similar to the concept of "reframing"); naming and shaping identity; engaging dialogue about difference; creating equitable governance mechanisms; and weaving multiple worlds together through interpersonal relationships. Although these five practices build on the steward and mediator roles, they are catalytic in that they try to proactively produce constructive collaboration.

The most surprising outcome of our interviews was the degree to which the workforce leaders we interviewed perceived themselves as change agents or innovators and the methods they used to catalyze innovation. As one leader articulated, "WIBs have a broader impact – if you take that role seriously you have to recognize that you are charged to be an influencer." Workforce leaders launched innovative approaches to job training and placement by courting specific stakeholders and framing the collaboration around these players:

> So it seems like it is so obvious and when I get together with people all over the country people would say: "How did you get bioscience to develop a curriculum for engineers?" The answer was: "Go to employers first, participate in their associations. Start with employers." Otherwise the systems can be beautifully designed programs serving needy populations with zero impact. Sometimes it is such stupid little things that prevent this – but when they do put in the time, it works.

As this quote suggests, workforce leaders understood that innovation comes about *through* collaboration.

Catalysts understand that collaboration and innovation can be a mutually reinforcing dynamic: innovation depends on collaboration, but collaboration is enhanced through innovation. In designing strategies to remain economically competitive and to forestall the effects of federal budget cutbacks, workforce leaders argued that collaboration gave them a competitive edge:

> I really believe that it is to our competitive advantage to be able to demonstrate that we can do something at a regional level because no one else can. [...] I want to be ready when our federal funds diminish to be able to turn to our local constituents to say that we are important.

Faced with economic uncertainty, this workforce leader viewed regional collaboration as a tool for attracting future investors when federal funds run dry. At the same time, many collaboratives developed products to attract partners and promote interest. One leader commissioned a "commute pattern analysis" to compel participation in a regional collaborative and to "show that employers didn't care whether people lived in this city or that – they wanted skilled workers." Another commissioned a report "to raise the visibility of an issue that for the most part was a challenge" to sell. The leader deliberately "included quantitative information around the impact and the opportunity it would have on the local and regional economy." By commissioning a report, generated by an impartial third-party and comprised of "hard facts," the leader was able to reach partners that had previously been unsympathetic to the collaborative's goals:

> The report had a unique value in that it put [the issue] in the framework of dollars and sense. It talked about the econ[omic] benefit in millions of dollars in taxpaying workers in the economy and that raised the interest of people who otherwise say [it] is a social service. This report allowed us to generate a greater level of interest and use it as a convening piece. We went on a campaign of briefings to anyone who would listen to us about what this report said. When we implemented things we referenced the report ... It allowed us to have an audience with various key stakeholders within various systems; resulted in contextualizing the degree to which adult literacy plays; and allowed stakeholders to consider the ways in which [the issue] played in their areas.

Catalytic leadership will exploit possibilities for positive interactions between expanding collaboration and innovative action.

In fact, it is because they prioritize innovation that workforce leaders pride themselves on thriving in conditions of uncertainty. As one leader stated:

> In an environment of complexity rigidity is not a strength. You have to have flexibility, the ability to assess a situation and use these assessments creatively. Where there is agility and flexibility, you have opportunity.

Rather than hiring an expert to head a collaborative, offered one leader, "you really want the ability to learn quick. Someone who is good at piloting, testing, running a lab – that kind of person is better suited for being a leader in a complex environment."

How would the contrasting leadership styles of neutral professional facilitator and organic leader affect the role of leadership catalyst?

Professional facilitators are trained to constructively mediate between stakeholders and help them to discover creative solutions to their problems. However, our expectation is that the neutral stance of the professional mediator places them in a position where they are less likely to take the initiative required by catalytic leadership. We also suspect that successful catalytic leadership often requires leaders to engage in "persuasion." The organic leader is more likely to possess the substantive knowledge, commitment, and relationships to effectively exercise the influence that a catalytic "value-creating" leadership role seems to call for.

Conclusion

Leadership is an important variable in explaining the success or failure of collaborative governance. We have argued that the distinctive quality of collaborative leadership is that it is *facilitative* rather than *directive* – it must create the conditions that support the contributions of stakeholders to the collaborative process and effective transactions among them. To better understand the character of facilitative leadership, we distilled three types of facilitative leadership from the existing literature on collaborative governance. A *steward* is someone who facilitates the collaborative process by protecting the integrity of the collaborative process itself; a *mediator* is a leader who facilitates by helping to arbitrate and nurture relationships between stakeholders; and a *catalyst* is someone who helps stakeholders to identify and realize value-creating opportunities. We proposed that facilitative leadership will typically require leaders to play all three of these roles but that antecedent conditions, systems context, and collaborative goals (service delivery, consensus-building, creative problem-solving) will influence the relative prominence of these roles. Innovation, we expect, probably requires greater emphasis on catalytic leadership.

We also extended our analysis of two different *styles* of facilitative leadership – the professional facilitator and the organic leader. The professional facilitator adopts a neutral stance towards outcomes, comes from outside the community, and is independent of any of the stakeholders. The organic leader comes from the stakeholder community, and can generally draw on extensive social capital, but may not be neutral with respect to outcomes. We argued that these two styles of leadership have different strengths and weaknesses. Both can serve as honest brokers, but the professional facilitator will have an easier time establishing their neutrality, but a harder time motivating and persuading stakeholders to make effective contributions. Organic leaders can cajole and mobilize, but may have trouble convincing stakeholders of their neutrality. Thus, the professional facilitator will probably not have much luck in convening stakeholders, but may do a good job of maintaining the integrity of the process. Organic leaders may do a good job convening collaborative forums, but may also become the target of distrust as collaboration unfolds. With respect to mediation, professional facilitators will easily stand "above the fray" and will have the professional skills to effectively mediate. Organic leaders, however, may have advantages in arbitrage that requires translation between different specialized idioms. Finally, with respect to catalytic leadership, our expectation is that organic leaders will have the advantage, since recognition of value-creating opportunities often requires a deep familiarity with the substantive issues at stake. Our expectation is that collaborative governance that aims for creative problem-solving will require strong catalytic leadership from organic leaders.

Our interviews with collaborative leaders of Workforce Investment Boards (WIB) reinforce our view that collaborative leadership must be facilitative rather than directive. This is not surprising to us, but it is worth noting. Although elements of the Workforce Investment Act are mandated, effective collaboration necessarily entails a strong voluntary element. Regional collaboration, in particular, requires considerable facilitation to bring local jurisdictions to the table to work on a regional basis. Second, we find support in our interviews for all three kinds of facilitative leadership. The WIB leaders express ideas that conform to our expectations for the steward, mediator, and catalyst roles. The interviews suggest that these roles are not very clear-cut in practice, because it is often difficult to see where the stewardship role ends and the mediator role begins, etc. Clearly, the leadership of WIBs is complex and requires leaders to be flexible and adaptive, playing slighting different roles depending on the situation (the interests and motivations of stakeholders, the structure of the regional economy, the jurisdictional tensions between stakeholders). However, we found that the catalytic role of WIB leaders was strongly in evidence.

Although workforce development is, in part, a process of integrating service delivery, there are many challenges that must be addressed before this integration can take place. Addressing these challenges calls for WIBs to be creative and innovative in finding strategies that motivate integrated service delivery. Basically, this phase of creative problem-solving precedes the more technical and administrative details of working out common service delivery platforms. The relative salience of catalytic leadership in the WIBs provides some preliminary (but hardly conclusive) support for the idea that collaborative leadership that aims for (or demands) innovation will enhance the importance of catalytic leadership.

Bibliography

Ansell, C., & A. L. Gash. 2008. Collaborative Governance in Theory and Practice. *Journal of Public Administration Theory and Practice*, 18(4): 543–571.

Chrislip, D. D., & C. E. Larson. 1994. *Collaborative Leadership: How Citizens and Civic Leaders Can Make a Difference*. San Francisco, CA: Jossey-Bass.

Crosby, B. C., & J. M. Bryson. 2005. *Leadership for the Common Good: Tackling Public Problems in a Shared-Power World*. San Francisco, CA: Jossey-Bass.

Crosby, B. C. 2010. Integrative Leadership and the Creation and Maintenance of Cross-Sector Collaborations. *The Leadership Quarterly*, 21(2): 211–230.

Emerson, K., T. Nabatchi & S. Balogh. 2012. An Integrative Framework for Collaborative Governance. *Journal of Public Administration Research and Theory*, 22(1): 1–29.

Feyerherm, A. E. 1994. Leadership in Collaboration: A Longitudinal Study of Two Interorganizational Rule-Making Groups. *Leadership Quarterly*, 5(3/4): 253–270.

Huxham, C., & S. Vangen. 2000. Leadership in the Shaping and Implementation of Collaboration Agendas: How Things Happen in a (Not Quite) Joined-Up World. *The Academy of Management Journal*, 43(6): 1159–1175.

Luke, J. S. 1997. *Catalytic Leadership: Strategies for an Interconnected World*. San Francisco, CA: Jossey-Bass.

Mandell, M. P., & R. Keast. 2009. A New Look at Leadership in Collaborative Networks: Process Catalysts. Pp. 163–178 in J. A. Raffel, P. Leisink and A. E. Middlebrooks (eds), *Public Sector Leadership: International Challenges and Perspectives*. Cheltenham, UK: Edgar Elgar Publishing.

Matthews, N., & B. Missingham. 2009. Social Accountability and Community Forest Management: The Failure of Collaborative Governance in the Wombat Forest. *Development in Practice*, 19(8): 1052–1063.

Morse, R. S. 2008. "Developing Public Leaders in an Age of Collaborative Governance." Pp. 79–100 in Ricardo S. Morse and Terry F. Buss (eds), *Innovations in Public Leadership Development*. Armonk, NY: M. E. Sharpe.

Morse, R. S. 2010. Integrative Public Leadership: Catalyzing Collaboration to Create Public Value. *The Leadership Quarterly*, 21(2): 231–245.

Ospina, S., & E. Foldy. 2010. Building Bridges From the Margins: The Work of Leadership in Social Change Organizations. *The Leadership Quarterly*, 21(2): 292–307.

Page, S. 2010. Integrative Leadership for Collaborative Governance: Civic Engagement in Seattle. *The Leadership Quarterly*, 21: 246–263.

Scott, C. 2011. A Case Study in Collaborative Governance: Health Care Law Reform in Georgia. *Conflict Resolution Quarterly*, 28(4): 441–462.

Sørensen, E., & J. Torfing. 2009. Making Governance Networks Effective and Democratic Through Metagovernance. *Public Administration*, 87(2): 234–258.

U.S. Department of Labor. 1998. "White Paper: Implementing the Workforce Investment Act of 1998." Accessed June 5, 2017 at: <https://www.doleta.gov/usworkforce/documents/misc/wpaper3.cfm>.

Vangen, S., & C. Huxham. 2003. Nurturing Collaborative Relations: Building Trust in Interorganizational Communication. *The Journal of Applied Behavioral Science*, 39(1): 5–31.

Weber, E. P. 2009. Explaining Institutional Change in Tough Cases of Collaboration: "Ideas" in the Blackfoot Watershed. *Public Administration Review*, 69(2): 314–327.

LILLY LEMAY

8 The Practice of Collective and Strategic Leadership in the Public Sector[1]

ABSTRACT

Currently, a dyadic and hierarchical vision dominates in the literature on leadership as it does in the public sector (Gronn, 2002; Hiller & Vance, 2006). The transactional and transformational perspectives present leaders in relation with their subordinates or their supporters. Yet, that is a truncated vision of the reality because it disregards the situation and the other leaders present (Gronn, 2002, 2008; Raelin, 2005; Yukl, 1989). In the public sector, since the leaders have limited control (Moynihan & Wallace-Ingraham, 2004) and coexist collectively and in a dependent and independent manner (Raelin, 2005; Bourgault, 2007), we propose that different leaders interact in complementarity at different levels of the practice of leadership.

Introduction

In this chapter, I propose a conceptual model of the individual development of leadership in connection with the practice of collective and strategic leadership in the public sector. Using a case history, I conduct an exploratory and heuristic study that leads to adoption, in a first phase, of Kuhnert and Lewis's model (1987). According to them, leadership can develop in individuals throughout their professional evolution. They propose three levels of leadership practice, two of which are transactional types (imperial, which is a weak level, and interpersonal, which is a higher level), while the third one is

1   *The Innovation Journal: The Public Innovation Journal*: 14 (1), 2009, article 2 <http://www.innovation.cc/volumes-issues/vol14-no1.htm>.

a transformational type (institutional). I propose a model that has four levels of individual practice of leadership, two of which are transactional (technical and organizational) and two, transformational (political and institutional). In a second phase, an exploratory and heuristic study is conducted by looking at the case of cadastral (land register) reform in Québec, a strategic file managed by the same senior public servant I describe in the first part of the chapter on leadership development throughout a career. The results show that different levels of leadership practice are necessary to the management and implementation of a strategic file, and that if one or several levels of leadership are not assumed in a perspective of collective action, this has an impact on the overall performance.

This new proposal makes several contributions from the theoretical and conceptual point of view: it takes into account the organized dimension of the individual practice of leadership as a context for applying the individual development of leadership, in the context of the public sector. The model is a conceptual base to understand the practice of distributed leadership (cf. Gronn, 2002; 2008). It is a relevant model for the public sector as a field of action for leaders who share the same public service mission even if they are in different organizations. This model takes into account the opportunity (rather than the constraint) represented by the legal context of managers' accountability in the development of the practice of a collective and strategic leadership. I ultimately develop five main research hypotheses and five secondary hypotheses to test the generalizability of the results.

Individual Development of Leadership

Political Leader and Managerial Leader?

Two major streams define leadership in the public administration literature (Ketll, 2000: 10–11; 7–34):

(1) political leadership, as a traditional approach in the political science field that separates the political and administrative dimensions of

the public sector, the role of the administrative sphere being limited to implementing policy enactments in the purest hierarchical tradition of the bureaucratic ideal. Leadership is thus the prerogative of elected officials. This approach represents the dominant stream in the literature on leadership in the public sector. In particular, the author says that to preserve democracy, the administration must be instrumental and a-political, reserving the exercise of leadership to politicians (cf. Elcock, 2001) even if public managers are recognized as having an influential capacity (Cook, 1998; Van Wart, 2003);

(2) a second stream, which does not see public administration as being limited to an executant role but as having roles that are strongly and responsibly linked to public institutions. In fact, there is a dialectic tension between the instrumental (determinative) nature of public organizations and their influential nature (as stakeholders), the latter potentially being considered as a threat to democracy. This is why some prefer an instrumental-type public administration that is separate from policy. As Cook (1998) pointed out, there is nonetheless a distance between the rhetoric and the reality, and the instrumental and constitutive nature of public institutions is real. Public administration is an institution (Cook 1998) and, as such, managers are the guardians of the public good. Elected officials must standardize the conduct of public managers for an ethical, transparent, and responsible public management, which in turn responsible public management, which has an institutional responsibility. In other words, without taking the place or the political responsibility of elected officials, public managers, because they ensure the continuity of the government and have experience managing it, must exercise a formative influence throughout their work in their organization (Cook, 1998) and at the inter-organizational level, influencing the collective processes.

In practice, although the political and administrative responsibilities cannot replace each other, these two levels of action are consubstantial and reciprocal (Svara, 1998; 1999; 2001; 2006; Lynn, 2001), meaning that one needs the other in order to function, especially strategically. Moreover, even though the literature on leadership is abundant and the topic has garnered the attention of researchers throughout the twenty-first century, few studies take into account the particular context of the public sector. Nor do they take into account the dynamic of leadership practice in this context.

Political leadership can be seen not as an attribute linked to political status, but rather as linked to the personal style of the leader (Elcock, 2001): one who exercises power for personal purposes and one who targets the public interest. In the first instance, *public choice* theoreticians and their defenders in political science see leaders as *rational maximizers* who seek to optimize the loyalty of their supporters. Politicians' private interests remain subject to the electoral cycle (Fiorina and Schelpsle, 1989 cited by Elcock, 2001) and remain elitist (the oligarchy spoken of by Michels in 1915), while those of bureaucrats appear to be marked by the construction of organizational fiefs (Tullock, 1976 cited by Elcock, 2001). Political-type leaders must retain and develop the approval of supporters and, to do so, the Machiavellian vision is still the order of the day. According to Machiavelli, individuals are motivated by their personal interests first and foremost and the Prince cannot trust a servant who thinks of his own interests before those of the Prince. The Prince maintains the servants' allegiance by granting them favors in return (transactional leadership), and keeps them in fear of the consequences if they betray him or disobey his instructions (Tullock, 1976 cited by Elcock, 2001: 23). While even preserving an egoistic view of leadership, political-type leaders today have no other choice but to respond to a demand that did not exist in Machiavelli's time: a moral demand in terms of the public interest that must take precedence over individual interests. As Elcock (2001) explained, this demand is present in political discourse but, sometimes betrayed by certain actions, it now challenges managers of the public good. This is a classic problem : "that of how influence over government decisions should be divided between elected politicians and the career bureaucrats who advise them," even though the line that divides the political sphere from the administrative sphere varies over time and depending on the governments of the countries (*id.*).

Individual or Collective Process? Transactional and Transformational Practice?

Is leadership an individual or collective process in the public sector? Van Wart (2003: 23, 214–228) counted only twenty-five articles directly related to leadership in the *Public Administration Review* (out of 100 articles in sixty-one years). In the 1940s, some studies focused on the discretionary capacity of public managers (Finer, 1949 and Leys, 1943 cited in Van Wart 2003).

As Van Wart (2003) points out, leadership in the public sector is viewed monolithically and the various ramifications of leadership are not explored in different context on the basis of the different missions, organizational structures, accountability mechanisms, constraints or opportunities. A traditional hierarchical (top-down) view of leadership is still very present (Van Wart, 2003), which explains the absence of studies on the dynamics of leadership practice in the public sector. Yet in the current modernization of public functions where there are now additional public service actors (agencies, partners, ministries, community organizations, etc.), and where the notions of result, efficient and effective management, and quality of services and ethics are becoming the leitmotiv, there is a need to better understand the practice of leadership in the public sphere. Is it an influential process of one individual within a group (for dyadic perspective see Hiller, Day and Vance, 2006; Northouse, 2001, or Taggar Hacket and Saha, 1999 for example) or a collective process shared by a network of actors (collective perspective)? In either case, it is assumed that the success of the group depends on the success of the mission and is therefore a teleological phenomenon. (Yukl, 1989; Alban, Metcalfe and Alimo-Metcalfe, 2007).

In this chapter, I take the position that leadership is a collective process (Charan, 2006; Denis, Lamothe and Langley, 2001; Yukl, 1989) that involves both an individual dimension and a networking dimension, because the public service mission (healthcare, for example) is shared among different organizations.

The individual dimension includes both an operatory dimension and an interpersonal dimension. The operatory dimension – "how things get done and right," according to Zaleznick, 1977; Bennis and Nanus 1986 – is what some call "transactional leadership." The interpersonal dimension – "do the right things" (Bennis and Nanus, 1985 cited in Yukl, 1989) and "what things mean to people" (Zaleznick, 1977 cited in Yukl, 1989) – is what others call "transformational leadership" (Bass, 1985 cited in Yukl, 1989). Like Yukl (1989), in this chapter I consider the terms "managers" and "leaders" to be interchangeable rather than different. However, I propose that there are levels of development of leaders (Kuhnert and Lewis,

1987) and that transactional leadership is an operatory practice of a basic level while transformational leadership is a social practice of a more complex level. These levels of individual practice correspond to the leaders' talent and not to their formal position of power. Consequently, while the formal position should correspond to a level of leadership practice, in reality, the correspondence between the two is not automatic. Leaders are therefore those who, in the context of public management, exercise a level of leadership corresponding to their level of personal development in this regard whether it matches or not the position held. They exercise it in a complementary manner with the other leaders who have the same concern and outlook.

At present, a dyadic and hierarchical vision dominates in the literature on leadership just as in the public sector (Gronn 2002, 2008; Hiller, Day and Vance, 2006). The transactional and transformational perspectives present leaders in relationship with their subordinates or their supporters. Yet, that is a truncated vision of the reality because it disregards the situation and other leaders present (Raelin, 2005; Gronn, 2002; Yukl, 1989). A networking vision forecasts that in a given situation or problem, several leaders exercising different levels of leadership are called upon to intervene on the basis of their position of power or influence to provide effective leadership, so that the situation or the problem can be successfully managed. Networking leadership is distributed (Gronn, 2002) and includes the complementary exercise of transactional and transformational-type leaderships (Bass, Avolio, Jung and Berson, 2003). Collective leadership as defined here applies in particular to the public sector where leaders have limited control (Moynihan and Wallace-Ingraham, 2004), where leaders coexist collectively and in a dependent and independent manner (Raelin 2005), and were they are accountable.

In this chapter, I suggest first that leaders might have develop their leadership in an individual manner during their career. Second, since public sector leaders have limited control (Moynihan and Wallace-Ingraham 2004), they coexist collectively and in a dependent and independent manner (Raelin, 2005; Bourgault, 2007), and they are accountable, I propose that different leaders interact in complementarity at different levels of leadership practice and in an inter-organizational mode.

Methodology

A within-case analysis (Miles and Huberman, 2003) and temporal bracketing (Langley, 1999) are used in an exploratory study. To start with, we will introduce the case (or the history) of an illustrious carrier evolution of a senior civil servant renowned for his leadership qualities. The case proved to be a rich heuristic source for this exploratory study of the individual and collective practice of leadership in the public sector.

Two in-depth interviews lasting nearly six hours, the testimony of resource people and verification of the facts in public documents enabled us to establish the database. For interpretation, the data were reorganized in two phases: (1) based on categories identified by Kuhnert and Lewis (1987) (see below), and in a longitudinal horizon, I matched the type of position held with the type of corresponding issue, and I analyzed the purpose of the individual's action (subject – organizing process) and the means he took to act and successfully deal with the issue (object – content of experience); (2) this data analysis allowed us to adapt and enrich the matrix of the individual development of leadership by identifying four levels of practice adapted to the public sector (in addition to the "imperial" category that I consider as stage 0 of individual leadership which I retained from the initial matrix): technical, organizational, political, and institutional; (3) by using a real strategic file in the public sector, I analyze the interconnections and complementarity between the four levels of leadership practice in the public sector.

Individual Development of Leadership: The Kuhnert and Lewis Model (1987)

Kuhnert and Lewis (1987) proposed a constructive model of the individual development of leadership in connection with the practice of transactional and transformational leadership. Drawing on the works of Burns (1978) and Bass (1985) who themselves recognized degrees of application in the action of transactional and transformational leadership, and from the work of Kegan (1982), Kuhnert and Lewis (1987) proposed two stages of transactional leadership (imperial or weak, and interpersonal or high) and one stage of transformational leadership (called institutional) in the individual development of leadership. They linked these stages with a personal evolution dealing with the self (subject) and the content of experience (object) (Table 8.1) (see also Piaget, 1954). Burns (1978) and Bass (1985), along with their supporters, were concerned with the actions of leaders and their impact on the actions of others, seen as followers. However, they did not explain what generates the action of these leaders (Kunhert and Lewis, 1987), and this was not studied in a particular context like the public sector (cf. Van Wart, 2003).

Table 8.1: Leadership Stages and Personal Evolution

Stages of leadership	Subject	Object
Personal Transactional (lower-order)	Personal goals and agendas	Personal needs and feelings
Interpersonal (higher-order transactional)	Interaction-interrelations, mutual obligations	Personal goals and agendas
Institutional (transformational)	Personal standards and value system	Interaction-interrelations, mutual obligations

Source: adapted from Kuhnert and Lewis model (1987: 652)

In the constructive and developmental theory of personality (Kuhnert and Lewis, 1987; Kegan, 1982), individuals evolve according to the manner in which they construct or organize their experience about themselves and about their social and interpersonal environment. For Kegan and Lahey (1984, cited in Kuhnert and Lewis, 1987), leaders who have reached superior levels of development also utilize the preceding levels to construct reality. For us, this approach bases itself on the psychology of the development of

Jean Piaget (1954–1939), which is why I added arrows to indicate it. The "subject" column indicates what the subjects (the leaders) use to define themselves. The "object" column indicates the relational interface with others used by the subjects. As their leadership evolves, the individuals transcend what defined them to use it as a transitional object or means of interaction. At the imperial stage, the subjects define themselves by their personal goals and agendas and they negotiate with the others by utilizing the perceptions, the most strongly expressed needs and the feelings of these others to achieve their own personal agendas. In fact, this stage corresponds to an absence of leadership, but it can take on the appearances of leadership depending on the discourse or status of the individual if I equate the individuals' leadership to an authority relationship. At the interpersonal stage, leaders transcend their goals and agendas as personal agendas to make them a means of action, and they define themselves instead through their relations of mutual obligation with others. At the institutional stage, they transcend their relations of mutual obligation with others as a personal agenda to make them the means of their action, and they define themselves henceforth by their value system and their personal standards.

Individual Leadership Development and the TOPI Model

Career Path and Stages of Individual Development of Leadership:
The Case of a Senior Public Servant

With the model proposed by Kuhnert and Lewis (1987) as a starting point (see Table 8.1), I propose an exploratory study of the individual development of leadership applied to the public sector.

I present and analyze the career path of Guy Morneau, a senior public servant, and the stages of development of his leadership.

> I have had a very non-linear career path. I never had a dream, I never had a career plan as such, I knew what I liked, I knew what I didn't like. And that I think that was the best filter to guide me in my career.

This Québec career senior public servant did not experience the impe-rial stage, where managers define themselves by their personal goals and agendas and use the emotions of others to achieve their personal agendas. A graduate in industrial relations, he began his career at the *Ministère de la Justice* (Department of Justice), where he evaluated specific cases relating to staffing and salary and negotiated specific job categories like that of substi-tute attorneys. Although his position presented him with normative issues, he was already aware of his abilities, and he was already showing a potential for leadership at the institutional level. He was able to take advantage of the responsibilities linked to his work to learn and develop his leadership.

> I remember my first mandate I was at the courthouse in Montréal. They called the mandate "qualitative analysis of human resources." There were lots of problems occuring in the work experience but they did not know why. Was it about the com-petencies? The management? The relationships between employers and syndicate? Between employees or employees and bosses? There was a lot of dissatisfaction and grumbling. I made interviews, we discussed about their work, about their working conditions, etc. Finally, I conclude that the quality of management was the issue. There was a very big problem of management! The direction and orientation were not clear, priorities were not identified or were badly identified, etc. In that case, they needed some new managers.

> I worked there, in the research and analysis service, where the first issue was to solve non-traditional cases in organisational working. I managed a lot of various and dif-ficult problems.

> I noticed that I had a predisposition to deal with complex situations and to find solutions that complied with the spirit or the letter of the major policy frameworks in the machinery of government. I had to be imaginative and creative.

> I was always concerned with the big issues. I thought at the time that I would like to make a significant contribution to a particular field, the world of labor relations.

At the time, the *Conseil du Trésor* (Treasury Board) was given the responsibility to manage the human resources of the entire public service in addition to its traditional role of budgetary control. Major rounds of union negotiation were taking place at this time. He became a negotiator for the government. He reached the organizational stage of leadership where the economic issues of governmental organization are important, and where he worked mutually and reciprocally with the other actors: unionists and government ministers alike.

> I found myself, I'm not sure how, at the Treasury Board in 1977. We needed to bring some order to the public service, bring good common sense to labor conditions, reconcile union and employers' interests by taking into account the capacity to pay, with solutions consistent with the value of the work, and avoid having too much distortion between the public and private sectors.

> So quite young, I found myself with weighty responsibilities, and also in some delicate situations. For example, as a Treasury Board employee, I found myself in a position where it was impossible to tell my boss, the president of the Treasury Board, what I was doing, because I was in a secret round of negotiations. [...] And since I am naturally very direct, very frank, I was direct and frank with my boss, the minister in charge of the Treasury Board: "I didn't choose this situation. But I want to assure you that when I have settled everything, you will have all the information. And I hope to convince you that it's a good settlement. But, in the meantime, you have to trust me. If that's a problem for you, speak to the Premier. I can guarantee you, however, that nothing will be accepted by the management without you being informed."

> So, you see, this created some very delicate situations and I wasn't sure of getting out in one piece, at least as regards personal relations. It was very intense!

> These were above all human experiences because I worked with human beings. For example, in negotiation, it's all about the ability to establish relationships with people who have a mandate. I don't start by bringing prejudices to the table, because those people will feel it quickly. I have objectives, they have objectives, so it is about being able to achieve consensus. You have to find a way where you can meet and eventually find a respective advantage in agreeing on something. So, these experiences allow you to develop patience, the ability to listen and to communicate. Then you have to live with the decisions, even if a lot of people become critical: "You gave us this, you did that ..."

Here again, he demonstrated an ability to reflect; he understood the organizational issues but also the strategic and ideological ones. He was able to manage the mutuality of his interpersonal relations with the network of actors involved.

> I quickly understood through that experience, that when you rise to the red-folder level, you have to know your files thoroughly, and you must have the moral qualities

and good health to be always ready no matter what happens. It made me develop an ethic because in working on strategic files, there are always cases that must be arbitrated, or moments when you are very close to the political powers that you have to convince to do or not do something, or to do this or that. You have to be clear, use simple words and get to the point of your message because those people don't have five hours to give you. They need to quickly understand the meaning of things, to quickly understand the issues, all the nuances there might be, because they have decisions to make and because they are accountable for them. Your job is to make recommendations.

When the minister comes out of the Cabinet and you talk to him about a negotiation issue, he does not necessarily follow your argument, because he has his own common sense logic. He says to you: "Look, maybe you've been working on this for six months, but now the situation has changed, it no longer has anything to do with what I wanted to do." So, you have to really keep a cool head, be able to articulate, be disciplined, be a good communicator, be concise. These are qualities that I develop in the heat of action.

Even though his leadership evolved as his responsibilities increased, and he was now acting at a strategic level, he felt the need to work on more day-to-day files. He went back to practicing on an organizational level even though he continued to act strategically when he focused on governance.

I did that (negotiation) for seven years. It was an exciting period, but also morally and physically exhausting. It doesn't create a very interesting social life. You work with the Premier, with the president of the Treasury Board, you are in the news every day or every week. It makes for a somewhat artificial world. I felt the need to experience the reality on the ground, as it took place day to day and not in an artificial way like what we had in periods of negotiation.

Then, I found myself at the *Commission administrative des régimes de retraite et d'assurances* (CARRA – public sector pension and insurance plan administration) as vice-president of administration and development, in particular responsible for public sector pension funds. It was 1984. I managed between 200 and 300 people. That helped me understand management.

It was important for me that the employees subscribe to the objectives of the organization and that they develop a customer service focus. It was then that I started to be very meaningfully interested in governance, meaning that the administration is required to report to the members of the board of directors who have the power to decide whether to allocate the resources or not, whether to agree with the proposals that you made, or not. When you are president or vice-president, someone has to question your objectives at a given moment; you cannot be the only one to decide what is good or not. That is an exercise in humility that managers at all levels should engage in. It gives depth to things, and keeps you from getting carried away with things, that can prove to be big disappointments once they are put into practice. I stayed at CARRA for five years.

Guy Morneau displayed his ability to understand strategic issues, managerial issues, and operational issues alike. In government, he was recognized for his ability to solve complex problems.

One morning, the telephone rang. It was one of my friends, who had become a deputy minister at the *Ministère des Ressources Naturelles* (Department of Natural Resources): "Come see me, I need you." He offered me the job of assistant deputy minister for public lands ... Assistant deputy minister for public lands ... I had been responsible for negotiations and I had managed the public sector pension and insurance plan, what was the connection? I said: "But I don't know anything about that!" And he replied, "That's not what I want, it's not important that you know it. I have a problem, I want you to solve it," and he added, "There are not many people who can solve this problem because it's very complex." It was the reform of the Québec cadastre.

The TOPI Model: Individual Dimension of Leadership

This case study illustrates the development of leadership in a senior public servant who throughout his career was able to develop his leadership ability by seizing all the opportunities that were offered to him. From the beginning, he showed an institutional type of leadership potential by his preoccupation with making a contribution to the world of labor relations. This indicates that the levels of leadership development do not necessarily correspond to a status, although the position in a given situation can promote the exercise of leadership. In this respect, this case study illustrates the links between the talent of leader (innate) and the occupational position (acquired). This is to say that status is not enough to make a leader, but it is an opportunity for leaders to develop and actualize their practice with current issues, as was the case here. It also means that status does not necessarily guarantee the development of the leader. However, in the case presented here, the progression between the level of practice and the status demonstrates coherence and

pertinence between natural leadership ability and the capacity to actualize practice at progressive levels of the issues, which is a sort of ideal type.

This case study led us to adapt Kuhnert and Lewis's model (1987) to
propose a new model that takes into account the organized dimension of
the individual practice of leadership as a context for applying the individual
development of leadership (see Table 8.2).

Table 8.2: Individual Development of Leadership in Public Management

	Leadership practice	Issues	Subject (purpose)	Object (means)
Transactional	0. Imperial	personal	personal goals and agendas	perceptions, immediate needs, feelings
Transactional	1. Technical	normative	task, structures, economic transaction	normative goals and agendas
Transactional	2. Organizational	economic	mutuality, reciprocity of roles	task, structures, economic transactions
Transformational	3. Political	strategic	public service mission, public institutions	mutuality, reciprocity of roles
Transformational	4. Institutional	ideological	vision of society, society in the world	public service mission, public institutions

Source: the author

The TOPI model includes five levels of practice, three of which are
transactional and two, transformational. The levels of practice presented
here are linked to the attitude and conduct of individuals and not to the
status of an individual within an organization. I keep the "imperial" category
that I consider as stage 0 of individual leadership, which I retained from the
initial matrix. In the case studied, Guy Morneau, had never been at stage 0.

At level 1, leaders can differentiate their interests from those of others,
and they define themselves by the task they have to accomplish as well as
by their role within the structures and their professional activities. They
use their professional goals and agendas this time to successfully deal with
normative issues – it is the rule that conditions their action rather than

their personal goals and agendas as in the previous case. Guy Morneau was at this stage at the beginning of his career (as agent for human resources management in Ministry of Justice 1974–1976).

At level 2, they define themselves in relation to their role within a network of organized actors (mutuality, reciprocity of roles) and they use socio-technical systems (task, structures, professional activities) to act and successfully deal with economic issues. The meaning of the word "organization" here goes beyond the judicial idea of the term, to include, for example, the inter-organizational functional networks of the actors. Guy Morneau was at this stage of leadership when he was working at the Treasury Board (as responsible for public and parapublic sector's negotiation – 1976–1984). The levels of practice 0, 1 and 2 are transactional.

At level 3, leaders exercise a political level of leadership practice, the word "political" being related to the power to act or to influence organized society. They define themselves by the public service mission to be accomplished and by the public institutions, and they interact on strategic issues through the network of involved actors. Guy Morneau was also at this stage of leadership when he worked at the Treasury Board (1976–1984) and as vice-president of administration and development of CARRA (1984–1989). Like level 4 leaders, they are capable of acting on the basis of a higher common interest and they exercise a transformational type of leadership. At level 4, leaders define themselves on the basis of their vision of society or of their society in the world, and they interact through public institutions or the public service mission.

Interestingly, throughout his career, Guy Morneau always had in mind a vision at a societal level and a sense of public service mission, at the same time not forgetting to consider the stakes he had to deal with.

From Dyadic Leadership to Collective Leadership

In the public sector, the practice of leadership is conditioned by the coexistence of two logics: political and administrative, as I discussed earlier. These are two different operating logics in American literature on leadership that differentiate between political leadership (elected officials) and administrative leadership (managers).

The Cadastral Reform and Collective Leadership: Case and Discussion

This case study features the same senior public servant, Guy Morneau, and illustrates both the need to combine different levels of leadership to successfully handle a strategic file, at the transformational level, and the need to provide leadership at the transactional levels to successfully implement the strategy.

> In 1985, the government authorized the reform: it entrusted the MRNF (Ministère des Ressources naturelles et de la faune) with the responsibility of proceeding with the renewal of the cadastre of the territory and ensuring that the cadastral plans are updated regularly. (Vérificateur general, 2007–2008)

> When I began as assistant deputy minister in charge of the cadastral reform at the Department of Natural Resources (1989–1994), $50m of the $87m had already been spent ... and there were no results! I like that type of challenge. The file might seem dull, the foundation of all property land rights, but it is important because many economic activities are rooted in these rights. So, if there are problems in this area, there'll be problems elsewhere. Therefore, I tried to undertake the modernization of the Québec cadastre. It was a colossal operation.

> I started by asking a surveyor: "What is the cadastre?" He gave me the first definition. Then, another surveyor gave me another definition. Well! I saw three or four who gave me different definitions. Even the Minister of Justice had his own.

> I worked with surveyors and municipalities, who use the cadastre a lot to serve as property assessments for taxation purposes. Many people are affected by the cadastre, for the installation of power lines, for example. Those people needed the assurance that the reform would be done using generally accepted practices. It wasn't a question of going out to survey Québec and putting pickets everywhere, which is what the surveyors wanted to do. I said that with modern techniques I could use satellite positioning, I could use the existing technology to get measurements and be able to accurately build the cadastral map, to within a few centimetres, which was very important. It made sense to use geomatics.[1]

> But I had to convince the land surveyors that the technology had become essential. They were measurement specialists. In the past, when they came to "draw a line" in

any country road, they had to cut down the woods to see the post at the bottom and the post at the top. But what good is that, in ten years when the woods have grown back? They said to us: "It's always been done this way, so we'll keep doing it this way!" I had to use stratagems. They meant well because they had always done their work that way. So, we did a test with some surveyors in the field and surveyors using geomatics. The results were similar to within 30 cm. Geomatics could give probative value to the title deed.

We were at the beginning of geomatics at the time, and implementing a system like that for the cadastre was equivalent in 1990 to a $500 million dollar program that would take fifteen years with a temporary organization, then a team of fifty to sixty people would manage cadastral maintenance. But we had to pass a law. It was 1990, in the middle of a recession, so you can imagine, a project like that was not very *glamorous* for a minister. "The cadastre is very important, you're right, Mr Morneau, but it won't get me re-elected." "You're right – Madam Minister, it won't get you re-elected, but it is part of your ministerial responsibilities, and if there are problems with this file, it may give rise to more problems elsewhere in Québec."

We convinced Ms Bacon, who was minister at the time. We proposed the $500m cadastral reform project to the government. Everyone said to me: "You'll fall flat on your face, Morneau, they won't find $500m for that." I replied that we would solve the problems one by one, that we knew how we would finance everything: users would pay for the rights. It was a fair solution. Finally, we passed the law in the National Assembly, in favor of renewal of the cadastre (R.S.Q., Chapter R–3.1).

We were innovators and, at the same time, the first to establish a geomatics institute in Québec. As long as we were spending $500 million, we were going to enter the twenty-first century, not stay in the eighteenth century. Ms Bacon emphasized the benefits of this decision: "Once the reform is complete, Québec will assert its role in the protection of land rights."

"The implementation of these complex information systems will make it possible to develop here an easily exportable expertise both in geomatics and in the cadastral field, and will create interesting openings for Québec firms on the international market" (*Le Soleil*, December 19: B3) [translation]. Other countries closely watched what was happening here, in this matter, especially Russia and Switzerland, and Venezuela had already chosen to use Québec's expertise and technology (*Le Soleil*, February 28, 1993: B4) [translation]. This episode instilled a huge dose of change in the whole machinery, and particularly in cadastral management. We equipped ourselves to do geomatics and we changed the way all land surveyors in Québec operate.

The TOPI Model for Distributed and Strategic Leadership

While Mr Morneau was able to evolve his leadership throughout his career by taking advantage of the opportunities provided by the different positions he held, he had always had an institutional dimension that truly expressed itself in this episode: (1) It was an ideological issue linked to geomatics as a new practice, a source of innovation, a competitive advantage for Québec; (2) and it was a public service mission through both sound and efficient management of the territory (society), and the positioning of Québec as a leader in geomatics (society in the world). Simultaneously, he used technical leadership in the way he convinced the land surveyors to change their practice by innovating; and he used organizational leadership in his management of the various stakeholders (land surveyors, municipalities, and minister, in particular, their respective work, and the economics of the project). He was also able to act as a leader at a political level by utilizing the mutuality and reciprocity of the roles of the different actors (minister, municipality, land surveyors, and others). He had to marshal the different interests into a higher common interest.

He also exercised his institutional leadership by positively influencing the minister (the ministerial institution and the public service mission), who exercised her political leadership: considering the recession, it was strategically important to win the decision-making "battle" in Cabinet for the purpose of sound and efficient management of the territory.

This part of the case reflects not only a direct relationship between the hierarchical status and the level of leadership exercised, but, above all, between two adequate practices. The assistant deputy minister assumed an institutional level of leadership in this strategic file while the minister, as decision-making vector in government, assumed a political level of leadership. This does not mean that the minister had not reached an institutional level of leadership on a personal level, but in the conduct of this particular file, it was the assistant deputy minister who assumed this level of leadership while the minister assumed the leadership associated with her status. As institutional leader, the assistant deputy minister was able to understand the stakes at the political and organizational levels of leadership to resolve the problem.

Epilogue of the Case Study

The epilogue of the cadastral reform case illustrates however that leadership not assumed at the appropriate level of action can have significant consequences, not only in terms of efficiency (costs–resources ratio) but also in terms of effectiveness (quality of the reform in regard to the management of the territory).

> The audit reveals that there were significant gaps in the planning process, especially in the matter of risk analysis and initial cost estimates. The project was influenced, in part, by competition problems, the reduced number of suppliers (land surveyors) and the quality of some of the work, which contributed to the cost increase and to the extension of the deadlines initially forecast. (Vérificateur général, *Rapport à l'Assemblée nationale*, 2007–2008) [translation]

> The cadastral reform, begun in 1992, will cost nearly twice as much as what had been forecast. It was supposed to end in 2006 at a cost of $508m. But it will end only in 2021, and the cost will likely reach $980m, noted the Vérificateur general, Renaud Lachance, in his annual report. This situation is attributed to the existence of a "quasi monopoly" among suppliers. Suppliers formed a group and have secured 97 per cent of the contracts since 1994. Since 2000–2001, only one tender each was presented for almost all of the calls for tenders. Renaud Lachance asked Québec to envisage other approaches to promote competition. (*La Presse*, June 8, 2006: A4) [translation]

> The role of the *Ordre des arpenteurs-géomètres du Québec* (Order of land surveyors of Québec) [as professional order] is to monitor the quality of the services offered by the province's 972 professionals. The profession is very sensitive to legislative changes. Thus, the reform of the civil code, the cadastral reform, and the laws on the protection or development of agricultural lands, lead the experts to continually reposition themselves on the market. (*Le Devoir*, October 4, 1997) [translation]

> Questions were raised, yesterday, as to a possible collusion between the land surveyor firms that shared approximately 100 million dollars in contracts for the cadastral reform. "Maybe the land surveyors made their own rules among themselves, I don't know," stated the Deputy Minister of Natural Resources, Normand Bergeron, before the parliamentary hearing on public administration. "But I know that every time we went to call for tenders, there was only one bidder." [...] Yesterday, in the presence of the Vérificateur général, Liberal and Parti Québécois Members of Parliament questioned public officials for more than two hours on various aspects of the file: cost previsions, risk management, lack of reporting to the Secretariat of the Treasury

Board for several years. But the dramatic increase in land surveyors' fees starting in 1998 got the most attention. The hearing's Chair, Rita Dionne-Marsolais, even asked for the list of employees who left the Department of Natural Resources at that time. [...] The *Ordre des arpenteurs-géomètres* explains the situation as being due to the real estate boom in particular. Since the private sector is more lucrative, public contracts are less interesting for firms. (*Le Soleil*, October 19: 6) [translation]

In the initial management of the cadastral reform file, the key leadership practice was transformational (the assistant deputy minister, temporary title of the public servant handling the file, and the minister). After the institutional and strategic challenges were successfully dealt with, the transactional levels of leadership, that is the organizational level (the Department of Natural Resources and the Order of land surveyors of Québec (*Ordre des arpenteurs-géomètres) du Québec*), as well as the technical level of leadership (public servants) had to take over and manage the implementation of the cadastral reform by meeting the economic and normative challenges. Yet, we observe that due to the lack of leadership at the organizational level and at the technical level (at the ministry through the standards relating to competition as well as at the Order of land surveyors of Québec in relation to its members), there was a failure to manage the mutuality and reciprocity of roles between the ministry and the professional order in the management of public funds and the protection of the public in this matter.

For successful leaders at the transactional levels of leadership practice, this would have involved the ability to understand the economic and normative issues as well as the purposes and the means to achieve the strategy. Doubtless the Department and the Order of land surveyors needed to be aware of the overriding stakes of the reform (strategic and ideological) not only from the perspective of successful implementation of strategy and accountability but also from the perspective of individual development of leadership.

Figure 8.1 illustrates the collective organization of the levels of leadership practice. The levels of political, organizational, and technical practice are matched with types of pertinent and interrelated positions at the transactional level (accountability). The institutional level of leadership practice can be exercised at all the levels so long as the individual thinks and acts in regard to the global public service mission, knowing that the different levels of positions held permit the exercise of a descending or ascending influence.

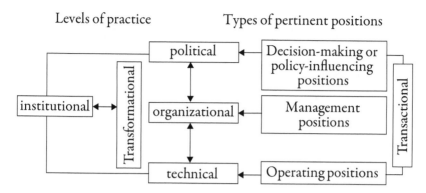

Figure 8.1: The collective practice of leadership.

Admittedly, hierarchy is typical in public management with its hierarchical operating structures. However, in a sectoral or inter-sectoral context where joint action is essential to fulfill the public service mission, the levels of leadership practice are necessary to develop and achieve the sectoral or inter-sectoral strategy. This model therefore applies both in an organizational context and in an inter-organizational context.

Contributions, Limitations, and Avenues of Research

This first phase of exploratory study has at least two important contributions. First, it proposes a new model of leadership that takes into account the organized dimension of the individual practice of leadership as a context for applying the individual development of leadership, here throughout the professional career. Of the debates about leadership reviewed by Van Wart (2003), the innate-acquired debate is irrelevant inasmuch as it is our position that the individual development of leadership (innate) is favored by the position held in an organization (acquired). The position fosters the increase of the influential capacity or the decision-making capacity, paving the way for taking on higher levels of issues. Second, it is a conceptual base to understand the collective and strategic practice of leadership.

Nevertheless, the exploratory and restricted nature of the study does not allow us to generalize the results. However, it does allow us to infer, in this first part, two main research hypotheses with secondary hypotheses in order to be able to generalize the results.

(1) Status does not necessarily reflect the individual level of leadership practice. In corollary:

> Managers accepting various levels of decision-making responsibilities should be capable of practising the corresponding level of leadership or situation.

(2) The individuals who succeed in developing their individual level of leadership practice over the course of their careers are leaders who understand the different levels of issues, both in a descending perspective and in an ascending perspective. In corollary:

> The higher the hierarchical status, the higher the level of individual development of leadership should be, in regard to the management and the successful resolution of key strategic problems.

(3) Leaders who are able to develop their leadership have naturally a sense of vision for society and public service mission as well as public institution. In corollary:

> People who are considering only personal issues, who defined them by personal goals and agendas, and use perceptions, immediate needs and feeling to act, don't have any vision of society nor have any sense of public service mission and public institutions.

These hypotheses could be dealt with separately or together depending on the research. A methodology combining questionnaires, case studies, perception studies and life stories could be made use of in various fields of application.

In the second phase, we outlined a particular event, the cadastral reform. I retraced the chronology of events, by identifying the actors involved throughout the events and their respective level of leadership based on the corresponding matrix in the new model. This allowed us to analyze different levels of leadership used, or not, by leaders during the cadastral reform as strategic file. Then I explain the study's contributions and limitations, and suggest future research avenues.

The exploratory study contains at least three important contributions. First, it enables us to propose a new model of leadership that takes into account the organizational dimension of the individual practice of leadership, here, a collective and distributed leadership at the (inter) organizational level in the public sector. The model compares and contrasts both the individual level of leadership practice and the individual's status or positioning in relation to other actors. The institutional level of practice, with the public service mission focus that it includes, can be found potentially or concretely at all levels of practice. It is the status or the capacity to influence that enables its actualization in action. Of the debates about leadership reviewed by Van Wart (2003), these results refer principally to strategic alignment (Technical-Organizational-Political-Institutional) as an object of leadership. In corollary, leaders can make a difference to performance by understanding the different levels of issues and by assuming their complementary role.

Secondly, while the results can be applied as effectively in the private sector as in the public sector, the model proves to be particularly relevant in the public sector where this strategic alignment involves leaders who are in complex organizations or in groups of organizations within operating super-structures. The public sector lacks post-bureaucratic models (cf. Josserand, Teo and Clegg, 2006) for its administrative operations and management. This model contributes an empirical understanding of collective and strategic leadership, from which it is distributed (Gronn, 2002) for effective post-bureaucratic management.

Thirdly, the model is an innovative and strategic way for the practice of leadership in the public sector since the legal context of manager's accountability in Québec.

Nevertheless, the exploratory and restricted nature of the study does not, for the moment, enable us to generalize the results. I therefore propose two main research hypotheses with secondary hypotheses in order to be able to generalize the results.

(1) While the transformational levels of leadership practice are necessary to resolve a strategic problem, the transactional levels of leadership must also be activated to effectively and efficiently implement it. In corollary:

> To act efficiently, transactional leaders must understand the overriding issues in addition to the issue of level of practice corresponding to their status or to their position of influence.

(2) Leadership that is not assumed or is poorly assumed at the appropriate level of the issue is positively linked to the failure of programs, policies or projects. In corollary:

> Effective staffing and promotion policies take into account individual level of leadership.

These hypotheses could be dealt with separately or together depending on the cases studied. A methodology combining questionnaires, case studies, perception studies and action research could be used in various fields of application.

Conclusion

In the chapter, I have first developed a conceptual model of individual development of leadership in the public sector. As to the debate about the best style of leadership to utilize, I infer from these results that it is a matter of aligning the right level of individual development of leadership with the type of position held. The case that I used allowed us to corroborate individual levels of leadership development and to identify three principal research hypotheses and three secondary hypotheses for future studies. I have made this an ideal-type case in the sense that it, typically speaking, illustrates the individual development of leadership of a manager throughout his career.

The model proposed implies an accountability linked here to the level of leadership development, which could be systematically taken into account during hiring or promotions to harmonize status with an adequate level of leadership practice.

Studies relating to the level of individual development of leadership, in connection with career progression, status, and the management of files, programs, policies or projects are needed to consolidate this conceptual model. I have proposed hypotheses to this effect.

Other studies to refine understanding of the model's operating mechanisms when different actors have to assume a collective and distributed leadership could also be conducted. The second section of the chapter proposes such a study with the case of the cadastral reform in Québec.

In a second time, the chapter enabled us to infer a model of collective and strategic leadership. The case presented corroborates the idea that while political and administrative responsibilities cannot or should not substitute for each other, these two levels of public action are consubstantial and reciprocal, meaning that one needs the other to function.

In terms of leadership, complementarity succeeds authority in public management. In the current context of public service transformation, accountability, and results-based management, the practice of collective leadership seems necessary to move beyond the traditional Weberian bureaucratic and hierarchical paradigm and to develop post-bureaucratic public organizations. The new research hypotheses that we have identified can be used for other studies linked to the practice of collective leadership and to its management.

Bibliography

Alban-Metcalfe, J., & B. Alimo-Metcalfe. 2007. Development of a Private Sector Version of the (engaging) Transformational Leadership Questionnaire, *Leadership & Organization Development Journal*, 28(2): 104–121.

Bass, B. M. 1985. *Leadership and performance beyond expectations*. New York: Free Press.

Bennis, W., & B. Nanus. 1986. *Leaders*. New York: Harper Perennial, Harpin Collins Publishers.

Bourgault, J. 2007. *Les facteurs contributifs au leadership du Greffier dans la fonction publique du Canada*. Administration Publique du Canada, 50(4): 541–571.

Burns, J. M. 1978. *Leadership*. New York: Harper & Row.

Charan, R. 2006. The collective leadership of boards. *Leader to Leader*, 46: 38–40.

Cook, B. J. 1998. Politics, Political Leadership, and the Public Management. *Public Administration Review*, 58(3) (May–June): 225–230.

Denis, J.-L., L. Lamothe & A. Langley. 2001. The Dynamics of Collective Leadership and Strategic Change in Pluralistic Organizations, *Academy of Management Journal*, 44 (4): 809–837.

Elcock, H. 2001. *Political Leadership*. Cheltenham, U.K.: Edward Elgar Publishing Limited.

Gronn, P. 2002. Distributed Leadership as a Unit of Analysis. *The Leadership Quarterly*, 13: 423–451.

Gronn, P. 2008. The Future of Leadership, *Journal of Educational Administration*, 46(2): 141–158.

Hiller, N. J., D. V. Day & R. J. Vance. 2006. Collective Enactment of Leadership Roles and Team Effectiveness: A Field Study. *The Leadership Quarterly*, 17: 387–397.

Kegan, R. 1982. *The Evolving Self*. Boston, MA: Harvard University Press.

Kettl, D. F. 2000. Public Administration at the Millenium: The State of the Field, *Journal of Public Administration Research and Theory*, 10(1): 7–34.

Kunhert, K., & P. Lewis. 1987. Transactional and Transformational Leadership: A Constructive/Developmental Analysis. *Academy of Management Review*, 12(4): 648–657.

Langley, A. 1999. Strategies for Theorizing From Process Data. *Academy of Management Review*, 24(4): 691–710.

Lynn, Laurence E., Jr. 2001. The Myth Of The Bureaucratic Paradigm: What Traditional Public Administration Really Stood For. *Public Administration Review*, 61(2): 144–160.

Michels, R. 1971 [1915]. *Les partis politiques: essai sur les tendances oligarchiques des démocraties*. Paris, France : Flammarion.

Miles, M. B., & A. M. Huberman. 2003. *L'analyse des données qualitatives*, 2nd Edn. Louvain-la-Neuve, Belgium: Université de Boeck.

Moynihan, D. P., & P. Moynihan. 2004. Wallace Ingraham Integrative Leadership in the Public Sector: A Model of Performance-Information Use. *Administration and Society*, 36(4): 427–453.

Northouse, P. G. 2001. *Leadership. Theory and Practice*. 2nd Edn. Thousand Oaks, CA: Sage.

Piaget, J. 1954 [1939]. *The Construction of Reality in the Child*. New York: Basic Books.

Raelin, J. A. 2005. We the Leaders: In Order to Form a Leaderful Organization. *Journal of Leadership and Organizational Studies*, 12(2): 18–29.

Svara, J. H. 1998. The Politics-Administration Dichotomy Model as Aberration. *Public Administration Review*, 58(1) (January–February): 51–58.

Svara, J. H. 1999. Complementarity of Politics and Administration as a Legitimate Alternative to The Dichotomy Model. *Administration and Society*, 30(6): 676–705.

Svara, J. H. 2001. The Myth of The Dichotomy: Complementarity of Politics and Administration in The Past and Future of Public Administration. *Public Administration Review*, 61(2) (March–April): 176–183.

Svara, J. H. 2006. Complexity in Political-Administrative Relations and the Limits of the Dichotomy Concept. *Administrative Theory & Praxis*, 28(1): 121–139.

Taggar, S., R. Hackett & S. Saha. 1999. Leadership Emergence in Autonomous Work Teams: Antecedents and Outcomes. *Personal Psychology*, 52(4): 899–977.

Van Wart, M. 2003. Public-Sector Leadership Theory: An assessment. *Public Administration Review*, 23: 214–228.

Yukl, G. A. 1989. Managerial Leadership: A Review of Theory and Research. *Journal of Management*, 15(2): 251–289.

Zaleznick, A. 1977. Managers and Leaders: Are they Different? *Harvard Business Review*, 55(5): 67–78.

PART IV

Innovation and Collaboration

J. TRAVIS BLAND, BORIS BRUK, DONGSHIN KIM,
AND KIMBERLY TAYLOR LEE

9 Enhancing Public Sector Innovation: Examining the Network–Innovation Relationship[1]

ABSTRACT

Communities around the country are facing an increasing number of problems for which traditional government action is failing. This has led to a growing realization that the public sector must increase its capacity to innovate. In an effort to do so, the public sector has increasingly turned to networks of public, private, and nonprofit organizations. While a considerable body of academic research has examined the relationship between collaboration and innovation, it has focused primarily on the capacity of networks to generate new ideas. Recognizing that innovation is a dynamic and iterative process, which includes the generation, acceptance, and implementation of a new idea or approach to an issue, we argue that previous studies have provided for a somewhat limited understanding of this relationship. Consequently, these studies have provided little to no practical guidance for public managers. To address this gap in the literature, the present study takes a first step in the development of a management perspective on the relationship between collaboration and innovation. In doing so, we present an exploratory case study of the Texoma Regional Consortium, a regional partnership that brought together Texas and Oklahoma workforce development efforts, that suggests the design, development, and institutionalization of specific mechanisms (integration, dialogue, and coordination) to facilitate the use of the network form of governance for the specific purposes of public sector innovation.

1   *The Innovation Journal: The Public Sector Innovation Journal,* 15(3), 2010, article 3
    <http://www.innovation.cc/volumes-issues/vol15-no3.htm>.

Introduction

Communities around the country are facing an increasing number of problems for which traditional government action is failing (Golden, 1990).
Consequently, it has become commonplace for one to hear that public
sector organizations are operating in a more unstable and volatile environment than at any time in history. This has led to a growing realization
that the public sector must increase its capacity to innovate. Scholars often
cite the need for innovation as a major reason for the emergence of the
network form of governance (Goldsmith and Eggers, 2004; Keast et al.,
2004; Kettl, 2002; Kickert et al., 1997; Osborne and Brown, 2005; Swan
and Scarbrough, 2005). In this study, we use the term network form of
governance to encompass all types of collaboration that bring people and
their organizations together to address the complex problems facing communities (Weiss et al., 2002).

Successful innovation represents the completion of a three-stage process: idea generation, acceptance, and implementation (Shepard, 1967).
To date, the literature has primarily focused on the capacity of networks
to generate new ideas (Goes and Park, 1997; Hardy et al., 2003; Swan and
Scarbrough, 2005). This has provided for a somewhat limited understanding of the network–innovation relationship. As argued by Van de Ven et al.
(2000), innovation requires more than the creative capacities to generate
new ideas. It also requires the managerial skills and talents to transform
new ideas into practice. Due to the limitations of previous studies, the skills
to facilitate and manage the entire innovation process, within networks,
remain somewhat underdeveloped.

To address this gap in the literature, this chapter reports on an exploratory case study in which we observed the network–innovation relationship
extensively. The central purpose of this study is to address the following questions: What is the relationship between the network form of
governance and innovation? How can networks be managed to address
the obstacles to innovation posed by the network form of governance? We
found that networked innovation requires the design, development, and
institutionalization of several processes that help facilitate the completion
of the innovation process. We call these processes *network–innovation*

mechanisms. To offer some practical guidance for public managers, we identify and illustrate several network–innovation mechanisms from the Texoma Regional Consortium.

Conceptual Framework

The concept of innovation has generated a vast amount of research. Yet, to date there is little to no consensus upon a definition (Damanpour, 1996). This does not necessarily reflect a weakness or defect in past research, but it does highlight the importance of understanding and defining innovation within a particular context. Two key aspects of this study create the context for this discussion: (1) this study's focus is public sector innovation; and (2) this study is interested in innovation at the inter-organizational or network level. Within this context, this study draws from several authors to define innovation as the generation, acceptance, and implementation of a new idea or approach to an issue, among social actors, that challenges the prevailing wisdom as it advances the public good and creates public value (Hannah, 1995; Light, 1998; Shepard, 1967; Osterlund and Carlile, 2005; Robertson et al., 2007; Van de Ven, 1986; Van de Ven and Angle, 2000).

To capture the essence of this definition, one must recognize the dual nature of this concept; that innovation is both a process and an outcome. Previous studies have tended to separate the different aspects of innovation. However, a better understanding of each is an important first step to understanding the network–innovation relationship.

Public Sector Innovation: An Outcome

Two important outcomes or expectations serve as a reminder of the ultimate rationale for public sector innovation. First, *innovation within the public sector should represent a new idea or approach to an issue, which challenges the prevailing wisdom* (Light, 1998). Becker and Whisler (1967) argue that innovation is literally the "first use" of a new idea or approach. Likewise, as Laurence Lynn defines it, innovation must be "an original disruptive act" (Light, 1998). This is an important distinction. Past studies have tended to define innovation as whatever is new to a given organization (Mohr, 1969; Shepard, 1967; Zaltman et al., 1973). When a public sector organization copies an innovation from another organization, that organization should not be deemed innovative. As noted by Paul Light (1998), this is merely an act of replication, not innovation. Considering the growing complexity of public problems, replication may not be enough.

Second, *innovation, within the public sector, should accomplish two things: (1) advance the public good; and (2) create public value.* Innovation, within the public sector, is just too expensive and time-consuming to be for the sake of mere novelty. Innovation, as suggested by Paul Light (1998) needs to be profitable to be worth doing in the private sector. Yet, in the public sector, innovations must accomplish something worthwhile. Thus, if a given act saves money but a segment of the population suffers as a result, it should not be labeled as an innovation. To do so, is to define innovation downward. Moreover, the creation of public value must be based on sound evidence that an innovation is likely to work. The potential costs of a failed innovation in the public sector are likely to be far greater than in the private sector. In the public sector, when an innovation fails a segment of the public is likely to suffer as a result.

Public Sector Innovation: A Three-Stage Process

As stated previously, innovation represents the successful completion of a three-stage process: idea generation, acceptance, and implementation (Shepard, 1967). When examined more closely, the processual nature of innovation provides a framework for enhancing our understanding of how innovations emerge, develop, grow, or are abandoned over time (Van de Ven et al., 2000). As outlined by Hannah (1995), ideas are generated through various personal or environmental stimuli in which individuals can play a number of different roles from initiator to champion to critic.

New ideas are then modified and shaped by various stakeholders, organizational routines, and external pressures eventually leading to a decision to accept or reject them. Once a new idea is accepted, the necessary resources and personnel must be gathered and put into place to implement them (Damanpour, 1991; Hannah, 1995). Figure 9.1 provides an overview of the different types of activities that may take place at each stage of the innovation process (Damanpour, 1991; Damanpour, 1996; Klein and Sorra, 1996; Pierce and Delbecq, 1977; Shepard, 1967; Van de Ven, 1986).

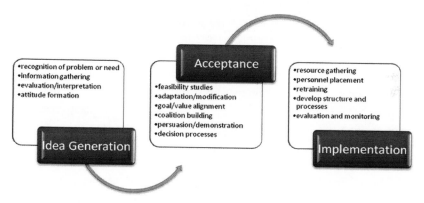

Figure 9.1: The stages of the innovation process. Source: authors.

For ease of understanding, the innovation process has been presented in a linear fashion. However, it typically plays out in more dynamic and iterative patterns where the different stages may overlap and merge into one another (Hannah, 1995; Shepard, 1967; Van de Ven, 1986). This represents a significant challenge for public managers who are responsible for both managing the innovation process and ensuring that its outcomes meet the unique expectations of the public sector. The following sub-section will review this literature to highlight the limitations of previous studies and introduce a new way to understand and approach the innovation process.

Previous Studies and Their Limitations

In *Bureaucracy and Innovation,* Thompson (1965) was one of the first authors to consider the obstacles to innovation within the bureaucratic organization and to offer some suggestions for changes that would facilitate innovation. This has led to an increasingly large amount of scholarly effort that has sought to identify the various organizational conditions that increase the likelihood and frequency of innovation. Despite these efforts, the findings remain somewhat scattered and provide a limited understanding of the innovation process. This has contributed to an unworkable solution for public managers.

In *Innovation and Organizations*, Zaltman et al. (1973) argue that an organization must alter its structure according to the demands of the various stages of innovation. The authors suggest that a more organic or less bureaucratic structure seems most appropriate for the generation of ideas. Then as the organization moves toward the implementation stage, more structure is necessary. Pierce and Delbecq (1977), argue that the successful completion of each stage of the innovation process seems to call for different attitudes, strategies, and structural conditions. In summary, an organization should be more open, diverse, and decentralized for the idea generation stage. Then as it moves to the acceptance and implementation stages, the organization should be more closed, centralized, and increasingly formalized (See Table 9.1). We refer to this as the structure-based view of innovation and we question whether this type of un-structuring and re-structuring is even possible.

Previous studies do not adequately account for the dynamic and iterative nature of the innovation process. This is largely due to the false assumption that each stage of the innovation process is distinctly separate from the others and occurs at different times with little or no overlap (Pierce and Delbecq, 1977). Moreover, these studies tend to overlook the collective and social aspects of the innovation process. Innovation, according to Cummings and van Zee (2005), is best understood as process that encompasses the interplay of social actors that share some commonality in practice. Reflecting this understanding, there are two key characteristics of the innovation process that warrant further consideration.

First, *innovation is a multi-level process. Innovation represents both an individual and collective achievement.* Van de Ven (1986) explains that, while the original conception of an innovative idea may be an individual activity, innovation is always a collective achievement because those ideas will have to be accepted and implemented by the whole of a group, organization, or collaborative. Likewise, as argued by Becker and Whisler (1967) innovation by its very nature is a cooperative group action. Secondly, *the different stages of the innovation process, and the levels at which they take place, are linked by various cognitive and social processes* (Becker and Whisler, 1967; Robertson et al., 2007; Shepard, 1967; Van de Ven, 1986). Within this context, this study concurs with Robertson et al. (2007) in suggesting that innovation is best understood as a reflection of a particular combination of flows of knowledge and information. This suggestion forms the basis of a new understanding and approach to the innovation process.

Table 9.1: Organizational Conditions Thought to Facilitate Innovation

Stage	*Organizational Conditions*	*Environmental Impact*
Idea Generation	Open/Diverse; Decentralized/ Participatory Culture; Structural Looseness/Low formalization	Increased Access to Knowledge and Information; Empowers/ Legitimizes Multi-Level Participation; Lateral Communication; Enhances Creativity; Growth in Professional Relationships
Acceptance	Singleness of Purpose/Closed; Centralization	Limits Conflict and Facilitates Commitment; Bounded Communication; Identifies Authority
Implementation	Formalization/Tightened Control	Specify Tasks, Roles, and Responsibilities; Areas of Specialization; Limits Experimentation

Source: the authors

A New Approach: The Knowledge-Based View of Innovation

Previous studies, which tend to promote a structure-based view of the innovation process, provide little practical guidance, for public managers, on the management of knowledge and information. This reveals the importance of a revamped understanding of the innovation process. It is important for one to understand that knowledge and information create the foundation of the innovation process. Moreover, knowledge and information are shaped by the ongoing experiences, interactions, and relationships of those involved in the process. A knowledge-based view of the innovation process forces public managers to visualize and understand the myriad of relationships that can enhance or restrict the flows of knowledge and information.

Two important assumptions about knowledge and information lay the foundation for this approach. First, an individual's knowledge and information cannot be separated from the specific social relations that are produced and reproduced through practice (Osterlund and Carlile, 2005). Second, as Groff and Jones (2003) suggest, unlike conventional assets, knowledge increases as it is shared. This raises several important questions for public managers to consider. How does information flow within the organization? To whom do people turn for advice? Are individuals and groups within the organization able to share what they know effectively? Does the organization have access to the necessary resources (i.e. knowledge, information, money, etc.)? Finally, how are these resources mobilized to effect change and innovate?

The successful completion of the innovation process hinges on the management of knowledge and information through shaping the experiences and interactions of the individuals, groups, and organizations that contain it. Public managers are responsible for creating an environment where different combinations of knowledge and information can come together, win acceptance, and mobilize the necessary resources to implement new ideas. A growing body of research now supports the notion that the network form of governance provides an optimal environment for this to take place (Goes and Park, 1997; Goldsmith and Eggers, 2004; Keast et al., 2004; Osborne and Brown, 2005; Swan and Scarbrough, 2005). For example, Swan and Scarbrough (2005: 914) argue that, because knowledge is more and more dispersed, innovations may require increased collaboration among groups and organizations that share a piece of a larger problem. In terms of the knowledge-based view of innovation, an important question must be considered: What is the relationship between the network form of governance and innovation? Further, what kinds of processes are needed to capitalize on the benefits of the network form of governance for the purposes of public sector innovation?

Networked Innovation: Potential Obstacles

While many studies have highlighted the potential benefits of the network approach for innovation, few studies have considered the potential obstacles that may arise (Swan and Scarbrough, 2005). When multiple organizations share in governance, they challenge existing patterns of organization and management. Recognizing these challenges is an important step to understanding and managing the network–innovation relationship. In regards to the flow of knowledge and information, what are the potential obstacles? We have identified three potential obstacles that form the basis of our empirical investigation: (1) a diversity of inputs; (2) incongruent goals; and (3) coordination.

Diversity of Inputs: The Failure to Communicate

Increased access to specialized knowledge, information, and expertise, resulting from the network form of governance, represents both an advantage and an obstacle for innovation. As Thomson and Perry (2006) indicate, the willingness to share information for the good of the partners is a distinguishing characteristic of networks. Likewise, the idea generation stage is largely dependent on an atmosphere that encourages and facilitates the sharing of ideas. However, one of the most significant challenges collaborating organizations face is associated with cultural and professional differences, which can create barriers to effective communication. Different organizations, and the individuals within them, may not share a common language and may make sense of, or define, problems differently. To build effective communication channels, public managers must effectively navigate cultural and professional differences to ensure that all participants are given a voice.

Incongruent Goals: Balancing Multiple Interests

Goldsmith and Eggers (2004: 41) highlight the fact that networks often encompass a diversity of actors whose goals may both overlap and differ. This is a major problem when network participants attempt to maximize their own interest. This is highlighted in the significant differences in interests among public, private, and nonprofit organizations. The central challenge in the development of meaningful innovation is determining how to achieve agreement without destroying the relationships and trust that are so vitally important to the network form of governance. With this in mind, reaching acceptance is unlikely when network participants fail to reconcile individual and collective interests to achieve goal congruence (Goldsmith and Eggers, 2004; McGuire, 2002; Thomson and Perry, 2006). Accordingly, public managers are charged with the difficult task of balancing multiple and, sometimes, competing interests.

Coordination: No One's in Charge

The "no one in charge" problem means that in networks the nature of authority differs from traditional organizations, which are typically based on superior–subordinate relationships (Keast et al., 2004; O'Toole, 1997a; O'Toole and Meier, 2004). In networks, command-and-control procedures typically are not an option. Networks require the coordination of efforts between different levels of government, nonprofits, and the private sector. When complexity is high and responsibility is unclear, as often is the case within networks, problems with coordination can undermine the innovation process (Goldsmith and Eggers, 2004).

In the next section, this study will offer an empirical investigation of the TEXOMA Regional Consortium (TRC) as an exploratory case study of the network–innovation relationship. Building on the knowledge-based view of innovation, the central purpose of this investigation is to report on how TRC addresses the potential obstacles to innovation posed by the network form of governance. In doing so, this section contributes to an improved understanding of the management of the network–innovation relationship.

Case Study: The Texoma Regional Consortium

This chapter presents the results of an exploratory case study of the Texoma Regional Consortium, the Southern Growth Policies Board's 2007 award-winning workforce development program. The choice of this Consortium developed as a means to study innovation that arose from the network form of governance. The Southern Growth Policy Board is a private nonprofit organization that provides a forum for partnerships seeking to strengthen economic development within a thirteen state region in the southern United States. The Consortium, formed in 2006, was chosen due to its innovative strategies, unique network structure, diversity of stakeholders, and the ability to work together despite the active rivalry between Northern Texas and Southern Oklahoma. Texoma consisted of entities representing higher education, K-12 education, business, government, and a variety of nonprofit organizations.

Methodology

Data was gathered during December 2007 and January 2008 from in-depth elite interviews, written documents, media reports, and a preliminary survey, focusing on the process of innovation as the unit of analysis. The managers of each workforce development board had been involved in the establishment of the network; they were ideally situated to assess the extent of success of inter-organizational efforts. Leaders and officials of fifteen TRC member organizations participated in a written pilot survey. Survey data provided baseline evidence about member affiliation, organization function, and opinions on the Consortium's success as a network.

Semi-structured interview questions were formulated to elicit information about the establishment of the network and its duration, the degree of network formality, network structure, institutional diversity, distinct participant roles, leadership structure and the perception of a lead organization, level of network stability, and process mechanisms.

Survey questions were based upon the overall objectives of the study, as well as prior literature (Donahoe, 2004). The resulting survey analysis identified common themes and patterns. Their work showed a high degree of inter-coder reliability.

Written notes were taken of all interviews with the verbal and written consent of the participating individuals. Interview notes were transcribed onto pre-developed data recording templates. Written documents that included meeting minutes, strategic plan documents, Consortium reports, and media articles were analyzed as a means of verifying the information provided by participants.

Background Information

The Texoma region, which encompasses thirteen counties between Dallas and Oklahoma City, is named for Lake Texoma, the large Red River reservoir located on the Texas–Oklahoma border. The region occupies an area about the size of Connecticut and Rhode Island combined (Poole, 2007). Like many other rural communities, the Texoma region, which is largely dependent upon petroleum, agriculture and ranching, mining, and manufacturing industries, has faced significant challenges. An aging workforce, increased numbers of low-skilled workers, a perceived lack of community support, and the relocation of highly skilled young workers to Dallas and Oklahoma City compound the economic development problems (Background Briefing Paper, 2006).

Globalization, economic recession, and technological innovations have caused the counties in the Texoma region to seek common workforce solutions. The Texas and Oklahoma workforce boards, thirteen municipalities, along with businesses, educational institutions, the Choctaw and Chickasaw nations, elected officials, and other stakeholders decided to form a two-state coalition in order to seek solutions to the regions' mounting workforce problem. Among the key goals, pursued by the TRC, are to create employment opportunities and to serve business needs by increasing the skills and availability of Texoma residents.

For its work, the Consortium has been recognized with several awards. This includes the *Best Practice* Honorable Mention of the National Association of Workforce Boards, the *Best Practice Award of* Texas Economic Development Council, and Innovator Award in Workforce Development presented by Southern Growth Policies Board. Accordingly, TRC has generated, accepted, and implemented a number of highly innovative approaches to workforce development and serves as model for networked-innovation.

Analysis and Finding: Fostering Innovation

Recognizing that innovation was not an inherent feature or function of networks, the TRC intentionally designed, developed, and institutionalized several processes to facilitate the completion of the innovation process. Management of these processes is central to deeming the network innovative. They suggest a long-term commitment to innovation. We call these processes *network–innovation mechanisms*. From the TRC case and supported by the knowledge-based view of innovation, we identify and illustrate three network–innovation mechanisms: integration, dialogue, and coordination.

Mechanism I: Integration

After reviewing the TRC, it became increasingly apparent that networking for innovation, especially at the idea generation stage, is highly dependent on the integration of knowledge and information from a diversity of inputs. Mechanisms of *integration* help to ensure that participants are given equal opportunity and consideration in sharing their ideas, suggestions, and concerns. These mechanisms help facilitate the development of inter-dependent relationships based on trust and professionalism, which are vital to open communication. In summation, mechanisms of integration help create value in participation and, thereby, enhance the flow of information and knowledge.

In their search for innovative ideas, the Texas Workforce Commission and the Oklahoma Department of Commerce developed a strategic part-nership with several different entities representing the public, nonprofit, and private sectors. Many of these partnerships are based on, or are extensions of, past relationships. This helped create the necessary pre-conditions for sharing knowledge and information: trust and interdependence (Bridging the Red River, 2007). In practice, the generation of ideas for year-to-year action planning, is supported by the belief that a diversity of voices and ideas boosts brainstorming capability. The survey showed that members strongly felt that collaboration, member diversity, and the overall culture of the TRC supported the idea generation phase. Three mechanisms of *integration* were identified within the TRC.

- *Empowering based on Increased Professionalism* – Surveyed members point to the fact that the Consortium limits any pre-occupation with status by empowering each of the participants as professionals. TRC does this by building trust with each of the participants and their orga-nizations, through the creation of sub-committees, so that they can take the lead in their area of expertise.
- *Using the Most of Past Relationships* – The majority of the TRC's bound-ary spanning efforts are based on past relationships. This limits uncer-tainty and helps create favorable pre-conditions for sharing information and knowledge.
- *Symbolizing* – The management within the TRC has worked to create a culture in which the participants realize that they are a part of some-thing important to the region. This is based on a shared belief that alone each organization is but only one piece of the puzzle. The TEXOMA symbol serves both as common identity and as a reminder of the value of participation in this effort.

Mechanism II: Dialogue

Innovative ideas needed to solve "wicked problems" thrive in cohesive, well-managed networks where members share an overall goal (Weber and Khademian, 2008). Surveyed members point to the fact that an overall sense of goal congruence is necessary for the organization to complete its mission. The overall goal for TRC, as written and stated by Consortium members, was to create common vision for a stronger economic future in the Texoma region. Achieving goal congruence can become a major obstacle in the acceptance stage of the innovation process within networks. Recognizing this obstacle, this study found that the TRC reached acceptance through the development of a joint understanding of the problems members faced. By generating new ways of seeing and understanding each problem, mechanisms of *dialogue* played a major role in this development.

Various levels of social interaction, cognition, and meta-cognition are necessary for the acceptance of ideas (Becker and Whisler, 1967; Shepard, 1967). In 2006, the Consortium held the first economic summit in which the stakeholders identified assets, obstacles, employment enhancement activities, development clusters, and a framework for future collaboration (Economic Summit, July 2006). At the summit, Consortium members used various strategies, employing large and small group cooperative discussion techniques, consensus-building activities, and feedback strategies (Manning and Rhoden, 2008). Specifically, discussion groups at the summit were asked to articulate strategies, develop methods that would sustain the work after the development of the plan, vet the group results, and provide feedback to the larger group (Economic Summit, July 2006). Varied organizational backgrounds enriched the conversation. Educators conversed with businesspersons, and workforce development personnel strategized with tribal chiefs. In the months that followed, groups assessed the information by continued communication between the sub-regional task forces and the larger Consortium.

Data from the summit were used to develop a report, "Bridging the Red River" (2007), which initiated the prioritization of strategies and the development of a vision. This eventually led to the formation of a unified workforce development plan for the Texoma region. Because of the size and diversity of the Texoma region, task forces and sub-regional committees led by chairpersons or champions, were created to write and communicate the goals, objectives, and action steps for the Consortium plan. By the spring of 2007, as the result of the second economic summit, TRC had put into place plans for implementation, monitoring, and program continuation (Poole, 2007; Economic Strategy Report, Spring 2007).

The large group continues to facilitate the interaction of different components of the workforce development plan. Group facilitation and consensus building strategies help maintain a cohesive sense of mission between the large and small working groups. The pilot survey showed that ideas are heard and represented within the group, the diversity of voices helps the brainstorming process, and that leadership encourages group consensus. Several mechanisms of dialogue can be drawn from this illustration.

- *Regular meeting institutionalization in the forms of the Summit, Sub-Regional Committees, Task Forces* – The TRC management has instituted meeting times that occur on a regular basis. These meetings stimulate dialogue and the exchange of ideas. In addition, the sharing and time together facilitates the growth of relationships and trust.
- *Appropriate Discussion Groups/Consensus-building techniques/ Brainstorming development* – The TRC management implements several discussion techniques to create a team atmosphere and get each participant involved in the process. This helps facilitate a joint understanding of problems and the acceptance of new ideas and approaches.

Mechanism III: Coordination

As a network, the TRC created a vision and produced a plan to support that vision. What the Consortium needed was an effective means of materializing or implementing this vision. While the literature suggests that the network structure may play a positive role in the innovation process (Zaltman et al., 1973; Pierce and Delbecq, 1977), problems may arise because, unlike traditional organizational structures, no one is in charge (Keast et al., 2004).

Thus, network structures will require several mechanisms of *coordination* to complete the innovation process. Consortium members used these mechanisms to perform the difficult task of mobilizing a number of different individuals and their organizations to get things done, while ensuring positive results. They must use them in a way that does not negatively influence the other stages of the innovation process.

TRC members have structured their network such that it has elements of an informal horizontal collaborative, while maintaining vestiges of a bureaucratic structure. Conversely, the configuration suggests a tight somewhat hierarchical structure, which can be observed in the operation of the core steering committee monitoring the work of smaller task forces and sub-regional committees (Economic Summit, July 2006). Likewise, the coordinators of the two state workforce boards play a leadership role in facilitating the development of the goals and objectives and communicating them to the different committees and working groups (Manning and Rhoden, 2008). It seems that the flexibility of the network structure makes this possible.

Decision-making in these types of arrangements, however, is not a given. A distinct decision-making framework has been set into place by TRC members that helped lead members through the creation of a workforce development plan. The TRC core steering committee serves as the proverbial network manager and provides some structure in organizing a variety of on-going regional activities. In this role, the TRC ... "continues to manage task force action steps, implement activities aimed at fostering regional collaboration, and provide on-going support to the Task Forces and their sub-regional committees in the form of fund-raising and leadership" (Bridging the Red River, 2007: 76). This framework equips the organization with a renewed knowledge base and the formation of a collective wisdom. This collective wisdom allows TRC the ability to work on difficult problems without losing the integrity of its network structure and culture. Two mechanisms of coordination were identified in this study.

- *Continued Tracking System through Annual Report/Website* – The TRC has developed several ways to track progress and share results with participants.

- *Instituting Legitimate and Core Steering Committee* – A small steering committee was developed to serve as the network manager and keep the Consortium on target. The committee still exists and remains legitimate because each member is actively involved in the different aspects of TRC. The committee has created a culture of innovation.

Discussion

This study discusses several points in regards to the relationship between the network form of governance and innovation. First, it emphasizes the role of management. The network structure alone does not ensure innovation. Although many studies suggest the network structure has a positive impact on innovation, many public organizations that adopt the network form of governance often fail to innovate. The structure or form of networks helps achieve innovation partially, but not entirely. It is important for one to understand the role of management in completing the innovation process. It was especially important then for those in the core steering committee and the workforce boards to facilitate the social interactions and help develop relationships between those involved in the process. These relationships enhance the sharing and emergence of knowledge and information, a vital component of innovation. The analysis of the TRC shows the importance of the three network–innovation mechanisms: integration, dialogue, and coordination.

Second, by analyzing the innovation process, this study explores the potential obstacles to innovation posed by the network form of governance. Many studies, to date, have failed to do so and provide for a somewhat limited understanding of the network–innovation relationship. This is largely due to innovation being viewed as an outcome rather than as a process with overlapping stages. To address this limitation, this study offers an in-depth review of the innovation process and its characteristics. In doing so, it focuses on the problems posed by the network form of governance for each stage of the innovation process and tries to identify several processes that address these problems. For example, as shown in the conceptual framework, the innovation process is comprised of three stages: idea generation, acceptance, and implementation. The structure of the network form of governance benefits the idea generation stage. However, the structure poses several problems for the acceptance and implementation stages. In other words, public managers should seek the design, development, and institutionalization of network–innovation mechanisms. These mechanisms can be applied to each innovation stage to help the network overcome obstacles as they arise.

Conclusion

This study examined how the flow of knowledge and information and the social interactions of the network form of governance intermingle to birth innovation. In the TRC case, innovation born of the individual and, to the larger extent, of collaborative achievement serves a worthwhile public purpose: to increase job opportunities and to spur economic development in the region. The study also showed that, in best-case scenarios, the network form of governance properly managed should increase the capacity for innovation.

At the same time, while the structural characteristics of the network approach are important, various processes or mechanisms help networks overcome any obstacles that may arise and support the completion of the innovation process. Thus, the central finding of this study is that *increasing the capacity for public sector innovation, through the network form of governance, requires the intentional design, development, and institutionalization of several mechanisms to facilitate the completion of the innovation process.*

The network–innovation mechanisms identified in our single-case exploratory study do not comprise an all-inclusive list of solutions for public managers. Yet, it does provide them with some practical guidance. The network–innovation mechanisms, offered in this study, lay the groundwork for the development of an improved understanding of the network–innovation relationship and the management of the network–innovation relationship.

Bibliography

Agranoff, R. 2007. *Managing Within Networks: Adding Value to Public Organizations.* Washington, DC: Georgetown University Press.

Aiken, M., & J. Hage. 1968. Organizational Interdependence and Intra-Organizational Structure. *American Sociological Review*, 33(6): 912–930.

Background Briefing Paper for the Texoma Regional Consortium. Accessed June 5, 2017 at: <http://www.workforcesolutionstexoma.com>.

Becker, S., & T. Whisler. 1967. The Innovative Organization: A Selective View of Current Theory and Research. *The Journal of Business*, 40(4): 462–469.

Beeby, M., & C. Booth. 2000. Networks and Inter-Organizational Learning: A Critical Review. *The Learning Organization*, 7(2): 75–88.

Bolman, L. G., & T. E. Deal. 2003. *Reframing Organizations.* San Francisco, CA: Jossey-Bass.

Bridging the Red River: A Regional Economic Strategy for the Texoma Regional Consortium. Accessed June 5, 2017 at: <http://www.workforcesolutionstexoma.com/Texoma_Economic_Strategy_Report_Final.pdf>.

Carlile, P. 2002. A Pragmatic View of Knowledge and Boundaries: Boundary objects in new product development. *Organization Science*, 13(4): 442–455.

Corwin, R. G. 1972. Strategies for Organizational Innovation: An Empirical Comparison. *American Sociological Review*, 37(4): 441–454.

Cross, R., A. Parker & S. Borgatti. 2002. A Bird's Eye View: Using Social Network Analysis to Improve Knowledge Creation and Sharing. *IBM Institute for Knowledge-Based Organizations*: 1–19. Accessed July 3, 2017 at: <https://www-07.ibm.com/services/hk/strategy/e_strategy/social_network.html>.

Cummings, S., & A. van Zee. 2005. Communities of Practice and Networks: Reviewing Two Perspectives on Social Learning. *KM4D Journal*, 1(1): 8–22.

Daft, R. L. 1978. A Dual-Core Model of Organizational Innovation. *The Academy of Management Journal*, 21(2): 193–210.

Damanpour, F. 1991. Organizational Innovation: A Meta-Analysis of Effects of Determinants and Moderators. *The Academy of Management Journal*, 34(3): 555–590.

Damanpour, F. 1996. Organizational Complexity and Innovation: Developing and Testing Multiple Contingency Models. *Management Science*, 42(5): 693–716.

Downs, G. J., & L. Mohr. 1976. Conceptual Issues in the Study of Innovation. *Administrative Science Quarterly*, 21(4): 700–714.

Economic Summit Report. Center for Regional Economic Competitiveness. Accessed April 29, 2008 <http://www.workforcesolutionstexoma.com/html/news.html> (no longer available).

Education Consortium in Durant. KXII–TV. Accessed June 5, 2017 at: <http://www.kxii.com/home/headlines/19867919.html>.

Goes, J. B., & S. H. Park. 1997. Interorganizational Links and Innovation: The Case of Hospital Services. *The Academy of Management Journal*, 40(3): 673–696.

Golden, O. 1990. Innovation in Public Sector Human Service Programs: The Implications of Innovation by Groping Along. *Journal of Policy Analysis and Management*, 9(2): 219–248.

Goldsmith, S., & W. Eggers. 2004. *Governing By Network: The New Shape of the Public Sector*. Washington, DC: The Brookings Institution.

Groff, T., & T. Jones. 2003. *Introduction to Knowledge Management*. Amsterdam: Butterworth Heineman.

Hannah, S. B. 1995. The Correlates of Innovation: Lessons from Best Practice. *Public Productivity & Management Review*, 19(2): 216–228.

Hardy, C., N. Phillips & T. Lawrence. 2003. Resources, knowledge and influence: The organizational effects of interorganizational collaboration. *Journal of Management Studies*, 40(2): 321–347.

Issacs, W. 1993. Taking Flight: Dialogue, Collective Thinking, and Organizational Learning. *Organizational Dynamics*, 22(2): 24–39.

Keast, R., M. Mandell, K. Brown & G. Woolcock. 2004. Network Structures: Working Differently and Changing Expectations. *Public Administration Review*, 64(3): 363–371.

Kettl, D. 1996. Governing at the Millennium. Pp. 5–18 in J. L. Perry (ed.), *Handbook of Public Administration*. San Francisco, CA: Jossey-Bass.

Kettl, D. F. 2002. *The Transformation of Governance: Public Administration for Twenty-First Century America*. Baltimore, MD: The Johns Hopkins University Press.

Kickert, W., E.-H. Klijn & J. Koppenjan. 1997. Introduction: A Management Perspective on Policy Networks. In *Managing Complex Networks: Strategies for the Public Sector*, 1–11. Thousand Oaks, CA: Sage Publications Inc.

Klein, K. J., & J. Sorra. 1996. The Challenge of Innovation Implementation. *The Academy of Management Review*, 21(4): 1055–1080.

Light, P. 1998. *Sustaining Innovation: Creating Nonprofit and Government Organizations That Innovate Naturally*. San Francisco, CA: Jossey-Bass Inc.

Manning, K., & B. Rhoden. 2008. Interviewed by J. T. Bland, B. Bruk, D. Kim, K. Lee & M. McGuire, 2002. Managing Networks: Propositions on What Managers Do and Why They Do it. *Public Administration Review*, 62(5): 599–609.

Moch, M., & E. Morse. 1977. Size, Centralization and Organizational Adoption of Innovation. *American Sociological Review*, 42(5): 716–725.

Mohr, L. B. 1969. Determinants of Innovation in Organizations. *The American Political Science Review*, 63(1): 111–126.

Osborne, S. P., & K. Brown. 2005. *Managing Change and Innovation in Public Service Organizations*. New York: Routledge.

Osterlund, C., & P. Carlile. 2005. Relations in Practice: Sorting Through Practice Theories on Knowledge Sharing in Complex Organizations. *The Information Society*, 21(2): 91–107.

O'Toole, L. 1997a. The Implications of Democracy in a Networked Bureaucratic World. *Journal of Public Administration Research and Theory*, 7(3): 443–459.

O'Toole, L. 1997b. Treating Networks Seriously: Practical and Research Based Agendas in Public Adminstration. *Public Administration Review*, 57(1): 45–52.

O'Toole, L., & K. Meier. 2004. Desperately Seeking Selznick: Cooptation and the Dark Side of Public Management in Networks. *Public Administration Review*, 64(6): 681–693.

Pattakos, A., & E. Dundon. 2003. Innovation in Government: Oxymoron or Core Competency? *Canadian Government Executive*, 10(3): 14–16.

Perkin, E., & J. Court. 2005. Networks and Policy Processes in International Development: a literature review. London: Overseas Development Institute.

Pierce, J. L., & A. L. Delbecq. 1977. Organization Structure, Individual Attitudes and Innovation. *The Academy of Management Review*, 2(1): 27–37.

Poole, K. 2007. Burying the Axe & Fording the River: A Tale of Regional Economic Cooperation. *Texas Business Review* (February): 1–6.

Powell, W., K. Koput & L. Smith-Doerr. 1996. Interorganizational collaboration and the locus of innovation: Networks of learning in biotechnology. *Administrative Science Quarterly*, 41(1): 116–145.

Provan, K. G., & P. Kenis. 2008. Modes of Network Governance. *The Jounral of Public Administration Research and Theory*, 18(2): 229–252.

Robertson, M., H. Scarbrough & J. Swan. 2007. Knowledge, networking and innovation: Developing the process perspective. *Working Paper*.

Shepard, H. A. 1967. Innovation-Resisting and Innovation-Producing Organizations. *The Journal of Business*, 40(4): 470–477.

"Strategic Action Plan." Southern Workforce Board. Accessed June 5, 2017 at: <http://www.swb-ok.com>.

Swan, J., & H. Scarbrough. 2005. The Politics of Networked Innovation. *Human Relations*, 58(7): 913–943.

Thompson, V. A. 1965. Bureaucracy and Innovation. *Administrative Science Quarterly*, 10(1): 1–20.

Thomson, A., & J. Perry. 2006. Collaboration Processes: Inside the Black Box. *Public Administration Review* 66(s1): 20–32.

Tornatzky, L., & K. Klein. 1982. Innovation Characteristics and Innovation Adoption-Implementation: A Meta-analysis of Findings. *IEEE Trans > Engineering Management*, 29: 28–45.

Van de Ven, A. H. 1986. Central Problems in the Management of Innovation. *Management Science*, 32(5): 590–607.

Van de Ven, A. H., & S. P. Marshall. 1990. Methods for Studying Innovation Development in the Minnesota Innovation Research Program. *Organization Science*, 1(3): 313–335.

Van de Ven, A. H., & H. Angle. 2000. An Introduction to the Minnesota Innovation Research Program. In *Research on the Management of Innovation: The Minnesota Studies*: 3–31. New York: Oxford University Press.

Weber, E., & A. Khademian. 2008. Wicked Problems, Knowledge Challenges, and Collaborative Capacity Builders in Network Settings. *Public Administration Review*, 68(2): 334–349.

Weiss, E. S., R. M. Anderson & R. D. Lasker. 2002. Making the Most of Collaboration: Exploring the Relationship Between Partnership Synergy and Partnership Functioning. *Health Education & Behavior*, 29(6): 683–698.

Zaltman, G., R. Duncan & J. Holbeck. 1973. *Innovation and Organizations*. New York: Wiley.

MARY ANN ALLISON

10   Criteria for Developing Mediated Urban
       Nervous Systems: A Complex Adaptive
       Systems Perspective[1]

ABSTRACT

As communication technology becomes increasingly sophisticated and hierarchical power diminishes in Western society, there is a concomitant increase in the complexity of public and private collective behavior and in the information and communication needed to support healthy cities. This chapter uses complexity theory to set forth a framework for mediated urban nervous systems which facilitate shared understanding and collaboration at all system levels in urban areas.

Introduction

There is a growing body of scholarship that enhances the understanding of communication in urban environments (Burd, Drucker, and Gumpert, 2007; Castells, 1996; Horrigan, 2001; Jeffres, 2003; Sassen, 2002; Sassen et al., 2007). The Urban Communication Foundation (Gumpert and Drucker, 2007) calls attention to the challenges to cities as healthy entities because cities face serious challenges from a number of internal and external sources.

This theoretical chapter brings together concepts and research from media ecology, complex systems theory, sociology, cybernetics, and human–computer interface design to propose an approach to monitoring and improving city health using feedback and feedforward mechanisms which

1   *The Innovation Journal: The Public Sector Innovation Journal*, 17(3), 2012, article 2
      <http://www.innovation.cc/francais/vol17-no3f.htm>.

simultaneously support management by government authorities, civil leaders, interventions by community groups, and the efforts of *bottom-up* emergent peer groups.

Systems researchers (Allison, 2005; Bar-Yam, 1997; Kauffman, 1993; Luhmann, 1989; Mainzer, 1996) argue that human groups – including cities – are living complex adaptive social systems. Thus, the literature on the complex adaptive systems (CAS) and evolution of emergent systems can be used as a framework to support urban communication systems which promote the health of a city as a whole as well as the residents and groups within and connected to it. It is both possible and desirable to consciously build elements of a city's mediated communication and information nervous system taking into account these characteristics, while simultaneously recognizing, connecting with, and amplifying elements which arise *unofficially*. The primary aim of this chapter is to put forward this framework and to illuminate some of the implications. To instantiate the possibilities, a review of a few examples of information and communication technologies (ICT) which facilitate intelligence in urban groups follows.

Context: Cities Change in Punctuated Equilibrium

As low-cost, easily portable ICT becomes simultaneously increasingly sophisticated, networked, and widely distributed, there are many important changes (Allison, 2005; Bar-Yam, n.d.a, b; boyd, 2006, 2008; Giddens, 2000; Laszlo, 1996, 2000; Levy, 1997, 1998, 2001) in the ways in which human groups – including cities – are organized.

In a multiple-cause and multiple-effect relationship characteristic of complex adaptive systems (CAS), there are, of course, other significant triggers of changes taking place in cities – as well as the larger social systems in which they are nested, such as nation states, and the smaller social systems nested inside them, such as neighborhoods. The development and diffusion of high-speed computing and graphic design, improvements in medicine, and developments in transportation contribute to the rapid increase in knowledge and ideas; communication, travel, and immigration; global commerce – all of which stress the traditional bureaucratic structure and formal processes of traditional city organization and governance.

Societies – and the groups within them – show increased complexity in a pattern of punctuated equilibrium – rapid bursts of change followed by periods of relative stability. Eldredge, Alcosser and Gould (1991) first described this pattern which they found in the fossil records of biological species. Additional studies (Allison, 2005; Bar-Yam, n.d.a; Laszlo, 1996) show that punctuated equilibrium theory is a useful explanatory model for the pattern of changes in human social systems.

Humans are now in a major transition point in human social systems – comparable to the rise of bureaucracy, manufacturing, and cities in Western society some 300 years ago. The challenges that cities face today, highlighted by the Urban Communication Foundation, are a part of this punctuation point. Affected by dramatically increased information and communication, higher structural complexity in an interconnected world, and increased flexibility and creativity at all systems levels, traditional city structures and process are reaching critical points of instability and will – along with the structures and processes within other levels of human social systems – move to the edge of chaos and then re-form in ways that will remain in comparative equilibrium until the next punctuation point.

One of the significant structural changes taking place now (Allison, 2005; Bar-Yam, n.d.a) is the reduction of authority and top-down hierarchical power. Alexander Dawoody (2011) describes the developing transformation of the traditional citizen or, in this case, urban resident, into a *global participant-observer.* Increasingly there is evidence of the power of global participant observers using widely disseminated, networked ICT to force transparency and accountability. This change is taking place not only in Tunisia and Egypt (Smith, 2011) but also – with less violence but no less persistence – in North American cities. Chicago, Seattle, and San Francisco (Montalbano, 2010) are among the latest cities to open city data sets to the public.

In addition, Saskia Sassen draws attention to the fact that "the capabilities for global operation, coordination, and control contained in the new information technologies ... *need to be produced*" (italics added; Sassen,

2001:). If cities cannot rely only on top-down authority to accomplish this production, how are they to proceed? As hierarchical power diminishes, there is a concomitant increase in the complexity of public and private collective behavior.

Those cities that are able to adapt rapidly to this change in structure and process internally (as a node in a global network) will be healthier and more successful. It is important, therefore, to understand the nature and criteria for physical and digital urban spaces which facilitate cooperation, productive emergence and civic collaboration.

It is not only the internal organization of cities – with the new emphasis on the flocking mechanisms of cooperation, emergence, and civic collaboration – that is changing as a result of the current punctuation. The importance of city-to-city flows is increasing. Now, in addition to connecting generally with their peers, healthy communicative cities connect with specific partners, developing expertise and strength. Healthy cities recognize specialized relationships and build on family ties; flows of commercial, political, and artistic information; travel and immigration patterns; and, of course, established commercial ties. The expertise arising from the deep structure of these flows is significant. Returning to Sassen, "focusing on cities allows us to specify *a geography of strategic places at a global scale, places bound to each other* ..." (italics added; Sassen, 2001:1).

Periods of Comparative Equilibrium in Recent Social Evolution: *Gemeinschaft, Gesellschaft, Gecyberschaft*

In his seminal work, *Community and Society* – in the original German, *Gemeinschaft und Gesellschaft* – Ferdinand Tönnies (1996) created names for two distinctive periods in the punctuated equilibrium of Western society. Tönnies' *Gemeinschaft* corresponds with the time when villages were the dominant form of social organization and agriculture was the primary form of production. Tönnies' *Gesellschaft* is defined by the emergence of bureaucracies, cities, and manufacturing. To honor Tönnies, the currently emerging period of dynamic stability has been named *Gecyberschaft* – ge-cyber-schaft, an American word modeled on the earlier German terms (Allison, 2005). The *Gecyberschaft* period is characterized by flexible groups of purpose, information and service industries, and the primacy of relationships. Co-evolving with the increasing complexity of their environments, *Gecyberschaft* cities will feature innovative forms of organization; increased structural complexity and flexibility; and – because they use information more effectively – will have greater autonomy than cities in earlier times.

Framework: The City as a Living, Complex Adaptive System

By categorizing cities as living complex adaptive systems (Luhmann, 1989), city leaders, urban planners, and residents gain access to the robust literature in complexity (Aldrich and Ruef, 2006; Bar-Yam, 2005; Goldstein, 2008; Goldstein et al., 2010, Glor, 2008; among many others).

Drawing on complexity theory and earlier work in social systems (Allison, 1997, 2005), the following framework was developed for use in understanding and enhancing cities and their communicative capabilities. There are thirteen characteristics of CAS which are particularly useful when examining human groups organized in cities. These characteristics are listed below in ascending order of system level and are followed by a brief description of the consequences for cities. Note that the characteristics which pertain to the lower levels of systems also characterize the higher levels, but the reverse is not the case.

There are four salient characteristics at the level of *physical systems*:

(1) *open*: Because city boundaries are permeable, cities take in and give out matter, energy, residents, and visitors, and, of special significance here, information and communication.
(2) *dynamic and non-linear*: The city, as an entity, as well as the systemic properties of the city as a whole, change over time. Forecasting accurately at this level of complexity is difficult; scenario-planning is more likely to be effective.

(3) *nested*: Cities are composed of smaller systems such as neighborhoods, church congregations, business organizations, and NGOs, each of which has unique identities and system properties. Cities are included in larger systems such as nation-states and federations. These larger systems also have unique characteristics.

(4) *dissipating and emergent*: Cities use (dissipate) energy in order to maintain themselves as a city. This applies to both emergent and more consciously directed elements.

Three complex adaptive system characteristics which are significant in urban areas emerge with the rise of *biological systems*:

(1) *irreversible*: In cities, history matters. Past structures, processes, and events (real and imagined) are essential components of a city's present and future organization.

(2) *cognitive*: Here the word cognition is used as Maturana and Varela (1980) and Capra (1996) define it. By perceiving certain changes in the environment and adjusting structurally, a *cognitive* plant grows toward sunlight. No *conscious* learning is required. In a process termed structural coupling, an organism's structure results in part from what it has perceived in the environment. Its structure is coupled to – but not determined by – the environment. Similarly, cities respond to changes in the environment whether or not directed to do so by the mayor or city council.

(3) *autopoetic and self-referential*: Each city is a unique system, with a beginning and an end in time as well as in space. Cities are self-bounded (they do not necessarily respect legal boundaries), self-generated (although they may be governed; the government does not create the city), and self-perpetuating (cities maintain themselves unless there are catastrophic changes).

Both enabling and constraining cities, three organizational capacities arise at the level of *human social systems:*

(1) *symbolic and language*: Human cities could not exist without human use of symbols and language.

(2) *technological*: In addition to language, technologies – both processes and physical technology – are essential to cities.

(3) *autonomous with regard to meaning/purpose:* People and groups generate meaning and purpose internally. Humans choose when and how to cohere. Authority does not insure cohesion. Even less can it mandate cooperation or emergent organization.

The pace of social evolution is not uniform. As cities move fully into the *Gecyberschaft* age, urban residents are able to change consciously many of the city's systemic parameters. *Gecyberschaft* groups, including cities, can develop this capacity. Particularly important in this context are the following three system characteristics:

(1) *far from the physical*: Healthy cities in the *Gecyberschaft* era are less dependent on starting conditions, especially physical conditions. ICT flows rise in importance, subsuming flows of matter and energy, as do human flows of residents and visitors.

(2) *continuously realigned*: Increased flexibility and higher levels of organization enable conscious coordination of meaning-making and alignment of purposes at multiple, nested system levels. Groups of purpose (transient groups formed around a specific purpose) in, for example, neighborhoods, businesses, peer cities and at nation-state level form shifting alliances as changing meanings and related purposes are negotiated. This might be pictured as multiple flocks shifting in tune with the environment and changing human purposes in a complex dance.

(3) *capable of consciously mediated reorganization*: For the first time, with education and intention, cities can become capable of conscious social evolution which includes both structural reorganization and coordination with emergent organization. There are early examples (Allison, 2006; Denning, 2006; Huston, 2006) where groups show the capacity to consciously select from social forms of organization characteristic of the current and earlier ages. For example, a group could choose *Gesellschaft* bureaucratic structure and process to achieve certain objectives, such as financial control; *Gemeinschaft village friends and family* norms for other objectives, such as developing trust and the close relationships which enrich lives; and *Gecyberschaft groups of purpose* and

hastily formed networks (HFNs) for still a third type of situation in which the environment is complex and rapidly changing and which requires voluntary collaboration, for example, when responding to earthquakes.

Vannevar Bush accurately predicted in *As We May Think* (1945) that individual human capacities could be greatly extended by the *memory extender* (*memex* is the name he used for what is now a combination of personal computers and the Internet). Taking into account the characteristics of cities as living complex adaptive systems with the capacity for continuous realignment and consciously mediated reorganization, it is posited that the capabilities of living cities can be significantly enhanced by the conscious development of mediated urban nervous systems, connecting, and supporting all of their many parts.

Selected Considerations in Developing Urban Nervous Systems

During development, it is important to conceptualize and to work at several levels simultaneously. As with any living system, work first in areas where there is interest and support, while, at the same time, building and linking to the fundamental capacities and bearing in mind the longer-term goals of group intelligence. Each urban system will evolve in response to its unique environment.

The Basics: Cybernetics, Feedback, and Feedforward

In developing the field of cybernetics, Norbert Wiener was among the first to point out the importance of structure in understanding and predicting the performance of a system, writing that "Cybernetics takes the view that the structure of the machine or of the organism is an index of the performance that may be expected from it" (Weiner, 1954: 57).

The importance of the structure of the system's means of perception is especially important. If an entity does not perceive something internally or in its environment, it cannot react or respond to it. Groups that have no structure in place to support balloting cannot function as democracies. In a time when there is no single central authority, cities that do not develop robust means of perception, feedback, and response which can be easily used by leaders, residents, and visitors who gather in bureaucracies but also in flocks, schools, and swarms will be handicapped.

In addition to drawing on the environment for the matter/energy used to maintain its existence as an entity, human communities interact with their environments – changing and being changed by them. Cyberneticists, information theorists and systems thinkers (Bateson and Bateson, 2000; Bednarz, 1988; Shannon and Weaver, 1999; Von Bertalanffy, 1976; Wiener, 1954) have illuminated the importance of information and the ways in which systems receive, structure, and use their perceptions of the environment. As Wiener notes, "Information is a name for the content of what is exchanged with the outer world as we adjust to it, and make our adjustments felt upon it" (Weiner, 1954: 17). Thus, when examining the interaction of cities and their environments, it is important to attend to a city's ability to:

- sense and model information from the environment (Bednarz, 1988; Shannon and Weaver, 1999; Richardson, 1984);
- respond to information about the system's environment (Beniger, 1986; Humphrey, 1992; Searle, 1984);
- get feedback on the results of its actions (Von Bertalanffy, 1976; Wiener, 1954); and
- evaluate alternative actions, learn, and generate meaning and purpose (Bednarz, 1988, 1990; Luhmann, 1989; Searle, 1984; Senge, 1990; Scharmer, 2007).

In addition to feedback mechanisms, *feedforward* procedures enable systems to respond to a specified change in the environment or in the system itself in a pre-determined way. This capacity assists groups to maintain stability or to respond quickly to anticipated but infrequent events. Both feedback and feedforward capabilities are important factors in group effectiveness.

More than the Basics: Supporting Cooperation and Group Intelligence

The Institute for the Future (IFF) (Saveri, Rheingold, and Vian, 2005; Saveri, Vian, Cascio, Kollock, Michalski, and Rheingold, 2007 a, b) has conducted several broad studies of the characteristics which support the emergence of cooperation and participation in human groups. In addition to independently confirming that tracking feedback loops and instituting feedforward mechanisms which highlight important thresholds support system or group intelligence, IFF studies (Saveri et al., 2005: 28–29) suggest that a series of specific sensing abilities are critical to the formation of emergent group intelligence. These include the ability to identify key thresholds for achieving *phase* shifts in behavior when shifting goals, processes, or organizational structure is desirable; methods of supporting transparent identities for those seeking to participate in urban activities; and techniques for converting present knowledge into deep memory and universally accessible memory.

In short, it is important for cities to provide for residents and visitors a *mediated nervous system* which – through near real-time reporting of the status of incoming and outgoing flows, the activities of internal bureaucracies and more fluid groups of purpose, feedback concerning the effectiveness of the city's activities, and protective feedforward trigger points – facilitates fluid co-evolution with the changing environment. The hypothesis is that this mediated nervous system will be a *sine qua non* for healthy, successful cities in *gecyberschaft*.

Salient Implications for Mediated Urban Nervous Systems

In this section, the thirteen characteristics of living complex adaptive social systems are revisited, this time extending the implications beyond cities as a generic classification to the implications for cities and urban areas with the goal of developing effective mediated nervous systems.

At the level of *physical systems*:

(1) *open*: It will be difficult to block communication, whether or not desired at the city level, sensing and filtering information is important so that key messages are visible.

(2) *dynamic and non-linear*: The systematic sensing and reporting of key systemic characteristics is of fundamental importance.

(3) *nested*: Systematic sensing and reporting of key characteristics at multiple levels with correlations (agreement and divergence) are important. Transparent and accessible identity and membership traits facilitate participation. Organization and individual identity should be *knowable*, searchable, and visible (with some individual control).

(4) *dissipating and emergent*: The resources required to support pattern sensing as well as act on the information received are key. Cities should establish common resources whenever possible.

At the level of *biological systems*:

(1) *irreversible*: Individuals and groups must take negative, as well as positive, history into account. Building on positive history – information flows and human connections already in place and Sassen's (2008) deep knowledge, as examples – is likely to facilitate urban health. Cities should enable persistent memory in all systems.

(2) *cognitive*: Cities are not able to divorce themselves from the environment and so must sense and work with their surroundings. City intelligence should sense and plan for strengths and weaknesses. Feedback and feedforward mechanisms are essential.

(3) *autopoetic and self-referential*: Urban groups should understand any homeostatic processes already in place and add to them. Intelligence systems should be able to sense emerging boundaries. Groups must choose formal boundaries carefully.

At the level of *human social systems*:

(1) *symbolic and language*: Urban groups should attend to symbols and languages in use and those needed. Education is a key resource. Monitoring systems should sense changes in use of symbols and language.
(2) *technological*: Communicative cities will attend to both process and physical technology development, as well as physical and digital divides.
(3) *autonomous* with regard to meaning/purpose: Individual and group identity and transparency is very important. Transparent methods of social accounting will facilitate cooperation and purpose sharing.

At the level of *gecyberschaft* groups:

(1) *far from the physical*: It is often easier to attend to the physical or to measure those elements such as financial data which lend themselves to reporting. Tracking and reporting on areas that are more difficult to measure but key to a balanced picture will provide a more complete urban nervous system. City leaders should consciously extend processes developed for the digital world to the physical world and vice versa.
(2) *continuously realigned*: Healthy cities set up systems and platforms for easy participation, open economy, and distributed authority/decision-making. In addition, they enable coordination and cooperation at all levels. Communicative mediated intelligence systems sense and report on peer-to-peer production.
(3) *capable of consciously mediated reorganization*: The most effective urban intelligence systems sense and report on thresholds, phase shifts, and transition points (identifying and searching for trigger points is essential to success in this area).

The salient characteristics of living complex adaptive systems, along with the concomitant consequences for cities and selected implications for communicative cities, are summarized in Table 10.1.

Table 10.1: Characteristics of Living Complex Adaptive Cities with Salient
Implications for Healthy Cities

Characteristic	*Consequences for Cities*	*Selected Implications for Healthy Cities*
Level 1: Physical Systems		
1. Open	City boundaries are permeable (open to matter/energy and information).	• Difficult to block communication, whether or not desired • At city level, sensing and filtering important
2. Dynamic and non-linear	The city and the systemic properties of the city both change over time.	• Systematic sensing and reporting of key characteristics important
3. Nested	Composed of smaller systems (e.g. neighborhoods) with unique properties; included in larger systems (e.g. nation-states) with unique properties.	• Systematic sensing and reporting of key characteristics at multiple levels with correlations (agreement and divergence) important • Identity and membership facilitate participation: "knowable," searchable, visible (some individual control)
4. Dissipating and emergent	Emerging directed and undirected systemic patterns draw on internal or external matter/energy and information; cities require energy.	• Resources required to support pattern sensing as well as act on the information received • Establish common resources whenever possible
Level 2: Biological Systems		
5. Irreversible	History matters; the past is an essential component of city present and future organization.	• Take negative history into account • Build on positive history (flows already in place; Sassen's deep knowledge) • Enable persistent memory

Characteristic	Consequences for Cities	Selected Implications for Healthy Cities
6. Cognitive	Cities respond to changes in the environment with and without conscious human intervention. Cities are structurally coupled with their environment.	• Cannot divorce the environment and so must sense and work with • Sense and plan for strengths and weaknesses • Feedback and feedforward essential
7. Autopoetic and self-referential	Cities are unique systems with a beginning and an end (in time). Cities are self-bounded, self-generated, and self-perpetuating. Homeostatic processes help to absorb change.	• Understand homeostatic processes already in place; add to them • Observe emerging boundaries; choose formal boundaries carefully
Level 3: Human Social Systems		
8. Symbolic and languaged	Human use of symbols and language is essential to cities.	• Attend to symbols and languages in use and those needed • Insure education • Sense changes in others' use of symbols and language
9. Technological	Technologies – both process and physical – are essential to cities.	• Attend to both process and physical technology development • Attend to physical and digital divides
10. Autonomous with regard to meaning/ purpose	People and groups generate meaning and purpose internally. Humans choose when and how to cohere.	• Individual and group identity and transparency important • Transparent methods of social accounting facilitate cooperation and purpose sharing

Characteristic	Consequences for Cities	Selected Implications for Healthy Cities
Level 4: Gecyberschaft Groups		
11. Far from the physical	Cities are less constrained by their initial starting conditions, especially physical circumstances, than they were in the past.	• Communication flows are critical to urban health • Extend processes developed for the digital world to the physical world and vice versa
12. Continuously realigned	Conscious autonomy, meaning-making, and alignment of purposes resides at multiple, nested systems levels (e.g. individual, neighborhood, businesses, city, nation-state, global federations).	• Set up systems and platforms for easy participation, open economy, and distributed authority/decision-making • Enable coordination and cooperation at all levels • Sense and report on peer-to-peer production
13. Consciously mediated reorganization	With education, cities are capable of conscious evolution including structural reorganization and adaption to changing purposes.	• Sensing and reporting on thresholds, phase shifts, and transition points (trigger points key)

Source: the author

Theory in Action

While it outside the scope of this chapter to address the practical implementation of these models, as part of the conclusion it is important to review a few instances of urban ICT. There are many examples of government-directed or NGO-led top-down but generally inclusive ICT efforts, including as examples, those cities winning the Intelligent Community Forum's (n.d.) annual awards which rate (1) broadband infrastructure, (2) knowledge workforce, (3) innovation,

(4) digital inclusion, and (5) marketing of the many cities using a balanced scorecard approach (Allison, 2008; Arveson, 2003; Kaplan and Norton, 1992) which takes into account multiple indicators of success.

ICT which facilitates urban collaboration, feedback, and feedforward is less well documented. Table 10.2 lists a few examples to instantiate some of the possibilities.

Table 10.2: Examples of Collaboration, Feedback, and Feedforward in ICT

Project Name/ url	Overview	Characteristics
Big Box Evaluator <http://www. bigboxevaluator.org/ about-big-box.php> (no longer available)	• Enables residents of an area to consider the implications of big box retail stores, especially their effect on the economy, environment, and character of the local communities	• Foundation-sponsored • Scenario-planning • Leading indicators • Feedforward
DataSF <http://www.datasf.org/>	• Enables anyone to search the datasets available from the City and County of San Francisco	• Foundation-sponsored • Access to data • Promotes innovative app development • Feedback • Potential for feedforward
Gapminder – Urbanization <http://www. gapminder.org/videos/ gapmindervideos/ gapcast-2-urbanization/> Gapminder – World <http://www.gapminder. org/tools/#_locale_ id=en;&chart-type=bubbles>	• Easy to understand, compelling data visualization • Clear pictures, some extrapolation of leading indicators • Presents UNDP Millennium typical correlations: education, GDP, life expectancy	• Foundation-sponsored • Traditional information with excellent visual correlations • Lagging indicators • Feedback

Project Name/ url	Overview	Characteristics
Participatory Chinatown <http://www.participatorychinatown.org/>	• Social virtual world • Single or multiple players • Avatars complete a task in one of several choices of roles, then comment on community-planning	• Foundation- and university-sponsored • Feedback and feedforward
Interobang <http://playinterrobang.com/> (no longer available)	• Students (grades 6–12) complete real-world missions to win prizes • Game combining virtual and "real world" activities	• Foundation- and big business-sponsored • Local and global • Community- and service-focused • Teaches collaboration and problem-solving
Ten by Ten <http://www.tenbyten.org/10x10.html> (no longer available)	• Automated feedback based on weighted linguistic analysis of RSS feeds of top stories from Reuters World News, BBC World Edition, New York Times International • Automated selection of the top 100 words with corresponding images	• Art, programming, and research centre • Lagging indicators, indicating attention • Feedback • Feedforward indicators could be added

Source: the author

Conclusion

This chapter presents a framework for thinking about urban ICT based on the idea that cities are living complex adaptive systems. In addition, it is argued that it is important for cities to foster the development of mediated nervous systems. Such systems may provide government authorities, civil leaders, community groups, residents, and visitors with the results of traditional ICT as well as collaborative, feedback, and feedforward mechanisms, fostering an ability to adapt to highly complex, rapidly changing environments.

Notes

(1) *Groups of purpose* (Allison, 2005) are not related to kin-ties, geography, or bureaucracy. They often arise in electronically mediated communication. *Hastily formed networks* (Denning, 2006; Huston, 2006) are multi-organization groups that come together to create coordinated action in unforeseen crises or opportunities.

(2) The author wishes to express her thanks to the Urban Communication Foundation for supporting research in the field of urban communication.

Bibliography

Aldrich, H., & M. Ruef. 2006. *Organizations Evolving.* 2nd Edn. Thousand Oaks, CA: Sage.

Allison, M. A. 1997. The Power of Changes in Communications: Human Groups as Complex Adaptive Systems. Paper delivered at the annual conference of the New York State Communications Association, September 19–21, Monticello, NY.

Allison, M. A. 2005. "Gecyberschaft: A Theoretical Model for the Analysis of Emerging Electronic Communities." *Dissertation Abstracts International,* 65 (11A), 4366 (UMI No. 3155725).

Allison, M. A. 2006. Hastily Formed Networks and Groups of Purpose. *Reflections,* 7(2). Cambridge, MA: The Society for Organizational Learning.

Allison, M. A. 2008. Measuring Urban Communication: Frameworks and Methods for Developing the Criteria for The Urban Communication Foundation Communicative City Award. *The International Communication Gazette,* 70(3–4): 275–289.

Arveson, P. 2003. "A Balanced Scorecard for City & County Services." Balanced Scorecard Institute. Accessed March 1, 2011 at <http://www.balancedscorecard.org/> (no longer available).

Bar-Yam, Y. n.d.a. Complexity Rising: From Human Beings to Human Civilization, A Complexity Profile. Accessed June 9, 2017 at <http://necsi.org/projects/yaneer/Civilization.html>.

Bar-Yam, Y. n.d.b. Significant Points in The Study of Complex Systems. Accessed June 9, 2017 at <http://necsi.org/projects/yaneer/points.html>.

Bar-Yam, Y. 1997. *Dynamics of Complex Systems*. Reading, MA: Addison-Wesley.

Bar-Yam, Y. 2005. *Making Things Work: Solving Complex Problems in a Complex World*. Brookline, MA: Knowledge Press.

Bateson, G., & M. Bateson. 2000. *Steps to an Ecology of Mind: Collected Essays in Anthropology, Psychiatry, Evolution, and Epistemology*. Chicago, IL: University of Chicago Press.

Bednarz, J. 1988. Information and Meaning: Philosophical Remarks on Some Cybernetic Concepts. *Humankybernetik* Band 29-Heft 1 (Copy provided by the author).

Bednarz, J. 1990. System and Time: The Function of Time in Meaning-Constituting Systems. *Kybernetes*. 19(4): 35–45. (Copy provided by the author.)

Beniger, J. 1986. *The Control Revolution: Technological and Economic Origins of the Information Society*. Cambridge, MA: Harvard University Press.

boyd, d. 2006. Friends, Friendsters, And Top 8: Writing Community into Being on Social Network Sites. *First Monday*, 11–12 (December).

boyd, d. 2008. *Taken out of Context*. Ph.D. Dissertation. University of California, Berkeley, CA. Accessed June 9, 2017 at <http://www.danah.org/papers/>.

Burd, G., S. Drucker & G. Gumpert (eds). 2007. *The Urban Communication Reader*. Cresskill, NJ: Hampton Press.

Bush, V. 1945. As We May Think. *Atlantic Monthly*, July. Accessed June 21, 2017 at <http://www.theatlantic.com/doc/194507/bush>.

Capra, F. 1996. *The Web of Life: A New Scientific Understanding of Living Systems*. New York: Anchor Books.

Castells, M. 1996. *The Information Age: Economy, Society, and Culture: Vol. 1: The Rise of the Network Society*. Oxford: Blackwell Publishers.

Dawoody, A. R. 2011. The Global Participant-Observer: Emergence, Challenges and Opportunities. *The Innovation Journal: The Public Sector Innovation Journal*, 16(1), article 9 <http://www.innovation.cc/volumes-issues/vol16-no1.htm>.

Denning, P. J. 2006. Hastily Formed Networks: Collaboration in the Absence of Authority. *Reflections*, 7(2). Cambridge, MA: The Society for Organizational Learning.

Eldredge, N., M. Alcosser & S. Gould. 1991. *Fossils: The Evolution and Extinction of Species*. New York: Harry N. Abrams.

Giddens, A. 2000. *Runaway World: How Globalization is Reshaping our Lives*. New York: Routledge.

Glor, E. 2008. Toward Development of a Substantive Theory of Public Sector Organizational Innovation. *The Innovation Journal: The Public Sector Innovation Journal*, 13(3), article 6 <http://www.innovation.cc/volumes-issues/vol13-no3.htm>.

Goldstein, J. 2008. Introduction to Complexity Science Applied to Innovation – Theory Meets Practice. *The Innovation Journal: The Public Sector Innovation Journal*, 13(3), article 1 <http://www.innovation.cc/volumes-issues/vol13-no3.htm>.

Goldstein, J., J. Hazy & B. Lichtenstein. 2010. *Complexity and the Nexus of Leadership: Leveraging Nonlinear Science to Create Ecologies of Innovation*. New York: Macmillan.

Gumpert, G., & S. Drucker. 2007. *Urban Communication: Proliferating Worldviews in the Urban Landscape*. National Communication Association call for papers. Accessed September 28, 2007 at <http://64.112.226.77/one/nca/nca07/index.php?click_key=1&cmd=Multi+Search+View+Program+Load+Box+To+View&program_box_id=30574&PHPSESSID=9329df707ab10806ce01516c3890obof> (no longer available).

Horrigan, J. B. 2001. *Cities Online: Urban Development and the Internet*. Washington, DC: Pew Internet & American Life Project. Accessed August 5, 2007 at: <http://www.pewinternet.org/pdfs/PIP_Cities_Online_Report.pdf> (no longer available).

Humphrey, N. 1992. *A History of the Mind*. New York: Simon & Schuster.

Huston, T. 2006. Enabling Adaptability and Innovation through Hastily Formed Networks. *Reflections*, 7(2) 9–22. Cambridge, MA: The Society for Organizational Learning.

Intelligent Community Forum. n.d. *Intelligent Community of the Year, 2010*. Accessed June 30, 2017 at <http://www.intelligentcommunity.org/>.

Jeffres, L. 2003. *Urban Communication Systems: Neighbourhoods and the Search for Community*. Cresskill, NJ: Hampton Press.

Kaplan, R., & D. Norton. 1992. The Balanced Scorecard: Measures That Drive Performance. *Harvard Business Review*, January–February (71–80).

Kauffman, S. 1993. *Origins of Order: Self-Organization and Selection in Evolution*. New York: Oxford University Press.

Laszlo, E. 1996. *Evolution: The General Theory*. Cresskill, NJ: Hampton Press.

Laszlo, E. 2000. *Macroshift 2001–2010: Creating the Future in the Early 21st Century*. Lincoln, NB: iUniverse.com, Ind.

Lévy, P. 1997. *Collective Intelligence: Mankind's Emerging World in Cyberspace*, trans. R. Bononno. New York: Plenum Trade.

Lévy, P. 1998. *Becoming Virtual: Reality in the Digital Age*, trans. R. Bononno. New York: Plenum Trade.

Lévy, P. 2001. *Cyberculture*, trans. R. Bononno. Minneapolis: University of Minnesota Press.

Luhmann, N. 1989. *Ecological Communication*, trans. J. Bednarz. Chicago, IL: The University of Chicago Press.

Mainzer, K. 1996. *Thinking in Complexity: The Complex Dynamics of Matter, Mind, and Mankind*. Berlin, Germany: Springer-Verlag.

Maturana, H. R., & F. J. Varela. 1980. *Autopoiesis and Cognition: The Realization of The Living*. Boston, MA: D. Reidel Publishing.

Montalbano, E. 2010. San Francisco Mayor Proposes Data Transparency Law; Gavin Newsom's Datasf.Org Online Repository Has Spurred Developers to Build More Than 50 New Applications Providing Online Services for City Residents. *InformationWeek*, October 28. Accessed June 9, 2017 at <http://www.informationweek.com/applications/san-francisco-mayor-proposes-data-transparency-law/d/d-id/1093720?>.

Richardson, J. (ed.) 1984. *Models of Reality: Shaping Thoughts and Action*. Mount Airy, MD: UNESCO, Lomond Books.

Sassen, S. 2001. The Global City: Strategic Site/New Frontier. *Seminar 503: GLOBALIZATION: A symposium on the challenges of closer global integration*. Accessed September 6, 2007 at <http://www.india-seminar.com/2001/503/ 503%20 saskia%20sassen.htm> (no longer available).

Sassen, S. 2008. *Territory, Authority, Rights: From Medieval to Global Assemblage*. Princeton, NJ: Princeton University Press.

Sassen, S. (ed.). 2002. *Global Networks, Linked Cities*. Oxford: Routledge.

Sassen, S., L. De Cauter, M. Dehaene & J. Urry. 2007. *Power: Producing the Contemporary City*, ed. Berlage Institute. Rotterdam, the Netherlands: Ai Publishers.

Saveri, A., H. Rheingold & K. Vian. 2005. *Technologies of Cooperation*. Palo Alto, CA: Institute for the Future (SR–897).

Saveri, A., K. Vian, J. Cascio, P. Kollock, J. Michalski & H. Rheingold. 2007a. *Ten-year Forecast: Culture: Digital Native, Civic Spaces*. Palo Alto, CA: Institute for the Future (SR–1064).

Saveri, A., K. Vian, J. Cascio, P. Kollock, J. Michalski & H. Rheingold. 2007b. *Ten-year Forecast: Methodology: The Open Economy Toolkit*. Palo Alto, CA: Institute for the Future (SR-1064).

Scharmer, C. O. 2007. *Theory U: Leading from the Future as it Emerges*. Cambridge, MA: The Society for Organizational Learning.

Searle, J. 1984. *Minds, Brains and Science*. Cambridge, MA: Harvard University Press.

Senge, P. 1990. *The Fifth Discipline: The Art & Practice of the Learning Organization*. New York: Doubleday.

Shannon, C., & W. Weaver. 1999. *The Mathematical Theory of Communication*. Champaign, IL: University of Illinois Press.

Smith, C. 2011. Egypt's Facebook Revolution: Wael Ghonim Thanks the Social Network. *The Huffington Post*. Accessed June 9, 2017 at <http://www.huffingtonpost.com/2011/02/11/egypt-facebook-revolution-wael-ghonim_n_822078.html>.

Tönnies, F. 1996. *Community and Society*, trans. C. Loomis. New Brunswick, NJ: Transaction Publishers.

Von Bertalanffy, L. 1976. *General System Theory: Foundations, Development, Applications*. New York: George Braziller.

Wiener, N. 1954. *The Human Use of Human Beings: Cybernetics and Society*. New York: Da Capo (Plenum Publishing).

MIE PLOTNIKOF

11 Negotiating Collaborative Governance Designs: A Discursive Approach[1]

ABSTRACT

This chapter addresses the design and implementation issues of collaborative governance, a public management practice aimed at involving stakeholders in problem-solving and public innovation. Although aspects of, for example, stakeholder inclusion and power are conceptualized in the literature, these issues remain challenging in practice. Therefore, the interest in understanding the emerging processes of collaborative governance is growing. This chapter contributes to theorizing discursive aspects of such processes by conceptualizing and exploring the meaning negotiations through which collaborative governance designs emerge and change. The findings of a case study of local governments' efforts to innovate quality management in education through collaborative governance suggest that such form of governance is continually negotiated in communication during both design and implementation phases. Through the meaning negotiations of local designs, discursive tensions and resistance generate changes in the organizing. The chapter shows that a discursive approach offers concepts valuable for refining the understanding of the emergence of collaborative governance in practice, and proposes approaching this process as organizing accomplished through and complicated by endemic meaning negotiations and change.

Introduction

The need to deal with complex problems in contemporary society has given rise to a growing interest in collaboration across the public, private, and nonprofit sectors (Ferlie, Hartley, and Martin, 2003; Osborne, 2006; Christensen and Lægreid, 2011). As such, collaborative governance

---

1   *The Innovation Journal: The Public Sector Innovation Journal*, 20(3), 2015, article 2.

initiatives emerge in public organizations with the aim of involving stakeholders in co-creating solutions for problems related to issues of policy and
service innovation (Ansell and Gash, 2008; Sørensen and Torfing, 2013).
The assumption is that inter-organizational collaboration can co-create
public value and innovation through:

> [A]n emergent process – one driven more by a concern about solving certain common
> problems than by a desire to respond to narrowly conceived incentives. This emer-
> gent process of bringing together parties to identify opportunities for public value
> creation leads to strong demands for a kind of "simultaneous engineering" [...] as a
> process of collaborative design. (Ansell and Torfing, 2014: 10)

However, in addition to its potential, the literature highlights considerable challenges of multi-actor interactions and interests. These issues are
addressed in conceptual and practice-based models as design and implementation issues in terms of, for example, stakeholder inclusion, decision-
making processes, power relations, and trust-building (Vangen, Hayes, and
Cornforth, 2014).

As such, social interaction within and between collaborations is
stressed as the potential source of both success and failure owing to actors'
idea generation and value creation, but also interest conflicts, and goal
confusion (Bryson et al., 2012). For instance, various actors concerned
with healthcare issues, such as nurses, doctors, politicians, and patient
organizations, may have different definitions of a shared problem. Through
collaboration, they engage in dialogue that may broaden their understandings of both the problem and its possible solutions. However, this may also
cause misunderstandings, frustration, and ineffective work. Despite efforts
to theorize such aspects in terms of design and implementation issues, the
practices to organize this form of governance remain tricky accomplishments (Huxham, Vangen, and Eden, 2000; Vangen and Huxham, 2011).
Thus, a growing interest in understanding the emerging processes of collaborative governance designs and their socially dynamic and open-ended
generative mechanisms is stressed (Ansell and Torfing, 2014: 3; Bryson et
al., 2012: 24). This makes communicative interactions and discourse critical
aspects to consider in relation to design and implementation in collaborative
governance theory and practice (Purdy, 2012). However the conceptualizing

of such is under-developed and their significance to understanding the organizing of this form of governance remain unexplored in greater detail.

In light of this, the chapter contributes with theorizing and unfolding communication and discursive aspects of the emerging processes of collaborative governance designs with the aim of understanding such accomplishments more detailed. In so doing, it draws on organizational discourse studies of inter-organizational collaboration and change, although these are not particularly concerned with public organizations (Hardy, Lawrence, and Grant, 2005; Thomas, Sargent, and Hardy, 2011). These offer useful concepts of communication and meaning negotiations, with which the chapter explores how collaborative governance designs emerge, are organized and change. The findings are based on an ethnographic case study of two local governments' collaborative governance practices in an effort to innovate quality-management methods for public daycare services in Denmark. Here daycare is a central welfare area, as up to 97 per cent of all children up to six years old are enrolled in daycare services. As such, these both ensure the gender equality in the labor force and serve as part of the overall Scandinavian education model (Plum, 2012).

This study shows that collaborative governance emerges through complex communicative processes of meaning negotiations, in which discursive resources and tensions of resistance are produced and generate change – both during processes of designing and implementing "final" designs. This proposes to approach the issues of collaborative governance designs as ongoing processes of organizing rather than clearly demarcated processes of "design" and "implementation." The findings demonstrate how managers and others negotiate the local design of collaborative governance through multiple communication modes such as meetings, minutes, posters, emails, and booklets, through which managers include or exclude collaborative stakeholders. Furthermore, the study shows the ways in which collaborative governance designs are negotiated during implementation also. In these negotiations across actors, time, and space, tensions of competing public management discourses generate power-resistance relations that affect the process. Thereby the chapter adds to the literature on collaborative governance by offering useful concepts for theorizing and unpacking issues of design and implementation, as they are negotiated in practice, which strengthen our understanding of the processes involved in enabling particular collaborative governance designs.

The structure of the chapter is as follows. I first address the literature on design and implementation issues in collaborative governance. I then present concepts from extant discourse studies on inter-organizational collaboration and change through meaning negotiations. Subsequently, I describe the empirical case, methods, and analyses, and then present the findings. I discuss the contributions and implications for theory and practice in the conclusion section.

Design and Implementation Issues in Collaborative Governance

Although variations appear, a recognized definition of collaborative governance is that it comprises various forms of networks and partnerships that gather actors from across "government/public agencies alongside private and not-for-profit stakeholders in the collective crafting and implementation of public policy" (Vangen, Hayes, and Cornforth, 2014: 1240). As such, it is often contrasted to more hierarchical organizing and forms of control associated with traditional public administration and new public management (NPM) and instead seen as part of a more flexible form of new public governance (NPG) (Ansell and Torfing, 2014; Ferlie, Hartley, and Martin, 2003; Osborne, 2006), which is developing currently due to: "the growing complexity of pertinent public issues and a high degree of interdependence among stakeholders' interests" (Choi and Robertson, 2014: 224). The potential of bringing various stakeholders together is that their diversity and interdependence may contribute to public value and innovation. However, this may also lead to conflicting interests, goal confusion, and power struggles. Consequently, social interactions within and across collaborations are stressed as potential sources of both success and failure (Huxham, Vangen, and Eden, 2000; Ansell and Gash, 2008; Purdy, 2012). The literature thus conceptualizes key design and implementation issues critical to enhance collaborative governance theory and practice.

One stream of studies makes such effort by combining theoretical concepts of new public governance, innovation, and design (Ansell and Torfing, 2014; Ansel and Gash, 2008; Hartley, Sørensen, and Torfing, 2013). Thereby a link between collaborative governance and public innovation is explained through three generative mechanisms, which are: synergies of multi-actor processes, learning through collaborative communication, and the commitment to building consensus. As such, these mechanisms are stressing the potentials of the social interactions in this form of governance, and they are taken to emerge through and form collaborative design processes encompassing problem/future orientations in the invention of new solutions, heuristic devices to co-create and explore tangible ideas, and interactive arenas that include all relevant actors (Ansell and Torfing, 2014: 11–12). Thereby the emergence of collaborative governance is conceptualized in terms of generative mechanisms and design components. In so doing, the significance of open-ended and socially dynamic aspects of collaboration are highlighted, however their theorizing and complications are not unfolded in greater detail.

Another recent literature review of more than 250 studies of various forms of collaborative governance and public participation offers a set of design guidelines (Bryson et al., 2012). This study unfolds design and implementation issues such as aligning designs with local problems, involving stakeholders, managing power relations and social dynamics. The guidelines are built into a cycle of design and redesign, as opposed to a step-by-step template; the authors stress it as an: "ongoing, active process of *designing* (*verb*), which is typically iterative and involves testing various ideas and prototypes before settling on the 'final' design (a noun)" (Bryson et al., 2012: 24). This latter study accumulates insights from multiple studies to enhance the link between theory of design and implementation issues and practice. Although, they offer instrumental guidelines, they also stress the significance of the ongoing social interactions affecting the designing and implementing.

In addition, another stream of studies also discuss the design and implementation issues identified in the literature on collaborative governance and, more generally, on inter-organizational collaboration (Vangen, Hayes, and Cornforth, 2014). They outline the following critical issues: the degree of stakeholder inclusion, collective decision-making, power relations, trust-building, the distribution of public resources, policy-oriented goals, public leadership, and accountability. These issues are viewed as marking crucial choices that affect the tricky multi-actor processes of collaboration, therefore, for success. This is because it is through the interaction amongst actors within and in between collaborations that idea generation and co-creation, as well as interest conflicts and goal confusion emerge and affect the design, implementation, and outcomes (Vangen and Huxham, 2011; Vangen and Winchester, 2013). This stream of literature argues for the significance of design choices in relation to socially dynamic tensions and power relations between actors and organizations from different settings and hierarchical structures. Nonetheless, the ways in which discursive powers and resistance are produced and negotiated between actors and affect the designing of collaborative governance are underexplored (Purdy, 2012).

As such, the literature is developing concepts to enhance the theory and practice of collaborative governance with regard to the socially dynamic and open-ended aspects of design and implementation, as it is acknowledged that such issues remain tricky accomplishments in practice (Huxham, Vangen, and Eden, 2000). However, the social interactions and communication through which this form of governance is emerging in daily, even mundane practices are under-theorized, although they are considered critical constituents to the accomplishment of collaborative governance.

Taking a Discursive Approach: Exploring Meaning Negotiations

In this regard, this chapter unfolds a discursive approach to study the communicative processes through which particular collaborative governance designs gets organized through everyday interactions. I argue that this is valuable for strengthening the understanding of the emerging processes and issues constitutive to collaborative governance design and implementation.

The interest in discourse within collaborative governance literature has mainly been concerned with how new public governance discourses of, for example, public participation, collaboration, and innovation "bears down" and affect local public policy and management (Skelcher, Mathur, and Smith, 2005; Newman et al., 2004). Such studies argue that "discourses of innovation [...] do not merely describe pre-existing practices, but bring them into being, 'ordering' contingent elements into relational systems of meaning" (Griggs and Sullivan, 2014: 21). Another study covers "three rule-giving discourses [and] provides a deeper understanding of the forces shaping the design of the new collaborative institutions" (Skelcher, Mathur, and Smith, 2005: 580). These studies identify macro discourses as constitutive forces behind general types of collaborative partnerships in, for example, U.K. national policies. However, they say little about the emergence of collaborative processes in the everyday practices involved in designing and implementing such.

In addition to these studies, the discursive theorizing of inter-organizational collaboration is developing, although not specifically in relation to public organizations (Hardy, Lawrence, and Grant, 2005; Koschmann, Kuhn, and Pharrer, 2012). Along with other discourse studies on organizational change (Thomas, Sargent, and Hardy, 2011; Grant and Marshak, 2011), these studies offer concepts to approach collaborative communication, meaning negotiations and resistance – issues that are key to refining the understanding of collaborative governance as it emerges in particular local designs. In such studies discourse is defined as a set of correlating texts and associated practices of producing, distributing, and consuming those texts, which altogether brings organizational ideas and objects into being (Hardy, Lawrence, and Grant, 2005: 61). Such texts may both take the form of writing, speech acts, non-verbal communication, *and* visuals, and symbols, and thus constitute the communicative interactions and conversations of the involved actors as they engage in collaborations. This definition is intriguing, as it advocates turning toward the discursive and material practices through which texts are interrelated in various communicative actions and events across time and space, and thereby shape the organizing processes of particular designs. Two related concepts are relevant to such a study: text-conversation dialectics and meaning negotiation.

Two studies, in particular, focus on inter-organizational collaboration in terms of a text-conversation dialectic (Hardy, Lawrence, and Grant, 2005; Koschmann, Kuhn, and Pharrer, 2012). Despite certain differences, both studies conceptualize this dialectic as constitutive of inter-organizational collaboration through the ways in which discourse, as a set of interrelated texts, is (re-)produced and/or changed through participants' conversations and other discursive practices that affect the formation of collaborative processes and events across time and space. Hardy, Lawrence, and Grant (2005) conceptualize this dynamic in relation to effective collaboration and a collective identity. They argue that effective collaboration is produced discursively through two entangled stages. The first stage entails the communication of a collective identity to the actors involved, while the second involves communication regarding the ways in which the collective identity can be translated into innovation through other discursive practices, depending on different styles of speech and discursive tensions. Koschmann, Kuhn, and Pharrer (2012) develop a model demonstrating the constitutive nature of the text-conversation dialectic in collaborative processes of value creation, which they argue depends on the production of a collective agency across collaborative members. Both studies highlight the complex, ongoing emergence of collaboration through text-conversation dialectics. This entails a nuanced understanding of dialogue as not necessarily consensus-driven, but as characterized by meaning negotiations producing discursive tensions between multiple, possibly conflicting views and positions related to the issues at hand.

Related discourse studies concerned with organizational change expand this point by conceptualizing change as multi-story processes that emerge in ongoing meaning negotiations producing discursive tensions and power-resistance relations (Thomas, Sargent, and Hardy, 2011; Grant and Marshak, 2011). The meanings of a change program, such as a collaborative governance initiative, are negotiated through interactions among actors that in so doing use and produce relevant texts. Meaning negotiations are both active resources in and effects of text-conversation dialectics, by which discursive tensions are produced between the positions and interests made relevant. In turn, these tensions produce further negotiations and through these communicative processes normative directions for change and collaborative outcomes are constructed. These studies thus stress that meaning negotiations are infused with power-resistance relations, although not necessarily in a repressive way, rather in a co-productive, generative way, as suggested by Foucault (1980: 142). This implies that some actors may be in a privileged position (e.g. managers) to negotiate meanings with other actors, but that does not mean that they necessarily set the collaborative direction – rather this study argues that in organizational changes of, for example, a collaborative design initiative struggles over meanings are to be expected:

> Such struggles are not necessarily negative or repressive, however, because there is always a creative potential to power-resistance relations as meanings are reordered and renegotiated – power-resistance relationships are thus enabling as well as restraining. (Thomas, Sargent, and Hardy, 2011: 24)

Following this, analyzing collaborative processes by the concepts of text-conversation and meaning negotiations therefore also entails following such struggles over meaning, including their creative potential. Such concepts are useful, then, not only to examine how collaboration becomes effective or change, but also to explore the communication through which particular collaborative governance designs emerge, are negotiated, and change. They direct the analysis to follow the design and implementation processes as they are communicated in diverse modes such as documents, meetings, emails, prototypes, etc. to unpack when certain meanings are fixed or changed, how ideas and decisions are made, and how the organizing of certain designs are interacted and accomplished. This suggests exploring emergence through communicative processes of meaning negotiations, including the discursive tensions and power-resistance relations that may generate designs of such form of governance.

Research Methods: Data Collection and Analysis

The present chapter is based on a qualitative case study of two local governments' efforts to develop quality-management methods in daycare services through collaborative governance. In Denmark child daycare is governed by national law and handled by local public departments. Each local department consists of a head along with managerial consultants, whom I will refer to as public managers, as they have the public managerial responsibility. A department encompasses a number of daycare centers in which daycare managers and professional teachers work with children. Daycare departments are accountable to a division head and a political committee for the quality of service provided by the daycare centers. Since 2004 a range of quality-management methods, including educational plans and quality inspections, have been introduced. Such practices are widely debated among professionals, managers, politicians, and researchers (Plum, 2012). Some view these methods as meaningless forms of control and useless paperwork that limit the teachers' time with the children, require translation into a more managerial format by the daycare departments, which is taken to provide little useful information for policy-makers.

In continuation of a public-sector reform in 2007, two local daycare departments and the Danish Union of Early Childhood and Youth Educators established a partnership to innovate new quality-management methods that incorporate stakeholders' perspectives on daycare quality. From 2010 to 2013, these two departments developed collaborative governance designs through meetings, laboratory workshops, and conferences concerning existing and new quality-management methods, as well as their likely potential and challenges. Some work involved several stakeholder groups, such as public managers, daycare managers, professionals, children and parents, politicians, and union representatives. Other activities involved only specific groups.

In 2012, politicians in both municipalities decided to develop collaborative governance designs as new quality-management methods. Moreover, in 2013 and 2014, the management teams were made responsible for designing and implementing collaborative governance events, which were called "daycare marketplaces." During the designing both small-scale events with few stakeholders and large-scale events for all stakeholders were organized. At the marketplace events, daycare managers and teachers discussed the quality of their work with other stakeholders, including other daycare staff, politicians, parents, and public managers, instead of accounting for it in written reports that are revised by public managers and presented to politicians. Accordingly, new quality accounts emerged in videos, pictures, narratives, and dialogues in workshops and meetings.

I conducted varying forms of fieldwork from 2010 to 2014. In some periods, I undertook ethnographic participant observations at city halls and daycare centers following the idea-generation and design phases of collaborative governance. This involved shadowing participants during and in between collaboration, engaging with and interviewing participants, plus gathering documents and other objects that emerged as significant to the designing. Methodologically, this data collection combined discursive approaches and organizational ethnography (Fairhurst and Grant, 2010; Grant and Marshak, 2011; Ybema et al., 2009), and aimed at producing rich data of everyday interaction as well as communication across time and space. The data-set resulted in audio and video recordings, field notes, actors' reflection notes, emails, visuals (e.g. participant-driven images, photos, and posters), reports, and organizational charts. The fieldwork focused on the meanings and matters that were explicitly negotiated between actors, as well as implicit elements and enactments that might not have been intentional but that nonetheless affected the work.

The analysis began with a construction of a timeline in order create overview of what happened when, with whom, and through which interactions (Hardy and Thomas, 2014). While in the field, I had noted times at which "new" quality-management methods was an explicit topic and when collaborative designs and implementation was in question. Therefore, I also highlighted data related to idea generation and design. I then reviewed all data to ensure that I had included significant data sources that might not have been noticed otherwise. My final dataset included six laboratory workshops, four formal collaborative governance events (including daycare marketplaces), sixteen design and management team meetings, six daycare meetings on quality management, and twelve single/group interviews with public managers (division heads, department heads, and consultants) and daycare managers. Data sources include field notes, audio and video recordings, organizational charts, website information, photos, a partnership article for a national magazine and partnership newsletters, meeting minutes, posters, and booklets.

In the analysis, I searched for text-conversation dialectics and meaning negotiations to study the emerging processes of collaborative governance. To do so, I undertook multiple analytical iterations to construct and qualify patterns (James, 2012). From the iterative analyses two clusters became evident: one on designing, the other on implementing. The first encompassed text-conversation dialectics and meaning negotiations related to idea-generation, to problems of existing quality-management methods and potentials of new collaborative methods and their design. This part of the analysis primarily draws on data from 2010–2012, as design was an explicit topic at that time. The other cluster concerning the implementation of a final design of the daycare marketplace primarily draws on data from 2013–2014. This comprise of interactions negotiating issues of implementation such as the purpose and legitimacy of the design, as well as its accomplishments. In both parts the communication related to issues such as trust versus control, top-bottom dynamics and collaboration versus hierarchy invoked discursive tensions that either explicitly related to NPM and NPG discourse, or that echoed issues, which the literature diagnose in relation to these public management discourses (Ferlie, Hartley, and Martin, 2003; Ansell and Torfing, 2014).

Findings

The findings are presented in two sections exploring how collaborative governance design and implementation processes emerged through various communication and meaning negotiations. The first focuses on how actors negotiated meanings of possible solutions to their problems of quality management in daycare, as well as how the design of collaborative governance emerged as a solution in meetings, text production, and managerial decisions. This elucidates the communication of ideas and decisions to solve quality management problems associated with control by designing collaborative governance events. In this case, managers sometimes included stakeholders in the idea generation and designing, while at other times they excluded them. The second section shows the ways in which a "final" collaborative governance design was legitimized and accomplished through discursive practices of booklets, articles, invites, meetings, and collaboration. This elucidates the various communication involved in implementing the design, however, it also shows that even during implementation, the design of collaborative governance remained subject to meaning negotiations, which affected and changed its organizing continuingly. During both design and implementation discursive resources created tensions and resistance that sometimes enabled the emergence of collaborative governance, sometimes restrained it. The examples provided are used because they elucidate the emerging processes of design and implementation, while unfolding their interrelations and socially dynamic complexity.

Negotiating the Emerging Collaborative Governance
Designs: Bringing Ideas to Life

In the following I look into communications in which ideas for addressing problems of quality management were negotiated and how this affected the development of specific collaborative governance designs. The problems of existing quality-management methods were described as meaningless control rather than useful information about quality, for example, in quality reports called education plans. As such, negotiations regarding what counted as meaningful became central to designing collaborative governance as a possible mean for innovating new quality-management methods.

The local governments addressed the problems of quality-management methods and ideas for potential solutions through meetings, workshops, conferences, and manager-written documents (e.g. meeting minutes and booklets), including interactions between public managers, politicians, daycare staff, and daycare union representatives. At a management meeting early in the partnership (2010), a department head explained the problems of existing methods to a consultant who just started that:

> I am working as an economist and I am annoyed with the quality measurements we are using. I have been in situations where we measure things that do not make sense.

For example, the education plans – they can be meaningless ... We need to be very critical, I think, when we start new things.

The department head described existing quality measurements and quality accounting as meaningless, and in this statement his position as an economist became a resource to strengthen this argument that downplayed the use of measurements to manage quality in a meaningful way. The point that their idea-generation in relation to new methods needed to consider the purpose of methods became defining for the emerging process as the "meaning" was negotiated throughout the design phase. For example at an inter-organizational conference (2011), the idea of establishing collaborative governance as a new, more meaningful quality-management method was discussed, after daycare staff presented daycare quality from their educational perspective – and not in written reports. That presentation included pictures and videos from daycare life. In the audience were politicians, public managers, and union representatives, who then discussed collaboration as possible a solution to their problems:

> Union representative: Does what we have seen here explain the education professionalism in a way that helps you reconsider your quality-management methods?
> Division head: I have a dream [laughter] Well, I don't think I need to say more, because there is major potential for collaboration to result in a common language that includes the public managers, the politicians, and the daycare staff. That includes communication among staff, children, and parents in a way that ... When sitting in the council chamber as a politician and deciding on something that affects other stakeholders, you know the consequences and you are informed by other information sources than a budget alone ... It is not easy, especially because finances are lacking, but I have a dream!
> Department head: I still really like quality management, I need a job tomorrow, right? [laughter]. No I think such form of governing is important, the question is how? I don't want education plans to be for the sake of public managers or politicians ... I am much more interested in finding methods that create value for the people that it is all about – and that is not me. I just need to know that what is going on in daycare reflects educational knowledge. In reality I think that all of us just want to know that daycare is offering children a good life.

At this conference actors negotiated the meanings of ideas for new methods that could be considered more meaningful than existing ones related to control, measurements, and budgeting. The division head stressed collaboration and common language as potential methods for qualifying political decision-making by adding educational insights relevant to budgeting. By referring to the idea of collaboration and common language as a "dream" he both stressed it as positive solution and as challenging to accomplish due to lacking resources. The department head altered the understanding of quality management as necessarily being problematic by using humor. In so doing he legitimized some sort of quality management, without directly agreeing but neither rejecting the idea of collaboration and common language as the solution. Instead he contrasted the meaning of quality management from being for the sake of policy-makers and managers to creating value for stakeholders, and most importantly assuring the good life of children. Thereby he shifted the focus to the purpose of the method, rather than deciding on specific methods. In this conversation the problem–solution negotiation was nuanced, as the department head resisted echoing the problem as "quality management" per se, and thereby the discussion of new methods shifted focus from being an issue of managerial control to one of creating public value. In effect, the meaning of new quality-management methods became to create value and reflect knowledge, but how was not settled yet.

In both municipalities, the meaning of new methods were negotiated in relation to purpose, with the result that focus was shifted from control to value and insights in children's life. Thus, laboratory workshops were organized to generate and discuss ideas for new quality-management methods, and between such the management teams summarized ideas in meeting minutes, which were then discussed at managerial meeting. During the managerial meeting the managers designed a workshop to explicitly explore "meaningful" knowledge concerning daycare quality from the different stakeholders' perspective and thereby generate ideas for new working methods (2012). The department head welcomed with the statement:

> At our last meeting, we focused on what politicians want to know about how children benefit from being in daycare and how they might use that knowledge in policy making. We also discussed what daycare teachers and managers want to present to politicians. That gave rise to a few themes that we sent out as background material for the meeting today. I concluded last time by stressing that we need to move away

from the laboratory to tangible experiments on accounting dialogically for children's benefits from daycare in a meaningful way. How can we organize large-scale dialogues that include the political committee, public managers, daycare managers, teachers in the municipality, and others who are involved in this work? What we need to do today is to generate ideas ... to begin moving from discussions toward developing tangible models of what can be meaningful. We won't make a decision today. Rather, the ideas generated today will be followed up by formal decision-making procedures, both administratively and politically.

In this extract, the department head framed the idea-generation of new methods in two ways; he linked the idea-generation of tangible methods to stakeholders' view on what knowledge about children's daycare life can be useful for in political work, and he stressed the decision about these methods were to be made separately. This framing invited actors to participate in generating method and design ideas and pushed the need to become tangible in terms of organizing, however, it clearly demarcated that influence was limited to this matter. In the following workshop, three groups brainstormed on ideas, which they then presented to the other groups on posters. The management team revised those presentations and posters in meetings and minutes afterwards, by which they concluded that four tangible ideas concerned different forms of collaborative governance, including recurring ideas for a daycare marketplace with different design issues associated.

As such, collaborative governance emerged as a solution to problems of quality management through these interrelated communications. Along the way some parts of the designs were explicitly negotiated between actors, and at other times, meanings were fixated through textual practices summarized by managers. In an email, the managerial consultant later (October 2012) described that:

It has been politically decided that in the future we are to design collaborative governance (instead of written quality reports) to evaluate the quality of daycare in a more dialogue-based, narrative manner. This is a shift from public managers' translation of quality to politicians toward letting teachers and managers discuss the benefits of daycare with politicians, parents, public managers, children, and colleagues. We will work with the design from this point on and until the implementation of daycare marketplace next summer.

For this matter a design team including both public managers and daycare managers collaborated, and the meeting minutes and posters from earlier workshops were used to fixate what could be negotiated and what could not. The following discussion took place at such a meeting (2013):

Public manager: I have hung up these posters with ideas for collaborative governance designs because we now have to come up with concepts for how to bring them to life. We have to return to these posters with ideas for the daycare marketplace and the knowledge needs of stakeholders ... We have looked at them a couple of times, but this is just to remind us about the ideas for developing the design. There were different ideas for collaborative governance events – a children policy day, a daycare fair, the life of children in daycare, and a marketplace. That is what we need to work with now ... We have discussed the name and decided the "daycare marketplace" is a quality-management community that should be designed as a structured process aimed at evaluating education planning. We have a guide that helps daycare staff to summarize results and quality, which might be used for presentations at the marketplace, right? In that guide, the children's voice is also stressed in terms of accounting for the senses of seeing, feeling, tasting, and listening. You were part of developing that – can you say more about it?

Daycare manager A: Yeah, it was not to only having the quality accounting be in written form but to also be able to evaluate through dialogue and to use the senses. This is because politicians say: "Well, this is affecting me. This is making me curious, making me think more about daycare ... that is, when children are documented in narratives, via photos or in other ways."

Daycare manager A: Yes. I remember one of the politicians bringing a booklet from one of our daycare excursions to a political meeting – he thought that was quality too. So, we need to remember that such things are a good starting point for talking about quality.

Daycare manager B: I agree because sometimes I fear that this will be the same kind of control, just in a different way.

Public manager: Yes, we must be careful, right? That's why we need other methods, right?

Daycare manager B: Yeah exactly, because when we are talking, I'm thinking they still want it in writing.

Public manager: No, it doesn't say that anywhere, but you need to summarize and conclude on the quality – you can do that on tape.

Daycare manager A: That is exactly what you can do.

Daycare manager C: Or you can videotape the children and then analyze it.

Public manager: Yeah.

> Daycare manager C: We can develop quality-management methods through IT ... technological advancements, like iPads and videos, etc. right?
>
> Public manager: Yeah, if you start developing your quality accounting in that way that's great to use in a daycare marketplace.

In the design meetings, documents were used to steer the process and as such they created the discursive space for maneuvering; as the conversation shows, the name and design was negotiable, but the concept of a marketplace was not in question, however its purpose as a collaborative governance event of quality management was. During the meetings the public manager held a privileged position insofar as she could refer to texts, for example, posters that legitimized certain design ideas and choices, while rejecting others. For example she summarized their definition of this form of collaborative governance as a structured evaluation community concerned with education plans, and stressed its purpose as more meaningful due to its ability to communicate quality by addressing the "senses" in relation to demonstrating the results of children's time in daycare. This point was backed up by a manager, who argued for its positive effects on politicians. However, it was also challenged by another daycare manager, who questioned whether the daycare marketplace – despite its collaborative mode –could still become a controlling quality-management method.

The negotiations affected the designing in two ways: the meaning of control was linked to writing which thus became negative and thus not something to be demanded for the daycare marketplace – as this was to be designed as more meaningful than earlier methods, although the manager stressed a demand to summarize and conclude. The other effect was that a negotiation of methods to communicate quality through other modes than writing was generated which led to a design that included multimedia presentations during the marketplaces. As such, the daycare manager challenged the conversation by questioning the differences between earlier quality-management methods and the potential of collaborative governance to form more meaningful methods. But her resistance was not destructive; rather it generated a nuanced dialogue on how the new design might avoid becoming a form of control, and how quality might be presented in ways other than written reports. This leads to design ideas about videotaping children and analyzing the video footage. After this meeting the public manager decided that multi-media should be used to support the collaborations of marketplace. But she also stressed a need to ensure that a constructive but critical discussion about quality was enabled during the marketplace in order for it to be evaluative and not just "a sunshine story to promote one's daycare center." Thus a design issue also became to prepare and enable daycare staff to deal with constructive criticisms possibly emerging during the dialogues with other stakeholders. Therefore, the public managers decided that the design needed to include external facilitators to support the collaborations and respectful critique, while also pushing for critical discussion and reflection.

Through different communicative practices actors negotiated meanings of quality-management methods and how they could design collaborative governance events related to different purposes. They discussed how collaborative governance, as a solution, could be designed as a more meaningful quality-management method than existing ones. Various discursive resources were used such as education plans, quality measurements, law, posters with ideas and meeting minutes, through which discursive tensions were constructed in terms of control and measurements versus dialogue and collaboration associated to competing ideals of NPM and NPG. As such, the collaborative governance ideas and designs emerged through complex, interrelated interactions between both human and non-human actors, as meanings were negotiated, nuanced, and retained. Along the way power-resistance relations appeared between diverging meanings, which generated both challenges and nuances in the communication that became constitutive to the emerging processes of collaborative governance. However, as the public managers were the ones concluding and writing minutes, their positions were defining; they decided to negotiate meanings of ideas for collaborative governance with other actors when it was useful, but they also used their privileged position to steer and make certain conclusions on their own.

Negotiating the Implementation of a "Final" Design:
Accomplishing the Marketplace

As shown above, a final design of the marketplace had been developed through meaning negotiations to become a solution to quality-management methods related to written reports and control. However, as this section unfolds, the design was negotiated and changed throughout its implementation too – both in relation to what its purpose was and in relation to how the organizing of collaboration became accomplished at certain daycare marketplaces. First, I briefly elucidate the negotiations of purpose in relation to legitimizing the implementation of a final design of marketplaces, and then I unpack the communicative practices that became critical to accomplishing the collaborative organizing of daycare market-places during 2013 and 2014.

Even during the implementation, the management teams struggled to legitimize the collaborative governance design of daycare marketplace. They experienced concurrent demands to still use quality-management methods associated with NPM, and they still negotiated the design, although they were already implementing it. This was addressed at network meetings between the management teams:

> Public manager A: This marketplace is a collaborative method of evaluating education plans, and until now I have steered the design enough to say it's about evaluating the education plans and not about promoting the daycare sector as a political agenda. It is about educational quality right? I don't know if I can maintain this design all the way. Because the department head really wants to show things off to the politicians. And I'm actually now using [the written reports] by turning it around and saying: "well that's in the quality report," so it might suddenly become an asset.
> Public manager B: Well that's great for you!
> Public manager A: I wrote this report that I was so frustrated, but now I can say: "Well, you can read it there."

At such meeting the managers discussed diverging meanings of the purpose of quality management and their effects on implementing collaborative gov-ernance events as a new working method. The manager explained that she had steered the design of the marketplace in order for it to be implemented as collaboration about education quality rather than political agendas, but that she was struggling with the department head, who was trying to change the design towards a political agenda, although they had started its implementation. However, she resisted this by turning attention to the written forms of quality-management methods associated with control, which she had been frustrated with doing, and argued that the political agenda was accounted for there. During this meeting and at other meetings, the public managers referred to an article to legitimize the implementation of a certain design of the daycare marketplace, instead of changing it to include political agendas and more writing. The article was written by the two local governments and published in a national public-management magazine in the spring of 2013. It stressed that:

> In many municipalities, surveys, tests, measurements, and quality accounting take up a lot of time among teachers and other frontline workers. But with all the paperwork aimed at managing quality, the management agenda has become a challenge. [W]hat if the actors instead began to collaborate on new, more meaningful – and effective – methods of governing and developing local services like daycare? And what if public governance could build on trust rather than control?

By referring to the article the managers created discursive tensions of diverging meanings of written reports and collaboration, and in doing so they produced resources to resist efforts to change the implementation of certain designs, they had developed. In this way the article was used when the final designs of daycare marketplaces became questioned during implementation, and as such it became a discursive resource to legitimize implementing a certain design and thereby shifting away from practices of control that were often associated with NPM.

The final marketplace design was presented in various documents and in the invitation sent to stakeholders, including daycare staff, parents, union representatives, politicians, and public managers from various welfare services related to daycare. The invite used photos of children, text, and images of the location to explain the organizing of two collaborative processes: booths in which daycare staff were presenting and discussing their work on education plans with attendees, and workshops in which they evaluated their educational practices to support children's development and learning in dialogue and reflection with attending stakeholders. At such a daycare marketplace in 2014 attended by around 400 stakeholders, a daycare center, for example, presented their work with the natural sciences in such a booth. The staff used various materials from nature (e.g. leaves, branches), technology (e.g. computers), visuals (e.g. videos, pictures), and writing (e.g. booklets) to engage in inter-organizational dialogues with attendees. The computer showed videos of day-trips to the woods, and the booth was built from natural materials, including wooden sticks and plants. The posters contained pictures of animals and the accompanying text describing them. The booths materialized the design as spaces for collaborative dialogues, in which the materials became discursive resources concerning quality. A politician opened the marketplace by saying:

> This daycare marketplace is a replacement of the yearly quality reports sent to us politicians. Previously, every daycare center was required to write a quality report evaluating their work with education plans. That report was sent to the administration, and summarized and presented for the committee. This daycare marketplace gives us an opportunity to see with our own eyes, to enter into a dialogue, and to hear you talk about what is happening in the daycare centers. It is considerably more interesting for us to experience it this way. It is great to see the support for this event. Furthermore, I think this is a unique possibility for the daycare staff to share knowledge and inspire each other ... We also have a lot of parents here – and although I cannot distinguish the various stakeholder groups from each other, I hope you are all well represented! I think that this daycare marketplace ... shows that daycare is much more than nursing and looking after kids. It is so much more substantial, as there is so much focus on learning and development, which is great to see. Thank you for that!

In her statement, she stressed the significance of experiencing daycare quality rather than reading about it. Her contrast of the design to written reports indicated it was a more meaningful quality-management method as it offered "a more interesting experience" and knowledge sharing between stakeholders. These strengths of the design were associated with the social interactions of stakeholders, but, as such, they also indicated the weaknesses; the accomplishment of the design depended on and changed through negotiations in both the booths and the workshops.

The workshops were designed to assure an in-depth presentation of educational quality by daycare staff which was then to frame dialogues between attendees. Prior to the events all attendees had signed up for specific workshops, so the management teams could assure that all stakeholder-groups were parts of the collaborations in workshops. Managerial facilitators also attended in case the dialogues needed to be framed or steered. However, in some of the workshops, the interactions of the attendees became defining for the collaborations. For example one workshop became more of an interrogation, because an attendee insisted on asking critical questions throughout the session while another was changed from being a PowerPoint presentation and collaboration facilitated through questions and answers to a collective motor skill exercise.

At the latter workshop the daycare staff, three teachers and a manager, presented their education plans and practices with children by means of a PowerPoint presentation and a video, which showed a motor-skill program developed with a group of children. The teachers talked about developmental theories and learning goals that were the basis of their efforts. They also handed out a questionnaire with attention points which attendees could reflect upon and discuss during the workshop. On the walls there were photographs hanging and texts explaining educational activities concerning "body and movement." As the presentation ended and the discussion between the daycare presenters and participants were to begin, silence broke out however. The daycare manager asked if anybody had any questions, and the managerial facilitator asked a few questions, but collaboration between the attendees and the presenters did not seem to happen, until one of the teachers turned around and started the video again. The video showed teachers and children engaging in a collective dance-balancing-act used to train motor function skills. She then said out loud: "This may look easy, but it's really hard. Why don't we all get up and use our motor functions – and then we can sit down and talk about the quality it brings to life?"

This invitation caused tumult; some people laughed, others looked a bit confused, and some looked at the door, until an attendee said: "All this writing is no good anyway" and stood up. The presenting teachers moved some chairs around, and the attendees started to get up, and next they all started to move around like the children in the video in between chairs and each other. Afterwards some people sat down again, others kept standing, and this more informal placement of the actors in the room that did not look like a meeting room anymore, produced new conversations. The attendees were smiling, looking around and talking to each other. Then the daycare manager asked about the experience of "sensing" one's own body in relation to discussing the work with children on the subject matter. This caused laughter and then a few other teachers, a politician and a parent started asking questions and discussed the presentations. This lead to a dialogue about the educational plans and their theories of motor function skills in connection to cognitive skills. The workshop ended up taking longer time than planned, and a smaller group of attendees, including a public manager and a politician, stayed in the room afterword and discussed visiting the daycare facilities.

Thereby the more and less (dis-)organized interactions became critical for the accomplishment of this collaborative governance event; the design was renegotiated across through both presentations, PowerPoints, photographs, questionnaires, videos, dance-balancing acts and the actors' movements as well as chair-arrangements. Altogether, this changed the design of collaboration and its dialogues. Along the way tensions were created between "sitting down" and "standing up" to engage in quality, as well as "writing," and although some of the attendees seemed to resist the invitation to engage in that type of collaboration, the mentioning of writing became a discursive resource that changed the events.

Likewise, interactions in the booths differed. Some were busy, while others were more or less empty which demanded that daycare staff called for attention. During this event, I shadowed the department head and the division head, who strolled around the booths, discussing current changes in the political committee and a forthcoming national education reform in relation to their efforts to challenge NPM practices and various forms of control. Ironically, these actors often missed the opportunity to practice collaborative governance, as they passed by booths without conversing with other stakeholders, by which their interaction rejected the organized dialogic opportunities. At one point, however a teacher interrupted them and pulled them into her booth to show a natural science project. She showed pictures and videos of children learning to climb trees, playing with natural materials, and learning about the seasons. Interestingly, this dialogue emerged due to the unpredictable involvement of a teacher who resisted hierarchical relationships in order to collaborate. Her interruption shifted the two heads' attention to the quality and value sought, created and communicated by various materials. Thereby her involvement changed the heads' participation and, as such, the interactions shaped the final design through both enabling and resisting changes.

In the case of daycare marketplaces, the design and implementation of collaborative governance emerged through meaning negotiations regarding quality-management methods in terms of "control by writing" versus "trust by collaboration." Thereby discursive tensions associated with NPM and NPG were produced and infused the communication with power-resistance relations, which both enabled and restrained the organizing of collaboration. Sometimes collaboration was seen as an innovative solution, at other times the collaborative designs were questioned as another form of control, and so this form of governance became constituted through more and less inter-related communication creating tensions between competing public management discourses and related practices of quality management in daycare. The socially dynamic strengths and weaknesses of the design became critical to its situated organizing within and across both workshops and booths.

In managerial network meetings during 2014, the management teams reflected upon the feedback of the implementation in the marketplace, and its success. Although stakeholders such as politicians, teachers, parents, and union representatives had expressed their satisfaction with the events, the division head and department head expressed doubt about collaborative governance as a quality-management method, and they had requested a new search for quality-measurement methods, which caused frustrations amongst the managerial consultants, who had developed the collaborative governance designs. This point became evident in an email from one of the management teams after their evaluation of marketplaces, concerning the next steps of their collaborative governance practices:

> We are to design a version 2.0 of the daycare marketplace based on our experiences and future needs. We have not started it yet but, unfortunately, we cannot rely on this design as the only quality-management method used to evaluate education plans in daycare. We are also asked to find other quality-measurement methods, but believe me, I am fighting.

During 2014 both local governments initiated renegotiations of new design and implementation processes for collaborative governance events as quality-management methods, as well as searching for new quality-measurement methods. As the email indicates, however, these new initiatives to redesign collaborative governance alongside other working methods associated with measurements produced resistance that may well affect the emerging organizing of changed designs and implementations.

Discussion: Design as Ongoing Organizing

The findings showed that collaborative governance practices emerge, are organized and change through the ways in which both their design and implementation are subjects for ongoing meaning negotiations in various communications across actors, time, and space.The first section elucidated how the meaning negotiation of the problems in existing quality-management methods connected to control, such as written reports, led to collaborative governance as a more meaningful solution. Furthermore, that negotiations of the design were affected by this contrast between what was considered controlling methods and collaborative methods, the tensions of which produced resistance, but which also generated nuances and changes significant to the design. The second section elucidated the meaning negotiations of designs occurring during implementation, firstly in relation to fixating the purpose of the design, which produced tensions between a political agenda and educational quality. The findings demonstrated the ways in which the accomplishment of a "final" design was still negotiated when it was being implemented – in this case during interactions across the booths and workshops at the daycare marketplace. In the communication of both the design and implementation, the use of discursive resources produced tensions and power-resistance relations associated with hierarchical control and NPM versus collaboration and NPG. These affected the meaning negotiations of design issues considered significant prior to the marketplaces, as well as the interactions that organized and changed the collaborations during marketplaces.

These findings suggest that collaborative governance does not necessarily emerge during demarcated phases and issues of design and implementation, but rather during ongoing organizing accomplished and complicated through endemic meaning negotiations and changes. This point relates to the current discussion of design and implementation issues of this governance form (Ansell and Torfing, 2014; Vangen, Hayes, and Cornforth, 2014; Bryson et al., 2012). In the discussions the socially dynamic, open-ended and iterative processes involved in the accomplishment of such designs are stressed, as is the need to theorize these processes further. Adding to the discussion, I will argue that we may both understand and conceptualize new aspects of design and implementation issues if we approach them as ongoing organizing processes constituted through various discursive practices emerging across actors, time, and space. This point echoes the practice-based theorizing of collaborative governance (Huxham, Vangen, and Eden, 2000; Vangen and Huxham, 2011) which argue to strengthen the understanding of this governance form through studying everyday interaction. This also stresses a cross-fertilizing potential in relation to discourse-based studies of inter-organizational collaboration (Hardy, Lawrence, and Grant, 2005; Koschmann, Kuhn, and Pharrer, 2012).

Many of the design and implementation issues covered in the literature concern the social dynamics of stakeholders involved in collaborative governance, and how design choices related to social interactions, communication, and power relations may affect and change the collaborative governance processes and products (Purdy, 2012; Bryson et al., 2012; Vangen, Hayes, and Cornforth, 2014). In this regard, the study has argued for a discursive approach because it pays attention to the formations of and struggles over meanings – with sensitivity to divergence as well as convergence, in the production of design ideas, choices, decisions, and enactments (Hardy, Lawrence, and Grant, 2005; Koschmann, Kuhn, and Pharrer, 2012). This offers concepts with which to explore the production of discursive power that may legitimize some design choices, while excluding others, as for example Purdy (2012) encouraged. By extension, the present chapter has demonstrated the potential in unfolding the communication of certain problems and possible solutions through which particular collaborative governance designs emerge, are negotiated, and change in discursive tensions and power-resistance relations. In particular, it allows for in-depth exploration of the meaning negotiations of certain issues emerging across actors, time, and space, that become constitutive to the organizing of such governance form.

By elucidating discursive aspects, the notion of generative mechanisms (Ansell and Torfing, 2014) can be unfolded analytically and nuanced theoretically. In this regard, this chapter has demonstrated the importance of power-resistance relations and discursive tensions as constitutive to changes in the emergent organizing of collaborative governance. As shown in the findings, these elements highlight both the restraining and generative dynamics of meaning negotiations, the exploration of which adds empirically grounded understandings of the significance of discourse in relation to developing this form of governance. In so doing, this study also addresses extant research on collaborative governance as a public-management discourse (Griggs and Sullivan, 2014; Skelcher, Mathur, and Smith, 2005). Not in order to either affirm or reject the macro discourse diagnosed, but rather to take another starting point and thereby show how and what kinds of communicative practices and discursive tensions emerge and become relevant across actors, time, and space. These practices and tensions constitute the emerging design by organizing particular collaborative governance events, which are more and less associated with certain macro discourses.

Conclusion

This chapter has explored theoretical and practical issues related to collaborative governance design and implementation. It has argued that a discursive approach adds a detailed understanding of the complex communicative practices constitutive to such form of governance and its socially dynamic and open-ended emergence. Drawing on extant organizational discourse concepts it has unfolded the meaning negotiations across both social and material practices that affect the emergence of particular collaborative governance designs. The findings of a case study demonstrated how managers and others negotiated local designs of collaborative governance through multiple communication modes including interaction, writing, visuals, and technology, by which managers both included and excluded collaborative stakeholders in the designing. Moreover, the findings showed that such design is continuingly negotiated – also during its implementation as the stakeholder interaction affect the organizing and accomplishment of a "final" design. During the negotiations across actors, time, and space, discursive tensions related to competing public management discourses and power-resistance relations were elucidated by the ways in which they generated changes in the design.

The strength of present discourse approach is that it attends to every-day interactions and communication to refine the understanding of the emergence of collaborative governance. As such, the study contributes by offering both theorizing and empirical exploration of the meaning negotiations constitutive to design and implementation choices. This also highlights the discursive tensions and power-resistance relations that generate changes concerning issues significant to this form of governance in terms of, for example, trust, control, and dialogue. This adds to the current studies (Ansell and Torfing, 2014; Bryson et al., 2012; Vangen, Hayes, and Cornforth, 2014) as an approach for studying governance designs as they emerge, are negotiated, and change through more and less ordered communicative practices across actors, time, and space. Moreover it suggests understanding such as ongoing organizing processes accomplished through and complicated by endemic meaning negotiations and change, rather than distinct phases of design and implementation.

That being said, the study is limited as a normative conceptualizing or instrumental guide; this is neither its scope nor aim. Nonetheless, it proposes that involved actors may reflect upon the open-ended and changing organizing of such form of governance (Vangen and Winchester, 2013), as they engage in negotiating meanings and matters of their local designs. Moreover, future research may pay further attention to the more or less (dis-)organized and (un-)intended communicative practices emerging across actors, time, and space, as particular governance designs are becoming. This would generate a stronger focus on the constitutive effects of situated meaning negotiations and their (re-)production of competing public management discourses and related power-resistance relations. Thereby we may produce multifaceted insights on the emerging processes of collaborative governance – and the particular design and implementation issues that will be negotiated and thus become significant, as diverse stakeholders engage in co-creating public value and innovation.

Bibliography

Ansell, C., & A. Gash. 2008. Collaborative Governance in Theory and Practice. *Journal of Public Administration Research and Theory*, 18(4): 543–571. Accessed June 7, 2017 at: <http://jpart.oxfordjournals.org/content/18/4/543> doi: 10.1093/jopart/mum032.

Ansell, C., & J. Torfing (eds). 2014. *Public Innovation Through Collaboration and Design*. New York: Routledge.

Bryson, J. M., K. S. Quick, C. S. Slotterback & B. C. Crosby. 2012. Designing Public Participation Processes. *Public Administration Review*, 73(1): 23–34. Accessed June 7, 2017 at: <http://onlinelibrary.wiley.com/doi/10.1111/j.1540-6210.2012.02678.x/abstract> doi: 10.111/j.1540-6210.2012.02678.x.

Choi, T., & P. J. Robertson. 2014. Caucuses in Collaborative Governance: Modelling the Effects of Structure, Power, and Problem Complexity. *International Public Management Journal*, 17(2): 224–254. Accessed June 7, 2017 at: <http://www.tandfonline.com/doi/abs/10.1080/10967494.2014.905398>. doi: 10.1080/10967494.2014.905398.

Christensen, T., & P. Lægreid. 2011. Complexity and Hybrid Public Administration – Theoretical and Empirical Challenges. *Public Organization Review*, 11(4): 407–423.

Fairhurst, G. T., & D. Grant. 2010. The Social Construction of Leadership: A Sailing Guide. *Management Communication Quarterly*, 24(2): 171–210. Accessed June 7, 2017 at: <http://mcq.sagepub.com/content/24/2/171>. doi: 10.1177/0893318909359697.

Ferlie, E., J. Hartley, & S. Martin. 2003. Changing Public Service Organizations: Current Perspectives and Future Prospects. *British Journal of Management*, 14(s1): 1–14. Accessed June 7, 2017 at: <https://www.researchgate.net/profile/Ewan_Ferlie/publication/228134311_Changing_Public_Service_Organizations_Current_Perspectives_and_Future_Prospects/links/02e7e5227815b0d31b000000/Changing-Public-Service-Organizations-Current-Perspectives-and-Future-Prospects.pdf>.

Grant, D., & R. J. Marshak. 2011. Toward a Discourse-Centered Understanding of Organizational Change. *Journal of Applied Behavioral Science*, 47(2): 204–235. Accessed June 7, 2017 at: <http://jab.sagepub.com/content/47/2/204>. doi: 10.1177/0021886310397612.

Griggs, S., & H. Sullivan. 2014. Necessity as the Mother of Reinvention: Discourses of Innovation in Local Government. Pp. 19–40 in C. Ansell & J. Torfing (eds), *Public Innovation through Collaboration and Design*. New York: Routledge.

Hardy, C., & R. Thomas. 2014. Discourse in a Material World. *Journal of Management Studies*, 52(5): 680–696. Accessed June 7, 2017 at: <http://onlinelibrary.wiley.com/doi/10.1111/joms.12113/abstract>. doi: 10.1111/joms.12113.

Hardy, C., T. B. Lawrence & D. Grant. 2005. Discourse and Collaboration: The Role of Conversations and Collective Identity. *The Academy of Management Review*, 30(1): 58–77.

Hartley, J., E. Sørensen & J. Torfing. 2013. Collaborative Innovation: A Viable Alternative to Market Competition and Organizational Entrepreneurship. *Public Administration Review*, 73(6): 821–830.

Huxham, C., & S. Vangen. 2000. Ambiguity, Complexity and Dynamics in the Membership of Collaboration. *Human Relations*, 53(6): 771–806.

James, A. 2012. Seeking the analytic imagination: Reflections on the process of interpreting qualitative data. *Qualitative Research*, 13(5): 562–577. Accessed June 7, 2017 at: <http://qrj.sagepub.com/content/early/2012/06/11/1468794112446108.full.pdf>. doi: 10.1177/1468794112446108.

Koschmann, M. A., T. R. Kuhn & M. D. Pharrer. 2012. A Communicative Framework of Value in Cross-Sector Partnerships. *The Academy of Management Review*, 37(3): 332–354.

Newman, J., M. Barnes, H. Sullivan & A. Knops. 2004. Public Participation and Collaborative Governance. *Journal of Social Policy*, 33(2): 203–223. Accessed June 7, 2017 at: <http://journals.cambridge.org/action/displayAbstract?fromPage=online&aid=212889&fileId=S0047279403007499>. doi: 10.1017/S0047279403007499.

Osborne, S. 2006. The New Public Governance? *Public Management Review*, 8(3): 377–387.

Plum, M. 2012. Humanism, administration and education: the demand of documentation and the production of a new pedagogical desire. *Journal of Education Policy*, 27(4): 491–507. Accessed June 7, 2017 at: <http://www.tandfonline.com/doi/abs/10.1080/02680939.2011.640944>. doi: 10.1080/02680939.2011.640944.

Purdy, J. M. 2012. A Framework for Assessing Power in Collaborative Governance Processes. *Public Administration Review*, 49(3): 675–689.

Skelcher, C., N. Mathur & M. Smith. 2005. The Public Governance of Collaborative Spaces: Discourse, Design and Democracy. *Public Administration*, 83(3): 573–596. Accessed June 7, 2017 at: <http://onlinelibrary.wiley.com/doi/10.1111/j.0033-3298.2005.00463.x/full>. doi: 10.1111/j.0033-3298.2005.00463.x.

Thomas, R., L. D. Sargent & C. Hardy. 2011. Managing Organizational Change: Negotiating Meaning and Power-Resistance Relations. *Organization Science*, 22(1): 22–41.

Vangen, S., & C. Huxham. 2011. The Tangled Web: Unraveling the Principle of Common Goals in Collaborations. *Journal of Public Administration Research and Theory*, 22: 731–760. Accessed June 7, 2017 at: <http://jpart.oxfordjournals. org/content/22/4/731>. doi: 10.1093/jopart/muro65.

Vangen, S., J. P. Hayes & C. Cornforth. 2014. Governing Cross-Sector, Inter-Organizational Collaborations. *Public Management Review*, 17(9): 1237–1260.

Vangen, S., & N. Winchester. 2013. Managing Cultural Diversity in Collaborations. *Public Management Review*, 1–22.

Ybema, S., D. Yanow, H. Wels & F. H. Kamsteeg. 2009. *Organizational Ethnography Studying the Complexity of Everyday Life*. London: Sage Publications.

PART V

Innovative Approaches

FRANCES WESTLEY AND NINO ANTADZE

12   Making a Difference: Strategies for Scaling Social Innovation for Greater Impact[1]

ABSTRACT

This chapter explores the strategies and dynamics of scaling up social innovations. Social innovation is a complex process that profoundly changes the basic routines, resource, and authority flows, or beliefs of the social system in which it occurs. Various applications of marketing and diffusion theory are helpful to some extent in understanding the trajectories or successful strategies associated with social innovation. It seems unwise, however, to rely solely on a market model to understand the dynamics of scaling social innovation, in view of the complex nature of the supply–demand relation with respect to the social innovation market. Instead, the authors propose a distinctive model of system transformation associated with a small but important group of social innovations dependent on discontinuous and cross-scale change. This chapter focuses on the challenge of scaling up social innovations in general and in particular the dynamics of going to scale.

Defining Social Innovation

Social invention abounds. In communities across the world, individuals daily come up with new ideas, large and small, for improving their lot and the lot of those around them, in response to locally perceived problems or social needs. Such inventions may thrive locally without any attempt at scaling up or generating a broader impact. Sometimes, however, they spread to other individuals or organizations, whether as the effect of a deliberate strategy or simply through a process of diffusion. More rarely, such inventions succeed in having a lasting or revolutionary impact: they challenge

1   *The Innovation Journal: The Public Sector Innovation Journal*, 15(2), 2010, article 2 <http://www.innovation.cc/volumes-issues/vol15-no2.htm>.

and change the very institutions that created the social problem which they address. When this happens it can be argued that social innovation has occurred. Social innovations involve institutional and social system change, they contribute to overall social resilience, and they demand a complex interaction between agency and intent and emergent opportunity. Each of these three aspects will be considered in turn.

A. Social innovation is a complex process of introducing new products, processes or programs that profoundly change the basic routines, resource and authority flows, or beliefs of the social system in which the innovation occurs. Such successful social innovations have durability and broad impact.

The terms *social enterprise, social entrepreneurship*, and (increasingly) *social finance* are often used interchangeably with *social innovation*. It is clear, however, that any sophisticated understanding of how novelty transforms complex systems requires great conceptual precision. A *social enterprise*, though it may respond to social needs, is a privately owned, profit-oriented venture which markets its own products and services, blending business interests with social ends. The Canadian Centre for Social Entrepreneurship (2001: 2) considers social enterprises as fitting the notion of hybrid organizational models which "fuse innovative, entrepreneurial practices with a commitment to both social and economic return on investment."

Whereas the concept of social enterprise is primary focused on organizational form and mission, *social entrepreneurship* is a human-centered concept that highlights the personal qualities of a person who starts a new organization (Phills et al., 2008). Martin and Osberg (2007: 30) note that "any definition of the term 'social entrepreneurship' must start with the word 'entrepreneurship.' The word 'social' simply modifies entrepreneurship."

Consequently, the emphasis on profitability is one difference between social enterprise, social entrepreneurship, and social innovation. Social innovation does not necessarily involve a commercial interest, though it does not preclude such interest. More definitively, social innovation is oriented towards making a change at the systemic level. As Phills et al. (2008: 37) explain, "unlike the terms social entrepreneurship and social enterprise, social innovation transcends sectors, levels of analysis, and methods to discover the processes – the strategies, tactics, and theories of change – that produce lasting impact."

Undoubtedly these three notions are closely related to each other. For example, a social entrepreneur can be a part of a social enterprise and, at the same time, can contribute to the promotion of social innovations. As Westall (2007: 2) notes, "Each of these terms reflects different cuts, or perspectives, on reality."

Figure 12.1 illustrates which sectors of the system are addressed by the social entrepreneur, social enterprise, and social innovation. It also explains on which scale the above-defined three concepts introduce innovation. Whereas social entrepreneurship focuses on an individual and social enterprise addresses organizations, social innovation strives to change the

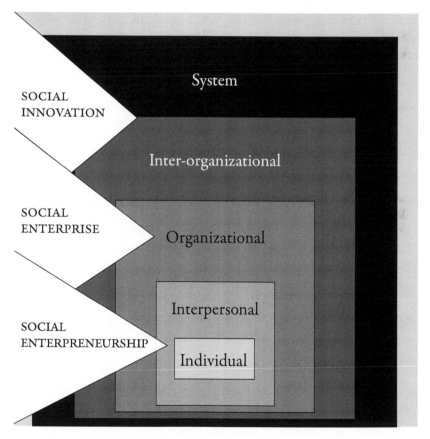

Figure 12.1: A systemic view of innovation. Source: based on Westall, 2007.

way a system operates. Consequently, social entrepreneurship and social enterprise operate within the larger framework of "wider trends of thought and practice" (Ibid.). As Leadbeater (2007) suggests, the policy on social enterprise should be developed within the boundaries of a wider strategy on social innovation. Moreover, inventions will hardly achieve a significant impact unless they are supported within the frameworks in which they operate (Westall, 2007: 11). Similarly, Marhdon et al. (2010: 13) consider that successful innovations must be viewed within the larger setting of "industrial and national systems and structures" in which they unfold.

Of particular interest in this chapter are those innovations that address seemingly intractable social problems such as homelessness, poverty, and mental illness. In these domains, the social sector struggles often with band-aid solutions which address the immediate symptoms but not the underlying causes. So, for example, social service organizations struggle to find financial support for those suffering from mental illness without addressing the economic system that excludes them from the mainstream economy. Indeed it can be argued that the established institutions – those taken for granted in the community – are often the source of such intractable problems. Real innovation without change in these institutions is therefore unlikely.

When a social innovation has a broad or durable impact, it will be *disruptive and catalytic* (Christensen et al., 2006); it will challenge the social system and social institutions that govern people's conduct by affecting the fundamental distribution of power and resources, and may change the basic beliefs that define the system or the laws and routines which govern it. While many smaller innovations are continually introduced at all scales, it seems most important to consider those innovations that have the potential to disrupt and change the broader system. To do so, a social innovation must cross multiple social boundaries to reach more people and different people, more organizations and different organizations, organizations nested across scales (from local to regional to national to global) and linked in social networks.

B. The capacity of any society to create a steady flow of social innovations, particularly those which re-engage vulnerable populations, is an important contributor to overall social and ecological resilience.

In the broadest sense, social innovation is urgently needed to solve the complex social-ecological problems facing the world. Since the advent of the world financial crisis in the fall of 2009, commentators have spoken of the possibility of a *perfect storm*: the intersection of rapid climate change, decreasing fossil fuel supplies, food shortages, and economic collapse – and the extreme difficulty of really understanding the dynamics of these problems, due to their complexity (Carpenter et al., 2009). Traditional, disciplinary-based science has done a poor job at illuminating these intersections. Thinkers about social-ecological resilience and complex systems, however, have for several decades been describing just such interconnecting systems and possibilities (Gunderson et al., 1995; Walker and Salt, 2006).

The exclusion of large parts of the world's population from basic economic and ecological services increases the vulnerability of the whole to *perfect storms* and hard losses of resilience. Re-engaging vulnerable populations in our mainstream economic, social, and cultural institutions, not just as recipients of services or *transfer entitlements* (Sen, 1981) but as active participants and contributors, is, therefore, intimately tied to social-ecological resilience. It is not accidental that much of social innovation addresses this kind of re-engagement; reintegrating the poor, the homeless, the mentally ill, and the lonely into community. But from another point of view, it seems clear that if the generation of novelty is largely dependent on the recombination of existing elements (Arthur, 2009), then as these groups are excluded from contribution, their viewpoints, their diversity and the potential for specific local contributions are lost as well. So social innovation not only serves vulnerable populations, but is served by them in turn. And, since resilience of linked social-ecological systems is dependent on the introduction of novelty in the back loop, resilience is also increased by that re-engagement (see Figure 12.2).

C. While social innovation has recognizable stages and phases, achieving durability and scale is a dynamic process, which requires both emergence of opportunity and deliberate agency, and a connection between the two.

Human beings are inventive. The capacity to explore new possibilities to create and to change is part of what defines our species. Humans are also a social species, highly dependent on each other for the creation and

The relationship between resilience,
vulnerability, and social innovation

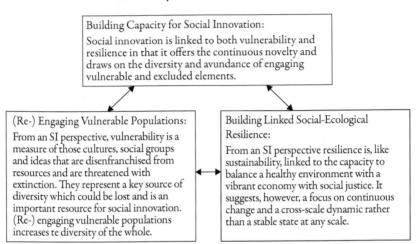

Building Capacity for Social Innovation:

Social innovation is linked to both vulnerability and resilience in that it offers the continuous novelty and draws on the diversity and avundance of engaging vulnerable and excluded elements.

(Re-) Engaging Vulnerable Populations:

From an SI perspective, vulnerability is a measure of those cultures, social groups and ideas that are disenfranchised from resources and are threatened with extinction. They represent a key source of diversity which could be lost and is an important resource for social innovation. (Re-) engaging vulnerable populations increases te diversity of the whole.

Building Linked Social-Ecological Resilience:

From an SI perspective resilience is, like sustainability, linked to the capacity to balance a healthy environment with a vibrant economy with social justice. It suggests, however, a focus on continuous change and a cross-scale dynamic rather than a stable state at any scale.

Figure 12.2: The relationship between resilience, re-engagement of vulnerable populations, and social innovation. Source: the authors.

maintenance of the world in which we live. The rules and beliefs which make up cultures both define and limit people and at the same time provide the material they need to create novelty. This has been defined as the paradox of agency (Friedland and Alford, 1991; Powell and DiMaggio, 1991; Sewell, 1992; Holm, 1995; Seo and Creed, 2002); that as individuals, as social beings, people are both deeply conditioned by and dependent on the continuity and stability of the social systems they have invented. Additionally, they are capable of altering these through both conscious and unconscious effort.

A social system may be defined as any organized assembly of human resources, beliefs, and procedures united and regulated by interaction or interdependence so as to accomplish a set of specific functions. Social systems are complex, having multiple interacting elements, and to survive they must be adaptive, ever evolving to adjust to emerging needs of the subsystems (organizations or individuals). Each social system is defined by its boundary and may be observed at various degrees of focus. An observer can *zoom in* to look at systems as small as a family, or *zoom out* to look at systems as broad as the globe. Each social system has its own character or identity, which can be analyzed in terms of its culture – beliefs, values, artifacts, and symbols; its political and economic structure – the pattern by which power and resources are distributed; and its social interactions – the laws, procedures, routines, and habits that govern social interaction and make it predictable. These three aspects of social systems, in their most established and taken-for-granted forms (political structure, religious or value heritage, economic markets, laws of public conduct) are often referred to as institutions (Giddens, 1976).

For institutions and social systems to remain resilient, therefore, a continuous integration of novelty is necessary. As Parsons (1951) indicated, healthy functioning social systems at all scales need to behave strategically, pursuing *goal-related activity*, adapting to *changing circumstances*, maintaining *integration* of the system, and ensuring continuity *(latency)* through pattern maintenance and social memory. How that novelty enters our social systems and transforms them, as well as how human agency plays a role, is key to understanding social innovation.

Innovation has been widely studied and appears to have a variety of phases and stages. This has perhaps been best described in the literature on continuously innovating firms (Kantor, 1983; Van de Ven, 1986; Dougherty, 1992; Dougherty and Hardy, 1996; Van de Ven et al., 1999). Innovation can be encouraged by a design that fosters competition between multiple teams all attempting to develop the best idea or model; this been called the exploration phase (March, 1991) and is characterized by numerous experiments, some successful, others not, as an individual or team attempts to move from idea to a prototype that can be tested in production. At some point choice favors one or several of these experiments and diverts all resources towards exploiting the possibility of these ideas in the form of new products or processes. As the product or process moves into the production or exploitation phase, the prototype is further modified and the organization gains experience at production, becoming more efficient until the product or process can be replicated with maximum efficiency and hence profitability. Its fate then rests with the market. If demand increases then more of the product is produced. Eventually, however, demand will decrease due to dynamics of the larger market, the competitive context, or changing social and economic conditions. The firm with only one product will therefore go out of business. To be resilient over long periods of time, the firm must be able to generate new products or variations of old products in response to this shifting demand context.

This model of innovation can be represented in the four-box cycle in Figure 12.3. This is known as the *adaptive cycle*, and it provides a heuristic for understanding the dynamics that drive both continuity and change. It is best understood as a diagram that charts this dynamic at a single scale or in a single system. It could represent the evolution of a single innovation from idea to maturity, or the organization that designs and delivers that innovation. It is important to the idea of resilience – that capacity to adapt to shocks and changes, while preserving sufficient coherence to maintain identity – that the four phases are not represented as linear but rather as an infinity loop. Once an idea or organization reaches the maturity (conservation) stage, it needs to release resources for novelty or change and re-engage in exploration in order to retain its resilience. The release and reorganization

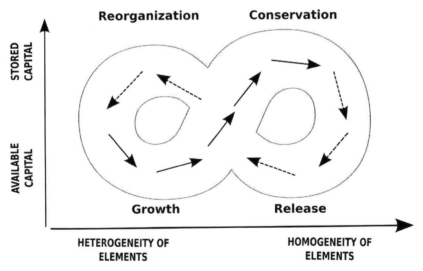

Figure 12.3: The adaptive cycle: A theory of the relationship of transformation to resilience in complex systems. Source: based on Holling and Gunderson, 2002: 34.

phase is often termed the *back loop*, where non-routine change is introduced. The exploitation and conservation phases are often termed the *front loop*, where change is slow, incremental, and more deliberate.

Making a Bigger Difference: Strategies for Scaling Out and Up

In this section, we first review the literature on scaling out of social innovations through employing market mechanisms. Next, we distinguish scaling up dynamics from scaling them out, and discuss the role of institutional entrepreneurship in scaling up social innovations through institutional transformations.

Market Mechanisms and Scaling Out

One model of how social innovations increase their impact is closely tied to the idea of social markets. As Mulgan et al. (2007: 11) explain, successful social innovation is not only a result of a brilliant idea or hard work of an individual. Successful social innovations are achieved through the interplay of *effective demand* (the *pull* factor) and *effective supply* (the *push* factor). Demand becomes effective when it is backed with purchasing power – when those who recognize the need to address a given problem are willing and able to pay for it. These may be direct customers (members of the public who are prepared to pay for certain products or services) and indirect customers (organizations which pay on behalf of those members of the public who are not able to pay themselves). On the other hand, effective supply refers to the innovations that are "made workable and useful." Such innovations should fit well within the scope of the existing demand and demonstrate their effectiveness and ability to be applied and implemented (Mulgan et al., 2007: 11). "The combination of 'effective supply' and 'effective demand' results in innovations that achieve social impact and, at the same time, prove to be financially sustainable" (Mulgan et al., 2007: 11).

Aside from being directly related to the supply–demand relation, the growth of innovation can be viewed from the perspective of the organizational form that it adopts. Mulgan et al. (2007) propose a spectrum of models of innovation growth that are spread between low control and high control. Between the extremes of the spectrum, three different models of growth are placed: uncontrolled diffusion, more directed diffusion by a *parent* organization (e.g. promotion through formal networks, licensing, franchising, multiplication including federations), and organizational growth (see Figure 12.4).

The above categorization of scaling up strategies assumes that the organization that is fostering and attempting to scale the innovation

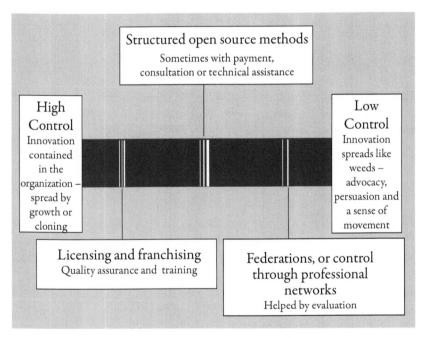

Figure 12.4: A spectrum of models of social innovation growth.
Source: based on Mulgan, Ali, Halkett and Sanders, 2007.

will continue to propagate a single innovation or group of innovations for the same market. One example of such an organization is L'Abri en Ville (<http://www.labrienville.org>), an innovative initiative based in Montréal, which creates co-operative living arrangements for persons suffering from long-term mental health challenges and seeks to increase its impact by helping other communities adopt the model. Similarly, Roots of Empathy (<http://www.rootsofempathy.org>), a Toronto organization dedicated to reducing bullying in elementary schools, has not only achieved dramatic results locally but has also spread its school program around the globe. This kind of growth might be called expansionary innovation.

Other organizations follow different trajectories. In Kitchener, Ontario, The Working Centre (<http://www.theworkingcentre.org>) has developed a series of products for homeless or vulnerable people living in the inner city core. They began with an employment center and drop-in center, then expanded to a café, a soup kitchen, a craft co-op, a bicycle repair shop, an organic garden and transition housing, as the need arose. This could be termed evolutionary innovation. An innovative organization such as Santropol Roulant (<http://www.santropolroulant.org/2006/E-home.htm>), an award-winning meals on wheels program in Montréal that also builds intergenerational partnerships, has such a demand for its services that it continues to expand to meet those needs. This might be called incremental growth. Ultimately, there are organizations that increase the impact of their innovations by changing both the product and the market. These are total innovators. This final approach will be discussed in more detail below.

Beyond the Market Model for Social Innovation: Institutional Change through Scaling Up

Despite the appeal of a market model to explain how social innovations go to scale, there are limitations to the application of a straightforward supply–demand dynamic to a social innovation context. There are at least three interlocking dynamics that affect the relationship between the supply and demand for social innovation (see Figure 12.5). The first, labeled Dynamic

A, is the hypothetical notion that a vulnerable group or intractable social issue *demands* social innovation for its breakthrough. In response to this *demand*, the social-entrepreneurial organization produces a *supply of social innovation*, which attenuates the needs of the vulnerable groups. Dynamic B, on the other hand, suggests that this supply, since it cannot be financed by the users themselves, needs sources of financing which come from governments or charitable foundations (or both). This funding is triggered by grant applications or proposals, the success of which depends not only on the evident needs of the vulnerable client group, but also on the skills of the grant writers in mediating such needs so as to fit the priorities of the government programs or the sponsoring foundations' strategies. This perception of priorities is in turn affected by Dynamic C, the capacity of news media or research unit to set the agenda for the government and foundations with respect to a particular vulnerable group or issue. At times, governments and foundations will fund research specifically to assess such needs, but again, the *feedback* is mediated by the capacities of the researcher.

All the mediators identified in Figure 12.5 – governments, foundations, media, and think tanks – introduce distortions into the market relationship as they act as proxy *buyers* for the vulnerable populations who are the identified end users of a social innovation.

Marhdon et al. (2010: 17) note that government policy-makers pay more attention to the factors associated with the supply, rather than to the demand-oriented policies (see also Georghiou, 2007: 4). Governments are often in the position to *purchase* innovative programs or products on behalf of the populations they represent but do not always see themselves as in the market for innovations. Governments are generally constituted as the *guardians* of the public good (Jacobs, 1992), leaving the private sector to respond to the demand for product and process innovation (Fontana and Guerzoni, 2008). Governments are also prone to more stringent requirements for accountability, and are uncomfortable with the uncertainty associated with radically innovative ideas. At best, therefore, governments are likely to fund incremental innovations, thus reducing the uncertainty associated with any novel product or process. This does not mean that governments, which are major purchasers as well as the primary regulators in the market, cannot significantly influence "the possibilities for innovation" (Georghiou, 2007: 14); however, they are unlikely to reflect existing

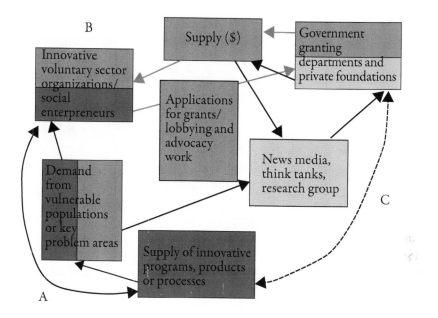

Figure 12.5: Three interactive dynamics affecting the relationship between supply and demand for social innovations. Source: the authors.

demand for the innovation through their purchasing or funding programs. Although the reasoning behind the market model is clear and logical, it cannot be seen as an accurate representation of the real-life market.

The media, and to some extent think tanks, act as a proxy for advertising in the sense that they stimulate *buyers* (government, foundations) to purchase social innovations on behalf of the poor, the homeless, the disabled, the mentally ill, or some other identified user group. However, they publicize the demand, not the solutions (supply). One of the challenges of social innovation is that many innovative solutions never come to the attention of the *big buyers* (i.e. the funders), but rather languish at a local level. Some think tanks such as Stanford Center for Social Innovation and Skoll Forum have attempted to redress this problem by creating forums to publicize the inventions of social entrepreneurs. The question remains however, whether the funders are using this publicity as a means of identifying solutions to the problems with which they are concerned.

In some documented cases, the government can intervene directly to raise awareness of solutions, using social marketing strategies (Weinreich, 1999, p. 3). Some well-known examples of social marketing campaigns are the campaigns for energy conservation and health promotion (e.g. drug abuse, physical activity), largely government-sponsored exercises (Health Canada, 2000). But this begs the question of the government's desire to truly support social innovations, particularly those radical enough to challenge current institutional arrangements.

Lastly, the supply of social innovation is not only dependent on mediated demand but on continuous support from funders, who are not the end users. An innovation may be successful insofar as it is in demand by its end users or consumers; but success of this sort does not automatically translate into additional income for further production or product development. That comes in the forms of grants, subsidies, and awards, the availability of which is not necessarily governed by end-user demand, but often by other concerns such as political stability, foundation strategy, or internal changes in programs or priorities.

In sum, the amount of mediation involved in the complex contexts where social innovation is needed means that demand is a *very vague* notion (Mowery and Rosenberg, 1979: 104) and is therefore "not necessarily the sole, or even the principal, determinant of the scale and direction of inventive and innovative activity" (Freeman, 1979: 206). The sheer complexity of these dynamics suggests that a strategy of supply and demand needs to be elaborated with other perspectives. In particular, we suggest the importance of models that incorporate discontinuous and emergent properties of innovation. Why do some innovations have an impact which far outreaches the numbers of people involved and which seems to depend on a *tipping point* dynamic (Gladwell, 2002) rather than a diffusion pattern?

Institutional Entrepreneurship: Scaling Up through
Institutional Transformation

It is in the nature of the social innovation market, as a complex system, to be highly dependent upon place and time. "Timing can be all-important, and many innovators consciously 'park' their ideas for years until the time is right" (Mulgan et al., 2007: 12). Social innovations do not necessarily generate the sorts of products or services that are always of interest to the market; they are born in a certain context, under certain circumstances, and in response to certain needs or problems. Although a social innovation in the later stages of its diffusion may be spread on a larger scale (in terms both of geography and of the numbers of actors involved), its emergence and diffusion are dependent on existing frameworks and opportunities. Whether or not the innovation has a broader social impact, however, is dependent on the interplay of political, social, economic, and cultural factors. The synergy of these factors results in the growth of certain innovations when the "efforts and interest of several actors coincide" to achieve a desired effect (Dalhammar et al., 2003: 9, Marhdon et al., 2010). Others, equally deserving, may fall by the wayside.

This, in part, is a symptom of the inherent complexity of the social innovation process. One example of a simple process is baking a cake. A recipe is used that identifies the components of the system (flour, milk, eggs) and a set of steps for relating these components in time and space so as to produce the desired product (the cake). Carefully following the steps of a good recipe will produce a good result nearly every time. A good analogy of *complicated* processes is sending a rocket to the moon. Much more expertise is required and much more coordination to connect the various experts into a unified design team. Still, once that is accomplished and a set of designs is in place, many rocket ships can be produced and the risk of failure is reduced. Achieving *complex* processes is more like raising children: success with one is not a guarantee of success with another, and recipes or blueprints are of limited value. Managing an ever-evolving and emerging relationship between parent, child, and the broader social context lies at the heart of this process. Unforeseen shocks or discontinuities can derail the relationship, changing the rules at any point. Outcomes remain uncertain (Westley et al., 2006).

Action and impact in complex processes are not governed by straightforward cause-and- effect relationships. A good idea, the resources to develop it, leadership capacity, and drive – all must be combined with *opportunity*, which can be recognized and seized but not directly controlled

(Westley et al., 2006). Moreover, as the innovation changes and evolves through its development, other kinds of opportunity become necessary (Bacon et al., 2008). Durability, scale, and impact depend not only on the degree of engagement with the broader social context but upon engagement of a *different kind*. Eventually, there must be a disruptive encounter with power, routine, and beliefs, though this may be subversive as opposed to revolutionary (Mumford, 2002). The transformation and action leading up to this disruptive encounter may be termed *scaling up*. How does such transformation unfold?

If the adaptive cycle can be used to understand phases and stages of developing a social innovation, the *panarchy* model can be used to understand how sudden transformations and disruptions occur. Panarchy draws attention to the dynamics of such cross-scale strategies and processes (Gunderson and Holling, 2002) and the possibility of sudden cascades of change.

Cross-scale dynamics in ecological systems are a key component of resilience. From the microscopic level of bacteria to the life and death of whole forests, systems existing at separate scales do not cycle together. The same may be said of social systems. Individuals, groups, organizations, institutions (such as economies, cultural systems and legal systems) go through cycles at different rhythms. Much deep novelty or transformations, therefore comes from *cross- scale* interactions, which Holling terms *panarchy*, named after the Greek god Pan, god of chaos and play. Under certain circumstances, novelty at lower levels can create a revolt at higher levels, pushing the broader system into release (Westley, 2002). Cross-scale interactions can operate in an opposite fashion as well, however, restricting novelty by a process of remembrance (Figure 12.6).

Agency, as mentioned earlier, clearly plays a role. Social innovation requires a variety of actors, working in concert or separately, if it is to have the kind of impact suggested above. Among these are the inventors, sometimes called *social entrepreneurs:* the individuals who initiate or create innovative programs, products, or processes and seek to build an initial organization that can bring that innovation to market. Increasingly research has indicated that among their key characteristics is their capacity to work in highly complex conditions (Goldstein et al., 2008). However, equally

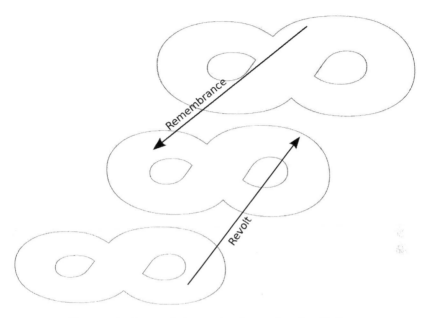

Figure 12.6: Cross-scale interaction. Source: based on Holling,
Gunderson and Peterson, 2002: 75.

important to social innovations that have the broad impact described above
are the *institutional entrepreneurs:* those individuals or networks of individuals who actively seek to change the broader social system through
changing the political, economic, legal, or cultural institutions, in order
that the social innovation can flourish (Dorado, 2005). Occasionally, individuals have the skills of both the social and institutional entrepreneurs,
but generally it is wiser to think of actor nets or groups behind successful
social innovation.

However, in complex systems, no change can be accounted for by
agency alone. Agency must coincide with opportunity that is a feature of the
broader social and institutional context (Westley et al., 2006; Rhodes and
Donnelley-Cox, 2008). Social innovation can be aided by market demand,
which is one form of such opportunity we have explored at length above. It
can also be aided by political demand, another form of opportunity, and by

cultural demand in the form of a breakdown in sense-making or meaning. These dynamics are complex and difficult if not impossible to manipulate directly. However, if the focus is on disrupting the larger institutional context, it appears that this can occur by connecting the innovation to political, cultural or economic opportunities that exist irrespective of the volume of adoption. Sudden tipping points or cascades of change that are discontinuous, that is, not the result of an incremental model of adoption or diffusion of innovation can then occur (Gladwell, 2002).

Strategies for connecting innovation to these other opportunity contexts defines institutional entrepreneurship. This role involves a set of skills including pattern recognition, resource mobilization, sense-making, and connecting (Dorado 2005). It involves a deliberate focus on *up-down* strategies of reflecting on and connecting to decision-makers and opinion leaders in policy, economic, and cultural arenas, engaging and questioning the strategic context of their decisions. It also involves recognizing local and *front line* innovations that promise institutional disruption, and selling these to the decision-makers/opinion leaders when windows of opportunity open (Burgelman, 1983). Institutional entrepreneurs therefore need to master a complex set of cultural/social skills (cognitive, knowledge management, sense-making, convening), political skills (coalition formation, networking, advocacy, lobbying) and resource mobilization skills (financial, social, intellectual, cultural, and political capital). Building capacity for social innovation in part involves increasing the representation of these skills among those interested in fostering broad-based change.

Conclusions

In the foregoing pages, the authors have explored a variety of aspects of social innovations in complex systems. *Social innovation* was defined as those processes, products, and initiatives which profoundly challenge the system that created the problem that they seek to address. For this category of innovation, the market model has some implications; but it does not provide an exhaustive explanation. Numerous intermediaries who distort direct supply-and-demand relationships confound market dynamics. Moreover, as complex dynamics, they demand models that account for fast and slow variables, discontinuities, relationships, and non-linear change. Models of resilience in linked social-ecological systems offer such a framework, which calls for close attention both to the institutional entrepreneur and to the strategies employed to link local innovation to global or national policies and economic structures.

Bibliography

Arthur, W. B. 2009. *The Nature of Technology: What It Is and How It Evolves.* New York: The Free Press.

Bacon, N., N. Faizullah, G. Mulgan & S. Woodcraft. 2008. *Transformers: How Local Areas Innovate to Address Changing Social Needs.* London: NESTA. Accessed May 3, 2017 at: <http://www.nesta.org.uk/transformers>.

Burgelman, R. A. 1983. *Managing Innovating Systems: A Study of the Process of Internal Corporate Venturing.* Ann Arbor, MI: University Microfilms International.

Canadian Centre for Social Entrepreneurship. 2001. *Social Entrepreneurship Discussion Paper.* No. 1. Accessed 2 May 2017 at: <http://webcache.googleusercontent. com/search?q=cache:jKg_41N4gV4J:citeseerx.ist.psu.edu/viewdoc/downloa d%3Fdoi%3D10.1.1.194.4683%26rep%3Drep1%26type%3Dpdf+&cd=1&hl=e n&ct=clnk&gl=ge>.

Carpenter, S. R., C. Folke, M. Scheffer & F. Westley. 2009. Resilience: Accounting for the noncomputable. *Ecology & Society,* 14(1): 13.

Christensen, C. M., H. Baumann, R. Ruggles & T. M. Sadtler. 2006. Disruptive innovation for social change. *Harvard Business Review,* 84(12): 94–101.

Dalhammar, C., B. Kogg & O. Mont. 2003. Who creates the market for green products? Proceedings for Sustainable Innovation, October 27–28, Stockholm, Sweden. Accessed May 3, 2017 at: <http://portal.research.lu.se/portal/en/publications/ who-creates-the-market-for-green-products(bdee96e3-76ec-4ca1-8408-b4f-8c3ae6f0c)/export.html>.

Dorado, S. 2005. Institutional entrepreneurship, partaking, and convening. *Organizational Studies,* 26(3): 385–414. DOI: 10.1177/0170840605050873. Accessed May 2, 2017 at: <http://journals.sagepub.com/doi/pdf/10.1177/0170840605050873>.

Dougherty, D. 1992. A practice-centered model of organizational renewal through product Innovation. *Strategic Management Journal*, 13(S1): 77–92. DOI: 10.1002/smj.4250131007. Accessed on May 2, 2017 at: <http://onlinelibrary.wiley.com/doi/10.1002/smj.4250131007/full>.

Dougherty, D., & C. Hardy. 1996. Sustained product innovation in large, mature organizations: Overcoming innovation-to-organization problems. *Academy of Management Journal*, 39(5): 1120–1153. doi: 10.2307/256994. Accessed May 5, 2017 at: <http://amj.aom.org/content/39/5/1120.short.>.

Fontana, R. & M. Guerzoni. 2008. Incentives and uncertainty: An empirical analysis of the impact of demand on innovation. *Cambridge Journal of Economics*, 32(6): 927–946. DOI: <https://doi.org/10.1093/cje/ben021>. Accessed on May 10, 2017 at: <https://academic.oup.com/cje/article/32/6/927/1711270/Incentives-and-uncertainty-an-empirical-analysis>.

Freeman, C. 1979. The determinants of innovation: Market demand, technology, and the response to social problems. *Futures*, 11(3): 206–215 <https://doi.org/10.1016/0016-3287(79)90110-1>. Accessed May 10, 2017 at: <http://www.sciencedirect.com/science/article/pii/0016328779901101>.

Friedland, R., & R. R. Alford. 1991. Bringing society back in: Symbols, practices, and institutional contradictions. Pp. 2320–2363 in W. W. Powell & P. J. DiMaggio (eds), *The New Institutionalism in Organizational Analysis*. Chicago, IL: University of Chicago Press.

Georghiou, L. 2007. *Demanding Innovation: Lead Markets, Public Procurement and Innovation*. London: NESTA.

Giddens, A. 1976. *New Rules of Sociological Method: A Positive Critique of Interpretative Sociologies*. London: Hutchinson.

Gladwell, M. 2002. *The Tipping Point: How Little Things Can Make a Big Difference*. New York: Little, Brown and Co.

Goldstein, J. A., J. K. Hazy & J. Silberstang. 2008. Complexity and social entrepreneurship: A fortuitous meeting. *Emergence: Complexity & Organization* (E:CO), 10(3): 9–24.

Gunderson, L. H., C. S. Holling & S. S. Light (eds). 1995. *Barriers and Bridges to the Renewal of Ecosystem and Institutions*. New York: Columbia University Press.

Gunderson, L. H., & C. S. Holling (eds). 2002. *Panarchy: Understanding Transformations in Human and Natural Systems*. Washington, DC: Island Press.

Health Canada. 2000. The Health Canada Policy Toolkit for Public Involvement in Decision Making. Accessed May 3, 2017 at: <http://www.hc-sc.gc.ca/ahc-asc/pubs/_public-consult/2000decision/index-eng.php>.

Holling, C. S., & L. H. Gunderson. 2002. Resilience and adaptive cycles. Pp. 25–62 in L. H. Gunderson & C. S. Holling (eds), *Panarchy: Understanding Transformations in Human and Natural Systems*. Washington, DC: Island Press.

Holling, C. S., L. H. Gunderson & G. D. Peterson. 2002. Sustainability and Panarchies. Pp. 63–102 in L. H. Gunderson & C. S. Holling (eds), *Panarchy: Understanding Transformations in Human and Natural Systems*. Washington, DC: Island Press.

Holm, P. 1995. The dynamics of institutionalization: Transformation processes in Norwegian fisheries. *Administrative Science Quarterly*, 40: 398–422. DOI: 10.2307/2393791. Accessed May 2, 2017 at: <http://www.jstor.org/stable/2393791?seq=1#page_scan_tab_contents>.

Jacobs, J. 1992. *Systems of Survival*. Toronto, Canada: Random House.

Kantor, Rosaberth M. 1983. *The Change Masters: Innovations for Productivity in American Corporations*. New York: Simon and Schuster.

Leadbeater, C. 2007. Social enterprise and social innovation: Strategies for the next ten years. A social enterprise think piece for the Office of the Third Sector. Cabinet Office, Office of the Third Sector, UK, November. Accessed May 3, 2017 at: <http://www.peopleproject.eu/wiki/PEOPLE%20WIKIS/socialentrepreneurship/mainSpace/files/Social%20enterprise%20and%20social%20innovation.pdf>.

March, J. G. 1991. Exploration and exploitation in organizational learning. *Organization Science*, 2(1): 71–87.

Marhdon, M., F. Visser & I. Brinkley. 2010. *Demand and Innovation. How customer preferences shape the innovation process*. London: NESTA. Accessed May 3, 2017 at: <https://www.nesta.org.uk/sites/default/files/demand_and_innovation.pdf>.

Martin, R. L., & S. Osberg. 2007. Social entrepreneurship: The case for definition. *Stanford Social Innovation Review*, 5(2): 28–39.

Mowery, D., & N. Rosenberg. 1979. The influence of market demand upon innovation: A critical review of some recent empirical studies. *Research Policy*, 8(2): 102–153. DOI: 10.1016/0048-7333(79)90019-2. Accessed May 3, 2017 at: <http://www.sciencedirect.com/science/article/pii/0048733379900192>.

Mulgan, G., R. Ali, R. Halkett & B. Sanders. 2007. *In and Out of Sync: The Challenge of Growing Social Innovations*. London: NESTA. Accessed May 3, 2017 at: <https://www.nesta.org.uk/sites/default/files/in_and_out_of_sync.pdf>.

Mumford, M. D. 2002. Social innovation: Ten cases from Benjamin Franklin. *Creativity Research Journal*, 14(2): 253–266. DOI: 10.1207/S15326934CRJ1402_11. Accessed May 2, 2017 at: <http://www.tandfonline.com/doi/abs/10.1207/S15326934CRJ1402_11>.

Parsons, T. 1951. *The Social System*. New York: Free Press.

Phills, J. A., K. Deiglmeier & D. T. Miller. 2008. Rediscovering social innovation. *Stanford Social Innovation Review*, 6(4): 34–43.

Powell, W. W., & P. J. DiMaggio. 1991. *The New Institutionalism in Organizational Analysis*. Chicago, IL: The University of Chicago Press.

Rhodes, M. L., & G. Donnelly-Cox. 2008. Social entrepreneurship as a performance Landscape. *Emergence: Complexity & Organization* (E:CO), 10(3): 35–50.

Sen, A. 1981. *Poverty and Famines: An Essay on Entitlement and Deprivation.* Oxford: Clarendon Press.

Seo, M., & D. Creed. 2002. Institutional contradictions, praxis and institutional change: A dialectic perspective. *Academy of Management Review*, 27: 222–248. DOI: 10.5465/AMR.2002.6588004. Accessed May 2, 2017 at: <http://amr. aom.org/content/27/2/222.short>.

Sewell, W. H., Jr. 1992. A theory of structure: Duality, agency and transformation. *American Journal of Sociology*, 98(1): 1–29.

Van de Ven, A. 1986. Central problems in the management of innovation. *Management Science*, 32(5): 590–607. DOI: 10.1287/mnsc.32.5.590. Accessed on May 2, 2017 at: <http://pubsonline.informs.org/doi/abs/10.1287/mnsc.32.5.590>.

Van de Ven, A., D. E. Polley, R. Garud & S. Venkataraman. 1999. *The Innovation Journey.* New York: Oxford University Press.

Walker, B. & D. Salt. 2006. *Resilience Thinking: Sustaining Ecosystems and People in a Changing World.* Washington, DC: Island Press.

Weinreich, N. K. 1999. *Hands-on Social Marketing: A Step-by-Step Guide.* Thousand Oaks, CA: Sage Publications.

Westall, A. 2007. How can innovation in social enterprise be understood, encouraged and enabled? A social enterprise think piece for the Office of the Third Sector. Cabinet Office, Office of The Third Sector, UK, November. Accessed May 3, 2017 at: <https://pdfs.semanticscholar.org/f62b/29e3bbac3c0617d7f6f916792 98790cf4e61.pdf>.

Westley, F. 2002. The devil in the dynamics: Adaptive management on the front lines. Pp. 333–360 in L. H. Gunderson & C. S. Holling (eds), *Panarchy: Understanding Transformations in Human and Natural Systems.* Washington, DC: Island Press.

Westley, F., M. Q. Patton & B. Zimmerman. 2006. *Getting to Maybe: How the World is Changed.* Toronto, Canada: Random House Canada.

PART VI

Diffusion of Innovations

EVERETT M. ROGERS, UNA E. MEDINA,
MARIO A. RIVERA, AND CODY J. WILEY

13   Complex Adaptive Systems and the Diffusion of Innovations[1]

ABSTRACT

The diffusion of innovations model (DIM) and complex adaptive systems theory (CAS) can be employed together in the construction of predictive or applied hybrid models of induced change in population behavior. In such interventions, differentiated heterogenous zones may act as catalysts for the adoption of innovation. The present study explores the actual and potential hybridization of these two systems theories, relying on illustrations from historical practical applications of DIM, particularly the STOP AIDS communication campaign in San Francisco, California.

The resulting co-theoretical model provides an analytical tool for students of innovation, particularly in the public sector, and especially in applications of network analysis predicated on a crucially defining feature of social networks, namely "the strength of weak ties" among their members. In cultivating network ties among heterogenous groups connected by common aims, it is here argued that the innovator may prompt and, to an extent, guide the complex emergence of innovation adoption in social systems. Commonalities in the concept of heterogeneity in CAS and in DIM is explored in depth, along its many dimensions, including membership and role heterogeneity, with a view to preliminary operationalization of diffusion-management principles.

Complex Adaptive Systems, Linearity, and Non-linearity

The *Complex Adaptive Systems (CAS) Model* was born of the scientific study of complexity. According to James Gleick, the inspiration for complexity science can be traced to John von Neumann's dynamic weather system

---

1   *The Innovation Journal: The Public Sector Innovation Journal*, Volume 10(3), 2005, article 3 <http://www.innovation.cc/volumes-issues/vol10-no3.htm>.

models of the 1950s at the Institute for Advanced Study in Princeton, New Jersey, an effort that, in turn, goes back to the work of the eighteenth-century philosopher-mathematician Laplace (Gleick, 1987: 14). The *diffusion of innovations* model, credited to Everett Rogers, delineates the process by which an innovation spreads via certain communication channels among members of a social system (Rogers, 2003). Diffusion phenomena bear a resemblance to complex adaptive systems. The purpose of the present study is to explore the relationship of the diffusion of innovations model and complex adaptive systems theory, and to consider the potentialities of a hybrid systems approach to managed innovation.

In order to discuss complex adaptive systems, one should first define simple linear systems by way of contrast. "In linear systems the relationship between cause and effect is smooth and proportionate. Linear systems respond to big changes in a big and proportionate manner and linear systems respond to small changes in an equally small and proportionate way" (Kiel, 1995). Most real-life situations, on the other hand, are complex. Small changes in initial conditions, and later interventions of whatever size, can result in disproportionately large effects.

A quadratic equation can demonstrate the transition of behavior from simple to complex regimes, and from complex regimes to chaotic ones. The equation is parameterized by $4 > a > 0$, and $s \in [0,1]$ where "s" is an infinite sequence of binary variables that describe the system – we will examine the quadratic equation $f(s) = as(1-s)$. Simple systems are those systems where $a < 1$. In simple systems $s = 0$ (Bar-Yam, 1997: 26–33) there is no fluctuation between states, and as a result all changes in the system are simple and occur linearly. However, a complex adaptive system comprises multiple agents dynamically interacting in fluctuating and combinatory ways, following local rules to maximize their own utility while also maximizing individual consistency with influences from network neighbors (Klein, Sayama, Faratin and Bar-Yam, 2002).

Complex systems are about relationships among members of a system, here taken to occur at $1 < a < 3$. In a complex regime, utility-maximization rules may make for movement from lower to higher levels of group cohesiveness and order. That order is marked by emergent self-organization, in relation to complex-network synchronization that is enhanced by heterogeneity

(Motter, Zhou and Kurths, 2004). When the resulting system can create emergent behavior capable of response to the environment, it is adaptive (Johnson, 2001). Beyond these parameters chaos begins, such that at $3<a<3.56994567$ "there is a bifurcation cascade with 2-cycles then 4-cycles" (Bar-Yam, 1997: 33) and increasing splitting and bifurcations, until at $a = 4$ cycles become chaotic (Kiel, 1995). Non-linearity is a constitutive feature of complex adaptive systems.

The Diffusion of Innovations Model

The diffusion of innovations model (DIM) is concerned with how *innovations*, defined as ideas or practices that are perceived as new, are spread (Rogers, 2003). *Diffusion* is the process through which an innovation spreads via communication channels over time among the members of a social system. This is a social sciences definition of diffusion, one that is not to be confused with the thermodynamic definition of diffusion. Diffusion occurs in complex systems where networks connecting system members are overlapping, multiple, and complex. Diffusion occurs most often in heterogenous zones, that is, transitional spaces where sufficient differentiation among network members comes to obtain. Such heterogenous network connections, which comprise the innovation-diffusion system, occur among innovators and other engaged members of target populations who, in Rogers's original formulation, are called "cosmopolites." Cosmopolites are locally networked system members with *heterogenous* weak ties to outside systems (i.e. reactivity to or interactivity with influences outside the system).

The first important diffusion studies were conducted some sixty years ago by rural sociologists who investigated the adoption of hybrid seed corn among Iowa farmers. In the ensuing decades, diffusion study has spread to public health, communication, marketing, political science, and most other behavioral and social science disciplines. To date, more than 5,200 diffusion studies have been published (Rogers, 2003). Diffusion investigations have typically focused on the order in which relatively cosmopolite and heterogenous individuals, organizations, or other units in a networked system adopt an innovation in a synchronous manner. Most of the innovations studied are technological in nature, but some are policy or other social-learning innovations. An example of policy innovation research concerns which of the fifty states in the United States adopt new programs and policies first (and thus are most innovative), which states follow this lead directly, and then which ones follow it indirectly (Walker, 1996). A key finding is that the states with the most heterogenous or variegated network links to adopter states are the most likely to adopt policy innovations.

Diffusion scholars have also studied why some innovations spread relatively rapidly while other innovations do so relatively slowly. Innovations that are perceived as (a) relatively advantageous (over ideas or practices they supersede); (b) compatible with existing values, beliefs, and experiences; (c) relatively easy to comprehend and adapt; (d) observable or tangible; and (e) divisible (separable) for trial, are adopted more rapidly (Rogers, 2003).

General Comparison of the Two Models

CAS and DIM are similar in several respects, and in a sense coterminous, since they share the ends of adaptation and adoption (emergence). The endpoint for complex adaptive systems is emergence out of disorganization into a more ordered system, with more adaptable patterning and better fit. The usual aim for a managed diffusion-of-innovations program is to effect a faster rate of adoption of a new idea or practice, resulting – it is hoped – in a higher-order, fitter system. It is at the threshold of criticality in both systems models that heterogeneity (adoption, mutation, or change) is rewarded, as members increase both individual utility and interdependency (Klein, Faratin, Sayama and Bar-Yam, 2003). Coalescence occurs at a point where individuals have risen to the group threshold of fitness and adaptation. It is also possible, however, for there to be collapse instead of development into a fitter large-scale system. Collapse often occurs because members were inhibited in their ability to adapt interdependently, failing to rise together to the minimum threshold of fitness required for adaptation or adoption.

Both DIM and CAS models are built on empirical observation of change, both can describe transitions occurring either naturally or as a result of directed change, and both can be statistically analyzed to infer population parameters for processes of change. Diffusion theory is concerned with change occurring among human agents or nodes in an interconnected network of communications, yet it can easily incorporate non-human intervention devices such as mass media or electronic technology as reactive agents (with reactivity defined as sensitivity to change). Similarly, complex adaptive systems may consist of human agents or non-human factors (such as epidemics, cells, and acts of nature), and even inorganic nodes (ideas, machines, computers, or information webs) in a reactive network. While CAS models originated principally in the physical and biological sciences and DIM in the behavioral and social sciences, they have converged to include or apply to a wide range of human (social) and non-human systems.

Comparing the Mathematical Foundations of the Two Models

Working models of either complex adaptive systems or diffusion processes prohibit hand calculations and require computer analysis when scaled to full size. Diffusion of innovation models were originally constructed and plotted in two dimensions (the number of adopters occurring over time) employing multiple-regression techniques and calculus-based rates of change. These early calculations of variables correlated with *innovativeness* (the degree to which a unit in a system is relatively earlier than other units in adopting an innovation or innovations) became cumbersome when a large number of independent variables were included in the analysis. Longitudinal computer simulations of diffusion processes have been conducted, but this approach is yet to make significant contributions to the understanding of innovation diffusion.

It is impossible to calculate the mathematics of a full-scale working model of a complex adaptive system by hand. Stuart Kauffman started designing rudimentary CAS models on paper in 1963 while in medical school, but it was not until he gained access to a computer that he was able to work iterations at scales that would properly test his theoretical model. If his theory had been incorrect, or if his trials had not evidenced self-organization in early iterations – reaching points of criticality in transitional heterogenous zones – his computer would not have been able to process the possible maximum number of iterations – 10 to the 29th power (Waldrop, 1992).

The mathematics necessary to identify a complex adaptive system's *strange attractor* ("strange" because it is orderly when it is expected to be random; attractor because it "attracts" or draws order to itself out of seeming chaos), called *phase-space reconstruction modeling*, requires computer analysis. A strange attractor is a three-dimensional plot of the "thumbprint" of a CAS that is derived from a phase-space reconstruction. In a simple system, a basin of attraction is formed like a depression in a three-dimensional space. The behaviors of individuals in the system gravitate to the basin like water flowing to a valley. In CAS, dynamics "may be described in terms of cycles and attractors" where space-time is found to be insufficient to account for the number of iterations of necessary cycles; thus it is found that part of the strange attractor lies in a fractal dimension (Bar-Yam, 1997: 116, and personal communication January 4, 2005).

Reconstruction of a CAS requires a minimum of three differential equations plotting the changing relationships among three variables, and the resulting attractor is plotted in three-dimensional space. Although it partially exists in another fractional dimension, the four dimensions are collapsed into three for purposes of illustration. Strange attractors in CAS will be discussed in this chapter in terms of their influence on large-scale behavior, and simultaneously the behavior at the micro and individualized system level that gives rise to large-scale behavior.

An example of phase-space reconstruction in epidemiological modeling was provided by Aron (1990), who demonstrated the effects of introducing a vaccine into a standard, seasonally forced population composed of what he called susceptibles, latents, infectives, and those who had become immune. As more and more members of the population were immunized, the vaccine inhibited the attractors of the disease (and its ability to self-organize or diffuse). Timing of the introduction of the vaccine was critical – if introduced at the wrong time, for example too late, it would lead to a weak change in the constellation of attractors, and that might still allow the disease to propagate according to its power law. This is because at earlier stages of diffusion, countering the disease requires a smaller number of vaccinations. Introducing a vaccine into the population early, timed to inhibit spread, is equivalent to introducing an innovation early, with diffusion able to perturb the social system and alter the shape of the attraction basin as desired. If vaccinations are introduced late in the spread of disease, after the basin of attraction grows and is strongly reinforced, then inhibition of the disease would require many more vaccinations.

Time Asymmetry and Reversibility in CAS and DIM

One test of a CAS is time asymmetry. Asymmetry in time occurs when a system passes a *bifurcation point*, a pivotal or decisional point where an option is taken over another or others, leading to time irreversibility. Irreversibility means that the system cannot be run backwards – rewound or reversed – so as to reach its exact initial conditions. Systems which, when run in reverse, do not necessarily or typically return to their original state are said to be asymmetric in time (Prigogine, 1997), and asymmetry in time is important in testing for a complex adaptive system. If system-time is symmetric in both directions, then it is reversible, and it is not a CAS but a deterministic system. Complex adaptive systems are asymmetric in time, irreversible, and non-deterministic. So, in a CAS one can neither predict nor "retrodict," even with infinite information on initial conditions, because the system "chooses" its forward path. Its "choice" is indeterminate, a function of statistical probability (Prigogine, 1997) rather than certainty.

Diffusion, like CAS, is asymmetric in time, irreversible, and non-deterministic. Time is an essential element in the diffusion process – indeed, the S-shaped adoption curve is graphed as the *rate of adoption over time* (Figure 13.1), and adopter categories are assigned on the basis of time (Rogers,

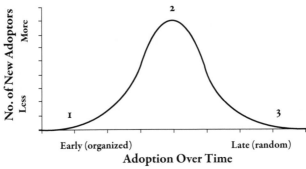

Figure 13.1: Normal distribution diffusion curve.

2003). At first glance, time might seem reversible in the diffusion process. The growth of an undesirable idea (such as use of a dangerous drug) can be halted or slowed using principles of diffusion theory. Analogously, certain manipulations may retard the complex adaptation, or self-organization, of a system. They do so basically by decreasing system variety and reactivity, building barriers to heterogenous interaction (i.e. external interactivity), removing therefore the prerequisites for complex-adaptive (self-organizing) activity. In neither instance, DIM or CAS, however, is there no true time-asymmetry, or reversibility. Even if there is complete discontinuation of a given practice, one cannot return to the conditions extant before the given innovation was introduced. The drug Thalidomide, for example, was banned once its dangers became apparent, but its social impacts, particularly its effects on mothers and their "thalidomide babies," could not be undone.

Variety, Reactivity and Heterophily in the Two Models

Variety and reactivity are prerequisites of CAS (Waldrop 1992: 314). Variety is defined in complexity science as a large enough and diverse enough pre-condition or population for emergence and adaptation to occur. Variety is found in diffusion theory as heterophily, or degree to which individual communicators differ along traits pertinent to predisposition toward adoption. A very high degree of heterophily will likely slow down diffusion, but some degree of heterophily among communicators is nonetheless necessary for an innovation to spread (that is, a source individual must know more, and is assumed to know more. about the innovation than a receiver one). Thus heterogenous interactions occur in heterogenous zones – as suggested previously, locations where members, in their variety, can react more sensitively, increase their fitness, and change in a way that enhances chances for survival or forestalls threats of extinction.

Reactivity in CAS entails sensitivity to change, which increases immediately before cascades between steps at system bifurcation points. Cascading mutation/extinction, or changes in individual species, results from reactivity to change and continues in step-like punctuated equilibria that approach the critical point of self-organization (in heterogenous zones). There is a gap that grows between these avalanches of mutations and step-up plateaus in systemic fitness thresholds. As fitness thresholds or plateaus step higher and higher, the cascades of change (between $1<a<3$ and $3<a<3.56994567$ in the quadratic equation $f(s) = as(1-s)$), with their draw on disposable resources, become larger and larger. Only those species (population categories) with sufficient disposable resources (adaptability to change) can survive at the higher fitness thresholds that occur during change cascades. In this view, only those capable of self-organizing emerge as "select." The cascading continues until the envelope function reaches the critical value fc of the system (Paczuski, Maslow and Bak, 1996), and it then stabilizes as a complex system.

The power law is discussed in more detail in the next section, *The Movement Toward Criticality*. When non-linear (complex) values of mutations/extinctions (self-change) are plotted in a quadratic iterative map $s(t) = as(t-1)(1-s(t-1))$, rewritten as $f(s) = as(1-s)$ (Bar-Yam, 1997: 26), bifurcation may continue until the system falls into chaos (Bar-Yam, 1997: 33). Similarly, in the DIM, innovations diffuse more rapidly and successfully in highly reactant social networks, through relatively heterogenous early adopters, who have the highest level of adaptability to change. They typically have high levels of disposable resources (high socio-economic status), relatively more exposure to adopters from other social networks, and the inclination to try new ideas (personality values and cosmopolite commu-nication behaviors) (Rogers, 2003: 288).

The highest reactivity across all adopter groups is found at the *critical mass inflection point*, point 2 on the S-shaped diffusion curve (Figure 13.2, see later). This is where cascades of change occur. The diffusion curve can be thought of as a smooth curve that passes through the step-up plateaus in systemic fitness thresholds. As the curve rises, certain thresholds are passed for adoption networks. These rising thresholds evoke adaptation (in the case of early adopters) or loss (for laggards). Granovetter (1978) discusses thresholds in terms of eliciting a critical mass of collective behavior. Critical mass is reached at the point where there are enough adopters that further diffusion becomes self-sustaining (Rogers, 2003). At the height of the adop-tion curve, the fittest members of the social network have self-organized (adapted) to the higher plateau of fitness and adopted the innovation. Bifurcation, or decision, points have been passed on the way at step-like critical-mass thresholds. Unfit adopters, those without sufficient capabil-ity or inclination to adopt, have been precluded from participating in the adoption of the innovation.

DIM requires a lower threshold of variety than CAS, yet some vari-ety is necessary in order for information exchange to take place between an innovation sender and an innovation receiver. The functionality of

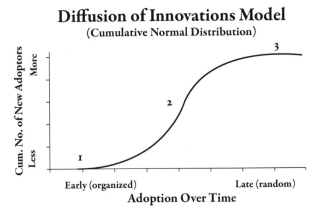

Figure 13.2: Cumulative diffusion ("S") curve.

heterophily and variety is consistent with Granovetter's *strength of weak ties* in networks (1973). A related finding of recent diffusion studies is that an innovation has a more rapid rate of adoption when it is easy to "re-invent." *Re-invention* is the degree to which adopters can change a new idea, practice, or technology as it diffuses (Rogers, 2003).

Before a complex system (a social network, a population, or cognition and motivation in an individual) can move into criticality, or complex adaptation, it must have sufficient variety or variability (degrees of freedom or heterogeneity), which can be translated as sufficient resources and inclination toward new ideas and heterophilous interactivity for internal organization (i.e. heterogenous mutation or adaptation toward self-organization). Similarly, diffusion is more rapid and effective (displays a higher degree of contagion) with a higher frequency of contact (interactivity) among heterophilous units in a system (Rogers, 2003: 19), a requirement that corresponds to that of variety in the CAS model (Granovetter, 1973). Both models require prerequisite internal conditions for their most favorable functioning, but diffusion can propagate reliably in low variety and low reactivity one-on-one environments, while a CAS may not. In some idealized hypothetical simulation, a CAS may begin to propagate if it only has one reactive element among a sea of "dead strings," but in other CAS simulations, such as in chemical reactions, there is a threshold floor beneath which propagation of reactivity will not occur.

In DIM, potential adopters, wholly located on the fringe or edge (the highest reactivity, heterogenous zone) of a system, are seldom certain about whether an innovation is a superior alternative to what they already have or do. Thus, potential adopters are not always able to easily ascertain the benefits of adoption. This imperceptibility or undecidability contributes uncertainty and a lack of guaranteed outcome from the point of view of the potential adopter – uncertainty is the degree to which a number of alternatives are associated with the occurrence of an event but the relative probability of the alternatives is unknown (Rogers, 2003). Uncertainty is a barrier to diffusion, and its antidote is information. A certain degree of uncertainty always characterizes an individual's perceptions of a new idea, practice, or technology, which is one reason why the diffusion process occurs gradually. Uncertainty is also a salient feature of complex adaptive systems, wherein uncertainty is a barrier to reactivity, and thus to emergence and criticality.

The Movement toward Criticality in CAS and DIM

Criticality is a three-or-more-variable interrelational location toward which complex systems migrate, in reaction to higher fitness requirements in the environment, in order to solve the problems of increasing complexity in increasingly difficult environments. The problem of adapting to increasing complexity is universally recognized as salient in today's world, as system complexity exceeds individual ability to process it sufficiently in real time (Bar-Yam, 1997; Toffler, 1970). The movement toward cognitive complexity may not be conscious; it may be an evolutionarily defined, heuristic if-then rule (Waldrop, 1992, "satisficing" in Simon, 1991).

Rules are structured to identify the direction of system rewards and are important in both models. In DIM, these rules are social *norms*, defined as established behavior patterns and expectations for members of a social system (Rogers, 2003). Rules cannot be violated in either theoretical model with impunity. Expectancy of rewards also prompts agents in a CAS to move towards criticality and to consider heterogenous ideas despite their uncertainty, or to adapt as a strategy to increase fitness. Agents develop strategies for fitness within boundaries, and "some strategies work better than others" (Waldrop, 1992: 310). Similarly, a population involved in innovation diffusion works within rule-sets to shift toward higher adoption rates, as rewards for adoption become widely known (and as uncertainty about such rewards for innovation decrease).

Agents in both models use rules to move toward fitness rewards located at the edge of a heterogenous zone, where criticality obtains. Changing an agent's strategic fitness has the effect of changing the fitness of adjacent agents: "As each agent develops, it changes the fitness landscape of all the other agents [in its local network] ... [When] a handful of species manage to find a temporary [local maxima, they are] locked in equilibrium" (Waldrop, 1992: 310–311). Agents move with their neighbors at a pace that varies by degree of proximity (Bar-Yam 1997, 2005), with the closest network neighbors mimicking movement most closely. Similarly, a synapse is part of the fitness landscape of its neighbors and contributes to the fitness of the entire neuronal system. Generally, a localized system exhibiting progressive and interreactive change "strategies" in movement toward maximum fitness will quit moving toward criticality when it reaches a local optimum if it is isolated from the larger population (Waldrop 1992: 311).

From the mid-1970s to the mid-1990s, scientists studied and described different phenomena of emergence of CAS out of chaos. Per Bak's sand pile analogies inspired Stephen Jay Gould and Niles Eldridge's ideas of "punctuated equilibria" in evolution. Bak worked with both of these scientists at the Santa Fe Institute in 1989, where he identified punctuated equilibria as indicators of self-organized criticality (Bak, 1996: 117–118). Bak also defined the signature $1/f$ *noise parameter* for a self-organizing system: In 1994, Bak, collaborating with Sergei Maslov and Maya Paczuski, discovered the power law: $f(t) = f_c - A \, (t/N)^{-1/(y-1)}$ (Bak, 1996: 169; Paczuski, Maslow and Bak, 1996). This power law describes the delta point for "cascades of change," as in the angle of repose of a sand pile (Gleick, 1987; Waldrop, 1992). By way of illustration and analogy, Figure 13.4 later in this study shows the power law for new HIV infections after the advent of the San Francisco *STOP AIDS* public education and prevention program.

The power law is a tool to identify when criticality is reached in a broad spectrum of systems such as "stock markets, [chemical solutions] ... and interdependent webs of technology" (Waldrop: 309): "Networks with power-law distributions are often referred to as *scale-free* networks" (Braha and Bar-Yam, 2004: 250; Barabasi and Albert, 1999). Maximum fitness, depending upon particular sets of boundaries, occurs "right at phase transition ... [and] the edge of chaos is actually where complex systems go in order to solve a complex task" (Waldrop: 313). As with CAS's *self-organizing* identifiers, the DIM employs measures of criticality and phase transition. Criticality and phase transition is to CAS as critical mass is to DIM.

Arrival at Self-Organized Criticality

Arrival at criticality and phase transition in CAS (critical mass in DIM, as just suggested) can occur relatively fast. It can occur immediately, as in sand piles, or very slowly, as in inter-generational cultural diffusion. In the case of the STOP AIDS program, to be discussed in a section that follows, criticality of new HIV infections occurred between 1978 to 1983, as the HIV virus multiplied exponentially over five years. On the one hand, the virus reached criticality before the STOP AIDS program diffused, and, on the other, the STOP AIDS program reached its own criticality or critical mass due to inoculation-like barriers in the form of safer-sex practices.

Per Bak distinguishes between types of self-organizing systems and their differing power-law exponents as classified by speed of formation. "The distribution of avalanche sizes is a power law with exponent 3/2 just like Henrik's random neighbor model ... The punctuated equilibrium evolution for a single species [in the Paezuski-Boettcher model] is ... 7/4" (Bak, 1996: 166–167). Maximum fitness occurs within particular boundaries "right at phase transition ... [and] the edge of chaos is actually where complex systems go in order to solve a complex task" (Waldrop, 1992: 313). Waldrop's finding coincides with the present chapter's: *Heterogenous areas are those where emergence is likeliest.* They are located in the CAS epoch, such as between $1 < a < 3$ and $3 < a < 3.56994567$ in the quadratic equation $f(s) = as(1-s)$.

Scale is an important consideration in many fields, as the scale may affect the behavior observed, and feedback processes can occur between system levels. Emergence in CAS is a bottom-up rather than a top-down process, that is, it goes from lower to higher scales. A number of units – cells, people, computer networks, synapses – interact locally, and each unit's actions contribute to the emergence of a global property at a higher level of organization and possibility. The sum of such microbehaviors produces a macrobehavior, and this global-level behavior feeds back to individual units at the lower level (Lewin, 1999). Local interactions are fine-scale-level behaviors, while the emergent level gives rise to global-scale behavior of higher-level fitness.

The observed system behaviors at these different scales are not necessarily the same. It is here where CAS differs from nested or scaled networks.

Behavior in CAS is scale-free (scale-free qualities of diffusion are discussed in the "Emergence and Feedback" section below). Macroscale propagation/adoption does not necessarily negate microscale volition (individual choices and propensities toward choice), although group norms from the macro-scale can strongly influence individual behavior through circular causation, feedback, and reinforcement.

Diffusion theory, like CAS, looks at both the fine and global scales of behavior and the relationships between them, and it illustrates emergent behavior and feedback when aggregates of individual behavior scale up to a similar behavior on a system level. Beginning with the level of local interactions, the fine scale, diffusion takes place through a network consisting of individual units (potential adopters). The adopter unit can be an individual or an organization ("individuals" hereafter, for simplicity). Each individual can be self-located in one of the five adopter categories (innovators, early adopters, early majority, late majority, and laggards) and the network provides connections through which an innovation spreads (Rogers, 2003).

As individuals adopt an innovation, their microbehavior contributes to the macrosystem-level scale of behavior. As the rate of adoption of an innovation accelerates and innovation diffusion takes off, emergent adoptive behavior occurs at the system level. As an innovation is adopted by additional individuals in a system, a feedback loop occurs in the diffusion process as observability and other attributes of the innovation process reduce uncertainties associated with the new idea, process, or technology. The progress – initiation and maturation – of adoption is seen in linear relationships between the quality and source of new information and a population's manifest propensity toward an adoption decision. This is an example of a scaled network.

The Micro Scale

Networks are an essential feature of a CAS. Without them, there would be no system. Networks allow the system to solve problems using the large numbers of individual nodes that have local interactions with other nodes.

The nodes themselves need not be "aware" they are contributing to this endeavor. They are following their own micromotivated rule-sets and interacting with local network neighbors. Such behavior allows the system to process information, and thus to learn. Moreover, CAS networks maintain their global behavior despite individual turnover (Johnson: 2001), even as complex mutual causation occurs at network levels. Diffusion theory is similarly dependent on networks in which individuals interact locally with their neighbors. Individual adopters are not usually cognizant of their contribution to a higher-scale order; rather, they make their decisions about innovations on the basis of their own perceived circumstances. As with CAS, network adoption of innovations is maintained despite population turnover, often for generations, even as different system levels influence one another.

An innovation comes into a system from outside, usually via an innovator or early adopter. Early adopters ("cosmopolites") are typically sufficiently respected in their local communities (relative to innovators and outsiders) that others are willing to follow their lead. They, then, function as role models. An early adopter may also be an opinion leader, and/or well connected, so that s/he has above-average network-connectivity in the system (Rogers, 2003). Early adopters are therefore highly reactive – heterogenous – and their behavior is conducive to reactivity in others, as they increase perturbation around themselves by virtue of their propensity to innovate. Once brought into the system, innovations diffuse through networks of social ties. These links include relatively strong ties with opinion leaders and weak ties among social subgroups, which bridge sub-networks that would otherwise remain unconnected. Granovetter discusses the importance of these interpersonal and inter-group heterogenous links in the diffusion process in his "strength of weak ties" theoretical argument (Granovetter, 1973).

A key feature of these links is the degree of homophily or heterophily between connected units. Homophily is the tendency to selectively interact with and learn from culturally similar others, so that degree of homophily refers to the extent of prior affinity among network actors, including proneness to accept innovation. Greater homophily allows for

greater ease of diffusion (although as previously stated, a degree of heterophily regarding an innovation is required for reactivity), while high
degrees of heterophily raise barriers to diffusion. At extreme values, high
heterophily makes diffusion almost impossible, as several studies illustrate
(Rogers, 2003).

In a CAS, as in DIM, the units interacting in a network require a
degree of variety – the network cannot link identical units. Heterophily
provides variety, and information processing allows even highly heterophilous pairs to interact, albeit indirectly through relatively more homophilous
links. The greater the homophily, the less the energy or effort required to
transmit information. For instance, individuals in a support group who are
homophilous in regard to the group subject (e.g. alcoholism) do not have
to expend undue effort explaining their situation; rather they can invest
themselves in working directly on their problem. A group of heterophilous
individuals (e.g. alcoholics and obsessive gamblers) would not be able to
work as efficiently.

An outsider, such as a change agent, needs to expend a large amount
of energy or effort when the agent and client are overly different in orientations and attitudes toward the given innovation. In addition to the specific
information the change agent must communicate about an innovation, s/
he must convey background information about the innovation if it is to
make sense to potential adopters. Failure to transmit all such information
can result in diffusion failure. An instance is found in the story of a public
health worker who attempted to persuade village women in Peru to boil
their drinking water (Rogers, 2003). Since the villagers lacked awareness of
science, she had to convey not only essential information about germs but
also the technological and scientific underpinnings of the proposed intervention in order to justify her call for boiling water for sanitation purposes.
Despite two years of intensive effort, the worker failed to prompt water-
boiling in the village. The cultural gap was too large for communication, and
hence diffusion, to occur. Uncertainty and suspicion served as protective
barriers buffering the indigenous system from excessive perturbation, or
shock. A social system needs time to absorb new information and integrate
change so as to maintain a reasonable internal stability.

The Macro Scale

In both the CAS and diffusion of innovations models, local interactions in networks lead to the emergence of global structures and behaviors at the next higher level of organization. As individual system units adopt an innovation, the innovation diffuses. Micro-scale behaviors – frequent instances of adoption – create macro-scale phenomena, such as the establishment of a consumer product standard. The often-cited triumph of VHS over Beta is a case in point.

The S-shaped curve represents cumulative adoption over time by members of a system. The two plateau segments (early and late in the adoption process, points 1 and 3) of the S-curve are relatively stable regions where it is difficult to change the system (Figure 13.2). These segments may be likened to attractors. An example is found in the diffusion of telecommunications innovations. A telephone is obviously useless for the first individual to own it, and even with a few adopters there persists a stable state of "non-telephony." However, telephones did diffuse globally with the rapid adoption of telephone use, whether through ownership or public-access pay phones. Thus, there was a linear stability plateau at low levels of adoption and usage in the early stage (point 1), followed by cascade of change (CAS emergence, point 2), ending in a linear stable stage again (point 3) after the market was saturated.

The "biggest bang for the buck" (whether in behavior change or chemical reactions) is found in the most externally susceptible and reactive, heterogenous, zone, the phase-state where cascades of change occur at the most rapid rate (point 2). Cascades of change occur as a system processes new information about an innovation, overcomes uncertainty, and in effect, makes a determination that operatively shifts the system from one attractor (point 1) to a new attractor (point 2). The state change could be from non-adoption to adoption of an innovation, or to a defining choice between two competing innovations or behavioral norms. Choice at the bifurcation point leads adoption and self-reorganization around the adoption and to arrival at self-organized criticality. Figures 13.3 and 13.4 compare points 1, 2, and 3 on the distribution curves for the DIM and CAS. It should be noted that the CAS and DIM models produce the same distribution curves.

Diffusion of Innovations Model

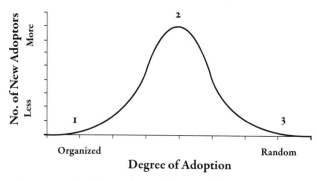

Figure 13.3: Distribution for the diffusion of innovations model.

Complex Adaptive Systems

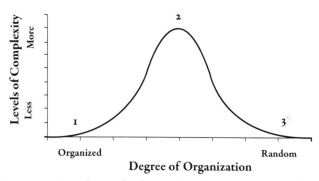

Figure 13.4: Distribution for the complex adaptive systems model.

When does the system as a whole make an adoption-decision? Where does it switch from one previously stable attractor toward another? The inflection point on the S-curve, about where critical mass occurs (Rogers, 2003), is the key point of interest (Figure 13.2). A continuing increase in the number of adopters, or synapses, or processing elements, increases the energy being processed in the local system at the inflection point. Until that point of critical mass is reached on the S-curve, the rate of increase in the number of adopters per time unit is nearly linear. Complexity begins at a threshold of non-linearity (So, Chen and Chen, 2005). In the diffusion system's rate of adoption, this critical threshold has also been called the *tipping point* (Gladwell 2002), a transitional inflection point associated with higher system reactivity, where system members are sensitive to change. At this conjuncture, the system exhibits the most change ("bang for the buck") for the least increase in energy – corresponding to heightened activity in the heterogenous (most externally interactive) zone. Once the rate of adoption in a system reaches critical mass at the inflection point, it is difficult or impossible to stop further phase transition around diffusion (Figure 13.5, see later). The eventual flattening of the curve owes to a decline in numbers of potential adopters, as the innovation is taken up by more and more adopters, and more easily so.

Emergence and Feedback

The micro and macro scales are connected, as individual actions aggregate to the macro level, al so called the large-scale level of a complex adaptive system. Within this system there is a type of feedback (strange attractor) that loops back to influence behavior on the micro or individual level. Feedback is a vital component of CAS – a large part of what makes a complex system adaptive (Johnson, 2001). As each individual unit makes a decision, that decision contributes to the emergence of further decision-action sequences on the macro or global scale. Conversely, the macro or large-scale behavior also influences microbehavior through strange attractors, though the two levels of scale do not necessarily change at the same rate.

Whereas a scaled network produces changes similarly at all system levels, a scale-free network, a complex network, is one where small changes on the individual level can cause large changes on the macro or aggregate level. A scale-free network operates according to the power law. We will offer an example of scale-free network diffusion in the discussion that follows of the STOP AIDS program. In terms of diffusion, individual adoption decisions at the micro level lead to the emergence of innovation adoption by the social system as a whole at the macro level. The S-curve and other aggregate measures are depictions of such macro-level phenomena.

Individual decisions of rejection or discontinuance on the micro level, on the other hand can grow to a failure of innovation adoption at the system level and thus to a failure of emergence, creating a flattened S-shaped curve (Figure 13.1). In this context, Rogers spoke of a "KAP-gap" (or "Knowledge-Attitude-Practice" gap), which he conceived of as a relatively homophilous zone where knowledge and attitudes are favorable toward adoption but insufficient for adoption. Rogers emphasized the importance of interviewing non-adopters and discontinuers and asking "why" and "when" and "under what conditions" failure occurred, to ascertain the reasons for failure and generally evaluate the diffusion campaign. Heterophilous members of a target population can be particularly helpful in offering information about determinative attitudes among non-adopters, because heterophilous members offer a dual outsider/insider view. Such interviews often led to a realization that the diffusion campaign targeted the wrong independent variables due to researcher misunderstanding of the culture of the target population – in particular a misunderstanding of that population's unique set of culturally defined meanings and felt uncertainties. Mistaken attributions on the part of designers of diffusion campaigns are usually the cause of diffusion failure, observed at the macro level as a marked flattening of the bell-shaped adoption curve (Medina, personal communication with Rogers, November 17, 2004).

Feedback from the macro level to individual units occurs in complex adaptive systems. In diffusion theory, one route for feedback is observability, as when a potential adopter observes influential people, such as celebrities or recognized experts, using the innovation. As the system adopts, individual adoptions are observable in this manner to an ever-greater degree, making for an increasingly rapid rate of change. The more observable an innovation (for instance, the use of cell phones), the easier it is for feedback to work. Poorly observable innovations, including many health prevention interventions, offer less noticeable feedback and diffuse more slowly. Trialability, or the opportunity to try a new idea on a small scale or in a short time (with less risk), also allows for feedback. A company may distribute free samples so that an individual consumer can try the new product, obtaining feedback from the trial. Feedback among individuals at the local micro scale is thus important; a primary means of local feedback occurs as adopters (and "rejecters") share their experiences with an innovation with others in their circle of acquaintances. A potential adopter may see someone else use an innovation (observability), or a tentative adopter may lend it to someone else to try out (trialability). Such feedback reduces uncertainty about the innovation, which may lead to more adoption through reinforcement.

Complexity science helps explain the establishment of order in a population where at first appears to be none, and where novelty or exception successfully challenges settled rules. The CAS model, like diffusion theory, works well when interrelationships among the members of a system are strong and dense, while allowing for action at the level of individual units (Stacey, Griffin and Shaw, 2000). For both models, prediction is weak when relationships are weak individuals in a system are isolated. CAS models break down or do not work when local units become isolated, or when relationships are broken, are locked into equilibrium, or fade out.

It is argued in this chapter that CAS models have the ability to inform diffusion models where diffusion processes are irregular. Furthermore, CAS provides an entirely new toolbox with which to model the diffusion process, essentially giving researchers a new way to look "inside the box," with a variety of population sizes at the scale of interest. For example, using the hybrid DIM–CAS methodology, one of the authors (Medina) is developing models that mathematically illustrate the process of attaining critical mass within small-group discussions. These models illuminate group norming communication dynamics. Formerly, such a process could only provide descriptive data, so that it was essentially a black box with regard to quantitative modeling and prediction. Likewise, the diffusion of an innovation amongst larger groups can be modeled with a DIM–CAS combined framework in a manner that provides greater insight into the mechanisms of diffusion and adoption. In the following section, a co-theoretical model is more explicitly built around an applied case study, the STOP AIDS experience in San Francisco.

Stop Aids

The STOP AIDS experience in San Francisco from 1984 to 1987 (Rogers, 2003; Wohfeiler, 1998, 2002) and subsequent HIV prevention interventions modeled after it (STOP AIDS II, 1990 to present), in several nations (Singhal and Rogers, 2003) and in certain social networks (Flowers, Hart, Williamson, Frankis and Derr, 2002; Kegeles, Hays and Coate, 1996; Kelly, Heckman, Stevenson, Williams, Ertl, Hays, Leonard, O'Donnell, Terry, Sogolow and Spink Neumann, 2000; Kelly, Murphy, Sikkema, McAuliffe, Roffman, Solomon, Winett an Kalichman, 1997; Kelly, Sogolow, and Spink Neumann, 2000; Kelly, Somlai, DiFrancesico, Otto-Salaj, McAuliffe, Hackl, Heckman, Holtgrave and Rompa, 2000; Kelly, St. Lawrence, Diaz, Stevenson, Hauth, Brasfield, Kalichman, Smith and Andrew, 1991; Kelly, St. Lawrence, Stevenson, Hauth, Kalichman, Diaz, Brasfield, Koob and Morgan, 1992; Miller, Klotz and Eckholdt, 1998; Sikkema, Kelly, Winett, Solomon, Cargill, Rofferman, McAuliffe, Heckman, Anderson, Wagstaff, Norman, Perry, Crumble and Mercer, 2000), have shown that the diffusion of innovations model can be applied effectively in public health and health policy settings.

These studies also suggest that planned diffusion closely parallels emergence in CAS. Diffusion begins in localized areas and spreads throughout a network, increasing in density unit adoption spreads. Adoption spreads as more and more members of a social network adopt, meeting an adoption threshold (Valente, 1995). In this manner, adopters influence others to adopt (Rogers, 2003). The STOP AIDS intervention was based on both the diffusion model and on social psychologist Kurt Lewin's strategy of changing behavior in small group networks (Rogers, 1994). STOP AIDS employed outreach workers who were gay, many HIV–positive recruit individuals to small group training meetings of from ten to twelve men (Yorke, 2003).

Meetings were held in homes and apartments along Castro Street and in other neighborhoods where gay men lived in San Francisco. Each meeting, led by a gay man (often one who was HIV–positive), featured explanation of the means of HIV transmission and of the importance of practicing safer sex. Each small group meeting ended with the individuals being asked to raise their hands (1) if they intended to practice safer sex, and (2) if they would agree to organize and lead a future small-group meeting themselves (Singhal and Rogers, 2003). The threshold for individual fitness, and survival, required a change in sex practices. These public displays of support for safer-sex practices created a type of emergent, macro-level normative pattern, a type of strange attractor for behavioral change in the larger community, and a complex adaptive system demonstrating the properties of a scale free network, a complex network.

Planners of the STOP AIDS intervention assumed that if they could reach a critical mass of opinion leaders in the city's gay community, the idea of HIV prevention would then spread spontaneously by interpersonal communication networks to others in the targeted population. Arenas, Danon, Diaz-Guilera, Gleiser, and Guimera (2003) found that community-size social networks exhibit scaling with a power law exponent in the range of −0.5 or −1. This scaling in the STOP AIDS program is illustrated in Figures 13.3 and 13.4. Scaling occurred both upwards as the virus spread and downwards as it was denied hosts due to safer-sex practices promoted by the program. Scaling down occurred at the power law exponent of −1.143, with adoption of a *shared commitment to safer sex* as the message reached critical mass in the city's gay community.

This diffusion process can be likened to "the symbolic [cultural] dynamics of a chaotic system [in its ability] to track a prescribed symbol sequence thus allowing the encoding of any desired message" (Yorke, 2003). Figure 13.5 (see later) illustrates log plots of the cumulative diffusion of the STOP AIDS program and its effects of declining rates of HIV infection, showing a power law regime with a fast decaying tail (Braha and Bar-Yam, 2004).

STOP AIDS reached over 30,000 of the total gay population is San Francisco of approximately 142,000. The rate of unprotected anal sex dropped from 71 per cent in 1983 to 27 per cent in 1987. With the decline of this means of transmission, the number of AIDS-related deaths per year dropped from 1,600 in the mid-1980s to only 250 in recent years (Wohfeiler, 1998, 2002). The application of diffusion of innovations theory, combined with networked Lewinian small-group strategies, in effect created strange attractors in large-scale population behavior, that is, new behavioral norms that attracted and promoted safer-sex behavior. These attractors were evident in the spread of safer-sex practices, a development that helped stem the epidemic (Figure 13.3).

An attitude, defined as a predisposition to action (Rogers, 2003), is, effectively, a reactive in the hybrid complexity-diffusion model here proposed. In the STOP AIDS case, the observability of the devastation caused by HIV/AIDS in San Francisco changed attitudes toward safer-sex practices (developed strange attractors within the large-scale that promoted such practices), and these strange attractors sped up the adoption of the innovation. Consequently gay men became much more willing to use condoms and to otherwise reduce risky behaviors to preserve their health and attractive looks, and to avoid sickness. Attitudes toward safer sex thus became socially embedded in the older gay men's population. Then, as conditions improved and the ravages of HIV/AIDS less visible, there came a new surge in infections in San Francisco. As new cohorts of younger gay men arrived in the city in the early 1990's, they identified the previous HIV/AIDS epidemic with the older gay community, whom they tended to stigmatize. Unwarranted negative word of mouth about the STOP AIDS program among young gays led them to shun adoption, and the adoption threshold therefore rose considerably for them (Erez, Moldovan and Solomon, 2004). Furthermore, in their time, these young gays could not observe the results of unsafe sex behaviors as readily as had their predecessors. The epidemic had been nearly eradicated. Clear-cut benefits to safer-sex adoption were less observable (Rogers, 2003). Hence, the younger gays did not adopt safer-sex practices, and rates of infection once again increased to epidemic level, until the STOP AIDS program was reinstated (Figure 13.5).

San Francisco's STOP AIDS intervention of the early 1980s was replicated in several developing countries (Singhal and Rogers, 2003). One program in the United States that was in part inspired by the STOP AIDS model was directed by Jeffrey Kelly and his colleagues (Kelly, Murphy, Sikkema, McAuliffe et al., 1997). In several U.S. cities, opinion leaders were identified and then trained in how to prevent HIV infection among gay men. Again, the objective was to reach a critical mass of at-risk individuals with prevention messages. The opinion-leader strategy is now being implemented and evaluated in at least five developing nations (Rogers, 2003).

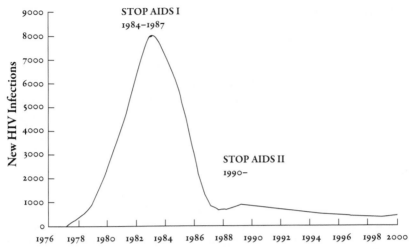

Figure 13.5: Changes in new HIV infections in San Francisco between 1977 and 2000
showing advent of STOP AIDS coinciding with decrease in new infections.

Analysis

The foregoing co-theoretical model links DIM to CAS and provides an
analytical tool for students of innovation, particularly in the use of public
sector collaborative networks. The interdependency of innovation networks and the heterogeneity operative in complex adaptive systems are
complementary. This analysis section discusses in detail how the combined
model of DIM and CAS offers the possibility of a deeper understanding
of diffusion in practice.

The coterminous processes of innovation-diffusion and complex adaptive systems leads, through phase transitions, to a more rapid rate of adoption or emergence, resulting in a higher-order, fitter system. Both models
are built on empirical observation of bottom-up change, both can describe
transitions occurring either naturally or as a result of directed change, and
both can be statistically analyzed to infer population parameters for processes of change. In CAS, the point attractor where organization is 100

per cent and complexity is equal to zero corresponds to the same point in DIM. At this point, an adoption begins to diffuse, organization is at 100 per cent (i.e. the original idea is still intact and has not yet been reinvented or reorganized) and the complexity of the social network among adopters is zero (Figure 13.4). It is here, at the beginning of both systems processes and at the corresponding point on the S-shaped curve, that *the rate of adoption changes little for every additional new adopter.* The rate of change at the beginning is particularly linear, attesting to the given system's status as a simple system (Bar-Yam, 1997). The *rate of adoption* changes less for each new adopter than it will at point two (Figure 13.3).

In CAS, at point two (Figure 13.4), the area where strange attractors and complex attractors are found at the most complex points on the curve is also the highest point on the bell-shaped curve. This area corresponds to that in DIM where the adopter network is the most complex, and where strange attractors are stabilized. Here there is the greatest increase in rate of adoption (where the slope is vertical, point two, Figure 13.1) for the fewest additional cumulative adopters: There is *increased sensitivity to change for the least increase in energy expended toward change.* This is the location of complexity where heterogeneity exists at the border of chaos – that area between simple systems and chaotic systems – the area of scale-free networks.

The disproportionate changes at different system scales or levels identify a scale-free network. The rate of adoption changes more for each new adopter than it did at point one, and the rate of adoption changes more for each new adopter than it will at point three. At point two, the bifurcation threshold has been passed for this population. There is no longer a question of whether diffusion will occur throughout the majority of the population: The population will continue to adopt due to the momentum that has been attained. Point two, the *inflection point* on the curve (Figure 13.1), is called the point of critical mass because it is where adaptation has met or exceeded the fitness threshold and "further diffusion becomes self-sustaining" (Rogers, 2003: 343). Point two is another dynamic juncture, a *heterogenous zone where the rate of change is non-linear.* At point two, the rate of change is nearly vertical – it approaches closest to infinity.

At point three in CAS (Figure 13.4), the area where 100 per cent randomness and zero per cent complexity occur, is the place where infinite attractors are found that cannot be modeled. This area corresponds to the same area in DIM, where an innovation has finished diffusing, and therefore the system is at zero per cent complexity – it has returned to a simple system and is again linear. There, perturbations are chiefly associated with resource scarcity or disinclination to new ideas among late adopters. At this place in the bell curve, diffusion as well as CAS cannot be modeled (Figure 13.4). At the correlating point three on the integral S-shaped curve (Figure 13.1), there is a flattened rate of adoption. That is, late in diffusion the speed of adoption is slowed and there are fewer new adopters. The rate of adoption changes less for each new adopter than it did at point two. The rate of adoption is stable, and the rate and quality of change is *rapidly linear*.

It is evident from the foregoing that both the DIM and CAS models can be used to describe behavioral changes in populations as well as other complex systems. The DIM has its strongest utility in the spread of new ideas, products, and practices. CAS may have the strongest value in the real-time monitoring of complex systems and in identifying early stages of phase transition into criticality. As defined previously, criticality or (interchangeably) critical mass is the point at which the random activity of unrelated elements in a system suddenly becomes more complexly structured and ends-oriented, as self-organization takes over. At criticality, a population's actions are no longer random, but rather take on a certain degree of predictability.

That phase transitions into higher levels of order can be anticipated, manipulated, and evaluated holds out significant promise for new applications in the social sciences and in social interventions. Future research might focus on the mathematical definition of zones of heterogeneity at the edge of adopter populations, where both uncertainty and sensitivity (or reactivity) to change are most acute, where the emergence of new attitudes and habits can be identified, and where communicative interventions can therefore be most cost-effective.

The STOP AIDS innovation spread rapidly because it was perceived by the gay community as relatively (a) advantageous over unsafe ideas or practices they superseded; (b) compatible with existing values, norms, beliefs, and life experiences; (c) easy to comprehend and adapt; (d) observable or tangible; and (e) divisible (separable) for trial and adoption (Rogers, 2003). The innovation operated like a vaccine in the CAS model, as more and more members of the gay population participated in the STOP AIDS program and adopted safer-sex practices, at the threshold of criticality (with reference to both DIM and CAS) where heterogeneity (adoption, mutation, change) was rewarded. Adaptation was rewarded as members increased both their individual utility (improved life expectancy, reduced fear and uncertainty) and the constancy and consistency of their interdependence (Klein, Faratin, Sayama and Bar-Yam, 2003).

During this complex transition, the utility-maximizing motivational rules (such as increased life expectancy) prompted individual-scale and group-scale movement from lower occurrence of safer-sex practices to higher levels of cohesiveness and order in group adoption of these practices). This new order was marked by *emergent self-organization*. Group adaptation to safer sex resulted from the increasing numbers and effective communication activities of highly connected sex health workers in the community. There was complex-network synchronization marked by role heterogeneity (in sustained interaction between health educators and members of the gay community; Motter, Zhou and Kurths, 2004). The resulting heterogenous system exhibited emergent patterned behavior that enabled the social group to respond more fitly to its environment, as a complex adaptive system (Johnson, 2001). If the social group was in fact a CAS, then a power law analysis should show it to be a scale-free network, one whose activity can be described by the power law. To test for this possibility, power law analysis was conducted by fitting a trend line of the least squares fit through data points (x, y), where x equaled the number of years since initiation of the STOP AIDS program and y equaled the number of new HIV infections. The following equation was applied: $y = cx^b$ where c and b are constants. Power law analysis yielded the following equation: $y = 10518x^{-1.143}$, with $R^2 = 0.9039$.

Ninety per cent of the variance was accounted for by the equation, showing a power law relationship between the STOP AIDS program and the sharply declining number of new HIV infections. Log plots of the cumulative distribution indicated a power law regime (Braha and Bar-Yam, 2004). The power law relationship between the STOP AIDS program and the decline in number of new HIV infections would indicate that there was a network of short-distance and highly connective iterative relationships between the health workers and members of the gay community (Braha and

Bar-Yam, 2004). Qualitative reports on the program tend to validate this assertion (Wohfeiler, 1998). Opinion leaders (highly connected, influential members of the target social group) became health workers and influenced large numbers in the gay community. Members organized in clusters around opinion leaders, and these clusters were highly connected to each other through those leaders. The health communication or diffusion work was iterative, in that it was conducted in virtually identical form in many, and often-repeated, small home gatherings. Pursuant to these conclusions the following graph, Figure 13.6, depicts the power law fit.

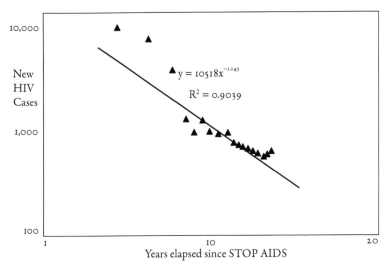

Figure 13.6: Power law fit between log of new HIV cases and log of time elapsed since STOP AIDS.

Conclusion

This conclusion section discusses in widely applicable theoretical terms how the co-theoretical model of DIM and CAS offers a deeper understanding of the theory and practice of diffusion. Recent treatments of STOP AIDS and kindred programs based on diffusion of innovations theory suggest that greater differentiation (heterogeneity) – by way of broader coalitions of activist groups armed with larger arsenals of proven interventions – makes for greater stability, sustainability, and effectiveness (a review of STOP AIDS and related literature is found in Bertrand, 2004; see also Wohfeiler, 1998; Essien, Linares and Osemene, 2000; and Wozniak, 2001); broad-based coalition-building is also the organizational and operational premise of the Global AIDS Alliance (Global AIDS Alliance, 2003). This finding, of the need for differentiated advocacy organization in the implementation of research-based interventions, is consistent with the proposition advanced in this chapter that heterogenous, transitional zones of innovation activity in networks can make for sustained efficacy in directed efforts at diffusion.

Bertrand indicates that "the changes in behaviour needed to halt the HIV/AIDS epidemic constitute what Rogers has labeled a 'preventive innovation,'" with the catalytic event occurring when "'trend setters' in a social network begin to model a new behaviour to others [and therefore] reduced uncertainty and altered the perception of what is normative ..." (Bertrand, 2004: 115). Bertrand adds that as prevention shifts from "predominant focus on individual behaviour to recognition of the importance of social norms in defining sexual behaviour," innovation diffusion is reasserting itself as a leading theory in the fight against HIV/AIDS (Bertrand, 2004: 120).

The increased heterogeneity of AIDS activism is, arguably, a major reason for the normative turn in applied diffusion theory. The greater breadth of membership strengthened the normativity and credibility of AIDS activism, and, in circular causation, greater credibility helps sustain AIDS advocacy. Bernardi (2003) has similarly found that the normative-structural characteristics of diverse social networks working in fertility-choice advocacy, and especially the inclusive quality and connective density of these family-centered networks, account for their effectiveness. Bernardi attributes their effectiveness to social-network synchronization.

In the CAS model DIM practitioners can now recognize the importance of heterogeneity and diversity – in modalities of social action, of ethical and cultural normativity, and of group membership – consistent with *law of requisite variety* (Ashby, 1970), which posits that system variation needs to match the corresponding features of environmental demands if organization and collective action are to be effective. Acknowledging the centrality of heterogeneity is also consistent with Actor-Network Theory, which, along with diffusion of innovations theory, points to the alignment of social and technical systems in *heterogenous networks*.

Heterogenous networks encompass interrelated structures of social relations, social values, and behavioral incentives and motivations, creating linkages to multiple chains of influence (Avgerou, 2002: 61). Arquilla and Ronfeldt (2001: 304) likewise argue that multiplicity or variety of network membership "permits division of labor and adaptation to circumstances ... The greater the differentiation of groups, the more likely the movement is able to offer something for every sympathizer to do to further the movement's goals."

In social action as in scale-free physical networks, heterogeneity enhances connectivity distribution and network synchronization. With sufficient differentiation, "synchronizability is drastically enhanced and may become positively correlated with heterogeneity," potentially reducing the costs involved in the creation of effective network ties (Motter, Zhou and Kurths, 2005: 334). As suggested throughout this chapter, in CAS a given system evolves in a non-linear, perturbable pattern of co-evolution among constituent elements.

In a differentiated network, typically marked by "the strength of weak ties," network synchronization is prone to emerge, rendering innovation relatively constant and, in that sense, sufficiently predictable for the purpose of program planning and projection (Cowan, Pines and Metzer, 1995). It is in this sense that Nobel Laureate Murray Gell-Mann (faculty member in Physics at the University of New Mexico and the Santa Fe Institute) writes (Gell-Mann, 1995) of "effective complexity" as a projection of a system's present-level complexity combined with the same system's "potential complexity." With STOP AIDS, effective complexity as a realization of potential complexity was attained when the social actors involved changed prevailing norms to a higher level of fitness, that is, the social network moved to a safer-sex-based normative system.

The foregoing suggests that applications of CAS to innovation diffusion can address not only the rate and sequencing of innovation adoption through the specification of threshold effects and phase transitions but also the acceleration of diffusion. The level of variety or heterogeneity among influentials' interpretations of the value of innovations counters prevailing norms and sensitizes the target population, increasing reactivity and bringing about *the early onset* of innovation adoption. After the stage here characterized as destabilization, the resulting quality and density of communications among all individuals (units of analysis, processing elements) in a given social network becomes more active, draws in more energy, and undergoes perturbation. At this juncture, norms are reorganized (redefined, modified) as new patterns of adoption emerge. It is in this vein that Ortiz-Torres, Serrano-Garcia, and Torres-Burgos (2000: 859) argue that working to change "sex-related social norms and normative beliefs" is subversive, because "rather than idealizing culture, it promotes changes that respect diversity within the culture and foster participation in the development of new cultural values, beliefs and norms."

What impact might a high level of heterogeneity – or, interchangeably, variety or variance – in the expected value of innovation have on diffusion? If expectancies are largely defined by groups and group norms, as Lewin argues, what happens when groups are moved by advocacy campaigns into uncomfortable zones of heterogeneity – for instance, when target populations are deliberately challenged – perturbed – and consequently change behaviors significantly (as did gay men in San Francisco between the 1980s and 1990s)? Do redefined group interpretations of what constitutes normative behavior lead to individual behavior change? How do perceived changes in the viability and normativity of available options affect the sequencing of choices associated with the adoption of innovations? Does heterogeneity of membership and roles in social networks make for variance of expectations and motivations (consistent with Lewin), as well as for more differentiated normative frames of reference?

Inevitably, the growth and diversification of AIDS advocacy groups and coalitions means that the movement has come to include disparate ethical standpoints and normative belief systems, numerous tested modes of intervention, and a wide array of social and institutional actors which despite their diversity share commitments around AIDS prevention and eradication. It is also the case, often commented, that AIDS is no longer – no longer seen as – strictly a "gay" disease, but rather one that affects the entirety of the population. Differently put, it is seen as differentially but universally affecting the entire population, including, in addition to gay men, heterosexual men, young adults, injection drug users, "sex workers," and other now-standard public-health group categories that, taken together, are virtually all-encompassing.

The preceding discussion suggests that a host of questions remain to be addressed in the innovation-diffusion field. These questions await the application of new mathematical and computational tools, and new theoretical perspectives. As to the first, there are numerous computational tools available, including self-organizing mapping systems, neural network software, and predictive network analysis software. As to the latter, it is suggested here that complex adaptive systems models provide a most promising theoretical and methodological source for innovation research. Under conditions we tentatively specify, the complex adaptive system and diffusion of innovations models are found to be essentially equivalent in important respects. Their synthesis and application could lend impetus to communicative action and advocacy efforts among a wide variety of social groups in varied contexts. It could also make innovation diffusion more predictable, and therefore more subject to planning, implementation, evaluation, and replication measures.

Bibliography

Arenas, A., L. Danon, A. Diaz-Guilera, P. M. Gleiser & R. Guimera. 2003. Community analysis in social networks. Accessed April 10, 2005 at: <http://complex. ffn.ub.es/cosin/publications.html> (no longer available).

Aron, J. L. 1990. Multiple attractors in the response to a vaccination program. *Theoretical Population Biology*, 38: 58–67.

Arquilla, J., & D. F. Ronfeldt. 2001. *Networks and netwars: The future of terror, crime, and militancy*. New York: Rand.

Ashby, W. R. 1970. *An introduction to cybernetics*. London: Chapman and Hall.

Avgerou, C. 2002. *Information systems and global diversity*. London: Oxford University Press.

Bak, P. 1996. *How nature works: The science of self-organized criticality.* New York: Copernicus.

Barabasi, A.-L, & R. Albert. 1999. Emergence of scaling in random networks. *Science*, 286: 519–512.

Bernardi, L. 2003. Social network influence on family and fertility choices. Paper presented at the International Social Network Conference, Sunbelt XXIII, Cancún, Quintana Roo, Mexico, February 13.

Bertrand, J. T. 2004. Diffusion of innovations and HIV/AIDS. *Journal of Health Communication*, 9: 113–121.

Braha, D., & Y. Bar-Yam. 2004. Information flow structure in large-scale product development organizational networks. *Journal of Information Technology*, 19(4): 244–265.

Cowan, G., D. Pines & D. Metzer. 1995. Complexity: Metaphors, models and reality. Paper in Santa Fe Institute Colloquium "Complex Dynamical Networks: Recent Developments," Santa Fe, New Mexico.

Erez, T., S. Moldovan & S. Solomon. 2004. Social anti-percolation, resistance and negative word of mouth. *Econophysics*, 4. Accessed April 11, 2004 at: <http://www.unifr.ch/econophysics> (no longer available).

Essien, E. J., M. W. Ross, A. C. Linares & N. I. Osemene. 2000. Perception of reliability of HIV/AIDS information sources. *Journal of the National Medical Association*, 92(6): 269–274.

Flowers, P., G. J. Hart, L. M. Williamson, J. S. Frankis & G. J. Derr. 2002. Does bar-based, peer-led health promotion have a community-level effect amongst gay men in Scotland? *International Journal of STD and AIDS*, 13: 102–108.

Gell-Mann, M. 1995. What is Complexity? *Complexity*, 1(1): 16–19. Accessed July 27, 2017 at: <http://www.ttivanguard.com/docs/phoenix99/complexity.doc>.

Gladwell, M. 2002. *The tipping point: How little things can make a big difference.* New York: Little, Brown and Co.

Gleick, J. 1987. *Chaos: The making of a new science.* New York: Penguin.

Global AIDS Alliance. 2003. *2003 Annual Report.* Accessed May 28, 2005 at: <http://www.globalaidsalliance.org/docs/2003annualreport.doc> (no longer available).

Granovetter, M. S. 1973. The strength of weak ties. *American Journal of Sociology*, 78: 1360–1380.

Granovetter, M. S. 1978. Threshold models of collective behavior. *American Journal of Sociology*, 83: 1420–1443.

Johnson, S. 2001. *Emergence: The connected lives of ants, brains, cities, and software.* New York: Scribner.

Kegeles, S. M., R. B. Hays & T. J. Coates. 1996. The Mpowerment project: A community-level HIV prevention intervention for young gay men. *American Journal of Public Health*, 86: 1129–1136.

Kelly, J. A., A. M. Somlai, W. J. DiFranceisco, L. L. Otto-Salaj, T. L. McAuliffe, K. L. Hackl, T. G. Heckman, D. R. Holtgrave & D. Rompa. 2000. Bridging the gap between the science and service of HIV prevention interventions to community AIDS service providers. *American Journal of Public Health*, 90: 1082–1088.

Kelly, J. A., D. A. Murphy, K. J. Sikkema, T. L. McAuliffe, R. A. Roffman, L. J. Solomon, R. A. Winnett & S. C. Kalichman. 1997. Randomized, controlled, community-level HIV-prevention for sexual risk behavior among heterosexual men in U.S. cities. *Lancet*, 350: 1500–1505.

Kelly, J. A., E. D. Sogolow & M. Spink Neumann. 2000. Future directions and emerging issues in technology transfer between HIV prevention researchers and community-based service providers. *AIDS Education and Prevention*, 12 (suppl. A): 126–141.

Kelly, J. A., J. S. St Lawrence, Y. E. Diaz, L. Y. Stevenson, A. C. Hauth, T. L. Brasfield, S. C. Kalichman, J. E. Smith & M. E. Andrew. 1991. HIV risk behavior reduction following intervention with key opinion leaders of population: An experimental analysis. *American Journal of Public Health*, 81(2): 168–171.

Kelly, J. A., J. S. St. Lawrence, Y. E. Stevenson, A. C. Hauth, S. C. Kalichman, Y. E. Diaz, T. L. Brasfield, J. J. Koob & M. G. Morgan. 1992. Community AIDS/HIV risk reduction: The effects of endorsements by popular people in three cities. *American Journal of Public Health*, 82(11): 1483–1489.

Kelly, J. A., T. G. Heckman, L. Y. Stevenson, P. N. Williams, T. Ertl, R. B. Hays, N. A. Leonard, L. O'Donnell, M. A. Terry, E. D. Sogolow & M. Spink Neumann. 2000. Transfer of research-based HIV prevention interventions to community service providers: Fidelity and adaptation. *AIDS Education and Prevention*, 12 (suppl. A): 87–98.

Lewin, R. 1999. *Complexity: Life at the edge of chaos*. 2nd Edn. Chicago, IL: The University of Chicago Press.

Miller, R. L., D. Klotz & H. M. Eckholdt. 1998. HIV prevention with male prostitutes and patrons of hustler bars: Replication of an HIV prevention intervention. *American Journal of Community Psychology*, 26(1): 97–131.

Motter, A. E., C. S. Zhou & J. Kurths. 2005. Enhancing complex-network synchronization. *Europhysics Letters*, 69(3): 334–340.

Ortiz-Torres, B., I. Serrano-García & N. Torres-Burgos. 2000. Subverting culture: promoting HIV/AIDS prevention among Puerto Rican and Dominican women. *American Journal of Community Psychology*, 28(6): 859–881.

Paczuski, M., S. Maslov & P. Bak. 1996. Avalanche dynamics in evolution, growth, and depinning models. *Physical Review E*, 53(1): 414–443.

Prigogine, I. 1997. *The end of certainty: Time, chaos, and the new laws of nature*. New York: The Free Press.

Rogers, E. M. 1994. *A history of communication study: A biographical approach*. New York: Free Press.

Rogers, E. M. 2003. *Diffusion of Innovations*. 5th Edn. New York: Free Press.

Sikkema, K. L., J. A. Kelly, R. A. Winett, L. J. Solomon, V. A. Cargill, R. A. Rofferman, T. L. McAuliffe, T. G. Heckman, E. A. Anderson, D. A. Wagstaff, A. D. Norman, M. J. Perry, D. A. Crumble & A. M. B. Mercer. 2000. Outcomes of a randomized community-level HIV-Prevention intervention for women living in 16 low-income housing developments. *American Journal of Public Health*, 19: 57–63.

Simon, H. A. 1991. *Models of my life*. New York: Basic Books.

Singhal, A., & E. M. Rogers. 2003. *Combating AIDS: Communication strategies in action*. New Delhi, India: Sage.

So, M. K. P., C. W. S. Chen & M. Chen. 2005. A Bayesian threshold nonlinearity test for financial time series. *Journal of Forecasting*, 24(1), 61–76.

Stacey, R. D., D. Griffin & P. Shaw. 2000. *Complexity and management: Fad or radical challenge to systems thinking?* New York: Routledge.

Valente, T. W. 1995. *Network models of the diffusion of innovations*. Creskill, NJ: Hampton Press.

Waldrop, M. M. 1992. *Complexity: The emerging science at the edge of order and chaos*. New York: Simon and Schuster.

Walker, R. M. 2006. Innovation Type and Diffusion: An Empirical Analysis of Local Government. *Public Administration*, 84(2): 311–335.

Wohfeiler, D. 1998. Community organizing and community building among gay and bisexual men: The STOP AIDS project. Pp. 230–243 in M. Minkler (ed.), *Community organizing and community building for health*. New Brunswick, NJ: Rutgers University Press.

Wohfeiler, D. 2002. From community to clients: The professionalisation of HIV prevention among gay men and its implications for intervention selection. *Sex Transm Infect*, 78 (Suppl 1): 176–182.

Wozniak, A. 2001. Literature review: Describing previous and ongoing mass media campaigns focusing on HIV/AIDS. Illovo, South Africa: ACT Mass Media Campaign/Abt Associates, November 2001. Accessed May 26, 2005: <http://www.aidsinfo.co.za/uploadfiles/PDF/MassMedia.doc> (No longer available).

Yorke, J. 2003. Communicating with chaos. Accessed July 27, 2017 at: <http://www-chaos.umd.edu/research.html#communication>.

MARK K. WARFORD

14 Testing a Diffusion of Innovations in Education Model (DIEM)[1]

ABSTRACT

This chapter reports on a questionnaire study based on the Diffusion of Innovations in Education Model (DIEM), and synthesizes research on educational innovations. The social system under study included foreign language teacher educators in eleven south-eastern states (N = 83). Regional foreign language teacher educators were targeted for gathering data regarding the ACTFL (American Council on the Teaching of Foreign Languages) Proficiency Guidelines (1986), a language-teaching innovation. In analyzing results, inferential statistics tested the weight of some of the DIEM's predictions about the nature of educational change. In terms of the model's predictions, state mandates appear to hinder rather than facilitate adoption. However, results support the DIEM claim that innovation knowledge is associated with its adoption. While the DIEM provides conceptual clarity to research on change in educational settings, its usefulness as a way to explain and predict the success or failure of educational innovations in attaining adoption remains to be verified.

Introduction

The educational research literature has underscored the shortcomings of American reform efforts (Fullan, 1993; Hall, 1992; Hansen, 1981; Sarason, 1990). Hall (1992) argues that a *development/implementation* imbalance, the notion that the incessant bombardment of practitioners with new ideas and practices, combined with their sense of low status, is to blame for

---

1   *The Innovation Journal: The Public Sector Innovation Journal*, 10(3), 2005, article 7 <http://www.innovation.cc/volumes-issues/vol10-no3.htm>.

resistance to change. The current gridlock may be ultimately due to a lack of attention to the practitioners' context (Carlson, 1964, 1968; Hall, 1992; Hansen, 1981; Miles, 1969; Rogers, 1995; Rogers and Jain, 1968; Sarason, 1990). Another factor undermining effective national-scale reform is the increase of state control over teacher education (Darling-Hammond, 1992, with Sclan; Early, 1993).

Diffusion of innovations or "DOI" theory presents a way of explaining and predicting the adoption or rejection of new ideas and practices. Rogers reports on the potential benefits of a systemic approach to educational research for a theory of DOI:

> An exciting potential contribution could be made by the education research tradition, stemming from the fact that organizations are involved, in one way or another, in the adoption of educational innovations ... organizational structures are inevitably involved in educational adoption decisions. (1995: 63)

Though it has precedents in educational research (Carlson, 1965, 1968; Hall, 1992; Huberman, 1983; Miles, 1969; Mort and Cornell, 1941), DOI, to date has not been employed to evaluate the spread of the many new educational ideas and practices that have disseminated in the wake of the Reform Movement of the 1980s. In testing a Diffusion of Innovations in Education Model (DIEM, Figure 14.1), the author administered a questionnaire regarding one such innovation, the ACTFL (American Council on the Teaching of Foreign Languages) Proficiency Guidelines (1986), to south-eastern foreign language teacher educators (N = 83; eleven states). The DIEM, in response to Rogers' (1995) call for a systemic perspective, considers both individual and socio-organizational variables affecting the impact of educational innovations. The following research question guided the investigation: How effective is the model developed by the researcher for the purpose of investigating the diffusion of innovations in educational settings as a tool for explaining the diffusion and adoption of the ACTFL Proficiency Guidelines? Results were used to investigate interaction between antecedent (background), diffusion process, and consequences (implementation)-related variables governing the success or failure of educational diffusion campaigns.

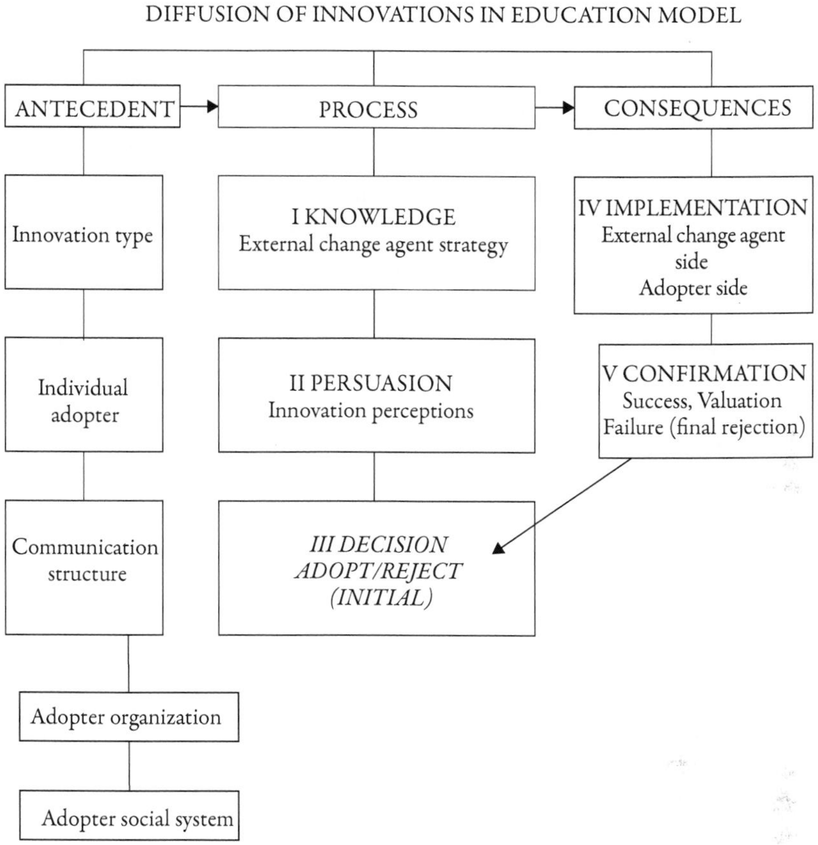

DIFFUSION OF INNOVATIONS IN EDUCATION MODEL

Figure 14.1: Diffusion of Innovations in Education Model (DIEM).
Source: adapted from Henrichsen, 1989; Rogers and Shoemaker, 1971.

Diffusion of Educational Innovations and Its Origins

The earliest trace of a diffusion of innovations research tradition originates in Europe. According to Rogers, French social scientist Gabriel Tarde (1903) discovered an *S-shaped curve* that governs the rate of *invention* and *imitation* diffusion (Rogers, 1995: 40) within a given social context. In American agricultural research, Ryan and Gross (1943, in Rogers, 1995) adopted the model as diffusion of *innovations*. Around the same time, Mort and Cornell conducted the first study of the diffusion of what he termed educational *adaptations*, in Pennsylvanian school districts, a study that led him to the following conclusion: "the succeeding waves of 'reform' which have come and passed in this century have left discouragingly little mark" (1941: 3). At that time, diffusion research's applications to educational reform efforts had yet to be exploited. As the researchers put it: "We have placed our faith in diffusion to a very high extent upon the initiation of individual communities and here given but little attention to the problem of how diffusion comes about" (1941: 25). Among factors influencing educational diffusion, Mort and Cornell found individual variables like teacher support of innovation and social variables such as tax and population base were facilitative variables. In the 1960s, Carlson (1965) described three barriers to change in the U.S. school system: the lack of a formal change agent figure in public school districts, the lack of a firm knowledge base in education, and the inherently dependent character of public education which diminishes the impetus for change. Miles (1969), taking a less deterministic stance, advanced strategies for creating more innovative school climates through a system of interrelated processes ranging from goal setting to implementing innovations and evaluating effects.

Review of the Literature

The goal of this study was to assess the diffusion and adoption of a language educational innovation, the ACTFL Guidelines as reported by south-eastern FL teacher educators. For this purpose, the researcher developed a model for diffusion of educational innovations from insights obtained from a review of related research. This Diffusion of Innovations in Education Model (DIEM) guided the development of a survey tool, which was designed to gauge respondents' perspectives on the diffusion of the guidelines within their area from the decision to adopt to implementation. The following review of the research on educational innovations is therefore organized according to the previously mentioned variable categories around which the model and the questionnaire were constructed: antecedent, diffusion process, and consequences.

Antecedent Variables

The success of a diffusion campaign depends on knowledge of the nature of the innovation as well as of the targeted adopters and their socio-organizational context. Because these are factors preceding the process of disseminating the innovation, they are referred to as *antecedent variables*. Antecedent variables include: the innovation, the targeted adopters and their socio-organizational contexts, as well as the flow of information about the innovation through various communication structures and channels.

THE INNOVATION

In early applications of DOI research to the field of education, Mort and Cornell (1941), as mentioned earlier, referred to innovations as *adaptations*. This practice appears to have died out in the 1960s. Carlson defines an *innovation* as "a new idea or practice" (1968: 10). Carlson further distinguishes between ideas and practices-based innovations, the former being more difficult to implement. Rogers (1995) asserts that hardware innovations, such as computer software or pesticides that are easily and readily employed, have the best chance of success and makes the further distinction between *idea- and principles-based* innovations, the latter being the most difficult to implement.

In this study, the innovation in question is the ACTFL Proficiency Guidelines (1986). Components of this language-teaching innovation include the Oral Proficiency Interview (OPI), designed to assess language learner proficiency, as well as proficiency-oriented instruction (POI), an approach to teaching that extrapolates pedagogical values from the tiers of proficiency advanced in the guidelines. Whereas the former, an example of a practice-based innovation, includes concrete support materials and clear parameters, the latter is the classic illustration of a principles-based innovation. Schulz (1986) describes how, at the Language Proficiency Assessment Symposium of 1981, over seventy definitions of proficiency in another language came to light. The debate over how to define this approach (Grosse and Feyton, 1991; Lange, 1988) has dramatized the difficulty of implementing a teaching innovation based on an elusive principle such as proficiency. Whether or not ACTFL's standardization of the proficiency principle had a substantial impact on the FL profession remains to be fully investigated. The same holds true for proficiency-oriented instruction.

DOI theory has also considered educational innovations in terms of the manner in which they are procured by practitioners, including its price tag (Emrick and Peterson, 1977; Mort and Cornell, 1941). The amount of adopter volition attached to the innovation and its adoption is also a significant factor. Whether an innovation is of an optional (individual decision), collective (group decision), or authority (mandated) variety is a factor of particular interest. Generally speaking, mandated decisions are associated with a high rate of diffusion and adoption (Rogers, 1995); however, Fullan (1993) argues to the contrary in the case of educational innovations. In the Southeast, only Florida tried to enforce the guidelines as a way of measuring the proficiency of learners in its schools. Whether this approach had a facilitative or inhibiting effect on the diffusion and adoption of the guidelines remains to be seen.

THE INDIVIDUAL ADOPTER

To the educational diffusion researcher, an adopting educator is governed by individual personality traits as well as characteristics governing their social and communication behavior. With regard to the former, innovativeness and a favorable attitude toward change (Rogers and Jain, 1968) are factors that facilitate adoption. Favorability may wane to the extent that educators feel overwhelmed by the increasing number of innovations to evaluate (Hall, 1992; Henrichsen, 1989), a reality illustrated by the tendency of educators to refer to new educational innovations as *bandwagons*. Rogers (1995) has identified the following personality traits of earlier adopters as enhancing educational diffusion: extensive formal education and literacy, empathy, open-mindedness, good abstract reasoning, a rational outlook, and intelligence (Rogers, 1995). The adopting educator also has certain inclinations in terms of their social behavior. Educators who favor networking on a broad, cosmopolite scale are viewed as key links in the diffusion and adoption chain, whereas those who are more conservative, locally affiliated are not (Rogers, 1995). With regard to educational innovations, Mort and Cornell advanced three categories of adopting teachers: followers, supporters, and neutrals (1941: 29).

ADOPTING SOCIAL SYSTEMS AND ORGANIZATIONS

In response to the growth of social learning theory, researchers have confronted the *social change* (Rogers, 1995: 6) dimension of DOI. According to Rogers, "there have been relatively few studies of how the social or communicative structure affects the diffusion or adoption of innovations in a system" (1995: 25). In DOI, social systems are defined as: "... a set of interrelated units that are engaged in joint problem solving to accomplish a common goal" (Rogers, 1995: 23) and exist within "the individual's personality, communication behaviour, and attitudes" (Rogers and Jain, 1968: 8). An impetus behind increased attention to social variables is criticism of an allegedly individualistic emphasis in diffusion survey design that tends to have a *pro-innovation* bias and neglects the question of what an innovation means to a particular social system (Rogers, 1995: 100).

Attention to social systemic variables is an important next step in educational diffusion research. As Rogers and Jain put it, "Such investigation will lead to theoretical understandings about the role of social structure on individual behaviour, as well as to practical insight about how to organize education in order to facilitate change" (1968: 10). Social systems may vary in openness to change (Rogers, 1995: 295). Mort and Cornell (1941) found higher population bases, concentration of citizens with a higher cultural level, tax leeway, wealth, and urbanness to be important social variables in the diffusion of educational innovations.

Within social systems, organizational factors present an important dimension of inquiry where educational innovations are concerned. Rogers defines an organization as: "a stable system of individuals who work together to achieve common goals through a hierarchy of ranks and a division of labour" (1995: 403). Rogers and Jain describe the growth of an organizational perspective in diffusion research: "Organizational theory, systems analysis, structural effects, and matrix multiplication," once "beyond the pale," have gained acceptance in DOI research (1968: 3).

An important aspect of an educational organization is its "makeup and norms" (Rogers and Jain, 1968: 8). For example, schools that are more traditional may differ from non-traditional schools in terms of having a faster rate of innovation diffusion (Henrichsen, 1989; Rogers and Jain, 1968). Leadership style is another relevant variable. Authoritarianism in the decision-making structure is negatively correlated with educational diffusion, whereas a more open leadership style based on the "principle of supportive relationships" (Likert, 1961: 103, in Rogers and Jain, 1968: 22) contributes to "full and efficient" diffusion (Rogers and Jain, 1968: 22). Rogers (1995) and Fullan (1993) both suggest that a more convergent style of educational leadership, connected across levels, facilitates diffusion. With regard to the potential of administrators in educational organizations to serve effectively as change agents, Carlson (1968) suggests that they are more likely to be gatekeepers while others like Fullan (2002) suggest that being a change agent is fundamental to the job description of principals. The presence of adaptive units in an organization has been also correlated with more efficient DOI (Rogers and Jain, 1968: 24). In addition, the size of the educational organization may also be a key factor (Rogers, 1995): "Larger organizations are more innovative" (Rogers, 1995: 379). Finally, staff characteristics like morale are important factors in educational diffusion (Carlson, 1969; Emrick and Peterson, 1977; Henrichsen, 1989).

The second language educational literature has underscored the importance of social systemic and organizational variables in the diffusion of language-teaching innovations (Henrichsen, 1989; Markee, 1997; Nunan, 1989; White, 1993). Henrichsen's (1989) study of the oral method's diffusion in Japan explains its demise in terms of American external change agents' lack of sensitivity to Japanese social and pedagogical norms. Nunan's (1989, in White, 1993) research on the Australian Adult Migrant Education Program reported that less hierarchical centre-periphery models are usually "widely adopted but poorly-implemented," limited by the "relative remoteness of change agents" (White, 1993: 252, citing Nunan, 1989). On the contrary, localized models showed greater teacher support and the development of teacher innovativeness.

COMMUNICATION CHANNELS

Communication channels represent another antecedent factor in DOI. According to Rogers, "there have been relatively few studies of how the social or communicative structure affects the diffusion or adoption of innovations in a system" (1995: 25). Communication channels include mass media, interpersonal networks that may be homophilous (identifying with one another) or heterophilous (no social identification), as well as "localite" or "cosmopolite" (Rogers and Jain, 1968: 11) networks. Within the communication structure there may also be certain cliques and chains that affect the diffusion rate. Some cliques, for example, act as gatekeepers, restricting the diffusion (Rogers and Jain, 1968, citing Mortimore, 1968). Mort and Cornell found that administrators restrict the diffusion process, "swayed by political influence" (1941: 210). In studying educational diffusion, communication channel considerations have led to the use of sociometric survey items like "Who first told you about ...?" or "who convinced you to adopt ...?" (Rogers and Jain, 1968: 7). Relational analysis clarifies the communication structure within the organization, deepening our understanding, for example, of the role of heterophily and homophily in communicating innovations. Heterophily and homophily respectively denote the extent to which two people communicating about an innovation identify with their interlocutor or perceive them as pertaining to a distant and or irrelevant social group.

Process

Process variables encompass all the activities related to a campaign to promote innovations to adopting systems beginning with increasing adopters' knowledge of the innovation, and ending with the decision to adopt or reject (Rogers, 1995). Time is a major focus during this stage. Carlson argues that "far more care needs to be exercised in pinpointing the time of adoption if diffusion studies are to provide a firm knowledge base" (1968: 9). The diffusion rate is not necessarily a question of when adoption takes place but rather *who* is adopting. The innovativeness of potential adopters – ranging from innovators, to early adopters, to early majority adopter, to late majority adopters, and ending with laggards (1995: 89) – influences the time it takes for an innovation to be adopted. Rate of adoption, as mentioned earlier, is represented in an S-shaped curve. Whereas *innovators* inhabit the low point of the S (the early stage of diffusion), *laggards* explain the point at the top of the S, as the last few are persuaded to adopt. The levelling phase of the *S* also indicates that an innovation has been institutionalized within the adopting system.

ADOPTERS' PERCEIVED CHARACTERISTICS OF THE INNOVATION

In addition to *who* adopts, the question of adopter perceptions of *what* is adopted is another significant factor that hinders or facilitates the flow of new ideas and practices. According to Rogers, an innovation is "an idea, practice, or object that is perceived as new by an individual or other unit of adoption" (1995: 11). Important criteria include: relative advantage (over previous practice), compatibility, complexity, trialability, and observability (1995: 21). Due, in part, to the increasing number of international diffusion studies (e.g. Henrichsen, 1989), cross-cultural variables have been determined to play a major role in determining an innovation's "compatibility with the values, beliefs, and past experiences of individuals in the social system" (Rogers, 1995: 4).

At the University of Texas at Austin, Hall, Rutherford, and George (1977) developed a Concerns-Based Adoption Model, which describes stages of teacher attitudes toward an innovation from finding out about it through extensive use. The first three stages of the CBAM, Awareness, Informational, and Personal, are measured by an instrument called the Stages of Concern (Soc) Questionnaire and follow the adopter side of the knowledge and persuasion process starting from the development of interest to the establishment of a personal assessment of adopting and its ramifications. In measuring process variables related to the decision to adopt, the authors developed the Levels of Use (LoU) inventory (Hord, Rutherford, Huling-Austin, and Hall, 1987). In the initial stages of the Lou, the teacher moves from a lack of interest (Non-Use) to an Orientation stage in which they begin to show interest in knowing more about the innovation. The decision to adopt is denoted by the formation of actual plans to use the innovation (Preparation stage). While the SoC and LoU are well-tested measures, they regard the decision as an individual act. From a DOI perspective, they are incomplete without recognizing the socio-organizational variables that impact educational diffusion.

THE CHANGE AGENT

In designing a diffusion campaign, disseminators must consider teacher innovativeness and attitudes toward the innovation, since patterns among teachers' "personality, communication behaviour, and attitudes" affect diffusion (Rogers and Jain, 1968: 8). If "precise goals of the new program being suggested – that is, have not planned adequately" (Rogers and Jain, 1968: 111), the status quo will reassert itself. In addition to underscoring the importance of external change agent staff size and experience (Emrick and Peterson, 1977), researchers have advanced ways to effectively manage the dissemination of an innovation. Rather than looking at change agent activity as a single action – an in-service workshop for example – change agents in educational settings should engage their activity as a relationship-building process (Frank, Zhao, and Borman, 2003; Fullan, 2001). According to Huberman (1983), teacher education programs that have engaged in extensive networking and dialogue with area schools regarding the design of innovations that serve a significant need have been more effective in leading educational reform. Successful diffusion depends on the methods employed and the extent to which change agents engage the adopting system's communication structure (Emrick and Peterson, 1977; Rogers, 1995) in promoting awareness. They should heed points of resistance (Rogers, 1995) and foster strong collaborative networks (Huberman, 1983; Hunkins and Ornstein, 1989). Though some argue that *all* education professionals are change agents (Fullan, 1993), DOI asserts that the utilization of opinion leaders and aides within the adopter social system is a more realistic strategy

(Rogers, 1995) than depending on the receptivity and cooperation across all of the stakeholders in educational adoption. Because opinion leaders and aides are more homophilous with adopters than change agents, they are more "able to influence other individuals' attitudes or overt behaviour informally in a desired way" (Rogers, 1995: 27).

Consequences

After considering the antecedent variables and following the stages of gaining knowledge about the innovation and being persuaded to adopt, DOI research considers the actual use of the innovation and its consequences. It is important to note that, although an initial decision to adopt has been made, that decision is often revisited after it has been tested. Rogers and Jain (1968: 25) call for more attention to the effects of adopting and implementing educational innovations: "What improvements in educational productivity or quality result from the adoption of each innovation?" The authors argue, "diffusion research has largely been a tool on the side of sources, not receivers of innovation diffusion" (Rogers and Jain, 1968: 1).

To enhance the fidelity of implementation to the intent behind its design, attention has been drawn to the systemic context of adopters. According to Markee, "the likelihood of an innovation being adopted is ... contingent on its ecological appropriateness in a specific context of implementation" (1997: 84). Warnings about overlooking the implementation factor date back to Mort and Cornell, in studying the diffusion of a number of educational innovations in the state of Pennsylvania, noted: "Communities were rather liberally credited when adaptations of the barest rudiments were in evidence" (1941: 29). Carlson states "school people seem quite prone to modify new practices in the process of adopting them. For example, what is called team teaching in one system is very different from what is called team teaching in another system" (1968: 12).

In educational settings, there is a tendency in the professional literature to look at the implementation process in terms of change agent assistance at the implementation stage as well as activities within the adopting or receiver organization. Fidelity of implementation, with all its contingent adaptations, depends in large part on the extent to which the external change agent guides the process vis-à-vis intensive, quality training, materials support, assistance, and follow-up (Emrick and Peterson, 1977). Keeping costs down is also a facilitative factor (Emrick and Peterson, 1977). In response to a tendency for DOI research to blame the adopter for lack of adoption, the emphasis has understandably shifted to change agent accountability for active dialogue with the adopter concerning the implementation process (Hunkins and Ornstein, 1989; Leithwood and Montgomery, 1980). Greater variation and re-invention should be tolerated among adopters in using a principles-based innovation (Rogers, 1995: 210, 166) as adopters will often struggle with the vagueness and/or abstraction involved in implementing such an innovation.

When meaning disparities develop between change agent and adopter, this often stems from ignorance of indigenous knowledge systems (Rogers, 1995: 241). Systemic and individual adopter variables interact to appropriate localized interpretations of the intentions behind the innovation. Rogers and Jain (1968: 27) distinguish between two dimensions of adopter implementation of an innovation: diffusion effects and consequences variables. The former refers to intermediate variables related to the receiver's experiences testing out the innovation, whereas the latter refers to ultimate consequences of implementation leading to final confirmation or rejection. According to Rogers (1995), true confirmation occurs when an innovation has been institutionalized to the point that it is no longer construed as a new idea or practice. According to Fullan (2001), adopter commitment is the key adopter variable determining whether or not an innovation survives the implementation process, thus producing lasting changes in educational practices.

Miles (1969) denotes several adopter organizational activities related to planning out implementation: goal setting, forecasting, diagnosing problems, as well as inventing and scanning solutions. The Levels of Use Survey (LoU) (Hord, Rutherford, Huling-Austin, and Hall, 1987) refers to this planning phase as the Preparation stage. During the subsequent early stages of testing out an innovation, vestiges of preliminary trials, called diffusion effects, may be well planned for, while others manifest themselves in surprising ways in the form of secondary diffusion (Emrick and Peterson, 1977), also referred to as unanticipated effects (Rogers, 1995). In terms of Hall et al.'s Stages of (Adopter) Concerns, this phenomenon denotes the fourth ("Management") stage in which the adopter moves beyond considering how implementation will affect them to using the innovation with their students. The LoU indicators applicable to this stage include the Mechanical and Routine stages, in which the teacher makes accommodations for the innovation and establishes a usage pattern.

A promising new perspective on implementation comes from recent investigations employing a social critical lens. Frank, Zhao, and Borman (2003) argue that implementation in educational organizations is an informal process driven by social relationships. Rather than looking at implementation as a decision wholly dependent on teacher cognition or governed by linear, managerial plans, the authors suggest that implementation is sustained or discarded largely due to collegial pressure or encouragement. Their study of social capital within an educational organization suggests that change agents should facilitate implementation indirectly by setting up contexts for informal staff communication about using the innovation.

There is some variation in evaluating the consequences of implementing of an innovation once an adopter has tried it out. In the program innovation literature, Leithwood and Montgomery (1980) argue that implementation is a dialogic process that necessitates careful collaboration between the external and receiver organizations and that "the nature and degree of implementation of program innovations" (p 193) must be established from the outset. On the contrary, Hall, George, and Rutherford (1977) denote this "Collaboration" stage of concern for adopters as a later phase of innovation use that follows a "Consequences" stage in which the teacher has had a chance to evaluate the innovation's effect on students. Thus, while collaboration appears to be a good thing in the educational diffusion literature, it is not clear exactly when and to what extent change agent–adopter collaboration needs to take place. In the final stage of the implementation process, the adopter assesses the overall consequences of using the innovation. In order for an innovation to be successfully implemented, it must find confirmation in its integration into the values and practices of the adopting entity, be it an individual teacher or an entire school district. In assessing the long-term consequences of implementing an innovation, adopters weigh three continua: desirable/undesirable; direct/indirect; anticipated/unanticipated (Rogers, 1995: 30–31). According to

Leithwood and Montgomery (1980), there are essentially three procedures to follow in assessing implementation: reviewing the original policy, reviewing the actual practice, and then identifying discrepancies.

Processes related to the consequences of adoption at its most mature stages include: clarifying, and routinizing/maintaining (Miles, 1969; Rogers, 1995: 403). The success of such self-sustaining activities eventually institutionalizes the innovation into the status quo (Rogers, 1995). Failure conversely leads to discontinuance or tabling (Rogers and Shoemaker, 1971). Within certain parameters, a certain amount of redefining/restructuring may take place in lieu of assessing the consequences of implementation. In Hall, George, and Rutherford's (1977), consequences-related variables are represented by the final three stages of adopter concern: a Consequences stage involving reflection and refining; Collaboration, which focuses on integrating one's implementation with colleagues; and finally, Refocusing, in which teachers carefully re-shape the innovation to better address their localized needs. With regard to the LoU (Hord, Rutherford, Huling-Austin, and Hall, 1987), the teacher moves from developing a routine with the innovation (Routine stage) to making refinements in order to optimize outcomes (Refinement stage). As the adopter matures in mastery, use involves more integration with colleagues' efforts (Integrative stage) and more evolved, carefully adapted versions of the innovation (Renewal).

Constructing the Model

After an extensive review of the research literature on educational innovation, the DIEM was constructed based on four criteria advanced by Henrichsen in his case study on the diffusion of the Oral Approach in Japanese English language teaching: a *coherent framework, abstractness, completeness, and predictability* (1989: 95). In order to be a complete account of educational innovation diffusion, Rogers' (1995) and Rogers and Jain's (1968) elements of diffusion (the innovation, communication channels, time, social system, diffusion effects and consequences) needed to be adapted in a way that reflects a full account of how diffusion works in educational settings. In particular, there is increased focus on two elements in particular, time and implementation. With regard to the time element of innovation diffusion, external change agent activities and strategies in designing effective promotional campaigns is amplified since it appears to have a significant effect on the success or failure of educational innovations (Emrick and Peterson, 1977; Fullan, 1993, 2001, Hall, 1992; Henrichsen, 1989; Huberman, 1983; Hunkins and Ornstein, 1989). Examples of external change agents in educational settings tend to be national level academic area professional organizations or policy-makers. There is also a closer focus on external change agent and adopter side activity related to implementing the innovation (Carlson, 1964; Emrick and Peterson, 1977; Frank, Zhao, and Borman, 2003; Hord, Rutherford, Huling-Austin, and Hall, 1987, Leithwood and Montgomery, 1980; Mort and Cornell 1941; Rogers, 1995) since this has been a persistent problem area in the arena of educational change, as well as measuring the extent to which adoption of an educational innovation may be confirmed as status quo in a particular socio-organizational context (Emrick and Peterson, 1977; Henrichsen, 1989; Hord, Rutherford, Huling-Austin, and Hall, 1987; Rogers, 1995, Rogers and Shoemaker, 1971).

According to Henrichsen, a true model considers "not only the forces that affect the change process but also the process itself" (1989: 69). In order to make the model more cohesive and coherent, the researcher has preserved the Rogers' (1995) model shares some common features with Henrichsen's hybrid model (1989) and the cross-cultural diffusion model it is based on (RandS, 1971), in particular, the delineation of antecedent, process, and consequences-related variables. Educational innovations, as is the case with innovations in general, do appear to be governed by a pre-existing context for adoption (antecedent variables). This context is governed by inherent characteristics of the innovation (Fullan, 1993; Rogers, 1995), the social (Emrick and Peterson, 1977; Rogers, 1995; Rogers and Jain, 1968; Mort and Cornell, 1941), the organizational (Carlson, 1965; Emrick and Peterson, 1977; Fullan, 1993; Henrichsen, 1989; Huberman, 1983; Rogers, 1995; Rogers and Jain, 1968), and the communication (Mortimore, 1969; Rogers, 1995; Rogers and Jain, 1968) structures in which teachers (Rogers and Jain, 1968; Hall, 1992; Huberman, 1983; Mort and Cornell, 1941) would use the innovation. With regard to diffusion process variables, the activity of an external change agent in promoting adoption of the innovation (Emrick and Peterson, 1977; Fullan, 1993, 2001, Henrichsen, 1989; Huberman, 1983; Hunkins and Ornstein, 1989; Rogers, 1995) and the extent to which teachers are open to it (Hall, Rogers, 1995). Finally, the model considers the consequences of implementing the educational innovation and appraisal of its long-term value as a pedagogical tool. Within these three dimensions, there may inevitably be overlap, for example between the adoption decision-making timeline and implementation factors (cited in the previous paragraph). In some cases, a given variable might have weight at more than just one stage or cross into another category. For instance, an innovation may have some pre-existing, inherent characteristics (antecedent variables). However, as established earlier in this chapter, what happens to an innovation as it begins to be defined by the adopter (process stage) and actually used (consequences), appears to create an often distinct entity altogether.

In terms of the tension between abstractness and completeness, relevant features culled from a review of the literature were carefully sorted according to their associated element of diffusion and the stage of the process they are associated with. The DIEM's greatest advantage for representing diffusion in educational contexts lies in its depth of consideration of organizational variables, as well as its increased attention to consequences, a step first taken by Henrichsen (1989). Such considerations are not guaranteed their deserved depth of treatment in any single diffusion model the researcher has investigated. The DIEM takes the central elements of educational diffusion through a sequential framework. Extensive empirical testing of the model will hopefully uncover some new connections between the variables under study.

Methodology

A census questionnaire entitled The Foreign Language Teacher Educator Survey was developed based on variables of interest in the DIEM and administered to the known population of south-eastern U.S.A foreign language teacher educators. When employed judiciously, "survey methods ... are often essential to gathering large-scale amounts of data as a basis for generalization" (Rogers and Jain, 1968: 4). Researchers may also feel compelled to conduct first hand observations of the educational system under study, interview members of the system, or review the system's documents (Emrick and Peterson, 1977). This is particularly important in measuring the consequences of adopting and implementing an innovation on the social system, a process Rogers (1995) relegates to more in-depth, case study methods, arguing that one-shot surveys will not suffice. It is hoped that the focus on one regional social system (the southeast) and the inclusion of opportunities for FL teacher educators to comment on the impact of the ACTFL guidelines counteract this limitation of the questionnaire method.

The researcher focused on the following research question: *How effective is the DIEM in explaining the diffusion and adoption of the ACTFL Proficiency Guidelines?* This question was divided, into seven sub-questions:

- *RQ3A:* As a principles-based innovation, do the guidelines yield, as predicted by the model, low scores on scale item measurements of the following perceived characteristics: relative advantage, compatibility, trialability, observability, and high ratings for complexity? With regard to the issue of complexity, will adoption, measured by integration in the methods course and other aspects of FL teacher education, as well as definitions of proficiency-oriented instruction, be idiosyncratic?
- *RQ3B:* Will respondents from states which have incorporated the proficiency guidelines as part of their educational policy (Louisiana, North Carolina, Florida) or curriculum framework (Georgia and South Carolina) or both (Florida) be more likely to adopt the guidelines and verify their acceptance and institutionalization in their area?
- *RQ3C:* How will knowledge of the guidelines and other ACTFL innovations correlate with adoption and integration by foreign language teacher educators?
- *RQ3D:* Are professional factors such as: length of tenure as teacher educator, overall experience in FL teaching, and level of involvement in FL professional organizations positively related to the guidelines' adoption and implementation?

- *RQ3E:* As population (urbanization) increases, does the likelihood of adoption and implementation of the guidelines also increase?
- *RQ3F:* Is there a relationship between the innovativeness and openness to change of the socio-organizational context of adopters and variables of adoption and implementation?
- *RQ3G:* Is adoption and implementation of the guidelines significantly higher and earlier among FL teacher educators housed in modern language departments than their counterparts in colleges of education, as suggested in the literature?

The population under study is the entire known population of south-eastern foreign language teacher educators (N = 83), defined as a full-time college faculty responsible for instructing the course on teaching FLs, in eleven regional states (Table 14.1). Though this was a parametric study, the small size of the population necessitated the use of more rigorous,

Table 14.1: Comparison of Survey Return Rate State-by-State

State	Possible # of returns	Actual # of returns	Response rate (%)
Alabama	6	5	83.33
Arkansas	4	4	100
Florida	7	5	62.5
Georgia	9	8	88.88
Kentucky	8	3	42.85
Louisiana	6	3	50
Mississippi	2	2	100
North Carolina	12	9	75
South Carolina	6	6	100
Tennessee	9	7	77.77
Virginia	14	8	57.14
Total = 11	Total = 83	Total = 60	Avg. = 72.3

non-parametric statistics. Thus, in interpreting the results, the researcher accepted increased risk of a Type I error (rejecting the alternative hypothesis of significance when it was actually correct). A total of sixty returns were received (72.3 per cent response rate). The return rate for each state was between 50 per cent and 100 per cent, except for Kentucky (37.5 per cent); therefore, results may not necessarily speak for this state. The next section focuses on questionnaire items designed to test the DIEM's validity.

Results and Discussion

RQ3A: As a principles-based innovation, do the guidelines yield, as predicted by the model, low scores on scale item measurements of the following perceived characteristics: relative advantage, compatibility, trialability, observability, and high ratings for complexity?

As indicated in Table 14.2, on a scale of 1–4, with a 1 indicating the highest degree of complexity and 4 the lowest, respondents rated Proficiency-Oriented Instruction 2.18 overall, suggesting that respondents view this innovation as somewhat complex. However, two write-in comments suggest that some respondents were not sure whether a "1" represented extreme complexity, the intended direction, or rather that such a score would indicate favorability in that area, thus indicating a lack of complexity. The same problem might also undermine the ratings of "Cost of implementation," which was rated the lowest (2.55), considering the high standard deviation ($\sigma = 1.13$). However, it is conceivable that one could implement proficiency-oriented teaching without investing heavily in training and materials. The guidelines were rated fairly low with regard to the criterion of "Compatibility with FL instruction in my area" ($x = 2.31$), which lends support to the findings of Grosse and Feyton (1991). With regard to the other categories, Proficiency-Oriented Instruction was rated rather favorably with regard to "Relative advantage over traditional instruction" ($x = 1.53$), Flexibility ($x = 1.94$), and "Observability of the results" ($x = 1.98$).

Table 14.2: Respondents' Ratings of Proficiency-Oriented Instruction

Innovation characteristic	N	Mean	Std Dev.
Cost of implementation	44	2.5455	1.13
Compatibility with FL instruction in my local area	52	2.3077	0.7286
Complexity	50	2.18	0.8254
Trialability (how easy is it to try out?)	51	2.1373	0.6639
Observability of results	51	1.9804	0.7613
Flexibility	52	1.9423	0.8498
Relative advantage over traditional FL instruction	53	1.5283	0.6681

(1 = highest; 4 = lowest rating in given category)

... also, will adoption, measured by integration in the methods course and other aspects of FL teacher education, as well as definitions of proficiency-oriented instruction, be idiosyncratic?

With respect to responses to the question "How would you define proficiency-oriented instruction?," nineteen respondents constructed their definition around the guidelines as a developmental framework for POI, an approach to assessment and instruction that factors in what students are capable of at a given level. Two respondents within this developmental framework-based definition emphasized that the guidelines are experientially, rather than theoretically derived (Omaggio, 1983). Among respondents to this question, seventeen stressed POI as guided by the goal of communicative competence (ability), defined often as *using or doing* with the language. Other definitions stressed POI as communicative, foreign language-immersed, or encouraging student communication in the foreign language (7). Six respondents indicated that they thought of POI as less explicitly focused on the grammatical structures of the target language (6). The rest of the definitions included elements of the following: focus on the modalities (4), focus on (real life) contexts, themes, or functions (4), the use of authentic materials (3), some emphasis on structural accuracy (2), and finally, the goal of FL proficiency (2). The criteria cited by FL teacher educators participating in this survey are either inherent aspects of the guidelines (i.e. the emphasis on a developmental framework, modalities) or from Omaggio Hadley's (1983, 1984, 1986) and Lange's (1988) writings on the pedagogical implications of the guidelines (i.e. emphasis on real/contextual communication, authentic materials). Thus, these would appear to be perfectly valid extrapolations of the original message about proficiency-oriented instruction that are readily available in the professional literature. Overall, FL teacher educators in the south-east U.S.A. voice a definition of POI that is consonant with the intentions of its originators (Leithwood and Montgomery, 1980) within the guidelines' given parameters and within the related literature. Therefore, it appears that the tendency for principles-based innovations to be randomly implemented does not hold true for the case of Proficiency-Oriented Instruction, according to FL teacher educators in the southeast US.

RQ3B: Will respondents from states which have incorporated the Proficiency Guidelines as part of their educational policy (Louisiana, North Carolina, Florida) or curriculum framework (Georgia) or both (Florida) be more likely to adopt the guidelines and report their acceptance and institutionalization in their area?

Analysis based on this question began with an Independent Samples t-test (Table 14.3). It was determined that if Florida, the only state where the guidelines had been mandated as a curriculum framework, did not show many significantly different means on measures of the guidelines' impact than those of the other regional states, then further comparisons would not be necessary. Two impact variables, the local foreign language supervisor and K-12 foreign language teachers, revealed significantly lower measures of the guidelines' impact. Contrary to Rogers' (1995) assertion that innovations backed by policy mandates are expected to show a higher rate of adoption, these results show exactly the opposite, suggesting that curricular mandates such as Florida's (derived from the guidelines) may have had a negative effect on the impact of the guidelines on K-12 foreign language education in that state (Fullan, 1993). However, though the comparison of means did pass the Equal Variances Test, it is difficult to say that five people (out of a possible total of seven) speak for the impact of the guidelines on K-12 education in the entire state of Florida.

Table 14.3: Results of t-Test for Independent Samples Comparing Florida with Other States' Average Scale. Measures of the ACTFL Guidelines' Impact (Equal Variances Assumed)

Impact variable	t	df	Sig. (2-tailed)	Mean difference
Impact of ACTFL Guidelines on local FL supervisor	−2.146	39	0.038	−0.9833
Impact of ACTFL Guidelines on local K-12 FL teachers	−2.202	47	0.033	−0.8500

RQ3C: How will knowledge of the guidelines and other ACTFL innovations correlate with adoption and integration by FL teacher educators?

Because the *Somewhat familiar with* ... and *Not familiar with* ... categories were seldom checked, these categories were conflated for data analysis purposes into two categories: *Very Familiar with* ... *and Somewhat to Not Familiar with* ... Only responses regarding familiarity with the ACTFL Guidelines were used for the test. In Chi Square analyses, familiarity was cross-tabulated with survey items #16 and #18–23, which include a series of dual response items asking the following questions:

- Have you implemented the ACTFL Proficiency Guidelines?
- Have you integrated the Proficiency Guidelines into your FL methods course?
- Have you played a role in promoting the ACTFL Proficiency Guidelines?
- Have you received training in use of the ACTFL Oral Proficiency Interview?
- Have you obtained official ACTFL OPI interviewer/rater status?
- Does your FLTE program test the oral proficiency of its candidates?
- Does your university/college's language department conduct exit OPIs for major? And finally,
- Does your FLTE program encourage teaching interns to continue to develop their proficiency?

The first three questions produced significant differences when paired with those who were very familiar with the guidelines. Though several rather low cell counts were noted, results suggest that those who were very familiar with the guidelines were more likely to be among those who claim to have promoted, implemented or integrated them into their FL methods course. This is in contrast to Wolf and Riordan's (1991) finding that suggested a negative relationship between knowledge and the guidelines' implementation.

RQ3D: Are professional factors such as: length of tenure as teacher educator, overall experience in FL teaching, and level of involvement in FL professional organizations positively related to the guidelines' adoption and implementation?

Because the intervals used for grouping lengths of experience in foreign language teacher education (FLTE) and foreign language education (FLED) contained groups that were too small for statistical comparison by range, a median split was conducted to bisect the FLTE group into eleven to fifteen years of experience and below, and sixteen to twenty years of experience and above. Likewise, the FLED group was divided into twenty-one to twenty-five years of experience and below, and twenty-six to thirty years of experience and above. These groups were then compared using a Chi Square test along the same items for RQ3C. Results (Table 14.4) show significant difference between expected and observed results, suggesting that FL teacher educators with the lesser overall amount of experience were more likely to be among those testing the proficiency levels of candidates. Because professional organizational activity was consistently strong among respondents, no meaningful statistical analysis could be conducted in that category. Because there was a nearly perfectly balanced representation of FL teacher educators with language and or literature doctorates and those with doctorates in education, an additional Chi Square analysis was calculated to see if such a professional background factor might be associated with the adoption and implementation of the guidelines for FL teacher educators. Results showed a difference just short of significant (.002 points) with regard to promotion of the guidelines. A significant difference would have suggested that those with an education degree were less likely to be among those promoting the guidelines. Due to the number and specificity of these factors, these results are inconclusive.

Table 14.4: Results of Chi Square Test of Variables of Adoption and Implementation versus Professional Background Factors

Grouping by Experience in FLTE			Does your FLTE program test the oral proficiency of its candidates?		Total
			Yes	No	
	1.00	Count	9	15	24
		Expected Count	12.7	11.3	24.0
	2.00	Count	20	11	31
		Expected Count	16.3	14.7	31.0
Total		Count	29	26	55
		Expected Count	29.0	26.0	55.0

Note: 1.00 = FL teacher educators with sixteen or more years of FLTE experience; 2.00 = FL teacher educators with less than sixteen years of FLTE experience.

Chi Square Tests	Value	df	Asymp. Sig. (2-sided)	Exact Sig. (2-sided)	Exact Sig. (1-sided)
Pearson Chi-Square	3.961[b]	1	0.047		
Continuity Correction[a]	2.951	1	0.086		
Likelihood Ratio	4.003	1	0.045		
Fisher's Exact Test				0.060	0.043
Linear-by-Linear Association	3.889	1	0.049		
N. of Valid Cases	55				

a. Computed only for a 2x2 table
b. 0 cells (.0%) have expected count less than 5. The minimum expected count is 11.35.

RQ3E: As population (urbanization) increases, does the likelihood of adoption and implementation of the guidelines also increase?

Because very few respondents indicated a rural or suburban work context, the categories of location were collapsed into *City over 100,000* and the rest of the respondents who reported either *City of under 100,000*, suburban, or rural. Respondents who checked off more than one response to this item were eliminated from this analysis, leaving two equal groups of twenty-six. In cross-tabulating location and items related to adoption and implementation, no significant differences were found between the observed and expected results. A t-test of the impact means (#27–28) of the two population groups likewise showed no significant factor for population grouping. This suggests that urbanization (Mort and Cornell, 1941; Rogers, 1995) may be overrated as a variable for this particular category of adopter and educational innovation. However, it is also possible that a scale with greater sensitivity to population variations might have produced different results.

RQ3F: Is there *a relationship between the innovativeness and openness to change of the socio-organizational* context *of adopters and variables of adoption and implementation?*

The ANOVA (Analysis of Variance) statistical operation was used to compare individual means of *support of innovation and openness to change* ratings with ratings of adoption and implementation. Respondents who reported having promoted the guidelines rated their support of innovations and openness to change significantly higher than those who did not ($x = 1.04$ vs $x = 1.50$); they also rated their communities' support of innovations and openness to change significantly lower than those who had not promoted the guidelines ($x = 2.72$ to $x = 1.87$). Respondents who indicated that they had implemented the guidelines rated their support of innovations and acceptance of change significantly higher (x = all "1s") than those who had not ($x = 1.66$).

Respondents who reported having received OPI training rated their respective State Department of Education significantly lower on the support of innovation and openness to change scale than counterparts who did not ($x = 2.58$ vs $x = 1.90$). Among those respondents who indicated having achieved official OPI rater/interviewer certification status, these FL teacher educators tended to rate superintendents significantly higher (x = 1.5 vs x = 2.55) and mentor teachers significantly lower (x = 2.75 vs x = 1.97) on the support of innovations and openness to change scale than counterparts who had not earned OPI certification. Respondents who indicated that they encourage FL teacher education candidates to continue to develop their proficiency-rated departmental colleagues higher on the scale of support of innovations and openness to change than colleagues who indicated that they did not (x = .161 vs 2.40). Finally, respondents who indicated OPI testing of FL majors were more likely to rate their superintendents higher than those who indicated that they did not (x = 2.07 vs 2.72).

Taken discretely, it is difficult to construct a meaningful interpretation of results of these tests. Given that there were a total of eleven variables along the scale questions about support of innovations and openness to change, and six variables to indicate adoption and implementation of the guidelines, it is not surprising that so many would show significant relationships. However, there is a pattern in the responses that indicates that adoption of the guidelines by FL teacher educators may be associated with a tendency to regard more localite groups (community, state departments of education, and mentor teachers) as less supportive of innovations and less open to change than non-adopting colleagues. Undermining this potential relationship is the fact that two of the adoption and implementation groups – those who obtained rater status and those who reported conducting exit OPIs for FL majors – reported higher ratings for their superintendents' support of innovation and openness to change than counterparts who had not implemented those derivatives of the guidelines innovation. Therefore, these results should be interpreted with caution.

RQ3G: Is *adoption and implementation of the guidelines significantly higher and earlier among FL teacher educators housed in modern language departments than their counterparts in colleges of education, as suggested in the literature?*

Respondents hailing from colleges or departments of education and those from language departments were selected for a Chi Square analysis. No significant differences were found between these groups when

connected with responses to survey items related to adoption and implementation. Due to the fact that many respondents reported preparation in
colleges of education and work in language departments and vice-versa, it
was determined that an analysis of the time of implementation along the
work context factor would not yield meaningful results.

Conclusions

It has been said that adaptation is an inherent characteristic of the way
new ideas and practices are communicated in the field of education (Hall,
George, and Rutherford, 1977; Mort and Cornell, 1941). In testing the
Diffusion of Innovations in Education Model, the researcher is therefore
not surprised to find areas where conceptual clarity still needs to be realized. There are two ways this can happen. First, the synthesis of studies is
limited by the lack of integration within research on educational innovations. Creating points of connection between researchers spanning a
broad geographic and temporal representation presents a significant challenge, somewhat like herding cats. Distinguishing stages of implementation
between diffusion effects and consequences, for example, is clearly difficult
in educational settings. Second, there is the issue of designing research
instruments for use with educators that toe the line between fidelity to
theoretical constructs of interest to researchers and a lexicon that adopting educators can connect with. For example, there was evidence of some
confusion as to how to treat Likert scale items measuring 1–4, lowest to
highest ratings when only one of five characteristics of an innovation under
study, complexity, may be perceived as a negative trait.

In spite of its limitations, results of the first questionnaire derived from
the Diffusion of Innovations in Education Model offers some insights into
which factors may help or hinder educational diffusion. For example, a
policy derivative of the innovation under study scored low on measures of
its impact on teaching within the state where the innovation was mandated.
Population base and innovativeness of the social context, once thought to

be major factors in educational diffusion and adoption, may not turn out to be so crucial. Also, in spite of early warnings that familiarity with the innovation under analysis appeared to negatively associate with adoption and implementation, the long-held DOI assertion to the contrary was borne out. Finally, there was a tendency for users and promoters of the guidelines to give low ratings to area education personnel, with the exception of superintendents, in the area of innovativeness and openness to change. Though these results are limited in their generalizability, they suggest that the nature of educational change is highly complex. While DOI provides a useful framework for conceptual clarity in designing and measuring the impact of educational innovations, it is clear that there are dynamic socio-organizational forces that are particular to the field of education – a finding that needs further verification in order to merit a significant contribution to a general theory of DOI. Such forces may not be unique to educational settings; they may have implications for any diffusion campaign that occurs on an inter-organizational level.

With regard to future questionnaire studies based on the DIEM, clearly a variety of innovations across a diversity of adopter settings need to be investigated in order to confirm or disprove the relative importance of the factors outlined in the model across a broader range of educational diffusion contexts. Will, for example, the same results hold true across educational innovations in a variety of academic settings? Also, to what extent is this study describing a phenomenon particular to schooling in the United States? In fact, the DIEM itself requires extensive review and reliability and validity testing by the educational research community.

Bibliography

American Council on the Teaching of Foreign Languages. 1986. ACTFL *Proficiency Guidelines*. Yonkers, NY: American Council on the Teaching of Foreign Languages.

Carlson, R. O. 1965. Barriers to Change in Public Schools. Pp. 3–8 in R. O. Carlson, A. Gallagher, Jr, M. B. Miles, R. J. Pellegrin & E. M. Rogers (eds), *Change Processes in the Public Schools.* Eugene, OR: The University of Oregon Center for the Advanced Study of Educational Administration (ERIC Document Reproduction Service No. ED 013 483).

Carlson, R. O. 1968. Summary and Critique of Educational Diffusion Research. Pp. 4–23 in Research Implications for Educational Diffusion: Major Papers Presented at the National Conference on Diffusion of Educational Ideas, March 1968. East Lansing: Michigan State University, Michigan Vocational Education Research Coordinating Unit (ERIC Document Reproduction Service NO. ED 026 535).

Darling-Hammond, L., with E. Sclan. 1992. Policy and Supervision. Pp. 13–29 in C. D. Glickman, Supervision in Transition: 1992 Yearbook of the Association for Supervision and Curriculum Development. Alexandria, VA: ASCD.

Earley, P. M. 1993. The Teacher-Education Agenda: Policies, Policy Arenas, and Implications for the Profession. Pp. 7–22 in G. Guntermann (ed.), *Developing Teachers for a Changing World.* The ACTFL Foreign Language Education Series. Lincolnwood, IL: National Textbook Co.

Emrick, J. A., & S. M. Peterson. 1977. Evaluation of the National Diffusion Network. Final Report. Volume II: Technical Supplement. Menlo, California: Stanford Research Institute, May (ERIC Document Reproduction Service No. 147 340).

Frank, K. A., Y. Zhao & K. Borman. 2004. Social capital and the diffusion of innovations within organizations: The case of computer technology in schools. *Sociology of Education,* 77: 148–171.

Fullan, M. 1993. *Change Forces.* Bristol, PA: The Falmer Press.

Fullan, M. 2001. *Leading in a Culture of Change.* San Francisco, CA: Jossey-Bass.

Fullan, M. 2002. The Change Leader. *Educational Leadership,* 59(8): 16–20.

Grosse, C. U. & C. Feyton. 1991. Impact of the Proficiency Movement on the State of Florida. *Hispania,* 74 (April): 205–209.

Hall, G. E. 1992. The Local Educational Change Process and Policy Implementation. *Journal of Research in Science Teaching,* 29(8): 877–904 <http://onlinelibrary. wiley.com/doi/10.1002/tea.3660290809/full>.

Hall, G. E., A. A. George & W. C. Rutherford. 1977. Measuring Stages of Concern about the Innovation: A Manual for Use of the SoC Questionnaire. Austin Research and Development Center for Teacher Education, University of Texas (ERIC Document Reproduction Service No. ED ED147 342).

Hansen, J. M. 1981. The Accidental Curriculum: The Unplanned nature of Curricular Implementation. *NASSP Bulletin,* 65(443): 16–21.

Henrichsen, L. 1989. *The Diffusion of Innovations in English Language Teaching: The ELEC Efforts in Japan, 1956–1968.* New York: Greenwood Press.

Hord, S. M., W. L. Rutherford, L. Huling-Austin & G. Hall. 1987. *Taking Charge of Change*. Alexandria, VA: Association for Supervision and Curriculum Development.

Huberman, M. 1983. The Role of Teacher Education in the Improvement of Educational Practice: A Linkage Model. *European Journal of Teacher Education*, 6(1): 17–29.

Hunkins, F. P., & A. C. Ornstein. 1989. Curriculum Innovation and Implementation. *Education and Urban Society*, 22(1): 105–114.

Lange, D. L. 1988. Some Implications for Curriculum and Instruction for Foreign Language Education as Derived from the ACTFL Proficiency Guidelines. *Die Unterrichtspraxis*, 21: 41–50.

Leithwood, K. A., & D. J. Montgomery. 1980. Evaluating Program Implementation. *Evaluation Review*, 4(2): 193–214.

Likert, R. 1961. *New Patterns of Management*. New York: McGraw-Hill.

Markee, N. 1992. The Diffusion of Innovations in Language Teaching. *Annual Review of Applied Linguistics*, 13(1): 229–243.

Markee, N. 1997. Second Language Acquisition Research: A Resource for Changing Teachers' Professional Cultures? *The Modern Language Journal*, 81(1): 80–93.

Miles, M. B. 1969. The Development of Innovative Climates in Educational Organizations. Menlo Park, CA: Stanford Research Institute (Eric Document Reproduction Service No. ED 030 971).

Mort, P. R., & F. G. Cornell. 1941. *American Schools in Transition: How Our Schools Adapt Their Practices to Changing Needs, A Study of Pennsylvania*. New York: Teachers College.

Mortimore, F. J. 1968. Diffusion of Innovations in Education in the Government Secondary Schools of Thailand. Unpublished doctoral dissertation. Michigan State University, East Lansing.

Nunan, D. 1989. Toward a Collaborative Approach to Curriculum Development: A Case Study. *TESOL Quarterly*, 23(1): 9–26.

Omaggio, A. C. 1983. Methodology in Transition: The New Focus on Proficiency. *The Modern Language Journal*, 67(4): 330–341.

Omaggio, A. C. 1984. The Proficiency-Oriented Classroom. Pp. 43–84 in T. V. Higgs (ed.), *Teaching for Proficiency, The Organizing Principle*. The ACTFL Foreign Language Education Series. Lincolnwood, IL: National Textbook Company.

Omaggio, A. C. 1986. *Teaching Language in Context: Proficiency-Oriented Instruction*. New York: Heinle and Heinle.

Rogers, E. M. 1995. *The Diffusion of Innovations*. 3rd Edn. New York: The Free Press.

Rogers, E. M., & N. C. Jain. 1968. Needed Research on Diffusion Within Educational Organizations (ERIC Document Reproduction Service No. ED 017 740).

Rogers, E. M., & F. F. Shoemaker. 1971. *Communication of Innovations.* 2nd Edn. New York: The Free Press.

Ryan, B., & N. C. Gross. 1943. The Diffusion of Hybrid Seed Corn in Two Iowa Communities. *Rural Sociology,* 8(1): 15–24.

Sarason, S. B. 1990. *The Predictable Failure of Educational Reform.* San Francisco, CA: Jossey-Bass.

Schulz, R. A. 1986. From Achievement to Proficiency Through Classroom Instruction: Some Caveats. *The Modern Language Journal,* 70(4): 373–379.

Tarde, G. 1903. *The Laws of Imitation,* translated by Elsie Clews Parsons. New York: reprinted 1969, Chicago, IL: University of Chicago Press.

Valdes, G. M. 1987. Florida: State of the Foreign Language Arts. Pp. 38–48 in T. B. Fryer and F. W. Medley, Jr (eds), *Planning for Proficiency: Dimension: Language; '86. Report of the Southern Conference on Language Teaching,* Atlanta, Georgia (ERIC Document Reproduction Service No. ED 337 010).

White, R. V. 1992. Innovation in Curriculum Planning and Program Development. *Annual Review of Applied Linguistics,* 13(1): 244–225.

PART VII

Innovation and Performance

ANGELO DOSSOU-YOVO AND DIANE-GABRIELLE TREMBLAY

15 Public Policy, Intermediaries, and Innovation System Performance: A Comparative Analysis of Québec and Ontario

ABSTRACT

Knowledge has become a fundamental resource of production in the economy; a major element for the innovation and the competitiveness of firms, regions, and nations. This knowledge is available through the interactions between firms themselves and with other organizations and stakeholders. These interactions often occur in places known as clusters and one of the main roles of the public bodies in economic development is to create a favorable environment to foster industrial and social development. Following the growing interest in industrial clusters, many regions have considered it as an interesting tool for public policy, but in many cases public policy has not integrated the knowledge of citizens or other stakeholders. Among these actors, we find what we call intermediary organizations (for example, professional associations, chambers of commerce, community organizations, and various new forms of governance networks), that contribute to the creation and the support of social dynamics within the networks of innovations and could be used more extensively in order to enhance public policy and introduce innovation in the public sector. In this chapter, we consider the role of the organizations at the meso level and we do a regional comparison in order to investigate the role of the intermediaries. We use the data from the survey of innovation completed in 2003 by Statistics Canada to compare Ontario and Québec, centering our analysis on the information and communication technologies (ICT) sector which is one of the most innovative in Canada. Our results show that the innovation performance relies on sources of information and high-skilled labor to innovate. Also important are factors such as the proximity of the universities and research laboratories, the presence of local and regional industrial associations, the presence of venture capital organizations, the presence of governments' organizations, as well as government financial assistance for research and development, but also new regulations that meet the firm's needs for intellectual protection. Thus, these are elements on which cluster policies should be centered. In such a context, cluster policies appear particularly pertinent, as this is one of the possible forms of public intermediation to be considered.

Introduction

Knowledge has become a fundamental resource of production in the economy; a major element for the innovation and the competitiveness of firms, regions, and nations. This knowledge is available through the interactions between firms themselves and also with other organizations and stakeholders that occur in places known as clusters. One of the main roles of the public bodies in economic development is to create a favorable environment to foster industrial and social development. Following the growing interest for industrial clusters, many regions have considered it as an interesting tool for public policy, and they have been created in various environments, including the City of Montréal (Klein and Tremblay, 2010; Tremblay and Cecilli, 2009; Britton, Tremblay and Smith, 2009). The theoretical contributions that are usually cited in the literature to explain the creation of clusters are based either on the concept of "industrial districts" introduced by Marshall (1994 [1890]), or on the competitiveness of local industries developed by Porter (1990) with his study on the competitiveness of the nations or on the concept of "Milieux innovateurs" from the Groupe de Recherche Européen sur les Milieux Innovateurs (GREMI).

As large factories are less effective and less flexible (Marshall, 1994 [1890]), it is necessary for public policy to try to support firms in adapting to the new economic context, and to try to divide the production process into several parts that can be done by small specialized firms. When these firms are localized in a geographical area, they tend to collaborate together. The result of this agglomeration of firms is the "cluster" or the "industrial district" which allows the firms to benefit from externalities like reducing cost of production, availability of the infrastructures, the services and knowledge. Porter explains the cluster phenomenon by the needs for the firms, regions, and nation to remain competitive in order to survive in the economy. He argues that clustering is a strategy, which will enable the firms to profit from competitive advantages in particular by increasing their productivity and their ability to innovate. However, this clusterization process often does not occur spontaneously and it is necessary for public policy to intervene to support such developments.

The approach of "milieu innovateur" is another approach which uses the territory or the "milieu" to explain the cluster phenomenon. This approach allows a broad understanding of the cluster, which includes not only firms but also different actors from the public sector. The GREMI group defines the "milieu" as a group of relations that occurs in a geographical area with a system of production, and a specific culture and actors (Maillat, Crevoisier and Lecoq, 1993: 4). In this approach, the cluster is the result of the "milieu." It develops because the "milieu" allows networks that create interdependences and cooperation between the different actors. We integrate the "milieu innovateur" approach with the innovation system approach (Freeman, 1987; Lundvall, 1992; Nelson, 1993; Edquist, 2001; Edquist and Johnson, 1997) to analyze the cluster. An innovation system could be analyzed at the national, local, sectoral, or technological level. Hence, we consider the cluster as a microsystem of innovation or reduced-scale national innovation system (Roelandt and den Hertog, 1999).

The literature on innovation systems also shows that the microsystems of innovation or clusters appear particularly in the "learning regions," which is a concept introduced by Florida (1995, 1998) and Baumfeld (2005) to emphasize the learning process that occurs inside a region but also within a cluster. This learning process occurs due to the diversity of social actors and stakeholders that collaborate together. The actors inside the cluster come from the private and the public sector. Among the actors that come from the public sector, we find the professional associations, the governmental economic agencies (e.g. Federal Business Development Agency), research institutions and venture capital organizations. At the regional level, these organizations contribute to the creation and the support of dynamics within what can be considered networks of innovations. These organizations are also called "intermediary organizations," defined as "an organization or body that acts as an agent or broker in any aspect of the innovation process between two or more parties" (Howell 2006: 720). They also play different roles such as sharing information about potential collaborators, facilitating transactions or mediation between different parties, and finally helping in accessing funding or support for innovation.

Because it is crucial for public policy to better understand the effectiveness of clusters, our chapter centers on the role of these intermediary organizations (or governance networks or bodies). The principal aim of this study is to investigate whether the intermediaries really influence the innovation systems' performance which we will evaluate qualitatively later in this chapter, by using the theoretical concept of the technological regimes (Nelson and Winter, 1982) and by focusing on the functions fulfilled by the organizations.

To our knowledge, very little research has been done on the relation between the role of the intermediaries and the performance of innovation in the microsystems or clusters, although some research was done within some sectors (Britton, Tremblay and Smith, 2009). Other authors have focused on innovation performance by comparing clusters within different regions (Spencer et al., 2010). One part of this literature has tried to identify these intermediaries and to describe in a theoretical way their role in the process of innovation (Doutriaux, 2003; Howell, 2006), while others have shown that these roles differ according to the macro, meso or micro level (Smedlund, 2006). In this chapter, we consider the role of the organizations at the meso level and we do a regional comparison between the Canadian provinces of Ontario and Québec in order to investigate the role of the intermediaries by focusing on the information and communications technology (ICT) cluster. Our aim is also to determine if an innovative collaborative policy such as the cluster policy can be useful to implement and produce innovative results in the process of public policy development. By cluster policy we mean all public initiatives, or incentives that contribute to the development of the cluster (for example subsidies, infrastructure development, incentives for industry-university collaboration, tax credit associated with a particular location, etc.). In order to test this hypothesis, we use the 2003 survey of innovation of Statistics Canada, which is the latest at the time of our study that focuses on the entire information and communications technology (ICT) sector. In the next section, we will define more precisely our theoretical framework.

Role of the Intermediaries and the Performance of the Microsystem of Innovation

In the literature on innovation systems, the system is either delimited by considering only the organizations, which intervenes directly in the process of innovation or with the integration of all economic and institutional structures, that intervene or influence the process of innovation. The institutions are the common practices, the routines, the established practices, the rules or laws which control the relations and interactions between individuals, groups, and actors (Edquist and Johnson, 1997: 47). Wolfe and Gertler (2003) consider that an innovation system at the national level includes several elements; namely, the private firms (R and D performers); the science and technology infrastructure; the government programs; the networks to facilitate knowledge and technology transfer; the education and training system; and the financial system for technology financing (see Figure 15.1).

In this chapter, we consider only the organizations that participate in the innovation process of the firm, going from the idea to the commercialization of a new product. We consider an innovation as a new commercialized product or a new manufacturing process. Moreover, as the firms don't innovate alone, we take into account the learning interaction that occurs inside (e.g. learning between employees) and outside (e.g. knowledge transfers with a university) the firm during the process. The organizations and the institutions are the components of the innovation system where three relations (Edquist, 2001) can be observed. These relations can be between the organizations, the organizations and the institutions, or the institutions themselves. Two organizations could have a market or non-market relation. The non-market relation usually allows to exchange for example tacit knowledge that is not available with market transaction. The relations between the organizations and the institutions are another type in the innovation system. The organizations fulfill different functions in the system that can be used by the institutions to evaluate them even if these institutions are created by the organizations (see Figure 15.2). There is also a last type of possible relation, which is between institutions.

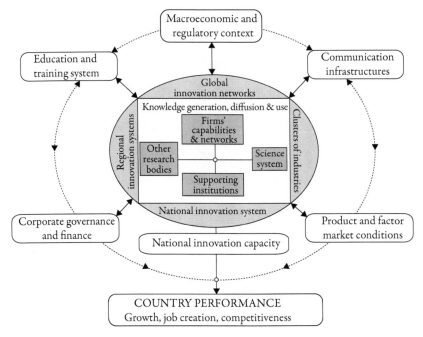

Figure 15.1: National innovation system. Source: D. Wolfe and M. Gertler. 2003. Policies for Cluster Creation: Lessons from the ISRN Cluster Initiative. *ISRN National meeting presentation.* Ottawa, Canada, p. 5.

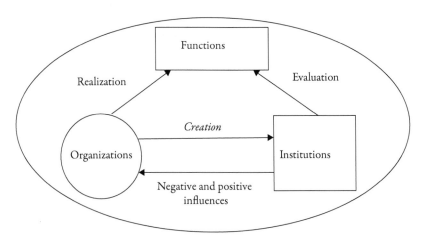

Figure 15.2: Microsystem of innovation. Source: the authors.

In this chapter, we evaluate the microsystem in the ICT sector in two ways. We base our performance evaluation on the availability of the essential resources for the innovation. For this, we use the theoretical concept of the technological regimes (Nelson and Winter, 1982). A technological regime is based on opportunities and appropriability conditions, the accumulation of knowledge and the characteristics of the knowledge base (Malerba and Orsenigo, 1990, 1993, 1997). The opportunities conditions determine the probability of the firms to innovate. Opportunities include the presence of sources of innovation such as the universities or research laboratory and an intense research and development. The appropriability conditions are the possibilities of protecting the innovation from the imitation. Moreover, we integrate the tacit knowledge, which is particularly essential for the innovation and which is an embodied knowledge. As the competences become also important for the innovators then the availability and the retention of competences or talents (Florida, 2002) become essential to allow the firms in the microsystem to innovate. To sum up, we consider in this chapter that innovation performance in the microsystem or cluster relies on the opportunities and appropriability conditions, on the competences, and the institutional environment. Therefore, we make the following proposals:

Proposal 1:   The performance of the microsystem of innovation depends on opportunities and appropriability conditions.

Proposal 2:   The performance of the microsystem depends on the availability of competences, the interactive learning, and the institutional environment.

As mentioned above, the organizations that are in the microsystem realize some activities, which are the functions of the system. Then, the second way we evaluate the performance of the microsystem is to see whether these functions are fulfilled correctly. The principal activities that are realized by the organizations include the supply of necessary resources for innovation (Johnson and Jacobsson, 2000; cited in Edquist, 2001: 9) and this is shown in the literature. A first group of researchers consider that these organizations, particularly the intermediaries play the role that consist in information diffusion, technology transfer and giving different kinds of support to the firms, while another group asserts that the principal role of intermediation is to fulfill the function of collecting, analyzing, and communication of the information (Howells, 2006). The diffusion and the technology transfer include the following activities: transmission of information, support in the decision-making, evaluation of new technologies, identification of the partners, technology transfer, and so on. Finally, the intermediaries support the firms in adapting the innovations to their specific needs, in being able to keep relations between the actors of the technological system.

In relation with this territorial dimension, Smedlund (2006) associates the role of the intermediaries to the regional dynamics, which are defined as: "The networks of production, development and innovation." Dynamics are based on tangible and intangible flows within the region that would not be possible without the networks or clusters, and their interactions. For Smedlund, the intermediaries contribute to the creation and the support of dynamics within the networks because they help in the formation of strategies of innovations between the actors, and the attraction and the retention of large firms with high intensity of Research and Development. The case studies done on the multimedia sector (Britton, Tremblay and Smith, 2009; Tremblay, Chevrier and Rousseau, 2004) illustrate well these roles. Finally, the intermediaries stimulate the social dynamics, which allows the creation, the evolution and the development of the microsystem because they support the diffusion of the information and the improvement of the knowledge base of the firms, the availability of competences and the continuous learning through interactions. We thus put forward the following additional proposals:

Proposal 3: The intermediaries have a positive impact on the opportunities and appropriability conditions.

Proposal 4: The intermediaries have a positive impact on the availability of competences, on the learning and the institutional environment.

Proposal 5: The intermediaries have a positive impact on the performance of the system (consequence of proposals 3 and 4).

These proposals will be evaluated hereafter in our case study.

Case Study: Comparative Cases of Québec and Ontario

The ICT sector is one of the most important parts of the Canadian national economy. It contributes significantly to the Gross Domestic Product (GDP) and is also an important source of jobs. The proof is that from 1977 to 2000, its part of the GDP increased by 19 per cent compared to 5.1 per cent for the whole Canadian companies (Statistics Canada, 2005: 190). Moreover, in 1999, this sector created 3.9 per cent of the jobs in the whole economy. According to Statistics Canada (2003: 12), the sub-sector of the services is more dynamic than the manufacture one in the ICT industry. The growth of the ICT sector was primarily due to the services during 1997 to 2003 when its part of the GDP increased by going from 3 per cent to 4.6 per cent compared to the manufacturing sub-sector, which decreased by going from 1 per cent to 0.8 per cent. At the provincial level, Ontario and Québec are the most important contributors in Canada in this sector with the incomes generated (respectively 40.1 per cent and 24.7 per cent of the incomes in 1999). That's why we chose these two regions for our comparative study.

Our research is based on the innovation data from the 2003 Survey of Statistics Canada in the ICT services industry, to which we had access. The

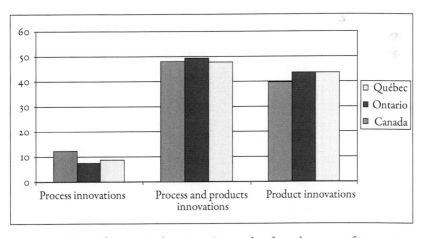

Figure 15.3: Type of innovation by region. Source: data from the survey of innovation, Statistics Canada (2004).

survey questionnaire is based on the indicators recommended in the Oslo Manual. The sample was built by considering only the establishments, which have fifteen employees or more and $250,000 of income. Therefore, out of a population of 4,504 companies in the sector of the services, the sample concerned 1,359 establishments. In this survey, the establishments, which are defined as innovators, are those that have introduced a new product in the market or have improved their process or built a new one during 2001 to 2003. We do a comparative analysis of Ontario and Québec in order to try to explain why a microsystem in a particular region may perform more than another one. In our case, the analysis of the performance in product and process innovation shows that Ontario performs slightly better than Québec when we take together product and process innovations (see Figure 15.3). However, if we consider only process innovations, then Québec performs better then Ontario. What explains this lag of performance? That's what we will try to explain in the following sections.

To be able to do that, as said before, we will evaluate the microsystem by analyzing mainly the opportunities and appropriability conditions. To these opportunities, we add the availability of competences and possibilities of learning. To the conditions of appropriability, we add the regulation environment. In the next sections, we will test our proposals. In the first part, we will analyze the conditions of innovation in order to support our proposals 1 and 2 and this part will be useful in complement of the second part to support our proposals 3, 4 and 5. In the second part, we will determine the role of the intermediaries on the performance of the microsystem. We will try to find out how the intermediaries realize activities or participate in the innovation process and consequently how they contribute to the innovation performance of the microsystem. This second part will allow us to support our proposals 3, 4 and 5.

Conditions of Innovation

CONDITIONS OF OPPORTUNITIES

Figure 15.4 shows that the sources of information that most used by the innovators are trade fairs and exhibitions, professional congresses and conferences, business associations, and consultants. For all these sources of information, Figure 15.4 shows that the percentages are higher in Ontario. Therefore, it is possible to predict that the advantages might be more important in Ontario in terms of the exchanges and the availability of information for the innovation. Consequently, this can be a first explanation of the disparity between Québec and Ontario in product innovation.

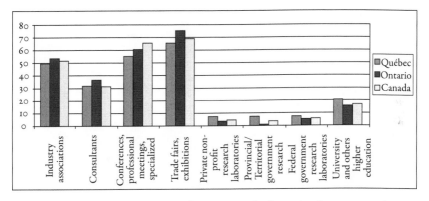

Figure 15.4: Organizations used as a source of information for process and product innovation by innovating firms. Source: data from the survey of innovation, Statistics Canada (2004).

In the knowledge economy, the availability of high-level competences and the possibility of improving these competences and of increasing the firm knowledge base in a continuous way with the training is essential for innovation and competitiveness. The regions, which have a quality human infrastructure, have competitive advantages because they are attractive for the firms, in addition to being a favorable milieu for innovation (Florida, 1995). Figure 15.5 shows that Ontario has higher competitive advantages than Québec in term of availability of high-quality competences; as the data show, there are more employees with a university diploma in Ontario than in Québec. This can be explained by the fact that Ontario seems to focus more on hiring skilled workers, on the creation of incentives to attract them or to retain them (see Figure 15.6). However, this can also be explained partly by the fact that as it is an English-language zone (versus French for Québec), it is easier

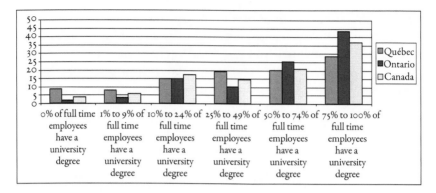

Figure 15.5: Availability of competences for process and product innovation.
Source: data from the survey of innovation, Statistics Canada (2004).

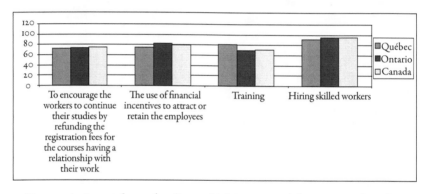

Figure 15.6: Success factors (medium to high importance) for process and product innovation – I. Source: data from the survey of innovation, Statistics Canada (2004).

to attract qualified workers from abroad; indeed Toronto is the main destination for immigrants in Canada.

This availability of competences helps with the knowledge diffusion through learning, which results in the interactions between employees but also with self-training. From this point of view, Figure 15.7 shows that in Ontario as in Québec different methods are used for that.

CONDITIONS OF APPROPRIABILITY

The method of protection, which is as much cited in Ontario as in Québec, is the confidentiality agreement. The proportion is slightly higher in Ontario

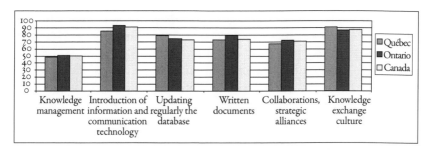

Figure 15.7: Success factors (medium to high importance) for process and product innovation – II. Source: data from the survey of innovation, Statistics Canada (2004).

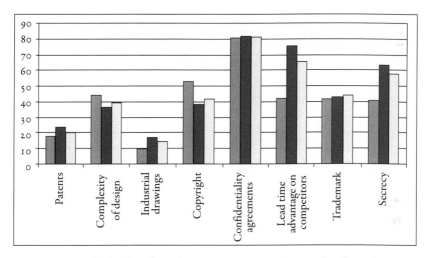

Figure 15.8: Methods of intellectual property protection. Source: data from the survey of innovation, Statistics Canada (2004).

(see Figure 15.8), however, it needs to be stressed that this question stresses more traditional sources of innovation protection, and not so much the new visions on sources of innovation, including the need for interactions as means for the diffusion of information. This could be the consequence of a lack of industry wide standards or government standards and regulation.

This seems to be the case in Québec and in Ontario but in a higher proportion in Ontario if we take into account the proportion of innovators, which consider this phenomenon as a barrier or an obstacle for innovation (see Figure 15.9). Finally, our analysis shows that the conditions of innovation are more favorable to the performance of the microsystems in Ontario. The opportunities contribute to a better availability of the sources of innovation and competences while the appropriability conditions allow the interaction for the exchange of tacit knowledge which is more vital for the performance of the microsystem. This analysis seems to show that our proposals 1 and 2 are supported.

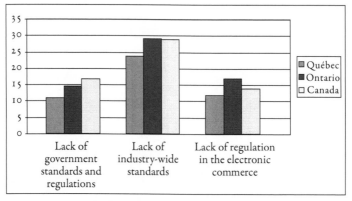

Figure 15.9: Obstacles (medium to high importance) for process and product innovation – III. Source: data from the survey of innovation, Statistics Canada (2004).

Impact of Intermediaries

Figure 15.10 shows that the success in innovation is related to the proximity of the universities and research laboratories as well as the presence of local and regional industrial associations. Doutriaux (2003) did an investigation on the role of universities in the development of clusters in Canada in the high technology industry. His study was based on the analysis of eleven clusters that were the most dynamic in Canadian high technology sectors during the 1980s and 1990s. He showed that the universities are important catalysts of the creation and development of firms in the high technology sector. Moreover, they participate in the construction of the local knowledge base that allows the clusters to develop and to grow.

Figure 15.10 shows us that industrial associations are intermediaries, which contribute more to the success of innovation. By considering the important role of these industrial associations, it seems that Ontario profits from it more than Québec as the data show in Figure 15.10. The venture capital organizations participate in innovation because they finance the innovation projects. The governmental organizations also take part in the innovation process, but this seems to be more efficient in the research and

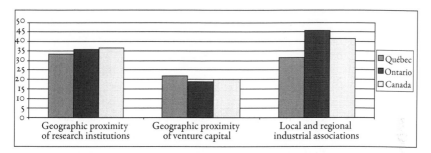

Figure 15.10: Success factors (medium to high importance) for process and product innovation – III. Source: data from the survey of innovation, Statistics Canada (2004).

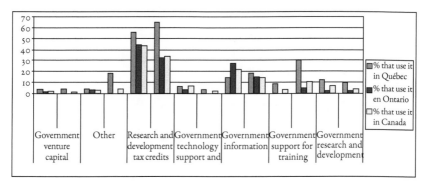

Figure 15.11: Use of governmental assistance. Source: data from the survey of innovation, Statistics Canada (2004).

development tax credits (see Figure 15.11). However, Québec firms use more governmental assistance than Ontarian firms for research and development.

It appears that the intermediaries take part in the process of innovation in various ways. It seems that industrial associations might have more impact on the performance of the microsystem. If we consider the data it is possible to predict that this impact will be more important in Ontario because of the proportion of innovators, which consider it as a success factor in process and product innovation. Finally, this analysis allows us to support our proposals 3, 4 and as a consequence support also proposal 5 However, it is important to mention that within the role of all intermediaries, the specific role of industrial associations seems to be very important.

Discussion

Considering the Ontario ICT sector as the most innovative based on the data on the performance in product and process innovation, we can analyze the difference with the ICT sector in Québec and draw some conclusions about the innovation performance factors associated with the environment of the firms. The success factors are the sources of information; the availability of high-skilled labor; and the industry regulation. The innovation performance relies on sources of information, particularly trade fairs and exhibitions, professional congresses and conferences, business associations, and consultants. Therefore, a cluster policy that focuses on these sources of information could be useful for economic development and the competitiveness of firms. In addition, as the firms in the cluster need high-skilled labor to innovate, a cluster policy that encompasses this objective would be helpful. An avenue for cluster policy would also be to establish new rules that meet the firm's needs for intellectual protection but also for financially accessible protection.

We have also analyzed the impact of the intermediaries in both regions and we have found several differences that also allow us to identify innovation performance factors, that are the proximity of the universities and research laboratories; the presence of local and regional industrial associations; the presence of venture capital organizations; and the presence of governmental organizations and public financial assistance for research and development. Therefore, a cluster policy should also focus on these actors. As our data indicate that the industrial associations, consultants, and trade fairs are important factors of innovation performance; these are elements on which cluster policies should thus be centered. In such a context, the cluster policies appear particularly pertinent, as this is one of the possible forms of public intermediation to be considered. The cluster model developed in Canada by the Innovation Systems Research Network is centered on the performance of firms and attempts to demystify the various factors that might explain this performance. The success or performance of a cluster is seen as being dependent on the performance of the individual firms that are part of the cluster, and this performance is moderated by cluster conditions and the environment of the firms. Amongst the factors, which are seen as having an impact on the firms, there are human and social capital, R and D capacity and infrastructure, information infrastructure, community resources and support, as well as government policies and programs.

Cluster development is obviously a long-term process that is based on the mobilization of key stakeholders in the community, or local or regional territory (Tremblay and Cecilli, 2009). In this context, Cassidy et al. (2005) have identified four stages: latent, developing, established, and transformation. While many writings on clusters are centered on established, long-existing clusters, there is now a recognition that clusters can be at different stages, and particularly that many are in the latent or developing stage in the new media or new creative industries (see for example Britton, Tremblay and Smith, 2009; Smith, McCarthy and Petrusevich, 2004; Tremblay, Chevrier and Rousseau, 2004; Gertler and Wolfe, 2005; Wolfe, Davis and Lucas, 2005). In any case, the interest here is on the role that local actors and stakeholders can play in policy development and economic performance. The main difference between the cluster view and other views of economic development or growth is the fact that it highlights the social and territorial nature of the innovation process, that we can call socio-territorial capital (Fontan, Klein and Tremblay, 2005).

This socio-territorial capital is seen as just as important a role as economic or financial factors (price, financial support, and so on), although it has not necessarily been as prioritized as the traditional factors. The territory is seen here as being more than a simple repository for economic activity and the role of social relations of production and interactions is highlighted. This explains that our view of creative clusters is largely centered on the analysis of social relations and interactions between actors and stakeholders.

Conclusion

In this chapter, we have tried to determine if and how intermediaries can have an impact on innovation and economic development, looking at the sources of innovation in Québec and Ontario, as well as the role of intermediaries on the performance of the microsystem of innovation. Our main objective was to investigate what type of information or resources appear crucial for innovation, and whether the intermediaries can have an impact on the performance in product and process innovation of the microsystem in the ICT sector, all this in order to determine if cluster policies, can be useful from this point of view. Indeed, cluster policies are based on collaboration and while they are often put forward in recent years, it is important to determine if the resources offered by clusters can indeed be useful. The data presented here seem to indicate that organization of trade fairs, exchanges with consultants and industrial associations do appear useful. As these elements are at the core of activities within cluster organizations and other similar intermediaries, it appears that cluster policies can most probably foster innovation and economic development.

We put forward five proposals, which we tried to test with our case study carried out with the survey of innovation done by Statistics Canada. In our research, we focused on the ICT sectors as it is an important sector for the Canadian industry but also in Ontario and in Quebec. We showed that many of the functions and roles of intermediaries can have an impact on innovation; they can create the dynamics within the microsystem and support the innovation activities. Therefore, they can influence the opportunities and appropriability conditions, the availability of competences and the learning, and finally the regulation in this environment. This leads to the conclusion that a cluster policy can be interesting to foster innovation in, as much as it favors collaboration between local actors and stakeholders and thus can contribute to create the conditions for innovation and economic development.

Our comparative analysis (Québec and Ontario) on the role of the intermediaries and their impacts in the process of innovation shows that these organizations can have a positive impact on the performance of the microsystem in product and process innovation. However, for the moment at least, this seems to be more the effect of industrial associations, than other actors. Our analysis of the data allows us to show that in this ICT sector at least the proximity and the exchanges between various actors and stakeholders contribute to the product and process innovation, and thus that collaborative innovation in the context of a cluster can contribute not only to policy innovation, but also to positive economic results.

To sum up, our analysis shows that the intermediaries can have an impact on the performance in product and process innovation in the microsystem, and more globally on a given industrial sector such as ICT, in as much as they do offer elements that contribute to innovation and are seen by firms as important factors of innovation. These elements are considered amongst the factors that can be supported by a cluster policy. It remains to be seen to what extent they are effectively put forward (Britton, Tremblay and Smith, 2009; Tremblay, Chevrier and Rousseau, 2004).

Bibliography

Baumfeld, L. 2005. *Balanced Scorecard für Regionen [Balanced Scorecard for Regions]*. Wien, Österreich: Leader.

Britton, J., D.-G. Tremblay & R. Smith. 2009. Contrasts in clustering: the example of Canadian New Media. *European Planning Studies*, 17(2): 211–235.

Cassidy, E., C. Davis, D. Arthurs & D. Wolfe. 2005. Beyond cluster – current practices and future strategies. Paper presented at the CRIC conference, Ballarat, Australia, June 30 – July 1, 2005.

Doutriaux, J. 2003. University-Industry Linkages and the Development of Knowledge Clusters in Canada. *Local Economy*, 18(1): 63–79.

Edquist, C. 2001. The Systems of Innovation Approach and Innovation Policy: An account of the state of the art. Lead paper presented at the DRUID Conference, Aalborg, Denmark, June 12–15, 2001.

Edquist, C., & B. Johnson. 1997. Institutions and organisations in systems of innovation. Pp. 41–60 in C. Edquist (ed.), *Systems of Innovation: Technologies, Institutions and Organizations*. London and Washington, DC: Pinter, Cassell Academic.

Florida, R. 1995. Toward the learning region. *Futures*, 27(5): 527–536.

Florida, R. 1998. Building the Learning Region. Paper presented at the OECD Symposium on the Learning Region, Jena, Germany, June 26, 1998.

Florida, R. 2002. The Economic Geography of talent. *Annals of the American Association of Geographers*, 92(4): 743–755.

Fontan, J.-M., J.-L. Klein & D.-G. Tremblay. 2005. *Innovation sociale et reconversion économique : Le cas de Montréal*. Paris, France: L'Harmattan.

Freeman, C. 1987. *Technology policy and economic performance: lessons from Japan*. London: Pinter Publishers.

Gertler, M., & D. Wolfe. 2005. Spaces of knowledge flows: Clusters in a global context. Paper presented at the conference Dynamics of industry and innovation DRUID Tenth Anniversary Summer Organizations, Networks and Systems, Copenhagen, June 27–29, 2005.

Howells, J. 2006. Intermediation and the role of intermediaries in innovation. *Research Policy*, 35(5): 715–728.

Johnson, A., & S. Jacobsson. 2000. The emergence of a growth industry: a comparative analysis of the German Dutch and Swedish wind turbine industry. Paper presented at the EUWEC Special Topic Conference Wind Power for the 21st Century, Kassel, Germany, September 25–27, 2000.

Klein, J.-L., & D.-G. Tremblay. 2010. Social actors and their role in metropolitan governance in Montréal: Towards an inclusive coalition? *GeoJournal*, 75(2): 567–579.

Lundvall, B.-Å. 1992. *National Systems of Innovation: Towards a Theory of Innovation and Interactive Learning*. London: Pinter.

Maillat, D., O. Crevoisier & B. Lecoq. 1993. Réseaux d'innovation et dynamique territoriale. Un essai de typologie. *Revue d'Économie Régionale et Urbaine*, 3(4): 407–432.

Malerba, F., & L. Orsenigo. 1990. Technological Regime and Pattern of Innovation: A theoretical and empirical investigation of the Italian Case. Pp. 283–306 in A. Heertje (ed.), *Evolving industry and market structures*. Ann Arbor: University of Michigan Press.

Malerba, F., & L. Orsenigo. 1993. Technological Regime and Firm Behaviour. *Industrial and Corporate Change*, 2(1): 45–71.

Malerba, F., & L. Orsenigo. 1997. Technological regimes and sectoral patterns of innovative activities. *Industrial and Corporate Change*, 6(1): 83–117.

Marshall, A. 1994 [1890]. *Principles of Economics*. London: Macmillan.

Nelson, R. R. 1993. *National Innovation Systems: A Comparative Analysis*. New York: Oxford University Press.

Nelson, R. R., & Winter, S. 1982. *An evolutionary theory of Economic Change*. Boston, MA: Harvard University Press.

Porter, Michael. 1990. *The Competitive Advantage of Nations*. New York: Basic Books.

Roelandt, T., & P. den Hertog. 1999. Cluster Analysis and Cluster-based Policy Making: The State of the Art. Pp. 413–427 in *Boosting Innovation: The Cluster Approach*. Paris, France: OECD.

Smedlund, A. 2006. The roles of intermediaries in a regional knowledge system. *Journal of Intellectual Capital*, 7(2): 204–220.

Smith, R., J. McCarthy & M. Petrusevich. 2004. Clusters or Whirlwinds? The new media industry in Vancouver. Pp. 195–232 in D. Wolfe and M. Lucas (eds), *Clusters in a cold climate. Innovation Dynamics in a Diverse Economy*. Kingston, Canada: Queen's School of Policy Studies and McGill-Queen's University Press.

Spencer, G., T. Vinodrai, M. Gertler & D. Wolfe. 2010. Do Clusters Make a Difference: Defining and Assessing their Economic Performance. *Regional Studies*, 44(6): 697–715.

Statistics Canada. 2004. Survey of Innovation 2001–3. Accessed June 27, 2017 at: <http://www23.statcan.gc.ca/imdb/p2SV.pl?Function=getSurvey&Id=7221>.

Statistics Canada. 2005. Coup d'œil sur le secteur des Tics [A look at the ICT sector]. Division des sciences, de l'innovation et de l'information électronique (DSSIE). Ottawa, Canada: Government of Canada.

Statistiques Canada. 2003. Innovation dans les industries de service du secteur des technologies de l'information et des communications (TIC); Résultats de l'enquête sur l'innovation [Innovation in the service industries of the Information and Communication Technology (ICT) sector: Survey results on innovation]. Working Paper. Division des sciences, de l'innovation et de l'information électronique (DSSIE). Ottawa, Canada: Government of Canada.

Tremblay, D.-G., C. Chevrier & S. Rousseau. 2004. The Montréal multimedia sector: District, cluster or localized system of production? Pp. 165–194 in D. Wolfe and M. Lucas (eds), *Clusters in a Cold Climate: Innovation Dynamics in a Diverse Economy*. Montréal and Kingston, Canada: McGill-Queen's University Press.

Tremblay, D.-G., & E. Cecilli. 2009. The Film and Audiovisual production in Montréal: challenges of relational proximity for the development of a creative cluster. *The Journal of Arts Management, Law, and Society*, 39(3): 157–187.

Wolfe, D., C. Davis & M. Lucas. 2005. *Global networks and local linkages: An introduction*. Montréal, Canada: McGill-Queen's University Press.

Wolfe, D., & M. Gertler. 2003. *Policies for Cluster Creation: Lessons from the ISRN Cluster Initiative*, ISRN National meeting presentation, Ottawa, Canada. Accessed October 30, 2011 at: <http://www.utoronto.ca/isrn/publications/NatMeeting/NatSlides/Nat03/Wolfe03_Lessons.pdf> (no longer accessible).

MICHAEL J. DOUGHERTY, PAMELA D. GIBSON GOFF, AND
DONALD P. LACY

16 Improving Performance and Accountability in Local Government with Citizen Participation[1]

ABSTRACT

Successfully engaging the public to shape the future of communities has increasingly become a challenge. Indicators of civic engagement, participation, and trust are showing decline. With the need to engender social capital to generate public involvement and input, it appears to be necessary to shift the pattern of public participation. To accomplish this, it will be necessary to bridge the gap between traditional governmental leadership theory and engaged community leadership. This proposed paradigm can potentially supersede existing models such as managerial-led efforts, legislative-led efforts, and limited community participation efforts. The broader participation activities have been the outgrowth of single-issue protests that broadened over time. Local examples from Virginia, Ohio, and West Virginia illustrate how this might be undertaken. Common factors include the need for flexibility, performance measures, and renewal. Monitoring and review are also advised. The outcome of these activities will help determine the eventual fate of this new civic process.

Introduction

One of the important challenges in the new millennium continues to be the finding of successful ways to engage the public in shaping the communities of the future. Building upon the social capital in a community is essential. Many indicators suggest that levels of civic engagement, civic participation, and

1   *The Innovation Journal: The Public Sector Innovation Journal*, 10(1), 2005, article 5 <https://www.innovation.cc/volumes-issues/vol10-iss1.htm>.

civic trust declined during the last two decades of the twentieth century. The decline in participation and trust revolve, in part, around the issues of programmatic and individual performance as well as the accountability of decision-makers and individuals for outcomes and actions. It will no longer be sufficient for public officials and local governments to demonstrate efficiency (doing more with less) and sound business principles (MBO, TQM, and High Performance). They must go further to demonstrate their accountability for the appropriate, proper, and intended use of resources.

What is the role of the citizen in a democratic society? The question is more than 2,400 years old and the debates on the topic have been lively. It is time to make a shift in the public participation paradigm as we move into a new century. The need to make the shift is created not because the old paradigms have failed but because the evolution of the civic culture has created a new operating environment for public officials and it demands a paradigm shift. The challenge is to shift the paradigm of the political system from the "expert/professional" model with institutional and functional separation of powers, roles, responsibilities, and duties to one that integrates the citizen into every aspect of governance. The traditional paradigm provides for linkages to citizens primarily through electoral politics, public opinion polls, customer satisfaction surveys, public hearings, organized group activities, and individual contacts. Consultation in the traditional paradigm is largely passive, while involvement is episodic.

Beginning in the early nineteenth century, two trends have dominated the political participation landscape in Western democracies. One of those trends has been the expansion of the franchise to include previously excluded categories of residents. The other trend has been the evolution of institutions that control access to political power such as political parties, interest groups, and entrenched bureaucracies. Further, the expansion of the franchise and the growth in population has reinforced the Federalists arguments for a republican form of government with elected representatives making decisions and citizens relegated to voting or other forms of participation such as public hearings, forums, petitions, protests, and service on volunteer boards, commissions, or similar types of activities. Political parties and other institutions for engaging citizens are very focused upon engineering majorities and minimizing the costs (especially time) associated with too much direct involvement. Government institutions are likewise reluctant to bear the costs associated with widespread engagement activities. Thus, the role of the citizen as an engaged partner in the governing process has been supplanted by governing through positional and organizational leaders who are bound by rules, procedures, and traditions that leaves governing to the "experts" (Lacy, Dougherty and Gibson, 2002). Citizens play a secondary role in setting agendas, developing budgets, implementing programs, or evaluating outcomes. Further, citizens have only minimal information about the details of the public's business except in an episodic manner often caused by some news story that focuses national, state, or local attention on an issue. The result in the minds of many citizens is that a wide gulf exists between the expectations associated with democratic theory and the practice of democracy in community governance.

Many community and public leaders as well as many public officials have realized that public participation is important in an environment where the citizens have a diminished trust in government and are demanding more accountability from public officials (Parr and Gates, 1989). Chrislip and Larson (1994) contend that the push for reform is a response to demands from citizens for an authentic role in improving their communities. Created by frustration with the status quo, "[c]itizens begin to collaborate because nothing else is working to address their concerns. And nothing else is working because there are significant obstacles or barriers to change that civic and political leadership, as traditionally practiced, have failed to overcome" (Chrislip and Larson, 1994: 15).

A study by the Kettering Foundation (1989) indicated that public administrators want relationships with citizens but found that they create delays and increase red tape. In turn, citizens felt that when their input was sought, it was rarely used to make administrative decisions. Some citizens felt that their concerns would be heard only if they organized into angry activist groups.

In an alternative paradigm, citizens would play a significant role at the strategic vision level. The professional literature and the participation awards from local government associations are filled with examples of significant levels of community involvement in various activities from strategic planning and visioning to single purpose activities in functional areas such as economic development, education, land use, and recreation. Administrators, elected officials, and community leaders have found that institutionalized neighborhood participation in the policy processes results in a more informed, effective, and participatory citizenry (Berry, Portney, and Thompson, 1993). In Nalbandian's research on new roles for local government managers, responding professionals said they could foresee a future in which citizens are fully engaged in local governance through organizations such as neighborhood councils and would increasingly take over many of the responsibilities traditionally associated with city councils and administrators such as setting priorities and evaluating service delivery (Nalbandian, 1999: 190).

The first change in an alternative paradigm must occur at the conceptual level where the public's business is the public's business. In the conceptual shift community residents will be actively encouraged to participate, invited into the process, and fully armed with the knowledge and information to make participation meaningful. Citizens will help define community goals, develop agendas, develop strategic initiatives, participate in and review implementation procedures, actively participate in the measurement of progress, and in assessing impacts of programs.

At the operational level, public officials will be engaged more frequently and effectively with citizens to understand the desires and expectations of community residents. In the new paradigm, the moral imperative for engaging community residents will shift to public administrators and managers. This holistic conceptualization will require effective managerial leadership "outside the policy implementation and management box."

Measures of performance and accountability traditionally have been the primary concern and central focus of public managers and administrators. They focused on short-term financial management and control in which accountability was defined in terms of accountants, budget analysts, and financial directors. Recently however, governments have extended their accountability focus to include concern for long-term management issues and public sector performance (Andrews, 2001: 10). Durant (1999) contends that accountability must be built into the entire program structure. Results from his research with the Maryland County Department of Health and Human Services indicate that reforms must be made to link strategy and structure, to think strategically about anticipating and overcoming obstacles, and to focus on processes rather than tasks (Durant, 1999: 331).

Kearns (1996), however, offers a more useful interpretation of accountability and performance. The approach "... embraces a broader conception of accountability – one that is perhaps messier than the precise operational definitions, but probably more consistent with the popular usage of the term." He contends that the popular view includes much more than the formal processes normally associated with the terms. He advances the proposition that:

> ... the term accountability generally refers to a broad spectrum of public expectations dealing with organizational performance, responsiveness, and even morality of government and nonprofit organizations. These expectations often include implicit performance criteria – related to obligations and responsibilities – that are subjectively interpreted and sometimes even contradictory. (Kearns 1996: 9)

The creation of the broader definition based upon popular interpretation provides a plausible explanation for part of the disconnection and distrust that citizens have toward their governments. Behn (2001) broadens the definition of accountability to include not only financial accountability, accountability for fairness (democratic governance), and accountability for performance, adding a fourth dimension as well: accountability for personal probity which requires incorporation of citizen interests into the accountability framework. Governments have internalized the concepts of accountability and performance in such a way that citizens do not perceive that public actions often conform to the popular expectations. The concept advanced by Kearns (1990) fits more closely into popular expectations and perceptions about the nature of the "social compact." Some scholars have found the broader view of accountability to be useful especially for overcoming some of the problems associated with traditional models of the governance process. Stivers calls these changed relationships "active accountability":

> Administrative legitimacy requires active accountability to citizens, from whom the ends of government derive. Accountability, in turn, requires a shared framework for the interpretation of basic values, one that must be developed jointly by bureaucrats and citizens in real-world situations, rather than assumed. The legitimate

administrative state, in other words, is one inhabited by active citizens. (Kearns, 1990: 247)

For the broader interpretation of accountability and performance to be useful and to satisfy popular interpretations of the terms, the entire governance paradigm needs to be redesigned.

While a paradigm shift and a redesign of process is important, leaders and public agencies must actively develop and use a wider variety of means and methods to inform and engage the public in public business. Leaders must find ways to engage all citizens by developing better and more frequent use of old tools such as surveys, advisory committees, performance review committees, and community forums to make participation more meaningful. The development of electronic communication and instant messaging hold great promise for the future if developed properly. Public access cable television has been around for a while, but public officials increasingly must make more effective use of websites, chat rooms, electronic bulletin boards, electronic town halls, email, and a myriad of other tools to communicate with, inform, and engage citizens. Decision-makers must be better prepared to meet the expectations and demands for higher standards of accountability and accessibility in the electronic age. Direct democracy offers the opportunity not only for citizens to become more informed but also for leaders, planners, and officials to ascertain what programs and decisions are important to citizens and to demonstrate and communicate performance and accountability in more meaningful ways.

Schachter (1997) puts forth the challenge that people should view themselves as owners of government, not mere customers of public services. Box (1998) advocates a citizen governance model of conducting the public's business. King and Stivers (1998) advance a model related to Box's also placing citizens at the center of the governing process playing an authentic role in policy formation. Chrislip and Larson (1994) advocate a fundamental orientation to public policy setting built on a collaborative relationship between citizens, elected public officials and public managers. At the heart of this discussion is an examination of the relationship between citizens, elected officials and public managers.

Nalbandian (1994, 1999), Golbembiewski and Gabris (1994), and Roberts (1997) also have furthered the discussion of governmental reform by focusing on the role of public managers. As citizen expectations for government and their role in government processes change, public leaders will be challenged to respond to those changes.

Drawing on both Schlesinger's cycles of political history model and Kaufman's model of shifts in public values, Box (1998) contends that these larger trends are mirrored at the local level. He maintains that we are currently "on the down slope of a long wave of local government reform, headed toward an uncertain destination" (Box, 1998: 18). What are the implications of this push for governmental reform? According to Box, "... it means redefinition of roles and processes of creating and implementing policy that are citizen centered rather than bureaucracy centered" (Box, 1998: 19). Thus, the current period of governmental reform focusing on changing the relationship between citizens and government serves as a springboard for developing the concept of citizen governance. Indeed, an enhanced concept of governance forms the foundation of Box's model of public management. Governance includes citizens, elected public officials, and public managers. That model is built on an expanded concept of governance that he refers to as "... the way citizens, representatives, and practitioners can join together in governing communities so that the strengths of each are brought to bear in addressing the challenges of the next century" (Box, 1998: 19).

Models of Community Planning and Engagement

For the engaged community to develop, grow, and flourish, professional administrators and managers must play a key role in the process to bridge the gap between traditional theory of governing and the practice of governing an engaged community. To support this argument, consider the following proposition about the governance process as we usually experience it.

Elected officials are focused most often upon engineering the calculus of majorities and building majority coalitions through electoral politics. Their goal is to seek followers and build a support base. Rarely are their goals to create partners in the governing processes. Professional administrators and managers must play the critical role in bridging the gap between the theory and practice of democratic governance. Public servants will need to guide elected officials through the mazes of citizen engagement while at the same time developing, fostering, and nurturing the civic participation processes in their governments. A dilemma that every public sector administrator faces is that of the appropriate role for their activities. The "Codes of Ethics" and "Standards of Conduct" from professional associations such as the International City/County Management Association and the American Society for Public Administration raise several "red flags" that cause some administrator to limit their active roles with citizen engagement processes.

Both conduct standards and ethics codes caution public sector managers about direct involvement in local politics. The challenge arises when administrators and managers try to provide leadership during situations where communities are divided and in conflict. In practice, however, local government administrators are already engaged in facilitative leadership at the community level, and for some it has become comfortable.

Many communities are involved in some forms of community engagement processes that involve residents in various aspects of the governance process. Virtually every local government is either required or empowered to appoint advisory committees. These citizen committees are most often appointed in specific sectors to provide advice on specific issues such as land use planning, zoning, recreation, transportation, economic development, and sometimes on budget and finance. Occasionally, and more often as a sporadic response to local situations, communities will engage in a more comprehensive strategic planning processes that engage a larger number of citizens in processes that are apart from the formal advisory structure. These broader community strategic or comprehensive planning process have not been studied as systematically as many of the sector specific planning processes. There are numerous case studies of the typical advisory or sector planning processes such as economic development, land use and recreation. Yet, there are few attempts to develop a systematic body of knowledge of local strategic or comprehensive planning processes that engage the community in non-traditional planning processes.

Several years ago, a team of educators whose members provided programs to assist community leaders and decision-makers in the process of community strategic planning began to explore the circumstances and conditions that surround the dynamics of community planning. The initial study was defined by team members in their roles as participant observers in projects with more than forty local governments in Virginia. The initial results for the framework were presented at a conference in Richmond, Virginia (Lacy, Dougherty, Gibson and Miller, 1993). Almost a decade later, a revised version of the model was presented at a Conference on Community Resource and Economic Development in Orlando, Florida (Lacy, Dougherty and Gibson, 2002). The various approaches observed among the local governments involved in this study illustrate the power of the participatory process.

During the study of the selected strategic planning efforts, a number of important indicators were identified to help evaluate the processes. These included the reason the process was initiated, who initiated it, and the likely outcomes. The process may be initiated to create a common community agenda or it may be used as a means to build teamwork among a locality's administrative staff. The process may be initiated by a member of the organization's governing board and/or by its Chief Administrative Officer (CAO). The process is most likely to be used following a change in the organization's political or administrative leadership or when the community is facing an operational environment that is either in crisis or stagnant. Finally, the process may produce a document designed to guide the future development of programs and policies. Alternatively, the process may be designed to provide for a significant reduction in the amount of conflict, tension, and stress that might exist either between or within three basic decision centers – members of the governing body, the administrative team and staff, and/or the community. The resultant classification of models of engagement includes four broad types of engagement that are discussed in the paragraphs that follow.

The traditional model is the *managerial model*. It is the most common of the four strategic planning models and is closely related to those strategic planning models found in the private sector. It is top-down, follows fairly rigid prescribed steps, is very linear in its application and provides very little room for meaningful stakeholder participation. The process is initiated by the community's CAO in order to accomplish one or more of the following purposes:

(1) to build a common agenda;
(2) to develop greater interaction and communication between members of the administrative team;
(3) to create a feeling of ownership towards the agenda for the members of the administrative team; and
(4) to develop and enhance teamwork.

This form of strategic planning is used most frequently when it occurs within six to nine months following a change in the organization's administrative leadership, or any time after there has been substantial turnover in key members of the organization's administrative staff. It is most effective when an organization exists in a very stable or stagnant operational environment that provides little motivation to search for innovative approaches to solve problems.

A second model is the *legislative model*. The second most widely used model, it usually is initiated to develop an action agenda to guide and direct the decisions of the organization's governing body and administrative team. Usually the organization's CAO and one or more members of the governing body initiate the process. It is most effective if used when the organization exists in an operating environment experiencing either rapid growth or significant decline, and the organization lacks an agenda for action. This second model of local government strategic planning is initiated to accomplish any combination of the following seven goals:

(1) to develop a common agenda;
(2) to explore the operational styles and establish operational guidelines;
(3) to create understanding between the organization's governing body and its chief administrative officer;
(4) to develop greater interaction and communication between members of the organizations governing body and its chief administrative officer;

(5) to develop and enhance teamwork;

(6) to develop community acceptance "buy-in" of an agenda for use by the organization's governing body and administrative team as a guide for making decisions and distributing resources; or

(7) to reaffirm and further legitimize an already existing agenda.

In some variations the process is initiated by members of the community's governing body. Under these circumstances the locality's CAO and administrative staff are likely to be actively involved in promoting the process. This type of application usually occurs when members of the local governing body have held office for an extended period. It is most effective when the organization exists in either a stable or stagnant operational environment with no signs of crisis. The results and outcomes of the strategic planning process in this situation include: the development of an agenda; the development of community acceptance, or "buy-in" of that agenda; and the legitimization of decisions made by the community's governing body and/or administrative team.

A third model is the *limited community participation model.* The process is characterized by the appointment of a Blue Ribbon Commission, usually composed of well-known or well-positioned community and business leaders. The select commission usually meets for a period of weeks or months, makes a report, and dissolves. The amount of community input is very limited in most cases with a limited number of community meetings, forums or surveys. Often the process is initiated to achieve one or both of the following two purposes:

(1) to open up the decision-making process and increase citizen participation and interaction with the governing body; or

(2) to generate harmony within the governing body and/or within the community.

Focusing on one of these two goals, members of the community's governing body usually initiate the process. The community's CAO and administrative staff also may be involved in initiating the process. This type of application usually occurs when there are some mild to moderately strong divisions between the governing body and the community. It is most effective if used when a community is experiencing stress during times of dramatic growth or decline. The application of a strategic planning process under these conditions typically results in the creation of a project report (usually very general in overall character and scope); reduced stress within the governing body and/or community; and the creation of common agenda shared between the governing body and community. For the most part, the activities surrounding the planning process continue for ten to eighteen months. After the citizens complete a report and present it to the governing body, the strategic planning activities begin to diminish.

The fourth model is the *community empowerment model*. It is built around extensive community participation and is designed as an empowerment process to develop a community agenda and engage the residents of the community over a long period of time. Usually the process is initiated by a proactive governing body. The organization's administrative team may be involved, but only at the request of the governing body. It is most effective if used when the community is not under significant stress and when there are no "open wounds" in the body politic. Also, its effectiveness is greatest when the community is broadly represented, and when the governing body legitimizes the process without exercising tight control over it. This type of application typically produces the following results and outcomes: a community agenda; a lengthy report that takes the governing body several work sessions to discuss and consider; and community cohesion achieved through a greater understanding of important community issues and processes. In the most successful cases an institutionalized process to ensure continued participation by residents is established. A review board or similar institution is created to provide for regular monitoring of the progress toward the goals that were established during the process.

Engaged Communities

Different forms of engagement from three states that occurred during the early years of the twenty-first century have been selected to illustrate the variety of forms of planned citizen engagement processes where community residents were encouraged to participate at every level.

In a project designed to help rural communities in Virginia develop the capacities needed to prosper in the Information Age economy, seven counties participated in this multi-faceted project in which citizens were given the leadership and technology training to run their own community networks (for a complete description of the project and evaluation, see <http://top.bev.net>). Whereas the immediate purpose of the project was to improve economic conditions through business listings and a virtual business incubator, it was the citizen visioning meetings, the discussion forum, and new access to governmental pages that stirred citizen dialogue. In many of these counties, citizens were given their first opportunity to ask questions about board agendas, the local school pages, and local government committees. Not only did they begin to ask questions, local leaders soon discovered that they were accountable for updating information and had to respond to this new electronic medium.

Coshocton County, Ohio, is another example of extensive efforts to inform and engage the community in the processes of developing a land use plan for the county. A Commission on Future Land Uses was appointed by the County Commissioners. The Commission, in turn, recruited more than 100 citizens to serve on Task Forces to prepare recommendations for eleven key areas of concern for land use. The meetings of the Commission and the Task Forces were announced on weekly radio programs and in weekly newspaper columns. The Commission took the initiative to post reports of each task force on an Ohio State University County Extension web site. The revised reports were posted periodically along with scheduled meetings so that interest citizens could stay informed during the fourteen month process. Such processes of using traditional committee structures, newspapers, radio, and community meetings that are supplemented with current electronic communication provide an insight into a new wave of possibilities of informing and engaging citizens.

The Ritchie County Development Authority in the Ohio River Valley of West Virginia decided to hold public meetings around the county it served. About 115 people participated in these sessions, with three of the meetings drawing over thirty people. While the overall document developed through the engagement process was not much different than if had been developed solely by the authority's board of directors, ideas put forth by residents were reflected throughout. This led to some different ideas – literally the last statement at the last meeting was something that had not been discussed previously and was incorporated into the plan. It also has increased the legitimacy and acceptance of the plan in the small, rural county. This in turn has permitted the development authority to seek project partners both among other organizations in the county as well as on a regional basis in its efforts to follow the recommendations put forth in the plan.

Nicholas County in central West Virginia undertook an eight-month strategic planning process to help determine its future direction. A select group of about thirty-five key individuals representing virtually every major concern was appointed to the Strategic Planning Committee by the County Commission. This group met in four work sessions – three to draft the plan and one to finalize it. The ideas and energy are reflected in a strategic plan that has been accepted by the County Commission and is expected to serve as a guide to the entire community.

Morrow County, Ohio, used an extensive process during six months to engage more than seventy five residents in a process to develop an economic development plan for the county. Extensive community survey work supplemented the numerous community meetings. The result was a plan that was adopted with considerably informed community support.

There are numerous examples of states and localities involving citizens in their planning processes. In the states of Minnesota and Oregon, the cities of Gresham, Oregon and Scottsdale, Arizona and Hillsboro County, Florida, strategic planning, budgeting, and benchmarking are combined into some of the best examples of broad-based approaches to incorporate citizens or stakeholders into the process. In each case, regular reviews of strategic goals and progress are conducted. Citizens are heavily involved in the processes of planning, budgeting, and evaluating progress. These five instances provide good examples of citizen engagement in strategic planning linked to budgets, benchmarks, and monitored by citizen review boards. In addition, each of these efforts has identified new governance processes in which citizens are improving governmental accountability through their participation.

Developing Patterns of Community Engagement

An examination of the various cases of community engagement provides some useful lessons about those factors and conditions that contribute to the success of engagement processes.

Flexibility is one of the key ingredients for establishing a successful community engagement process for any form of community planning. Each community or public sector organization with its unique blend of stakeholders/citizens, strengths/weaknesses, and decision-making roles/responsibilities must design and implement a process that will work effectively in its particular environment. A community that begins an engagement process must be prepared to modify whatever initial model is developed to guide the process. The group dynamics that often emerge during an engagement process are likely to alter different steps and objectives in the process. It may even be necessary to alter the timetables established for completing the process.

Further, developing *widely accepted measures of success or progress* is essential for sustaining community planning processes. The process must have a structure in which evaluation and accountability are part of the long-term process for sustaining increased levels of engagement. Unless community residents can see evidence that their participation has meaning and produces results, a greater degree of cynicism and withdrawal are likely to become part of the community landscape.

Planning initiatives must have *renewal mechanisms* built into the processes if they are to have longevity. Provisions must be made for some form of *progress review board or independent oversight committee* to continually monitor progress toward defined goals and strategic objectives. Further, the process should provide mechanisms to engage community residents in periodic reviews of the work from the original planning process by using a process similar to the original planning process. The emphasis on engagement and participation must be as strong as during the initial process. The timeframe for the review process can be shorter since the review would be based upon the work and documents from the earlier initiative. Too often there is little systematic effort to sustain the interest and momentum generated during the original planning process. It is not uncommon to hear community residents who are invited to participate in a community planning process say something like: "We have done that before and nothing has happened," or "Why should we bother? Nothing happened the last time we did this!" Residents most know that the process will continue through annual reviews and periodic periods of broadened engagement. Further, it is important to provide opportunities for those who want to continue to participate in some meaningful way to work toward the identified goals and objectives.

Too little attention is paid to the details of the types of leadership that are needed to create a successful effort to facilitate a community engagement process. When appointments are made to the "Commission on the Future," the "Strategic Planning Committee," or the "Steering Committee," it is important for the appointing authorities to treat their appointment decisions as personnel decisions with the same interest and concerns used to hire fulltime staff. Considerable time must be devoted to finding a broad representative mix of knowledgeable residents who are known to have the ability to work in a collaborative manner with others even in circumstances where they may disagree with the final decision. Selecting individuals with the appropriate leadership qualities are necessary to build a successful engagement process. Without good leadership, the community engagement process likely will not produce the desired result nor will it lead to a sustained process of engagement.

Thus, we have found that the governance process in which community planning is combined with benchmarking and performance monitoring, is a vital link for reconnecting citizens through the participatory process and for developing a more visible measure of accountability. Performance measures and benchmarks can be used effectively to build higher levels of trust among residents. We contend that these measures must be developed through negotiated processes where community residents are actively engaged to define desired outcomes, expected accomplishments, and acceptable results. Communities and governmental organizations that engage residents and partner with them in all aspects of programming and policy-making to define performance standards and measures of success will enhance, in very significant ways, public perception of accountability.

Morse (1996: 2) suggests that we need to build new patterns of civic interaction. She believes that, "[t]here are capacities that exist in every community that hold strong potential for building new patterns of inter-action that can renew our sense of responsibility and commitment to each other." Implied in these new patterns of civic interaction is the need for an expanded concept of citizenship. The convergence of a new leadership paradigm and demands by citizens for an authentic role in public decision-making calls upon the institutions of government and public officials to nurture these newly emerging sets of expectations of individual citizens and to build the intellectual, cultural, and institutional infrastructure to support the expectations of consultation and engagement. Also, implied in Morse's observation is the need for action, for a fully engaged pool of citizens. In other words, citizenship demands more than voting. Morse's statement also encompasses the concept of community and concern for the well-being of the community as a whole. In short, parochial interests must be weighed against the interests of a much broader community.

Making a shift in the paradigm as an intellectual construct is likely to be less of a problem than convincing elected officials and the public that there is reason to participate in a process that provides no assurances that something productive will result from the process. Programs that are designed to increase participation for the sake of participation are not likely to meet the criteria of "meaningful." Likewise, as Rosener (1978: 462) observes, mandating participation does not provide the assurance that quality participation will occur. The expanded concept of citizen participation must permeate the entire governance processes. Leaders in this new paradigm must utilize important civic skills such as: group formation and dynamics; problem solving orientation in group processes; active listening; willingness to accept differing views; and a mind-set that recognizes that public decision- making is messy and often contentious. Programs that rest solely on satisfaction surveys, benchmarking practices, or even electronic interaction provide only the limited possibilities available. Performance and Accountability must become everyone's responsibility in an expanded governance society. However, if citizens and leaders alike approach public processes with an eye toward the common good, the result can be very rewarding. Indeed, it can form the basis for strong and vibrant communities. By opening the entire governance structure to public participation through agenda setting, strategic planning, program evaluation, and monitoring, democratic governance can become a permanent part of our civic culture.

Perhaps there is greater reason for optimism than reflected in the assessment by Box (1998: 5) noted just a few years ago that we are "on the down slope of a long wave of local government reform." The blending together of traditional models of engagement with the potential of the electronic media is just beginning to feed and strengthen the engagement process. One of the interesting undercurrents during the past two decades has been the growing number of community groups, neighborhood associations and civic associations that have become standard features of many local landscapes. As these civic associations and local engagement groups mature the process of engagement will have a more formalized infrastructure just outside, but connected to, the governance structures of communities.

Many communities, such as Columbus, Ohio, have developed formal neighborhood governance structures that are staffed and supported by the city, but left to make local decisions or recommendations and function independently of city hall. The engaged community, often born in single-issue protests, is only in its infancy. However, it appears that many of these single-issue/episodic engagement processes have morphed into avenues for public officials to reach out and tap citizen interests, energy, and knowledge. These transformed civic impulses have become part of the more formalized infrastructure of civic engagement where citizens are brought in the governance structure through committees, commissions, and task forces or have become part of formalized neighborhood or civic associations. Only time will tell if the trend to engage communities can be sustained.

Bibliography

Andrews, M. 2001. Adjusting external audits to facilitate results-oriented government. *International Journal of Government Auditing*, 28(2): 10–13.

Behn, R. D. 2001. *Rethinking Democratic Accountability.* Washington, DC: Brooking Institute Press.

Berry, J. M., K. E. Portney & K. Thomson, 1993. *The Rebirth of Urban Democracy.* Washington, DC: Brookings Institution.

Box, R. C. 1998. *Citizen Governance: Leading American Communities into the 21st Century.* Thousand Oaks, CA: Sage Publications.

Chrislip, D. D., & C. E. Larson. 1994. *Collaborative Leadership: How Citizens and Civic Leaders Can Make a Difference.* San Francisco, CA: Jossey-Bass Publishers.

Durant, R. F. 1999. The Political Economy of Results-Oriented Management in the "Neo-Administrative State": Lessons from the MCDHHS Experience. *American Review of Public Administration,* 29(4): 307–331.

Golembiewski, R. T., & G. T. Gabris. 1994. Today's City Managers: A Legacy of Success-Becoming-Failure. *Public Administration Review,* 54(6): 525–530.

Kearns, K. P. 1996. *Managing for Accountability: Preserving the Public Trust in Public and Nonprofit Organizations.* San Francisco, CA: Jossey-Bass, Inc.

Kettering Foundation. 1989. *The Public's Role in the Policy Process: A View from State and Local Policy Makers.* Dayton, OH: Kettering Foundation.

King, C. S., & C. M. Stivers. 1998. *Government Is Us: Public Administration in an Anti-Government Era.* Thousand Oaks, CA: Sage Publications.

Lacy, D. P., M. J. Dougherty & P. D. Gibson. 2002. Models of Community Planning. Paper presented at Strengthening Communities, Enhancing Cooperative Extension's Role, National Community Resources and Economic Development Conference, Orlando, FL, February 24–27.

Lacy, D. P., M. J. Dougherty, P. D. Gibson & M. D. Miller. 1993. Strategic Planning: Alternative Models To Empower Communities. Paper presented at the Region IV Conference of the American Society for Public Administration Region IV Conference in Richmond, VA, September 30–October 1.

Morse, S. W. 1996. *Building Collaborative Communities.* Charlottesville, VA: Pew Partnership for Civic Change.

Nalbandian, J. 1999. Facilitating Community, Enabling Democracy: New Roles for Local Government Managers. *Public Administration Review,* 59(3): 187–197.

Parr, J., & C. T. Gates. 1989. Assessing Community Interest and Gathering Community Support. Pp. 55–58 in International City Management Association (ed.), *Partnerships in Local Governance: Effective Council-Manager Relations.* Washington, DC: International City Management Association.

Roberts, N. C. 1997. Public Deliberation: An Alternative Approach to Crafting Policy and Setting Direction. *Public Administration Review,* 57(2): 124–132.

Rosener, J. B. 1978. Citizen Participation: Can We Measure Its Effectiveness? *Public Administration Review,* 38(5): 457–463.

Schachter, H. L. 1997. *Reinventing Government or Reinventing Ourselves: The Role of Citizen Owners in Making a Better Government*. Albany, NY: State University of New York Press.

Stivers, C. M. 1990. Active Citizenship and Public Administration. Pp. 246–273 in G. L. Wamsley, *Refounding Public Administration*. Thousand Oaks, CA: Sage Publications.

PART VIII

Conclusion

JAMES IAIN GOW

17   Public Sector Innovation Theory Revisited[1]

ABSTRACT

The purpose of this chapter is to inquire into the state of public sector innovation (PSI) theory. Four authors, Rogers, Borins, Behn, and Glor and recent comparative governmental practices are chosen to represent a variety of approaches. This sample allows identification of both areas of consensus and of controversy in the field. Important disagreements remain about the defining parameters of PSI study and about the basic questions PSI studies should address.

Introduction

Innovation is a prime subject in our time. In business and government, it is held to be essential in the face of the massive and complex problems and the rapid pace of change in contemporary society. Innovation is thought to be the way to harness the creative potential of the human race in order to survive, to progress, and to prosper. A letter in the Montréal newspaper *Le Devoir* (April 26, 2013) noted that the Latin and Greek words for stupidity referred to immobility, lethargy or inertia, so we might infer that the opposite of stupidity would be mobility, energy, adaptation.

Public sector innovation (PSI) is a subset of all innovation. A Google search in July 2013, found references to 316 million publications, of which PSI constituted 4.4 million, or about 1.4 per cent of the whole, a small part,

---

1   *The Innovation Journal: the Public Sector Innovation Journal*, 19(2), 2014, article 1
    <http://www.innovation.cc/volumes-issues/vol19-no2.htm>.
    The author wishes to thank for their very useful comments Sandford Borins, Eleanor Glor, and the three anonymous evaluators.

but a big absolute number. In the final edition of his masterwork on the diffusion of innovations, Rogers (2003: 45–46) identified nine disciplinary fields producing the greatest number of studies, of which "marketing and management" accounted for 16 per cent. This group did not appear to cover the public sector, but some of the others include subjects like city managers, public health, and education. Publications on PSI thus appears rather marginal to the field of innovation studies.

Having written a book on the diffusion of administrative innovations among Canadian governments twenty years ago (Gow, 1994), I was curious to learn how the field had evolved since then. I wanted to see how the subject itself had changed, what are the main theoretical approaches, and what the outstanding unresolved issues. What follows is not a primer on all the contemporary theories of PSI. Instead, I have chosen five theorists and approaches in order to see what unites and what divides them. In part one, these authors and schools are presented briefly. In the second part, the contentious issues are examined with a view to exploring their potential for asking good questions.

Requirements of a Theory

The very first step in considering this subject is to enquire what we mean by theory. The root meaning is not controversial: the *Shorter Oxford Dictionary* gives, among others, one that fits our case, "A scheme or system of ideas or statements held as an explanation of a group of facts or phenomena." The operative word is "explanation"; the familiar expression "descriptive theory" is an oxymoron.

Theories use concepts to organize raw material into variables, abstract categories concerning causal variables (independent) and outcome variables (dependent). The common distinction is between deductive and inductive theories. In deductive theory, the hypotheses to be tested are drawn from postulates and principles that are held to be true while inductive theory builds up hypotheses from observation and adjusts them as experience dictates. Most social science is inductive, but there are important theoretical schools that are deductive. Both Marxism and Public Choice theories start from first principles and deduce their hypotheses. The theory of the class struggle, for example, made it very difficult for the leaders of the communist countries to accept that working class protests against their governments could be genuine.

Glor (2008: 3) recalls the advantages of inductive theory, since it is constantly adjusting itself to take account of new evidence. She also makes a distinction between substantive and formal theory. In her view, substantive theory relates to a substantive or empirical area, whereas formal theory is built on a formal or conceptual area. To her, substantive theory may be used to develop formal theory. Thus she considers that innovation theory is substantive, whereas organization theory is formal. This language is apparently used because she prefers to think of innovation theory as a more exploratory area, while formal theory is more abstract and parsimonious.

The more sticky question is that of prediction. Glor (2008: 4) states that a test of a theory may be its capacity to predict on the basis of a correct understanding of cause and effect Moreover, Kahneman (2011) has shown with devastating effect that the predictions of experts in finance, investment, psychology, and education are mostly no better than rolling dice. Their expertise, he found, could deliver protocols or algorithms which were very useful when combined with base line statistics, but did not constitute precise predictions in themselves. He found that "our insatiable desire for narrative" leads to "the illusion of understanding" and an overestimation of the orderliness of things. Taleb (2007) has a similar complaint about inductive theories: they do not prepare for "Black Swans" or extremely unlikely events.

In the present case, Wildavsky (1979: 139) has the last word: "The trouble with social interaction is that you don't know how it will turn out in advance."

A further obstacle was identified by a biologist cited with approval by Wildavsky (1979: 58): "the difficulty in most scientific work lies in framing the questions rather than in finding the answers." A reading of recent developments in public sector innovation theory, suggests that such difficulties plague the field. From the definition onwards, it seems difficult to know what are the right questions in public sector innovation theory.

Approaches to PSI

Everett M. Rogers

The first of our authors is the late Everett M. Rogers, often considered the dean of contemporary innovation studies. His book *Diffusion of Innovations* ran to five editions, from 1971 to 2003. A professor of communications, Rogers dealt relatively little with invention, and concentrated instead on the process of diffusion of innovations of all kinds, scientific, technical, social, managerial, and so on. One of his major contributions was to conduct a continuing meta-analysis of diffusion studies, from one edition to the next. For several editions, this allowed him to give a running score of support for and failure to support generalizations about which individuals were most likely to be innovative, their communication behavior, characteristics of adopted innovations, and of the social systems supporting them.[2]

From one edition to another, Rogers presented generalizations about personal and organizational variables that are independent variables explaining rates of innovation in organizations. Personal and social variables making a positive contribution to innovation rates were education, socio-economic status, cosmopolitan personalities, capable of abstraction, and empathy and open to change. Age was not a relevant variable. Organizations more likely to innovate were large, complex, with good interpersonal communications and unused resources ("slack"). Centralization and formalism were obstacles to innovation. For example, in the third edition (Rogers, 1983: 260–261), he noted that 74 per cent of the studies surveyed confirmed the positive relation between education achievement and innovation; for cosmopolitan personalities, the number was 76 per cent, while for larger size units, it was 67 per cent. The characteristics of the innovations themselves constituted another category of explanatory variables, such qualities as cost, compatibility, complexity, and trialability (see Chapter 13 of this book).

---

2   In the fifth edition (2003), Rogers abandoned the practice of listing raw scores and percentages of studies confirming or refuting these proportions, simply listing "generalizations" that were relevant (Chapters 5, 7).

Rogers presented the rate of adoption of innovations as a bell curve, with early, middle, and late adopters; he also developed an S-curve to track the cumulative rate of adoption. So his method was inductive, his reasoning was based on his own and others' observations. Rogers acknowledged a number of shortcomings in the approach he had developed: the main one was that the search for determinants had given inconsistent results (Downs and Mohr, 1976; Mohr, 1978). Rogers and Eveland (1978) argued that it was wrong to oppose personal and organizational variables, since they interacted. Indeed all of the independent variables interacted, so that diffusion research was complex. By the time of his final edition (Rogers, 2003: 106) Rogers felt that innovation research suffered from a pro-innovation bias, probably because of the bias of funding agencies. This situation led to a search for wider and faster solutions and willful ignorance about gaps in knowledge and about anti-diffusion programs against bad innovations.

My 1994 book was inspired by the Rogers approach. I was interested in the diffusion of innovations as cases of communication. How did ideas like the Planning– Programming–Budgeting System (PPBS), the Ombudsman, privatization of public corporations or program evaluation circulate and become adopted? I chose fifteen such cases from the years 1960 to 1990, and set out to see in what order the Canadian federal government and the provinces adopted them. Large governments were found to be the most innovative and each innovative idea was adapted to the needs of the adopting government. In the process of adaptation and adoption, central agencies had the last word. Patterns varied considerably: Ontario was among the early adopters, but was more spontaneous, less inclined than the others in this category to proceed after long preparatory studies; Québec was often in the first three adopters, but never the first (a trait that contradicted much casual analysis).

Sandford Borins

In the late 1990s Sandford Borins took a new tack in PSI work by doing a rigorous study of a complete population: he surveyed all the semi-finalists in the Ford Foundation's innovation awards competition in the United

States for the years 1990 to 1994 (Borins, 1998). He then compared these results with those obtained in two similar competitions organized by the Commonwealth Association for Public Administration and Management (CAPAM) (Borins, 2001). In this way, he had a stock of material available for statistical analysis.

Borins found a number of results that went counter to the current wisdom on PSI. The subtitle of his 1998 book was "How Local Heroes Are Transforming American Government." Contrary to the idea that most innovations are imposed on a reluctant bureaucracy, he found that half of the American innovations came from middle managers and frontline employees, and over 80 per cent of those in the CAPAM competitions. Politicians were originators of about one-fifth of the American group, but only about 10 per cent of the Commonwealth group. Agency heads were the originators of 25 per cent of the US group and 39 per cent of the Commonwealth one (Borins, 2001: 27). Managers were unlikely to propose changes in organization; these came from political leaders or boards of directors.

As opposed to the "managing by groping along" approach, Borins found that one-half of American innovations were the result of policy planning and that the majority of both samples used a systems or holistic approach. His conclusion was, "Integrity in innovation demands that one plan when it is desirable and possible to plan, but when it is not possible to plan, one experiments and learns from one's experiments" (Borins, 1998: 64). Planning was thought to be desirable in cases of large capital projects, involving partnerships or the coordination of many players. Innovations drawn from theory were in evidence in both social services and education. There was general agreement that successful innovations require measurable goals and regular monitoring of results. Outside evaluation was more likely to lead to replication of innovations.

Borins found that half of the obstacles to innovation came from within the organization. They were not primarily based on self-interest (union opposition was really negligible) but came mainly from philosophical objections and were amenable to both accommodation and persuasion.

So Borins produced studies that covered complete populations of given groups and were amenable to theory-testing (Loffler, 2001), much of the theory drawn from Osborne and Gaebler's *Reinventing Government* (1992). It had some weaknesses also: by the terms of the Ford Foundation program, no federal innovations were included; the group was self-selected and necessarily told us nothing about failures or about cases where new political department or agency heads put a stop to innovations already under way. Moreover, as Loffler (2001: 112) wrote, "local heroes may innovate with (ethical) integrity but not necessarily with (political) legitimacy."

However, these objections do not detract from the overall value of these innovative studies. Borins' work has to be considered in any discussion of PSI theory.

Robert Behn

Robert Behn has been writing about innovation for more than twenty-five years. He is presented here after the others because he is PSI's skeptic and iconoclast. His early and much-remarked article "Managing by Groping Along" (Behn, 1988), took aim at rational planning models of innovation. He claimed that managers do not know enough about the knowledge, customs, and preferences of their clients and employees to proceed in a rational manner. His model differed from Lindblom's "muddling through" and Peters and Waterman's "managing by walking around" because "groping along" was neither a method of policy analysis nor was it aimless wandering about. Behn wrote that what successful managers do is choose an ultimate goal and proceed by trial and error to reach it. They do so by choosing intermediate goals to be achieved and they use a wide variety of managerial tools along the way. In this way his model resembles the New Public Governance model of Jocelyne Bourgon, who proposes using case studies to widen the range of possibilities open to managers, rather than as models to be strictly imitated (Bourgon, 2011).

In a recent text, Behn (2008) adds to this model the idea that much of the knowledge needed to innovate cannot be written down, it is tacit. He cites the work of O'Dell and Grayson (1998), who claim that in all but the simplest cases, the most important information cannot be codified or written down. Their postulates for successful innovation include face-to-face contact from the beginning of a project, acceptance that a project will never be a one-time operation, but instead will need many steps and much attention along the way. As a result, Behn cautions that there must be "no unthinking mimicry," but instead adaptation to the point of "reinventing the wheel" (156). Behn's model places a premium on leadership, since it depends on the leader to develop the vision of his or hers organization's mission and lead by groping along (Behn, 1988).

Although it is not his most recent publication, Behn's overview of the contents of a book he and Alan Altschuler edited in 1997, gives a masterful résumé of the difficulties facing theorists of PSI entitled "The Dilemmas of Innovation in American Government" (Behn, 1997). Of the sixteen dilemmas he identified, the most important for this text are: the accountability dilemma, posed by proposing to allow mid-level and front-line managers to engage in political work like coalition building, partnering, co-developing policies, etc.; the failure dilemma, "The dirty little secret is that innovation requires failure" (15), which will be seized upon by the opposition and the media. Behn adds, "Like all true dilemmas, there is no way out"; the dilemmas of scale and decentralization; that of the priority to be given to action or to analysis; the question whether to repair an ailing organization or replace it; that of extrinsic (material) or intrinsic (personal satisfaction) rewards, which Behn regards as possibly the biggest challenge of all.

As we have seen, Borins' work challenges Behn's "managing by groping along" model. However, the list of paradoxes we have just touched on provides us with a number of controversies we will have to deal with in the following section.

Eleanor D. Glor

The fourth author retained is the founder and editor of *The Innovation Journal: The Public Sector Innovation Journal*, Eleanor D. Glor. In a series of articles since 2001, she has examined the epistemological bases of PSI theory (Glor, 2001a, 2001b, 2008). She shows how innovation studies can be seen as part of organization theory, management science, social learning and systems analysis, to which we might add administrative reform.

By taking a broader view of the subject, she has developed an inclusive theoretical approach that attempts to situate more detailed studies in its framework.

Glor chooses what she calls a grounded and substantive approach, which I take to be inductive theory, built on experience and literature, and progressively tested and modified. She does not want a priori theory to limit her research: "Others' theories and experience are of interest but should not be allowed to stifle insights generated by qualitative data" (Glor, 2008: 3).

For the purposes of this commentary, I can only produce the barest sketch of a far-ranging theoretical reflection. In Glor's system, there are three clusters of drivers or independent variables. The first of these deals with the motivation of individual members of an organization. The two well-known classes of motivation are retained: extrinsic, which are "arbitrary goals and rewards" coming from outside the individual, and intrinsic, which are self-determined, and relate to the interest of the work, the desire to participate in its orientation and personal ethics (Glor, 2001a; Chapter 2 of this book). The second cluster treats the organization and its culture, which is described as top-down or bottom-up.

The third cluster of influences or variables is called "challenge"; it conflates the characteristics or attributes of the innovation itself, the strategies for its introduction (incremental or more global), the degree of change introduced and the degree of power necessary to achieve it. For purposes of further testing, this variable is characterized as either minor or major (Glor, 2001b). Major challenges occur when risks are high, compatibility with existing values is low, a high degree of personal commitment is required, there is low relative advantage in the innovation and it is difficult to test. A minor challenge is the contrary of these properties and produces no big change in power relations in the organization.

The combination of these clusters leads to the identification of eight patterns of innovation that are presented in an ingenious three-dimensional model (Glor, 2001b). The eight patterns are called: reactive, active, necessary, imposed, proactive, buy-in, transformational, and continuous innovation. Glor (2001b) tested these categories on Canadian examples and found them useful. She considers that they may enable executives to identify anomalies and opportunities for intervention.

Glor wants theory to evaluate an organization's capacity for adaptation and survival (Glor, 2008). This "capacity for fitness" is to be found in organizational adaptability (variety, reactivity, and self-organized emergence), its capacity to communicate through feedback loops, and the magnitude of the challenge. Glor writes that resilience or fitness depends on the level of innovation activity: level 1 deals with activities, level 2 with structure, and level 3 with goals and identity. Fitness is judged to be greater if an organization can meet second or third levels of difficulty.

Much of the critical discussion of this approach must wait for part two, but some comments may be made here. While the innovation patterns have been chosen by rigorous combination of the three clusters of variables, the choice of names for them leaves one perplexed. What is the difference between necessary, imposed, and reactive innovations? What about combinations, as in the case of the man at Agriculture Canada who, upon learning that his job was soon to be cut, took the initiative to develop a public-private-partnership database for the Canadian government? It is classified as proactive, but there is an element of imposed change here also. What distinguishes reactive and necessary, active and proactive? At the least the number of choices that are to be made raises problems of instability of the classification.

Another problem comes from the complex nature of the "challenge" category, which has four distinct components: the attribute of the innovation itself, the strategies of innovation used, the degree of change involved and the use of power. Moreover, it turns out to be something that you learn after the fact: "Magnitude of challenge is identified by the magnitude of the change required of the organization ..." (Glor, 2008: 12). This seems to raise serious problems for the predictive capacity of the theory. The author's great merit, however, is to have systematized PSI theory and to have formulated propositions in ways that will allow testing and improving over time.

New Comparative Measurement Approach

In the past decade, Commonwealth and European governments have embarked on a new process based on the idea that effective measurement or monitoring of PSI in all public sectors will "allow for continuous improvement and international benchmarking" (Australia, 2011: 3). Governments in these countries, plus South Korea and the Organization for Economic Cooperation and Development (OECD), have been developing methodological frameworks for producing national indices of innovation and productivity. The OECD has published "The Oslo Manual" containing guidelines for collecting and interpreting national innovation data (OECD, 2005). In the United Kingdom, the National Audit Office did a survey of central departments and agencies in 2005 (National Audit Office, 2006), while the National Endowment for Science, Technology and the Arts (NESTA) did the same for the health and local government sectors in 2013 (Hughes, Moore and Kataria, 2013). The Australian study also cites a study by the European Community called the Innobarometer which surveyed 5,000 public sector bodies in public administration, higher education, local government and hospitals across the twenty-seven member states (European Commission, 2011). All of these studies indicate much activity in this field and support the idea that regular monitoring can identify trends and anomalies, which will produce occasions for PSI.

The results of these preliminary surveys differed somewhat from those we have seen so far. The EU study found that new laws and regulations were the single most important driver of innovation, followed by budget cuts. Such a response begs the question of where the new laws and regulations came from. The leading innovators were large national institutions. State institutions were just as likely to introduce innovations as independent decentralized ones. While managers cited lack of funding as an important obstacle to innovation, the survey results did not confirm this.

In the United Kingdom, the NAO study reported in 2006, found that the largest number of innovations involved agencies joining up to improve service delivery, the second largest to improve service delivery and the third to improve services for clients. In this self-selected sample, senior managers were by far the most numerous originators of the innovations, followed by other organizations and central agencies and ministers. The most important barriers to innovation were said to be working with stakeholders and private contractors. This audit study cited the complaint of one public servant who said, "Anyone who has worked in [my department] will say that we are all absolutely change weary and that the department in relation to the [lower tier public sector organizations] has done nothing but press changes (and some would call it innovation, I suppose) relentlesly" (NAO, 2006: 12).

In the NESTA survey of local and public health institutions (Hughes, Moore and Kataria, 2013), the main incentive was found to be customer satisfaction, but the largest impacts were efficiency and cost savings. A majority of new ideas came from outside the organization, with best practice information being the largest single source. The people who found this information were frontline staff and managers, followed closely by service users. The accent was on short-term improvements: restructuring was said to hinder innovation.

All these surveys found most innovations to be of the kind Borins found, improvements at the procedural level, dealing with efficiency, cost savings and better customer service. Surveys of national departments and agencies tended to find centralized sources of innovation, but when the NESTA study dealt with local government and health questions, frontline employees were slightly more likely than managers to be the originators of innovations, by way of their knowledge of best practices elsewhere.

Using mostly these five theories or approaches, I turn now to what are the outstanding unresolved differences in the field of PSI theory.

Litigious Questions in PSI Theory

It seems to me to be more useful to look at the most controversial or litigious questions in PSI theory-making than to dwell on some of the big questions that it has dealt with. While there is no doubt more to be learned about them, I do not find much division either in the question of which people are more innovative or that of what are the characteristics of successful innovations. There does not appear to be much change in the individual characteristics of innovative people: they are highly educated, intelligent, lacking in dogmatism, empathetic, capable of thinking in the abstract and cosmopolitan. Counterintuitively, age is not related to capacity to innovate (Rogers, 2003: 288–291).

There does not seem to be controversy about the steps involved in innovation and diffusion. Here again, we may take those identified by Rogers (Rogers, 2003: 16): knowledge, persuasion, decision, implementation, and confirmation or evaluation. Also, the characteristics of successful innovations do not seem to have changed over the years. As Rogers (2003:15–16) described them, they are: relative advantage (in terms of costs and benefits), compatibility with existing technologies and practices, "trialability" and ease with which they may be communicated to others. Behn (2008: 88) adds that the greater is the tacit dimension of an innovation, the greater is the need for face-to-face contact in promoting it.

Definition of Innovation

It is the most surprising lesson to learn on returning to PSI theory after twenty years, that there are major disagreements about the precise nature of the subject. I have long worked with the definition of Merritt and Merritt (1985: 11) that an innovation is "the introduction of a new idea, method or device" into a social unit. The change being introduced need only be new for the adopting unit, it may already have been in use elsewhere. This led Rogers and Kim (1985: 103) to distinguish between, "invention ... the process by which a new idea is created or developed, (and) innovation ... the process of adopting an existing idea."

This still seems a sensible distinction. The creativity quotient of invention is much higher than in innovation, where we may speak of early and late adopters, and where communication skills are more important than in the case of invention. At any rate, most of the innovation that occurs comes through diffusion, although there seems always to be an element of true creation or reinvention (Behn, 2008: 155–156) in the adoption of an innovation.

One thing that has happened in recent times is that the reference group has expanded. In public sector innovation in North America, the reference group has usually been similar organizations in one's own country. The Ford Foundation's criteria have limited the reference group to state and local governments in the United States. In her work on Saskatchewan, Glor, perhaps reflecting an Anglo-Canadian conditioning, limited her population to the first, second or third time a new policy, program or process was introduced in a government in North America (Glor, 2008: 7). As we may see from the report of the Australian government (2013), their reference group includes the European Community, The Organization for Economic Cooperation and Development, Scandinavian countries, South Korea, and the United Kingdom.

What this development suggests is that larger numbers of cases are going to be involved in comparisons and that the study of replication and diffusion will be on shakier ground. The plea of both Borins and Behn, despite their differences of view on planning or groping along, would seem to be to concentrate on your organization's need rather than to try to fit into some popular trend. It is interesting to note that, as decades of reform roll past, there is a general refusal to consider the undoing of past innovations as innovative (OECD, 2005). Deregulation and privatization of public enterprises may have seemed innovative to the governments of the 1970s and 1980s, but it is rare to find a study of innovations that would include them. It may be that the broader notion of reform is needed to include planned change that is not the adoption of a new idea, method or device, but the abandonment of a previous innovation no longer deemed desirable.

The most disturbing thing about the search for the proper definition of an innovation is the disagreement about how big or disruptive an innovation must be to be taken seriously. Behn (1997: 7) cites approvingly Lawrence Lynn (1999) who wrote; "Innovation must not be simply another word for change or for improvement, or even for doing something new lest almost anything qualify as innovation." Behn argues that, to be considered as an innovation, a change must be an original, disruptive, and fundamental transformation of an organization's core tasks." Even Borins, whose Ford Foundation group would seem to include many innovations that were neither fundamental nor disruptive, said that innovation, by definition, is controversial (Borins, 1998: 79).

Now it is understandable that analysts do not wish to be distracted by myriads of small, insignificant changes. However, this attitude seems to reflect a bias for big, heroic changes. One of Behn's dilemmas is the Scale Dilemma (1997: 19). The problem is, in Behn's view, that many small changes may not change mental paradigms. Indeed, perpetual innovation may "intensify the very practices that create high costs and low access in the first place." Such an approach reinforces the view of newly elected governments that some big, sweeping change is needed to make the administration more responsive, or less costly, or less intrusive in the lives of people and businesses.

It seems absurd to me to reject repeated acts of lesser innovation in the name of some larger cause. The taste for sweeping reforms has left public servants in Canada, the United States and Britain exhausted and demoralized. Obviously, senior managers must beware of self-serving minor improvements. But there is surely a case to be made that continuous improvement is a radical way to achieve important changes (Glor, 2001b: Tables 1 and 4). Moreover, large-scale, ambitious reforms have more serious consequences if they fail, not the least being increased cynicism among the public, the media and the political class.

It seems, therefore, that a large variety of innovations should be eligible for study. Obviously, some judgement must be made about which of them are significant, but I must reject the desire to retain only the fundamental transformations.

Conceptual Approaches to Innovation

Rusaw (2007, cited by Kuipers et al., 2013) identified four different approaches to innovation in the public sector: first, rational, top-down, planned change; second, incremental decentralized change, with emphasis on results; third, pluralistic, involving many models and actors, necessary and useful for complex problems; and finally, individualistic learning. The main controversy seems to be between what Kuipers (2013: 23) calls the heroic model based on strong leadership, and a less popular systematic decentralized, model, represented by Borins, and Rusaw). A second cleavage occurs between those who believe that successful innovation can only done by "groping along" to use Behn's phrase (including Bourgon and Paquet in Canada) and those, like Borins and several contemporary governments, who emphasize systematic measurement and planning.

This is one of those paradoxes that Behn (1997) identified. Borins is no doubt right that bottom-up innovations are more numerous than top-down central ones, but this requires important qualifiers. Most of the bottom-up innovations that he identified were managerial, coming in the wave of New Public Management reforms inspired by Osborne and Gaebler's 1992 book, *Reinventing Government*, and dealing with efficiency, savings, and service to clients (Hughes et al., 2013: 13–14). On the other hand, the European Innobarometer found that the single most important driver of innovation was reported to be changes in legislation and regulations and budget restrictions (European Commission, 2011). They also found that larger, central organizations were more likely to innovate and that state organizations were just as likely to innovate as decentralized public sector institutions.

It would seem then that lower-level innovators, Borins' "local heroes," should be encouraged, that their creativity is clearly needed in times of financial difficulties and public impatience with poor or inadequate service. The governments engaged in the new trend to measurement of PSI would agree.

However, although continuous improvement is an important and practical goal, it is not the whole story. Borins recognizes (1998: 84) that it is unlikely that managers will make the first move, when it comes to organizational change. Such changes were more likely to come from political leadership or from management boards. Similarly, Rogers (cited by Glor, 2001b) wrote that elites will screen out innovations that threaten the status quo. Moreover, we noted that several authors did not consider more modest kinds of change to be real innovation. The kinds of innovations that get tracked as "administrative reforms" are not often going to be initiated from below: budget systems like the Planning Programming and Budgeting System (PPBS), and other reforms like the Ombudsman, Access to Information, Equal Opportunity, reorganization, rules about whistleblowing, and deregulation.

So these are also important major innovations that have their place. Perhaps here the need is not to proceed at too rapid a pace with too many sweeping reforms or innovations that leave public servants exhausted and the public cynical about the capacity of the state to change. The last word goes to Borins (1998: 64): "Integrity demands that one plan when it is desirable and possible to plan, but when it is not possible to plan, one experiments and learns from one's experiments." It is a judgment call.

Further complications may be found to affect the argument about the relative merits of top-down or bottom-up innovation. Lynn (1997: 94) points out that there may be different priorities for different stages of the process; decentralization may be better for initiating a reform than for implementing it. The rate of adoption may be different from its scope. Kraemer and King (1984) found that in OECD countries policies favoring the use of computers in local government led to greater use than in the United States, but that American cities that adopted computers made much more advanced and extensive use of them. Also, in the case of reorganization of state governments, Garnett (1980) found that the presence of a national consulting organization led to a more comprehensive plan but a lower probability of adoption. Once again, it does not seem possible to choose one format over the other all the time, but it does seem likely that there will be more peripheral and bottom-up reforms than centralized ones and that they will be better adapted to local needs, at least those of local public servants.

Outcomes and Results

Everyone agrees that a successful innovation must meet measurable goals. Borins (1998: 119) found that having a formal evaluation increased chances of replication in the Ford Foundation competition. He also noted a number of positive side effects of successful innovations, such as empowerment, and education. In the Innobarometer Survey (European Commission, 2011), the 5,000 responding organizations in twenty-seven states reported rare negative effects. On the other hand, Kuipers et al. (2013) in their survey of a decade of literature on PSI, found that not all effects of planned change are reported.

In her recent *A New Synthesis of Public Administration*, Jocelyne Bourgon (2011: 38) proposes that as well as the intended policy results, PSI studies must consider the civic results that follow. These are the effects of innovations on citizenship, social capital and the quality of democratic life in a community. She acknowledges that this is another task calling on administrators to find balance: "Public administrators must mediate between better public policy results and a drive for efficiency gains in the short term with the need to achieve better civic results to build the capacity to achieve better public results over time." Unless these results are included in the measurement of specific goals, we can surmise that they will come a distant second to effectiveness and efficiency results.

A particular kind of result concerns us here. Glor, in her study of PSI theory (Glor, 2008) would like to be able to predict the "fitness" of an organization to adapt and to survive. Fitness would be found in two qualities, adaptiveness and communications. Adaptiveness "requires sufficient variety, reactivity and self-organized emergence"; the capacity to communicate includes being organized to receive feedback from both the internal and external environments. Fitness also needs to take into account the magnitude of the challenge facing the organization.

The problem with this is, as Glor acknowledges (2008: 10), that the ultimate test of fitness is survival over time. There is the well-known case that many of the "exemplary" companies identified by Peters and Waterman in *In Search of Excellence* (1982) were in difficulty of few years later (Wikipedia, 2013). More fundamentally, paleontologist Stephen J. Gould, to whom Glor refers, calls this search "the classic error of circular reasoning ... Survival is the phenomenon to be observed" (Gould, 1989: 236). In his reinterpretation of evolution, Gould claims that all the evidence gathered about the creatures whose fossils were found in the Burgess Shale shows that, despite their decimation, they were "adequately specialized and eminently capable" of survival (239). These two examples suggest how difficult it is to find the parameters for the study of survival. To these, we might add the most extreme cases of organizational reform when their boundaries or their identity disappear in the process.

Accountability and PSI

Two major problems occur when we consider accountability and PSI. First, innovation by public servants creates a challenge to representative government. As Altschuler (1997: 40) put it, "Society can scarcely have civil servants adjusting the criteria for welfare eligibility case by case or determining what procedures to employ in arraigning criminal suspects." This problem is not limited to innovation, but it seems certain to occur as governance arrangements link more partners to the public decision-making process.

The second problem is linked with the first. For all those who believe in learning by doing, or groping around, a huge difficulty is identified by Behn (1997:15): "innovation requires failure ... and ... even the smallest mistake in the public sector can be magnified into a major embarrassment or even a sensational scandal ... ."

There are partial answers, such as moving ahead with projects that do not require political or top-level support, and forging alliances with client and other groups, but if the elected officials are against, for reasons of philosophy or ideology, or if the experiment is caught up in partisan debate, it is unlikely to be judged on its merits as a learning experience. Behn's preference for a "compact of mutual, collective responsibility," organized about performance contracts (Behn, 2001: 126) only partially meets the need for some enforceable responsibility of the periphery to the center, at least in parliamentary systems, and it requires a level of trust and responsibility that we do not often see these days.

Creativity and Invention

Not much of the literature deals with the creativity dimension of invention or of adaptation of an existing idea, yet it is clear that it is a distinct process from diffusion, persuasion, and implementation. The new emphasis of governments and international organizations on measuring and codifying innovations surely does not include this stage. By keeping score, one may be able to identify areas that need attention, but not to come up with new solutions to the problems identified.

Creativity means breaking away from existing rules, practices or concepts, or crossing or mixing two or more elements not customarily linked. Arthur Koestler (1970) found this to be equally true in art, science, and humor. The process of seeking such new ideas is not the same as that for analysis and it is a well-established practice now to separate the stage of creativity, or brain-storming, from the subsequent stage of analysis, because analytical thinking may prematurely stifle creative thinking (Agor, 1984, 1985, 1989). In the case of Borins' study of Ford Foundation contestants, the illuminating idea was the New Public Management drawing its inspiration from business methods applied to the public sector (Borins, 1998). In the British case, the most important sources of new ideas reported to the NESTA study were best practices known to employees (Hughes et al., 2013: 16). The National Performance Review of Vice President Gore counted on new ideas being generated by boundary-crossing partnerships (National Performance Review, 1993). One of the reasons that cosmopolitans are more likely to be innovative is their openness to things happening elsewhere. Membership in professional associations also leads to the spread of new ideas.

The point here is not that the encouragement of creativity is controversial, although it may be if the metaphor being used is considered inappropriate (as many people thought about the idea of making government more like a business). The point is that it is a separate kind of activity that requires distinct attention. Perhaps that is why replication, imitation, and best practices are so popular: they involve minimum risk or departure from what works in a given field of activity.

Context

In my study of innovation among Canadian governments (Gow, 1994: 110, 134), I found it essential to consider the context in which an innovation was considered. Following the suggestion of Elkins (1983), I adopted a grid which asked about any innovation whether it originated within the organization or if the initiative came from outside it and whether its origins came from a power relationship (and therefore politics) or from a non-controversial technical problem. Only one of the fifteen cases studied had external and technical origins, and that was the information technology called at that time the electronic office, which was vendor driven. All the others had a political component. In contrast, Borins' study of *Local Heroes* (1998) dealt with innovations that were more managerial, local, and specific; even so, they ran into power considerations arising from internal resistance. To succeed with adoption and implementation, Borins recommended information, persuasion, and bargaining before trying to impose an innovation by authority (72).

What this latter menu indicates is that these proceedings are political not analytical or technical. As indicated, few of the innovations I studied were purely or mostly technical. It is one of the defining characteristics of PSI that even the most technical of dossiers may quickly become political, if stakeholders or the media decide to make it so.

The point here is that the context, along with the stage in the process, indicate what is the appropriate method for innovation: invention requires freedom to consider all possibilities, without immediate concern for technical or political rationality; analysis requires evidence-based scientific, legal and/or technical reasoning; while politics requires persuasion, negotiation, and bargaining.

Behn writes (1991: 215), "Context is everything." It does appear to be a determining element that decides what method is appropriate. I would add that on some of the classic dilemmas that we have encountered, such as central, top-down versus decentralized, bottom-up and planning versus groping along, these are also judgement calls, that give importance to leadership, even if we wish to avoid the "heroic model" of innovation.

Management is such a conglomeration of different activities and capacities, that one of the essentials of leadership is the ability to recognize when different kinds of activity are called for. Borrowing their classification from C. J. Jung, Rowe and Mason (1987: 140) argued that successful managers must be able to operate in the realms of both thinking and feeling, of intuition and analysis. Something similar occurs here, where analysis calls on verifiable facts and careful reasoning, whereas creativity and politics call for more intuition and empathy, or the ability to put oneself in another's shoes.

Conclusion

The purpose of this chapter was to return to the subject of PSI theory after two decades and to enquire into the state of theory at this time. I found that there does not seem to be much controversy about the kind of people who are innovative, the stages of innovation nor about the kind of innovations that are likely to succeed, but that on many other aspects of the question, there was surprising lack of agreement.

It seems that there is still important disagreement about what constitutes a true innovation, with the debate centering on the merits of a multitude of lesser improvements versus a smaller number of major, disruptive, changes. The debate continued between proponents of planning and those who think one must "grope along" by trial and error, and between those who favor top-down and those who prefer bottom-up processes. Everyone wants to have results on innovations measured, but there is not agreement about what should be included in these results nor about the criteria of success. Innovation seems to pose huge problems of accountability to some, but others act as if it were a false problem, noting that most innovations can be introduced without recourse to higher political and administrative authorities.

All of which leads to the following conclusion:

- when you have trouble defining the object of your studies and stating the problem to be solved;
- when you must depend on a certain kind of leadership for innovations to occur;
- when you must frequently deal with self-reporting, which may be a house of cards, and which does not include failures;
- when the context is one of political clash, media fault-finding and confrontational accountability;
- when at every stage of the process there are paradoxes to be faced;
- when you do not have a clear protocol to establish whether an innovation will do more harm than good.

Then, as Everett Rogers and colleagues put it (2005: 6) you have an indeterminate subject, like innovation itself. Systematic studies such as those of Borins are certainly to be welcomed, but they do not include the larger controversial innovations. Moreover, the imperative of local adaptation leads one to wonder if these innovations are really comparable (Pollitt and Bouckaert, 2004: 200–202). If the world is really composed of local heroes doing their own thing, and repeatedly reinventing innovations, it certainly complicates the task for researchers (not that that is a reason not to do it).

I am of the school of Kahneman (2011), Taleb (2007) and Gould (1989) that there is more chance in these matters than we wish to admit. Still, innovation occurs in the public sector and it behooves us to try to understand it. With the exception of the work of Glor (in its intention and scope), most of the studies in this area are designed to aid in the process of successful innovation. This is inevitable, as it is in all of the study of public administration, as governments and administrators search for ways to improve, to adapt, and to survive.

These observations bring us back to the initial step in theoretical reasoning which is, what is the question? Of the authors considered, Glor is the one who pays this the most explicit attention. She proposes that what we are looking for are patterns which, if accurate, will have some predictive power. Rogers came to think that the search was to understand the process rather than, as he had long believed, to identify the determinants or independent variables causing innovations. He also came to believe that there can be too much innovation, which adds to the list. Borins basically undertook to study how the most successful of the Ford Foundation candidates achieved their successes. He also noted (Borins, 2001: 9) that it would not be desirable to have a public sector "that is as unrelentingly innovative as the private sector." Behn's sixteen "dilemmas," can be reformulated as research questions. The various surveys by contemporary public bodies seem to take for granted that innovation is a good thing.

At the end of this reflection, the basic question that comes through from PSI literature is how to do it successfully. This, however, leads to several other questions. Of an innovation, we need to know if it is beneficial. That question breaks down into three others: Does it work? Do we like the result? What are the side effects? In this last case, I agree with Bourgon that we should look not only at the intended policy results of an innovation but also at the civic or democratic results. Another set of questions concern whether or not the innovation is replicable and how far reinventing or adaptation can go before the innovation becomes something else.

The question of how to create and sustain a culture of innovation is important. This includes getting the right mix of rewards (Glor) and as Borins says, finding the tools of persuasion and the accommodations needed to obtain the acceptance. We need to know how lasting the effects are. Do we need, with Tennyson, to worry "lest one good custom should corrupt the world"?

A question that probably escapes the realm of serious research is how to determine when not to innovate. It is the task of the public service to find the balance between adapting and preserving, between change and conservation, both in the name of the viability of the political system. Who is going to tell political leaders that there has been enough change for the present in the structures of the state, the content of the primary and secondary school programs, the financing of local government?

A key question facing managers concerns the correct identification of the context in which an innovation occurs. I remain persuaded, as I was in 1994, that there are three overlapping but different stages in an innovation, namely invention or creation, analysis, and negotiation, and that each requires different methods and capacities.

Governments, of course, will not wait for academics to sort out their differences before acting on what they see as an imperious need to innovate. Moreover, there is much interesting and informative research on PSI taking place. Even so, this return to the subject after twenty years leads me to think that PSI theory will not be able to advance much until progress is made on the controversial questions discussed here.

Bibliography

Agor, W. 1984. *Intuitive Management.* Englewood Cliffs, NJ: Prentice Hall.

Agor, W. 1985. Managing Brain Skills to Increase Productivity. *Public Administration Review*, 46(5): 864–868.

Agor, W. (ed.). 1989. *Intuition in Organizations.* Newbury Park, CA: Sage.

Altshuler, A. A. 1997. Bureaucratic Innovation, Democratic accountability and Political Incentives. Pp. 38–67 in A. A. Altshuler & R. D. Behn (eds), *Innovation in American Government: Challenges, Opportunities and Dilemmas.* Washington, DC: The Brookings Institution.

Altshuler, A. A., & R. D. Behn (eds). 1997. *Innovation in American Government. Challenges, Opportunities and Dilemmas.* Washington, DC: The Brookings Institution.

Australian government. 2011. *Measuring Innovation in the Public Sector: a Literature Review.* Canberra, Australia: Department of Innovation, Industry, Science and Research. <http://Innov.govspace.gov.au/files//2011/08/APSII-Consultation – Paper.pdf>.

Behn, R. D. 1988. Managing by Groping Along. *Journal of Policy Analysis and Management,* 7(4): 643–663.

Behn, R. D. 1991. *Leadership Counts.* Cambridge, MA: Harvard University Press.

Behn, R. D. 1997. The Dilemmas of Innovation in American Government. Pp. 3–37 in Alan A. Altshuler & Robert D. Behn (eds). 1997. *Innovation in American Government. Challenges, Opportunities and Dilemmas.* Washington, DC: The Brookings Institution.

Behn, R. D. 2001. *Rethinking Democratic Accountability.* Washington, DC: The Brookings Institution.

Behn, R. D. 2008. The Adaptation of Innovation: The Challenge of Learning to Adapt Tacit Knowledge. Pp. 138–158 in Sandford Borins (ed.), *Innovations in Government. Research, Recognition and Replication.* Washington, DC: Brookings Institution.

Borins, S. 1998. *Innovating With Integrity. How Local Heroes Are Transforming American Government.* Washington, DC: Gerorgetown University Press.

Borins, S. 2001. *The Challenge of Innovating in Government.* Arlington, VA: The Price Waterhouse Coopers Endowment for the Business of Government.

Borins, S. (ed.). 2008. *Innovations in Government. Research, Recognition and Replication.* Washington, DC: Brookings Institution.

Bourgon, J. 2011. *A New Synthesis of Public Administration. Serving in the Twenty-First Century.* Montréal, CA: McGill-Queen's University Press.

Downs, G. W., & L. B. Mohr. 1976. Conceptual Issues in the Study of Public Innovation. *Administrative Science Quarterly,* 21(4): 700–714.

Elkin, S. 1983. Toward a Contextual Theory of Innovation. *Policy Science,* 16(4): 367–387.

European Commission. 2011. *Innobarometer 2010. Innovation in Public Administration* Brussels: European Commission. Collected June 29, 2017 at: <ec.europa. eu/public_opinion/flash/fl_305_en.pdf>.

Garnett, J. L. 1980. *Reorganizing State Government: the Executive Branch.* Boulder, CO: Westview Press.

Glor, E. D. 2001a. Key Factors Influencing Innovation in Government. *The Innovation Journal: The Public Sector Innovation Journal,* 6(2): 1–20.

Glor, E. D. 2001b. Innovation Patterns. *The Innovation Journal: The Public Sector Innovation Journal*, 6(3): 1–42.

Glor, E. D. 2007a. Identifying Organizations Fit For Change. *The Innovation Journal: The Public Sector Innovation Journal*, 12(1): 1–25.

Glor, E. D. 2007b. Assessing Organizational Capacity to Adapt. *Emergence: Complexity and Organization* (E:CO), 9(3): 27–40.

Glor, E. D. 2008. Toward Development of a Substantive Theory of Public Sector Organizational Innovation. *The Innovation Journal: The Public Sector Innovation Journal*, 13(3): 1–28.

Gould, S. J. 1989. *Wonderful Life. The Burgess Shale and the Nature of History.* New York: W. W. Norton.

Gow, J. I. 1994. *Learning From Others. Administrative Innovations Among Canadian Governments.* Toronto, CA: Institute of Puublic Administration of Canada and Canadian Centre for Management Development.

Hughes, A. K. Moore, & N. Kataria. 2013. *Innovation in Public Sector Organizations. A Pilot Survey for Measuring Innovation across the Public Sector.* London: National Endowment for Science, Technology and the Arts (NESTA).

Kahneman, D. 2011. *Thinking Fast and Slow.* Toronto, CA: Doubleday Canada.

Koestler, A. 1970. *The Act of Creation.* London: Pan Books.

Kraemer, K. L., & J. L. King. 1984. National Policies for Local Government Computing: An Assessment of Experience in Ten OECD Countries. *International Review of Administrative Science*, 50: 133–147.

Kuipers, B. S., M. Higgs, W. Kickert, L. G. Timmers, J. Grandia & J. Van der Voet. 2013. The Management of Change in Public Organizations: A Literature Review. *Public Administration*, 92(1): 1–20. doi:10.1111/padm.12040. Collected July 11, 2014 at: <http://onlinelibrary.wiley.com/doi/10.1111/padm.12040/full>.

Loffler, E. 2001. Review of S. Borins, Innovating With Integrity. How Local Heroes Are Transforming American Government. *International Public Management Journal*, 4: 109–113.

Lynn, L. E., Jr. 1997. Innovations and the Public Interest. Insights From the Private Sector. Pp. 83–103 in A. A. Altshuler & R. D. Behn (eds), *Innovation in American Government. Challenges, Opportunities and Dilemmas.* Washington, DC: The Brookings Institution.

Merritt, R., & A. J. Merritt (eds). 1985. *Innovation in the Public Sector.* Beverley Hills, CA: Sage.

National Audit Office. 2006. *Achieving Innovation in Central Government Organisations.* London: The Stationery Office.

National Performance Review. 1993. *Transforming Organizational Structures.* Washington, DC: Office of the Vice-President.

O'Dell, C., & C. J. Grayson. 1998. If We Only Knew What We Know: Identification and Transfer of Internal Best Practices. *California Management Review*, 40(3): 154–174.

OECD. 2005. *Oslo Manual. Guidelines for Collecting and Interpreting Innovation Data.* 3rd Edn. Paris: Organization for Economic Cooperation and Development.

Osborne, D., & T. Gaebler. 1992. *Reinventing Government. How the Entrepreneurial Spirit is Transforming the Public Sector.* Reading, MA: Addison-Wesley.

Peters, T., & R. A. Waterman. 1982. *In Search of Excellence.* New York: Harper and Rowe.

Pollitt, C., & G. Bouckaert. 2004. *Public Management Reform. A Comparative Analysis.* 2nd Edn. Oxford: Oxford University Press.

Rogers, E. M. 2003. *Diffusion of Innovations.* 5th Edn. New York: Free Press.

Rogers, E. M., & J. D. Eveland. 1978. Diffusion of Innovations in Public Organizations, Perspectives on National R&D Assessment: Communication and Innovation in Organizations. Pp. 275–297 in P. Kelly and M. Kranzberg (eds), *Technological Innovation: A Critical Review of Current Knowledge.* San Francisco, CA: San Francisco Press.

Rogers, E. M., & J. Kim. 1985. Diffusion of Innovations in Public Organizations. Pp. 85–105 in R. Merritt and A. J. Merritt (eds), *Innovation in the Public Sector.* Beverley Hills, CA: Sage.

Rogers, E. M., U. E. Medina, M. Rivera & C. J. Wiley. 2005. Complex Adaptive Systems and the Diffusion of Innovations. *The Innovation Journal: The Public Sector Innovation Journal,* 10(3), article 3 (Chapter 13, this volume).

Røste, R. 2004. *Studies of Innovation in the Public Sector, a Literature Review.* Oslo, PUBLIN Report D 16. Collected July 11, 2014 at: <http://survey.nifu.no/step/publin/reports/d16litteraturesurvey.pdf>.

Rowe, A. J., & R. O. Mason. 1987. *Managing With Style.* San Francisco, CA: Jossey Bass.

Taleb, N. N. 2007. *The Black Swan. The Impact of the Highly Improbable.* New York: Random House.

Wikipedia. 2013. In Search of Excellence. Collected August 30, 2013 at: <http://wikipedia.org/wiki/In_Search_Of_Excellence>.

Wildavsky, A. 1979. *Speaking Truth to Power: The Art and Craft of Policy Analysis.* Boston, MA: Little, Brown.

Notes on Contributors

MARY ANN ALLISON, Ph.D., is Professor Emerita of Journalism, Media Studies and Public Relations at Lawrence Herbert School of Communication, Hofstra University, Hempstead, New York. She uses media theory, sociology, and complex systems theory to study the ways in which individuals, communities, and institutions are changing. Among her publications are "The Complexity Advantage: How the Science of Complexity Can Help Your Business Achieve Peak Performance," "Community Revitalization in New Cassel, New York," and "Primary Attention Groups: A Conceptual Approach to the Communicative Ecology of Individual Community in the Information Age."

CHRIS ANSELL is Professor of Political Science at the University of California, Berkeley. He is the author of *Pragmatist Democracy: Evolutionary Learning as Public Philosophy* (Oxford, 2011), which develops a Pragmatist approach to collaborative governance. He is also the co-author of the article "Collaborative Governance in Theory and Practice" (*JPART* 2008) with Alison Gash.

NINO ANTADZE is currently Visiting Assistant Professor of Environmental Studies at Bucknell University. Her scholarly work is situated at the disciplinary interface of environmental studies, human geography, and ethics, with the focus on environmental and climate justice. She earned Ph.D. in urban and regional planning from the University of Waterloo, Canada. She holds an MSc in Environmental Management and Policy from Lund University, Sweden and an MSc in Environmental Sciences and Policy from Central European University, Hungary.

J. TRAVIS BLAND is Assistant Professor in the Department of Public Administration at the University of Illinois at Springfield. He received his PhD from the Center for Public Administration and Policy at Virginia Tech. His research interests include the network approach to governance,

front-line behavior, social welfare, and the normative and ethical foundations of our Constitutional Democratic Republic. He is a contributing
author to *Community Action Leaders: Rooting out Poverty at the Local
Level* (Routledge, 2017) edited by Beverly Bunch and Dalitso Sulamoyo.
His research has been published in *Public Administration Quarterly*, the
Journal of Public and Nonprofit Affairs, and *Springer's Global Encyclopedia
of Public Administration, Public Policy, and Governance*. He can be reached
at: jblan7@uis.edu.

BORIS BRUK holds a PhD and Master's degrees in public administration from Virginia Tech and international studies from the University
of Wyoming. His research interests include public management reform,
comparative public administration and policy, citizen participation, innovation, and administrative ethics. Before coming to the United States, he
worked for a regional administration in Russia, first as a consultant in the
international affairs department, and later as an advisor to the head of the
department of economic development. In the United States, he has fulfilled
a number of teaching, research, and service roles in Wyoming, Virginia,
and New York. He currently works as a Neighborhood Naturally Occurring
Retirement Community Director at the Shorefront YM–YWHA and as
a Contributing Faculty in the Public Policy and Administration Program
at Walden University, USA.

ANGELO DOSSOU-YOVO, Ph.D., is Assistant Professor in the Department
of International Studies at York University, Glendon Campus. He currently
teaches management and entrepreneurship courses in the new Glendon/
EMLYON dual degree undergraduate program in international studies and business administration. He received his Ph.D. in Management
from Université du Québec à Montréal (UQAM, Québec) in 2011. His
research interests include cluster policies, the innovation process as well
as the growth process of small businesses in the high technology industry,
innovation systems and entrepreneurial ecosystems.

MICHAEL J. DOUGHERTY is Professor/Extension Specialist with the West
Virginia University Extension Service and the Davis College's School for
Design and Community Development. He has been there for over twenty
years. In that capacity, he works with local governments and community

organizations on a variety of issues related to administration, finances, and planning. His research interests include strategic planning and budgeting and financial management.

ALISON GASH is Associate Professor of Political Science at University of Oregon. She is the author of *Below the Radar: How Silence Can Save Civil Rights* (Oxford, 2015) and the co-author of the article "Collaborative Governance in Theory and Practice" (*JPART*, 2008) with Chris Ansell.

PAMELA D. GIBSON GOFF worked in the area of community development and governmental operations at Virginia Tech from 1989 to 2006. During this time, she developed and conducted seminars and workshops to support local, regional, state, and community operations. Her passion is citizen participation and leadership development in community planning programs. She currently works in human resources in the private sector and teaches classes on an adjunct basis.

ELEANOR D. GLOR spent her working life as a public servant in the Canadian public sector at four levels of government and has written about public sector innovation for publication since the 1980s. She ran the Innovation Salon, a dinner meeting on public sector innovation, for ten years. She is the publisher and founding editor of *The Innovation Journal: The Public Sector Innovation Journal*. She was for many years Adjunct Professor at the School of Public Policy and Administration, Faculty of Liberal Arts and Professional Studies, and is currently Fellow of McLaughlin College, York University, Toronto, Canada. Most recently she published *Building Theory of Organizational Innovation, Change, Fitness and Survival*, "What Happens to Innovations and Their Organizations?" (with Garry Ewart), and "Innovation and Organizational Survival Research," with Mario A. Rivera, a chapter in James D. Ward, *Leadership and Change in Public Sector Organizations: Beyond Reform*.

JAMES IAIN GOW is Emeritus Professor of Political Science at l'Université de Montréal. After five years as a Foreign Service Officer (1957–1962), he took a doctorate in political science at l'Université Laval, before joining the Department of Political Science at l'Université de Montréal. His principal publications are: *Histoire de l'administration publique québécoise, 1867–1970*;

Learning From Others: Diffusion of Administrative Innovations in Canada;
*From Bureaucracy to Public Management: the Administrative Culture of the
Government of Canada* (with O. P. Dwivedi); and *A Canadian Model of
Public Administration?* His current research interests are administrative
history, administrative innovation, ethics, and governance.

DONGSHIN KIM is Assistant Professor at Daegu University, Republic of
Korea.

DONALD P. LACY retired in 2007 as Associate Professor and the State
Leader, Government and Community Services with The Ohio State
University Extension, Community Development Program. His program
development and research focused on strategic planning, community
involvement/citizen participation, leadership development, performance
evaluation, and benchmarking. Prior to that, he taught in the Political
Science Department before transferring to the Community Resource
Development at Virginia Teach from 1966 to 1999 He retired as Associate
Professor Emeritus in 1999.

KIMBERLY TAYLOR LEE is a Ph.D. candidate at Virginia Polytechnic
Institute and State University (Virginia Tech). Her research interests
include educational policy, federalism, and ethics.

LILLY LEMAY, Ph.D., is Professor at École Nationale d'Administration
Publique (ÉNAP) in Québec, where she teaches courses in public management and strategic management. Her research interest is in strategic
management including knowledge management and innovation as well
as leadership as tools to do strategy.

KIMBERLY LUKASIAK is Master of Public Administration, School of
Environmental and Public Affairs, University of Nevada, Las Vegas
(UNLV).

UNA E. MEDINA was Everett Rogers' graduate assistant, and is a Ph.D.
candidate at the University of New Mexico.

MICHAEL MILES, Ph. D., is Emeritus Senior Faculty Member at the
University of Ottawa's Telfer School of Management where he taught

organization change, corporate governance and ethics and organization redesign. He has worked for over thirty years providing consulting advice related to high performance to Canadian corporations in the banking, petroleum, telecommunications, and high-tech sectors. In addition to his Canadian experience he has lived and worked extensively in Asia (Thailand, China, and Malaysia) and Europe (Romania and France). He has been active as a Board member for a number of nonprofit Boards and advises them on best practices. He completed his doctoral degree in Human and Organization Systems at the Fielding Graduate School in Santa Barbara, California and holds three management-related Master's degrees. In 2004 he was voted one of the top 20 "hottest/coolest" management professors in Canada by *Canadian Business Magazine*. Areas of his current research and consultancy activity include international leadership practice and business strategy (with a focus on China), cross-cultural business effectiveness, and the use of simulation to teach real-world business skills.

MAI NGUYEN earned her Ph.D. in Political Science from York University, Toronto. Her doctoral research concentrated on Canadian public adminis-tration and public policy, focused more specifically on Aboriginal peoples in the administrative process. Based on her doctoral work, she has pub-lished numerous journal articles on Aboriginal socio-economic issues. She continues to publish in the area of Aboriginal-state public consultations and its potential to deliver Aboriginal-based change. She currently works as a policy advisor for the Ontario Public Service.

MIE PLOTNIKOF is Assistant Professor in the Department of Leadership and Organizational Learning, University College Copenhagen (UCC), Denmark. She holds a Ph.D. in Public Management and Organization from Copenhagen Business School. Her main research field is organiza-tion studies with a specific focus on discourse analysis, qualitative methods, professional identity, subjectivity and power, and on the public policy area of education and its reform processes. She has published research articles in scientific journals such as the *International Journal of Public Sector Management*, *The Innovation Journal: The Public Sector Innovation Journal*, and *Nordic Journal of Working Life Studies*, as well as in international and Scandinavian anthologies on studying management and leadership.

Currently, she is working on a new project about power-resistance dynamics in cross-sector collaborations and in policy innovation.

MARIO A. RIVERA is Regents' Professor of Public Administration at the University of New Mexico and a specialist in change management and program and policy evaluation.

EVERETT M. ROGERS (deceased) was renowned for his pioneering and enduring contributions to Diffusion of Innovations Theory. He was Distinguished Professor and Regents' Professor of Communication at the University of New Mexico, USA, in the Department of Communication and Journalism.

CHRISTOPHER STREAM is Director at the School of Public Policy and Leadership, Greenspun College of Urban Affairs, University of Nevada Las Vegas (UNLV).

DIANE-GABRIELLE TREMBLAY is Professor of Labour Economics, Innovation, and Human Resources Management at the Télé-université of the University of Québec, Canada. She was appointed Canada Research Chair on the socio-economic challenges of the Knowledge Economy in 2002 (<http://www.teluq.uqam.ca/chaireecosavoir/>) and again in 2009, and appointed Director of a CURA (Community-University Research Alliance) on the management of social times and work–life balance in 2009 (<http://www.teluq.uqam.ca/aruc-gats>). She has published in various journals such as the *New Technology, Work and Employment*, *International Journal of Technology Management*, *Intl Journal of Knowledge-Based Development*, *Cities*, *International Journal of Entrepreneurship and Innovation Management*, and others. She has often been invited by print, radio, and TV media to comment on industrial policy issues, cluster policy, employment policies, etc.

MARK K. WARFORD, Ph.D., serves as Department Chair for Modern and Classical Languages, Buffalo State College, New York and teaches courses in Spanish and language pedagogy. He has published in the areas of applied linguistics, Spanish language pedagogy, educational innovation, teacher development, and sociocultural theory. His scholarly work has been cited in over 300 publications. With regard to educational technology, he certified as a peer reviewer for Quality Matters and serves as Research and Innovation Fellow for the Open SUNY Center for Online Teaching Excellence. In addition to delivering keynote addresses, presenting and chairing dozens of sessions at professional conferences from the regional to international level, Warford regularly leads workshops on a range of topics, including the promotion of student engagement and blended course design in online instruction, as well as FourSight, a model for organizational self-reflection.

FRANCES WESTLEY currently holds the J. W. McConnell Chair in Social Innovation and is the Director for the Waterloo Institute on Social Innovation and Resilience at the University of Waterloo. She is a renowned scholar and consultant in the areas of social innovation, strategies for sustainable development, strategic change, visionary leadership and inter-organizational collaboration. She received her Ph.D. in Sociology from McGill University (1978), her Master's degree in Sociology from McGill University (1975), and her B.A. in English Literature from Middlebury College (1970).

CODY J. WILEY is a dual Master's candidate in the Water Resources Program and Geography Department at the University of New Mexico, USA.

JESSICA WORD is Associate Professor in the School of Public Policy and Leadership at the University of Nevada, Las Vegas. She currently serves as the Director of the Nonprofit, Community, and Leadership Initiative and the Graduate Coordinator for the School of Public Policy and Leadership. She received her doctorate from the Askew School of Public Administration and Policy at Florida State University in 2006. Her research focuses on capacity building in the public and nonprofit sectors. Her work has been published in *Public Administration Review, Review of Public Personnel Administration, Personnel Review, Public Personnel Management, Journal for Nonprofit Management, Journal of Management, Spirituality and Religion* and *The Innovation Journal*. She has worked with such notable national nonprofits as the Girl Scouts of the U.S.A, Volunteers of America, and Opportunity Knocks on issues related to employee engagement and burnout.

Index